*Laying Down the Law*

JOHN F. MATTHEWS

# *Laying Down the Law*

## A STUDY OF THE THEODOSIAN CODE



*Yale University Press*
*New Haven &*
*London*

Set in Sabon type by Keystone Typesetting, Inc.
Printed in the United States of America.

Library of Congress Cataloging-in-Publication Data
Matthews, John (John Frederick)
Laying down the law : a study of the Theodosian code / John F. Matthews.
p. cm.
Includes bibliographical references and index.
ISBN 0-300-07900-1 (alk. paper)
1. Codex Theodosianus. 2. Roman law. I. Title.
KJA457 .M38 2000
340.5'4—dc21 00-035198

A catalogue record for this book is available from the British Library.

The paper in this book meets the guidelines for permanence and durability of the Committee on Production Guidelines for Book Longevity of the Council on Library Resources.

10 9 8 7 6 5 4 3 2 1

# *Contents*

# *Preface*

The Theodosian Code is a compilation, begun in March 429 and accepted for publication in the autumn of 437, of Roman imperial legislation of the period extending from Constantine the Great to Theodosius II. Remarkably, it is the first fully official collection of such legislation ever made, and forms a partial precedent to the more comprehensive and far more famous program of codification undertaken by Justinian a century later. In its present state, it contains more than 2,500 texts on all aspects of the legal, administrative, social, and religious life of the late Roman Empire and is a constant resource for historians, whose use of it is not however supported by a consistent understanding of the nature of the Code and how it was produced. *Laying Down the Law* is an attempt to provide such an understanding; it is a book about the Code itself and not about the Roman Empire portrayed in its pages. Whether the portrayal is accurate has long been at issue, and it is my belief that such a study as this is a precondition for the use of the Code as a historical document to describe and interpret the late Roman Empire and its society.

The book begins with a short chapter describing the political circumstances in which the Code was planned, prepared, and published—a time in which, at the initiative of the eastern court, the unity of eastern and western *partes imperii* was being promoted, as a matter both of ideology and of practical politics. The second chapter, "Emperors, Law, and Jurists," is an account of the nature of legal sources and the making of law in the Roman Empire. It leads to an attempt to characterize the juristic culture in which the Code was conceived but argues also that the initiation of the project at this particular time owed as much to political as to juristic ideals. The third chapter, "Senatus Amplissimi Gesta," describes the meeting of the Roman Senate in December 438, at which the Code was accepted in the west; this is a subject of general historical interest, since the record of the meeting, transmitted in a single manuscript, portrays senatorial procedure in a detailed and quite colorful way. The fourth chapter sets out the editorial principles laid down by the emperor and analyzes the composition of the editorial committees entrusted with the work. These four chapters form an introductory section to the book, of a general historical character.

Chapter 5 turns attention to the Theodosian Code itself and is constructed in three parts. It first describes the state of the transmitted text of the Code, with special attention to the work of Mommsen, and criticism of his method in one important matter. The second part of the chapter is an account of the contents of the first five books of the Code, which are incomplete in the manuscripts. In particular, the argument of these two sections supports Paul Krüger's restoration to these books of the Code of more than 230 texts from the sixth-century *Codex Justinianus* that were not included by Mommsen. The contents of the first five books are further elucidated by reference to the traditional order of the Praetor's Edict, and in the third part of the chapter this connection is used as the basis for an explanation of the arrangement of the Code.

Chapter 6, on the Sirmondian Constitutions, is also in three parts. The Sirmondian Constitutions are a collection of sixteen late Roman texts preserved independently of the Theodosian Code in a complete, or unedited, state. This permits a comparison with the edited texts in the Code, to yield controlled conclusions about the nature of the editorial methods used there. The first part of the chapter introduces the Constitutions, the second is a comparison of ten of the sixteen texts with their counterparts in the Theodosian Code, and the third draws general conclusions from the texts about the nature of late Roman legislation, its formal conventions, and its distribution. These two chapters are substantial in length and, inevitably, the most technical in the book. The topics can hardly be addressed otherwise.

Building on the third part of Chapter 6, Chapter 7 reverts to a more historical approach by reconstructing the notional "lifespan" of a late Roman constitution, from its conception and drafting to its publication and reception in the province or provinces to which it was sent. This chapter provides the fullest description of the administrative processes by which laws were prepared, and it addresses the question of the authors of the texts, whether quaestors or other officials in the emperor's service.

Chapters 8 and 9 address a variety of questions to the text of the Theodosian

Code itself. In the first part of Chapter 8, a single title is studied for what it has to say about the editorial process, to illustrate the sorts of error and confusion that can arise, and to raise some questions of editorial convention that may throw light on the general character of the Code; in the second, some laws excerpted by the editors and distributed in different parts of the Code are reassembled; in the third, some anomalies and inconsistencies in the editing are presented and their implications examined. In Chapter 9 are discussed four texts which, like the Sirmondian Constitutions, are preserved separately and permit the controlled study of editorial methods. The first of these four texts, the so-called Edictum de accusationibus, of which parts are attributed in the Theodosian Code to Constantine but which is also preserved independently in epigraphic sources, presents the issues in a particularly complex way and is given a full discussion.

Directly or by implication, the question of the sources of the Theodosian Code recurs throughout, and in the concluding chapter, Chapter 10, the arguments on this matter are drawn together. This chapter, and the whole book, come to an end with some (hesitant) guidance on the principles according to which the Code is best employed for the purposes of historical interpretation.

It will be clear to readers of the book, and those who know my previous work will expect, that it is written from a historical rather than from a juristic standpoint. I have no doubt that I have thereby taken insufficient account of much excellent work on juristic aspects of the Code, and I am aware that some rather famous names are absent from my footnotes. This does not at all mean that I underrate the importance of such work in understanding this difficult text, but I think it an important principle of method that once an approach has been defined, it should be adhered to. My method is historical and philological; I am not a legal historian and I have not pretended to be. I am well aware also of the loss of concentration that can ensue from the temptation to follow up every interesting side-issue that arises on the way, without the technical expertise that is required to do so adequately. I do not mean that a more discursive approach is always inappropriate, only that it is so in the present case. The Theodosian Code being by its nature a discursive text, this restriction has imposed a constant discipline.

For the same reason, I have exercised restraint in citing secondary works and confined myself to work that is directly relevant to the point at issue and have at all times kept the original text firmly in view. Nothing is easier in scholarly writing than to pile up references in footnotes. However, the Theodosian Code is a sufficiently complex subject as it stands. Often, the most that one can hope to achieve is clarity in the presentation of difficult arguments, and more is to be lost than gained by plunging the subject into a welter of scholarly references that may only deter the reader. I have however worked with constant reference to Mommsen's formidable Prolegomena to his edition of the Code, published in 1905. I have controlled my discussions with reference to Otto Seeck's *Regesten der Kaiser und Päpste,* written in 1919, vols. 1 and 2 of the *Prosopography of the Later Roman Empire* (1971 and 1989), André Chastagnol's *Les Fastes de la préfecture de Rome au Bas-Empire* (1962), the chronological registers in T. D. Barnes, *The New Empire of Diocletian and Constantine* (1982), and the commentaries of Alan Cameron and others in *Consuls of the Later Roman Empire* (1987). I also put on record how much I have learned from two Oxford doctoral theses with which I am proud to have been associated, and from the many discussions that they generated while they were being written; Benet Salway's "Creation of the Roman State, A.D. 200–340: Social and Administrative Aspects" (1994), and Simon Corcoran's "The Empire of the Tetrarchs: Imperial Pronouncements and Government, A.D. 284–324" (1992; published with this title in the Oxford Classical Monographs series, 1996). As my notes and bibliography will show, I have been much influenced by the published works and by the personal contributions of Tony Honoré and Jill Harries. Honoré's *Law in the Crisis of Empire, 370–455 A.D.: The Theodosian Dynasty and Its Quaestors* was published by Oxford University Press in the summer of 1998, in time for me to consult and where appropriate refer to it in the final revision of this book. That the same is true of Jill Harries' *Law and Empire in Late Antiquity* I owe to her kindness in sending me proofs of her book before its publication (by Cambridge University Press, 1999). It is a rather cheering coincidence, reflecting many years of friendship, and of discussion and exchanges of opinion among us, that these two books and mine have appeared so close together. It will be obvious to the reader that in their approaches they are independent and complementary; where we have discussed the same topics, the comparisons should prove productive rather than repetitive. I also make particular mention of the work of Boudewijn Sirks, for its care and quality, and for its demonstration that differences of opinion can be expressed with courtesy as well as frankness, and with amity. He is a legal historian, I a cultural and social one. We are both aware of what each has to offer to the other.

I have given translations of at least the more extended texts I have discussed. Those from the Theodosian Code are taken from the collaborative translation directed by Clyde Pharr and published in 1952, a monumental effort that has among late Roman historians achieved a more or less canonical status, and rightly so (it gives me recurring pleasure to see, in the library of the Department of Classics at Yale, bound copies of the typescript drafts of this translation, as they were sent to Michael Rostovtzeff as a member of the advisory committee of the project). If there are weaknesses in Pharr's translation, they do not show in the use that I have made of it. Other translations are taken or adapted from existing versions, and some I have done myself. All are identified where they occur.

I substantially began this work as the holder of a British Academy Research

Readership in 1988–90 and substantially completed it during my tenure of a fellowship provided by the Andrew W. Mellon Foundation at the National Humanities Center in North Carolina during the academic year 1995–96. To all of these, I express my thanks. The National Humanities Center was a wonderfully tranquil and enjoyable environment in which to spend serious working time, and I thank Bob Connor, the director of the center, and his staff, especially the librarians, Alan Tuttle, Jean Houston, and Eliza Robertson, for their help in making it so.

I have just said that I substantially began and completed my work in these periods of study leave. This is an oversimplification. It would have been better to admit that the time for reflection provided by them taught me the need to master the fundamentals of what progressively developed into a far more complex subject than I had anticipated. On so many matters, I found myself going back to the beginning, often in the diminutive Latin print of Mommsen's Prolegomena; for instance, it was only at the start of my time at the National Humanities Center that I fully realized the importance of understanding the textual history of the Code and the possibilities of using the Sirmondian Constitutions to explore it, and a lot of hard work followed from these realizations. It is with such avowals, and by appeal to other intervening duties both at Oxford and at Yale, that I would explain to the British Academy, to which I had amazingly proposed a study in four chapters, my failure to complete my research in anything like the time frame I had suggested, and to the National Humanities Center the fact that it is four years even since my fellowship there that I am bringing my book to publication. I am quite sure that without these opportunities the project could not have been undertaken at all, and I am grateful to the University of Oxford and to the Provost and Fellows of Queen's College, Oxford, who granted me the relief from teaching and other duties that allowed me to accept these awards. I also express my gratitude to my new colleagues in the Departments of History and of Classics at Yale University, and to the many friends that I and my wife Veronika Grimm have made here, for their academic and personal support, and to the warmth of their welcome in a new university, and in a new, or rediscovered, country. It is a source of pride to me that my book should be published by Yale University Press, and I thank Harry Haskell and his colleagues for their positive reception of what I am sure is the least "popular" book that I have written; I am particularly grateful to Susan Abel for her careful and sympathetic advice in preparing the book for publication. The title of the book I accept as a gift from my friend Noel Lenski, of the University of Colorado, who conceived it for a talk that I gave at Boulder in March 1996. Its doubly allusive character is perfect for the job in hand. I would never have thought of it myself, and I am very grateful to him.

I will not attempt a register of the friends, both students and colleagues, who, at points too numerous to note, have helped me with advice and encouragement. I ask them to be content with this general acknowledgement, and to understand that my final word is for Veronika, whose confidence that I could accomplish this difficult project, encouragement to continue it, and advice, love, and patience while I did so, have never wavered, and whose extraordinary mind and experience have enriched mine with endless insights on all manner of things, both solemn and frivolous. If, in this book, the former are more obviously on show, I am enough of a psychologist to know that I should thank her for both.

# *Abbreviations*

The following abbreviations, short titles and editions are of works used recurrently. Titles that occur only once or twice are given in full in the notes; others are self-evident.

| | |
|---|---|
| App. 1, 2 | *Appendices Legis Romanae Wisigothorum duae,* in Riccobono, vol. 2, pp. 667–79. |
| Barnes, *New Empire* | T. D. Barnes, *The New Empire of Diocletian and Constantine* (Cambridge, Mass., 1982). |
| Bruns | K. G. Bruns, ed., *Fontes Iuris Romani Antiqui* (7th ed., O. Gradenwitz, ed., Tübingen, 1909, repr. Aalen, 1969). |
| Chastagnol, *Fastes* | A. Chastagnol, *Les Fastes de la préfecture de Rome au Bas-Empire,* Etudes Prosopographiques, vol. 2 (Paris, 1962). |
| *CIL* | *Corpus Inscriptionum Latinarum.* |
| *CJ* | *Codex Justinianus,* ed. P. Krüger, Corpus Iuris Civilis, vol. 2 (Berlin, 1877, repr. 1967). |
| *Collatio* | *Mosaicarum et Romanarum Legum Collatio,* in Riccobono, pp. 539–89. |

| | |
|---|---|
| Corcoran, *Empire of the Tetrarchs* | Simon Corcoran, *The Empire of the Tetrarchs: Imperial Pronouncements and Government,* A.D. 284–324 (Oxford, 1996). |
| *CSEL* | *Corpus Scriptorum Ecclesiasticorum Latinorum.* |
| *CTh* | *Codex Theodosianus:* (1) *Theodosiani libri XVI, cum Constitutionibus Sirmondianis,* ed. Th. Mommsen with P. Meyer and P. Krüger (Berlin, 1905, repr. 1962); (2) *Codex Theodosianus,* ed. P. Krüger, fasc. 1 (Books 1–6) (Berlin, 1923); (3) Trans. Clyde Pharr, *The Theodosian Code and Novels, and the Sirmondian Constitutions* (Princeton, 1952, repr. New York, 1969). |
| *Frag. Vat.* | *Fragmenta Vaticana,* in Riccobono, vol. 2, pp. 463–540. |
| Gaius, *Inst.* | Gaius, *Institutes;* F. de Zulueta, *The Institutes of Gaius* (Oxford, 1946 and reprinted), vol. 1 (*Text and Translation*), vol. 2 (*Commentary*). |
| Harries and Wood (eds.), *The Theodosian Code* | Jill Harries and Ian Wood (eds.), *The Theodosian Code: Studies in the Imperial Law of Late Antiquity* (London, 1993). |
| *ILS* | H. Dessau, *Inscriptiones Latinae Selectae* (3 vols., Berlin, 1892–1916). |
| Jones, *Later Roman Empire* | A. H. M. Jones, *The Later Roman Empire, 284–602: A Social, Economic and Administrative Survey,* (3 vols. and maps, Oxford, 1964; reprinted in 2 vols., 1973). |
| *JRS* | *Journal of Roman Studies.* |
| *MGH, auct. ant.* | *Monumenta Germaniae Historica, auctores antiquissimi* (Berlin, 1877). |
| *Nov. Just.* | *Novellae* (that is, *Justiniani A.*); ed. R. Schöll and W. Kroll (Corpus Iuris Civilis, vol. 3, Berlin, 1895). |
| *Nov. Th./Val.* | *Leges Novellae divi Theodosii A./divi Valentiniani A.,* ed. P. Meyer, (*Theodosiani Libri XVI,* vol. 2, 1905). |
| *PG* | J.-P. Migne, *Patrologia Graeca.* |
| *PIR/PIR,* 2nd ed. | *Prosopographia Imperii Romani* (1st ed., ed. E. Klebs, H. Dessau, P. de Rohden, Berlin, 1897–98; 2nd ed., ed. E. Groag, A. Stein, L. Petersen, and others, Berlin, 1933– ). |

| | |
|---|---|
| *PL* | J.-P. Migne, *Patrologia Latina.* |
| *PLRE* 1 and 2 | *The Prosopography of the Later Roman Empire,* vols. 1 (A. H. M. Jones, J. R. Martindale, J. Morris), A.D. 260–395 (Cambridge, 1971); and 2 (J. R. Martindale), A.D. 395–527 (Cambridge, 1980). |
| Riccobono | S. Riccobono, J. Baviera, and J. Furlani, *Fontes Iuris Romani Ante Justiniani,* vol. 2 (2nd ed., Florence, 1968–72). |
| Seeck, *Regesten* | Otto Seeck, *Regesten der Kaiser und Päpste* (Stuttgart, 1919). |
| *Sirm.* | *Constitutiones Sirmondianae;* see under *Codex Theodosianus.* |
| *ZPE* | *Zeitschrift für Papyrologie und Epigraphik.* |
| *ZSS* | *Zeitschrift der Savigny-Stiftung, Römische Abteilung.* |

# I

## *The Historical Moment*

In the year 437 two envoys from the Roman Senate presented themselves at the court of Theodosius II at Constantinople. Men of greater or more pertinent distinction could hardly have been found. Both were senior senators from the best-established and most influential Roman families, whose careers had expressed the loyalty of their class to the western successors of Theodosius the Great through all the vicissitudes that befell them in the early fifth century. One of the envoys, Rufius Antonius Agrypnius Volusianus, had been prefect of Rome in 417, and praetorian prefect of Italy under Valentinian III in 428–29. He was a friend of the pagan poet Rutilius Namatianus, who wrote of his promotion to the urban prefecture, and is known also as a correspondent of Augustine.[1] The other envoy, Anicius Acilius Glabrio Faustus, though unknown to posterity through such literary connections, was if possible still more distinguished. He had been three times prefect of Rome, under the Emperor Honorius at some time in the period 408/23, under Valentinian as Caesar in 425, and for the third time under Valentinian as Augustus, between 425 and 437.[2]

The senators' distinction matched the occasion for which they had come to

1. *PLRE* 2, pp. 1184–85 (Volusianus 6); Chastagnol, *Fastes*, pp. 276–79 (no. 125).
2. *PLRE* 2, pp. 452–54 (Faustus 8); Chastagnol, *Fastes*, pp. 286–89 (no. 128).

Constantinople. They were there to attend a Royal Wedding. Valentinian was to fulfill his betrothal to his cousin Eudoxia, daughter of Theodosius II and his wife Aelia Eudocia. Now eighteen, Valentinian was the only son of the late Emperor Constantius and Galla Placidia, daughter of Theodosius the Great by his second wife. Placidia was thus half-sister to Theodosius' sons by his first wife, the emperors Arcadius (d. 408) and Honorius, but she could not have been more unlike them in character and ability.[3] Intelligent where they were dim, forceful where they were flaccid, Placidia was a woman of power and insight. In the years following the sack of Rome by Alaric, she had been first hostage, then wife of the Visigothic king Athaulf, who spoke publicly of his indebtedness to her political wisdom.[4] The murder of Athaulf as the victim of a Gothic feud brought to a premature end one of the most interesting and potentially one of the most important political alliances of the age. A son born to the couple died in infancy and was buried in a church near Barcelona, where Athaulf then held court.

After the death of Athaulf, Galla Placidia was restored to the court of Honorius at Ravenna. In 417 she married Constantius, a successful Roman general, of whom the contemporary historian Olympiodorus wrote a vivid pen-portrait. In his public progresses, said Olympiodorus, Constantius appeared "with downcast eyes and sullen countenance. He was a man with large eyes, long neck, and broad head, who bent far over the neck of the horse carrying him and glanced here and there out of the corners of his eyes so that he showed to all, as the saying goes, 'an appearance worthy of a tyrant.'" The contrast with his informal conduct in private is striking: "At banquets and parties he was so pleasant and witty that he even contended with the clowns who often played before his table."[5] It was also said that he regretted his promotion as emperor (in 421) because it deprived him of the opportunity to joke and laugh in public, as he was accustomed to. However, Constantius held the

3. Honorius is an unfortunately easy target. Gibbon wrote of him (*Decline and Fall,* ed. Bury, vol. 3, pp. 339–40) that, since in the course of a "busy and interesting narrative" he might forget to mention in its proper place the death of such an unobtrusive character, he would take the precaution of observing now (under the year 413) that Honorius survived the last siege of Rome by about thirteen years.

4. Orosius, *Historia adversus paganos* 7.43; see my *Western Aristocracies and Imperial Court, A.D. 364–425* pp. 316–18.

5. Olympiodorus, frag. 23 Müller/23 Blockley, trans. by Blockley ad loc., and by C. D. Gordon, *The Age of Attila* (1960), p. 38; Matthews, *Western Aristocracies and Imperial Court,* chap. 15, at pp. 377f. Placidia's alleged reluctance to marry Constantius (Olympiodorus, frag. 34 Müller/33,1 Blockley; Gordon, p. 43) may have owed something to a gloss put on the marriage at the eastern court, where Constantius' promotion as Augustus was not recognized.

imperial office for only a few months before he, too, died. Olympiodorus claimed what is not very likely, that he had at the time been planning an attack on the east, because it had not recognized his promotion.[6]

Widowed for the second time, Galla Placidia lived with her little son, her second child by Constantius, at her half-brother's court at Ravenna. At about the time of his fourth birthday in 423, in consequence of a quarrel between Placidia and Honorius leading to open rioting by their supporters,[7] Valentinian had been taken by his mother to the court of Theodosius II at Constantinople. There they lived as political exiles, but not for long. Theodosius had never recognized the claim of Constantius to the title Augustus, nor that of Galla Placidia to the title Augusta, and in consequence did not accept Valentinian as a legitimate successor. However, the situation changed when, later in 423, Honorius died and the throne was claimed by a usurper. Theodosius was then persuaded to undertake the restoration of Valentinian as emperor in the west, and to endorse his support by the betrothal of his young protégé to Eudoxia. The betrothal would restore the dynastic union of the Theodosian house under the guidance of its senior emperor and was a declaration of commitment to the political unity of the eastern and western empires. With the clear implication that Galla Placidia would act as regent for a child emperor, it was also a commonsense solution to a practical problem; there was no other obvious claimant in the imperial line, but no shortage of ambitious men of power in the west who might claim the imperial power for themselves.

After a successful campaign by Theodosius' generals, Valentinian was installed as Augustus in a ceremony held at Rome on 23 October 425. With this episode, Olympiodorus brought to its climax his fine history of these years, which he dedicated to Theodosius in about 437—a literary endorsement, in the Classical style, of imperial policy in the west. In a series of passages that, even in the fragmentary form in which they survive, are vivid testimony of the social and economic life of Rome in the period, Olympiodorus made much of the physical grandeur of the city and its great houses, and the apparently undiminished wealth of its senatorial class.[8] It was in the weeks leading up to the installation of Valentinian but while Theodosius' protégé was still in his previous rank as Caesar that Anicius Acilius

6. Olympiodorus, frag. 34 Müller/33,1–2 Blockley; Gordon, p. 44; Matthews, *Western Aristocracies and Imperial Court,* p. 378.

7. Placidia was supported by barbarian partisans acquired during both her marriages; Olympiodorus, frag. 40 Müller/38 Blockley; Gordon, p. 44.

8. Frags. 43–44, 46 Müller/41, 43 Blockley; Gordon, pp. 22–23; see my "Olympiodorus of Thebes and the History of the West (A.D. 405–25)," pp. 80, 88, and *Western Aristocracies and Imperial Court,* pp. 384f. For arguments in favor of a date of publication ca. 438, see F. M. Clover, "Olympiodorus of Thebes and the Historia Augusta."

Glabrio Faustus is recorded as holding his second prefecture of Rome.[9] We may assume that his duties would include collaboration with Theodosius' emissaries in preparing for the investiture and would have given an additional reason for his choice as senatorial envoy in 437. He knew Valentinian, was well connected with the Theodosian court establishment, and had some experience in planning grand public events.

The support of the eastern court for the western government nominally headed by Valentinian did not produce years of stable prosperity for the west. They witnessed a substantial weakening of authority, with loss of territories in Gaul, Spain and Africa; but the ideology running through these years, of an imperial unity based upon eastern initiative, was still intact when Valentinian traveled to Constantinople to fulfill his betrothal to Eudoxia.

The wedding, on 29 October, was a great state occasion. It is narrated in no contemporary source, but in the palace at Ravenna a series of mosaic pictures, now lost but described by the poet Merobaudes, depicted the occasion and the events that had led up to it. The mosaics showed the "exile" of Valentinian at Constantinople with Galla Placidia and his appeal to Theodosius, his restoration by the eastern government and the betrothal to Eudoxia. They further showed the baby daughter of the young couple, born probably in 438 and baptized in infancy. Dominating the composition, however, in the center of the ceiling were the Emperor Theodosius and his wife Eudocia, "like the bright stars of the heavens on high." It left no doubt which was the senior court, pre-eminent in power and authority.[10]

Merobaudes' description gives some faint impression of the pomp and ceremony with which the wedding of Valentinian and Eudoxia was celebrated.[11] The distinction of the western delegates, not simply as supporters of the Theodosian dynasty but as senators of Rome, *viri inlustres,* and the holders of five praetorian and urban prefectures between them, would ensure their rank among the dignitaries who attended it. They would certainly receive more deference than they were obliged to pay to others. They could claim precedence over all but the small elite of nonim-

9. *CTh* 16.5.62 (17 July).

10. Merobaudes, *Carmen* 1; ed. and trans. F. M. Clover, *Flavius Merobaudes: A Translation and Historical Commentary* (1971), pp. 11 and 16–27, but with some differences of interpretation, in which I acknowledge an unpublished paper by Alan Cameron; the "princeps" (v. 5) and "praeses" ("pro praeside nostro," v. 7) are Theodosius, and the "novus exul" (v. 8) is Valentinian. The identification of the main personnel in the poem by T. D. Barnes, "Merobaudes on the Imperial Family," *Phoenix* 28 (1974), pp. 314–19, is spectacularly misconceived.

11. According to the church historian Socrates (7.44), the wedding had been planned to take place at Thessalonica but was moved to Constantinople, "to avoid causing trouble to Theodosius."

perial candidates to whom the emperors had granted the consulship,[12] the current holders of the praetorian prefecture and the prefecture of Constantinople and the highest court offices in the east, and the imperial family itself. As the ceremonies moved between court and palace, city and church, they would have ample opportunity to observe the emperor and his wife, and perhaps to reflect, as cultivated senators, on her background as the former Athenaïs, the daughter of an Athenian professor of rhetoric, and on her considerable reputation in poetry and rhetoric.[13] It was perhaps with less sympathy that they viewed the "other empress," Theodosius' elder sister Pulcheria Augusta, who had many years ago dedicated herself to perpetual virginity (and persuaded her two sisters to do likewise) and had since then devoted herself to church building and good works, and to transforming her quarters into something more resembling a convent than part of the imperial palace. That was not, the senators might have told each other, how to keep the barbarian world at bay. With good reason or bad, rumors abounded that the two empresses were not friends, and their rivalries were (and still are) supposed to provide the key to court politics under Theodosius.[14]

Some also wondered, though none would have dared share their doubts with western visitors, about the relations between Theodosius and his wife. In the opinion of some historians, those suspicions were sharpened when early in 438 Aelia Eudocia left court to embark upon a pilgrimage to Jerusalem, but this is to read too much back from the events of five years later, when, after a scandal leading to the execution of a senior member of the imperial bureaucracy and the exile of her leading supporter to a remote and dangerous bishopric, Eudocia took up permanent residence in the Holy Land.

The pilgrimage of 438 should not be seen in the light of these later circumstances. Far from showing a rift between Eudocia and Theodosius, this highly ceremonious journey, it has been well said, was "a major public event for the eastern empire, the sequel to the wedding celebrations of the previous year"; indeed, the connection between the two events is made explicit by the church historian Socrates, according to whom Eudocia had vowed to make the pilgrimage once

12. The consuls of 437 itself, Fl. Aetius and Fl. Sigisvultus, were both *privati* but also western; they would not have attended the ceremonies, so that the senatorial delegates would not have been outranked by other westerners.

13. Anticipating Anna Comnena, she had among other works written verses on victories over Persia—Socrates 7.21.8 (*PLRE* 2, p. 409).

14. Kenneth G. Holum, *Theodosian Empresses: Women and Imperial Dominion in Late Antiquity* (1982), esp. pp. 123ff., with the criticisms of Alan Cameron, "The Empress and the Poet: Paganism and Politics at the Court of Theodosius II," *Yale Classical Studies* 27 (1981), pp. 217–89.

she had seen her daughter married.[15] The evidence leaves no doubt that the journey was designed for public appreciation. Nor was it merely a pilgrimage, but a calculated expression of the public ideology, in all its aspects, of the Theodosian regime. At Antioch, Eudocia delivered an oration in which, in a display of academic erudition that will have delighted the shades of her father, she claimed Antiochene blood on the grounds of the legendary role of the Athenians in founding the city.[16] In a traditional gesture of *philanthropia,* she presented funds to feed the people of Antioch and was honored by acclamations and by gilt and bronze statues.[17]

Moving on to Palestine, Eudocia prayed in the church of the Holy Sepulchre at Jerusalem, a scene later depicted in a mosaic or painting in a church at Constantinople. She attended the consecration of a church of St. Stephen and, returning the following year to Constantinople, carried with her relics of the protomartyr; she was received into the city with her holy spoils in a public ceremony of *adventus.*[18] For all the variety of its range of reference, Eudocia's conduct evinces nothing that does not reflect the culture of Theodosian Constantinople and express the claim of its rulers to dominion over all the cultural diversities of their still vast empire.

And this was not all, for it was also after the completion of the marriage ceremonies, presumably in November 437, that Theodosius summoned to his presence the chief western delegate, Faustus, and the praetorian prefect of the east, and before them, his imperial colleague Valentinian, and the assembled dignitaries, announced his intention to present to the world a compendium of Roman imperial law in sixteen books, to be called after himself. Valentinian, with the loyalty of a colleague and affection of the son that he now was, approved this project.[19] Theodosius now ordered to be conveyed "from his divine hand" to the praetorian

15. Socrates, 7.47; cf. E. D. Hunt, *Holy Land Pilgrimage in the Later Roman Empire,* A.D. *312–460* (1982), chap. 10 (p. 231); Holum, *Theodosian Empresses,* pp. 117, 185f.

16. I favor the interpretation of Cameron, "The Empress and the Poet," p. 278, rather than that of Holum, *Theodosian Empresses,* p. 117. Eudocia claims Antiochene descent in such a recondite way as to demonstrate that she was not actually an Antiochene.

17. G. Downey, *A History of Antioch in Syria,* (1961) p. 451; cf. pp. 355, 622 on the location of the statues outside the former Museion.

18. Holum, *Theodosian Empresses,* p. 189; Hunt, p. 233. On 28 January 438 in a similar ceremony the bones of John Chrysostom, who had died in exile in 407, were installed in the Church of the Apostles at Constantinople; Holum, pp. 184–85. On the arrival of relics in an adventus ceremony, see Sabine MacCormack, *Art and Ceremony in Late Antiquity* (1981), pp. 64f.; "Change and Continuity in Late Antiquity," *Historia* 21 (1972), p. 748.

19. "Quam rem aeternus princeps dominus noster Valentinianus devotione socii, affectu filii conprobavit." I take the narrative perfect tense "conprobavit" to indicate Valentinian's assent as having actually been given at this meeting, as it was described by Faustus to the Senate in December 438 (Chapter 3). When work on the Code had begun, in 429, Valentinian had not yet reached his tenth birthday.

prefects copies of the new codex. We may again indulge ourselves for a moment by imagining the scene, as a robed imperial functionary advances, takes the splendidly bound copies of the Code from the emperor and solemnly presents one to each recipient. It would be good also to picture, standing there in the *consistorium,* if that is where the ceremony took place, the high officials and other associates whom Theodosius was to thank, in his law of 15 February 438 validating the Code, for their work on the project—and one man in particular, Antiochus, also known as Chuzon, the inspiration and guiding spirit of the enterprise. He, if anyone, deserved a share in the achievement of this moment.[20]

The protocol of the situation as it affected Faustus and the eastern praetorian prefect offers an easy explanation for Faustus' promotion as prefect of Italy, Illyricum, and Africa.[21] It is possible, indeed, that this was his first official act in that capacity. An inscription from an Italian town in which the promotion is mentioned calls it an expression of the judgment of each part of the empire: "utriusque inperii iudicii[s] sublimitato." It may be seen, in the western perspective of the inscription, as a promotion to a western prefecture taking place at the eastern court.[22] Faustus' acceptance of the Theodosian Code, in the presence of both emperors, thus came from an equal basis in protocol with his eastern counterpart. His appointment as praetorian prefect has a further consequence, in that it enables us to plot his journey home, for this will certainly have been in the company of Valentinian and his new bride; indeed, in their historical perspective, attending emperors on their travels was just what praetorian prefects were for. We know that the imperial couple spent the winter at Thessalonica, and traveled to Ravenna, presumably by ship and by way of Salona and the imperial palace at Split, after the reopening of the seas in April 438.[23] Faustus would have to return to Ravenna with them: it was not until December that he was able to report the outcome of his eastern visit to the assembled Senate at Rome.

It was in this address to the Senate that Faustus, still in his capacity as praetorian prefect, presented the Theodosian Code to the western empire and accepted the

20. *Nov. Th.* 1, §7.

21. *PLRE* 2, p. 453; Chastagnol, *Fastes,* p. 288.

22. *ILS* 1283 = *CIL* 14.2165 (Aricia, Latium). Despite the comment in *CIL,* the phrase cited here should refer to the appointment to the praetorian prefecture rather than to the generic "tertio praefectus urbi" that precedes it, cf. *PLRE* 2, p. 453. The inscription does not mention Faustus' consulship in 438.

23. Marcellinus, *Chron.,* s.a. 437, 438; Mommsen, *Chronica Minora* 2, p. 79. In slightly discrepant passages, a law of Gratian (*CTh* 13.9.3), and Vegetius (4.39) define the season for sea travel as mid-April to mid-October, with extensions for the acceptance of cargo; see further Chapter 7 with n. 52. Similar considerations no doubt affected the arrangement of the wedding for October 437.

Senate's instructions for its further distribution (see Chapter 3). He was however without his fellow envoy Volusianus, who had fallen ill in the east and died, on 6 January 438.[24] We know this from the Greek *Life* of his niece Melania, who had heard of her uncle's visit from her ascetic retreat on the Mount of Olives and come to Constantinople to see him—and, in the event, to ensure that the old man, the last to maintain the pagan tradition of a great senatorial family, would die a professed Christian.[25] Given the circumstances and the endless pressure to conform, it was perhaps just not worth holding out any longer. In any case, the baptism, by Bishop Proclus of Constantinople, and the death of Volusianus on Epiphany 438, are among those symbolic episodes that seem too good just to have happened like that—taking Volusianus from old Rome to Constantinople, the new seat of power, from paganism to a deathbed baptism in the presence of a holy lady who, many years before, had abandoned worldly ambitions and the pride of her class and devoted her wealth to charitable works and the building of monasteries. Melania herself stayed at Constantinople for the prescribed forty days of mourning before returning to the Holy Land, in the meantime sharing her religious counsel with the "Christ-loving empresses" Eudocia and Pulcheria; strange obsequies for the old Roman, whose skeptical questions to Augustine after the sack of Rome by Alaric had had much to do with the writing of the *City of God*.[26] Augustine had in that work praised Theodosius the Great as a Christian ruler whose piety was expressed by the laws he had issued in favor of the Catholic Church. If during long winter evenings at Thessalonica Faustus thought to browse through the magnificent volume that he had received from the hands of Theodosius' grandson, he would have found the laws among the three thousand or more edited texts that it contained. If he read the work very attentively, he might even have found his own and his colleague's names in the Code as the addressees of laws issued in the name of Valentinian.[27]

A visit to Constantinople, the publication of a code of Roman law, the arrival of a holy lady, the death of a senator, an empress's journey to the Holy Land—one could hardly find more diverse associations for a Royal Wedding. It might be argued that such episodes are only incidentally connected, proof only of the obvious fact that Constantinople was a great capital city in which all sorts of activities

24. Against *PLRE* 2, p. 1185 and others, I accept the date 438 rather than 437 for his death; see Holum, *Theodosian Empresses,* p. 183f. with n. 39. Deaths of *legati* during absence on embassies are quite often recorded in the sources; cf. my article "Gesandtschaft," in *Reallexikon für Antike und Christentum* 10 (1977), col. 666.

25. *Life of St. Melania,* 50–56, in D. Gorce, *Sources Chrétiennes* 90 (1962), pp. 224–39. Melania must have come to Constantinople to see her uncle, not just because he was ill.

26. Peter Brown, *Augustine of Hippo: A Biography* (1967), pp. 300–303.

27. *PLRE* 2, pp. 453 (Faustus), 1185 (Volusianus).

took place, not all of them consistent or part of a single pattern. This would be an unduly casual attitude. Varied as they may be, these events are not disconnected. They are expressions of the complex cultural setting in which the Theodosian Code was conceived and implemented, and of the still more complex world that is reflected in its contents.

The Theodosian Code presents to us a double image. On the one hand, as an intellectual enterprise it belongs to a juristic tradition that was older than the Roman Empire itself and stands at the heart of its culture; on the other, it is the single most extensive expression that survives of a contemporary reality that had undergone radical changes in almost every dimension of experience. What follows, a description of the way in which the Theodosian Code was conceived, edited, and published, is a study of the first aspect rather than the second: of the Code as an intellectual enterprise rather than of the contemporary world that is portrayed in its pages. The interpretation of the world that is so portrayed has been, and remains, one of the most difficult challenges facing the late Roman historian, but it cannot be approached without an understanding of the nature of the text on which it is based. It is the purpose of the following chapters to work toward such an understanding.

# 2

## *Emperors, Law, and Jurists*

The Theodosian Code was initiated by a decision of the emperor Theodosius II, announced to the senate of Constantinople in a constitution of 26 March 429.[1] The instructions to the editorial commissions appointed then, and in a second law issued in December 435, were to assemble in a single volume all imperial constitutions of general bearing issued by Constantine and his successors up to that point, whether or not those were currently in force. The work would be a sequel to the codes of the jurists Gregorius and Hermogenianus, published under Diocletian in the 290s; and when it was finished, the three codes, together with the writings of the jurists, would contribute to a further volume, a comprehensive manual of law which would be a true guide to life, *magisterium vitae,* for future generations. This second, more far-reaching phase of Theodosius' project was never realized, but work on the first phase was finished by the late summer of 437. We have just seen how the completed Code was formally presented to the praetorian prefects of east and west at a ceremony held at Constantinople in November.

Even without the full text of the first five of its sixteen books,[2] the Theodosian

1. *CTh* 1.1.5, read to the Roman Senate in December 438 by the praetorian prefect Faustus (see Chapter 3).

2. A raw count of Mommsen's edition yields 2,515 texts, with 233 more to be added from the Codex Justinianus to the first five books and the beginning of the sixth (see Chapter 5).

Code contains more than 2,500 edited constitutions issued between 313 and 437, on a vast range of subjects on all aspects of the political, social and economic, cultural, and religious life of the Roman Empire in the fourth century and the early decades of the fifth. They are a goldmine of information for historians, who have exploited them avidly but, beyond issuing routine cautions derived largely from the preface of A. H. M. Jones' *The Later Roman Empire,*[3] have usually not shown the same eagerness to come to grips with the actual nature of the compilation and the process by which it was made. This is understandable. The Theodosian Code is not a welcoming text, and it is made no more so by the scholarly intensity and daunting presentation of Mommsen's edition. It is, however, critical that the historian approach the book with an understanding of how it was made and published, and why it takes the form it does.

We may take as a starting point the more comprehensive and better-known program of work undertaken by Justinian a century after Theodosius' time.[4] In this program, two categories of material can be identified. The difference between them is expressed—and was so understood by the Romans themselves—by the distinction between *ius,* the law considered as an interpretative discipline, and *leges,* the primary legislation upon which the interpretations were based. So, in the most massive of the volumes issued by Justinian, known as Digesta or the Digest, are excerpted the opinions of the jurists, with their supporting evidence, on the whole range of public and private law; while the Institutes, published simultaneously with the Digest in 533, are updated in the Institutes of Gaius, the most influential textbook of Roman law. These books form part of what is here defined as *ius,* law as an interpretative discipline, and were based on the published works of the legal writers of the Classical period, mainly of the second and early third centuries. A glance at the Digest will show that in their discussions of legal topics the Classical lawyers cited everywhere the pronouncements of Roman emperors. These were *sources* of law, and of all sources by far the most important; what raised them to the status of *ius* is that they had been tested, debated, and set in thematic legal contexts by jurists.

As for leges, the legislative texts themselves, the Codex Justinianus, which appeared in a revised edition in 534,[5] contained the pronouncements of emperors going back to the early third century, incorporating material from the Gregorian,

3. Preface, p. viii: "The laws . . . are clues to the difficulties of the empire, and records of the aspirations of the government and not its achievement."

4. See F. Schulz, *History of Roman Legal Science* (1946, rev. 1967), pp. 317–22; W. Kunkel, *An Introduction to Roman Legal and Constitutional History* (2nd ed., 1973), chap. 11 (pp. 163–76); and esp. Tony Honoré, *Tribonian* (1978).

5. The first edition of 529 does not survive—Schulz, *Roman Legal Science,* pp. 317f.; Honoré, *Tribonian,* p. 212.

Hermogenian, and Theodosian Codes; and in the Novellae, or Novels (New laws), is collected the legislation of Justinian himself from the years following the main work of codification. These two works, the Codex Justinianus and the Novellae, contained the texts of imperial legislation, without critical comment, except insofar as this was implicit in the selection of the texts for inclusion in the Codex Justinianus from the earlier compilations that provided its material.

Although more was originally intended, only the second category of text, that of primary legislation, is represented in the codification of Theodosius—in the Theodosian Code itself, in which is collected imperial legislation from Constantine to the reigns of Theodosius II and Valentinian III, and in the Novellae of these last emperors followed by those of their successors—indeed, it was the first Novel of Theodosius, of 15 February 438, that gave authority in the east to the Theodosian Code itself. Even allowing for the absence of the projected "magisterium vitae" of Theodosius, there is no suggestion that anything resembling the Justinianic program in scale or character was ever contemplated. The Theodosian Code does, however, differ from the work of Justinian (except the Novellae), in that it was largely based not on existing juristic writings and collections of texts, but on primary sources that had never before been brought together.[6]

The constitutional basis upon which the law was administered by the emperor was the concept of *imperium* inherited from the Roman Republic. In itself, imperium was not specifically power over jurisdiction but was what enabled a magistrate to perform all the various functions required by his administration—financial and, if need be, military, as well as judicial. Nevertheless, jurisdiction was always an important aspect, probably the most important single aspect, of these functions. On an ivory diptych of the early fifth century, the *vicarius urbis Romae* Rufius Probianus is shown as a judge in session, listening to petitioners and rendering judgment, while the proceedings are taken down by secretaries; his role is indicated by the ceremonial inkstand symbolizing his judicial powers (Figures 1 and 2). Indeed, in the later Roman Empire *iudex* was the usual generic term for a civil governor. Some civil governors (namely, praetorian prefects and the prefects of Rome and Constantinople), vicarii (like Probianus), proconsuls and *consulares,* were assigned powers to act as judges of appeal on behalf of the emperor and were so designated—"vice sacra iudicantes."[7]

As this phrase implies, the judicial role of the emperor was pre-eminent. Historically, from the time of Augustus, the position of the emperor too derived from his

6. I say "largely based," to allow for the likelihood that the editors of the Theodosian Code used existing collections as well as primary material (see Chapter 10).

7. Jones, *Later Roman Empire,* pp. 481–82. For Probianus, *PLRE* 2, p. 909 (Probianus 7). He may be the same Probianus who was prefect of Rome in 416 (p. 908; Probianus 1).

tenure of imperium, but of a special kind. It was defined as greater (*maius*) than that of any other magistrate, it was tenable for a longer period of time, and it was renewable; indeed, again following certain late republican precedents, it was formally detached from the need to hold any actual magistracy. By the second century, no doubt, only antiquarians thought of the principate as established in this way, and by the late empire it unlikely that anyone thought of it at all. Nevertheless, imperium was the foundation of the emperor's role in jurisdiction, which he exercised in the first place as a court of appeal against the judgments of lower (that is to say, all other) magistrates, later, and increasingly, however, as a judge of first instance in both criminal and civil cases.[8] By the early third century, and one would say much earlier, the legal authority of any imperial pronouncement was axiomatic; in the words of Ulpian, cited in the Digest, "Whatever the emperor has decided has the force of law"—"quod principi placuit legis habet vigorem" (Digest 1.4.1 pr.). Although it is often quoted as such, this is not a statement of the emperor's powers in general. It does not mean that the emperor could do whatever he wanted in any circumstances but was a precise statement of the principle that the emperor's decisions had the force of law because his imperium derived from a *lex*.[9]

In addition to adjudicating points of law, the emperors also made law. They did this, formally speaking, in two ways, the first arising from their role in jurisdiction. In this capacity they issued decrees, or *decreta,* which in their narrower sense were judicial decisions arising from cases heard by the emperor. These were classified as imperial *constitutiones* and, on the principle just outlined, possessed the force of law.[10] They also, much more commonly, offered responses in the form of rescripts addressed to individual petitioners. Although they were only supposed to have force in the case to which they applied, rescripts were displayed at the place where the judgment was given, where they could be read by the public and transcribed by lawyers for the sake of the precedents and statements of principle that they might contain. In such cases, they inevitably acquired legal force beyond the original circumstances in which they were issued.[11] The vast numbers and the technicality

8. For what follows see the discussion of the sources of law in Gaius, *Institutes* 1.2–7; de Zulueta, vol. 1, pp. 3–4, and vol. 2, pp. 13–23; F. Millar, *The Emperor in the Roman World* (1977), pp. 228–40, 507–37.

9. Compare Gaius, *Inst.* 1.5: "Constitutio principis est quod imperator decreto vel edicto vel epistula constituit; nec umquam dubitatum est quin legis vicem optineat, cum ipse imperator per legem imperium accipiat." On the scope and meaning of Ulpian's maxim, see esp. P. A. Brunt, "Lex de Imperio Vespasiani," *JRS* 67 (1977), pp. 95–116, at 110ff. For the juridical sense of *placere,* see A. Berger, *Encyclopaedic Dictionary of Roman Law,* s.v.

10. See Gaius, *Inst.* 1.5; Millar, pp. 239–40.

11. Gaius, *Inst.* 1.5 does not include rescripts in his list of legally authoritative *constitutiones*—though he was writing before the mature growth of the "rescript system."

The two leaves of the ivory diptych of Rufius Probianus, *vicarius urbis Romae,* show him in his role as judge. He is being addressed by rival advocates or petitioners, scrolls in hand (note, too, their individually characterized features), while two secretaries write down the proceedings on hinged wax tablets. Behind his throne, which stands on a low dais, can be seen the upper part of the ceremonial inkstand representing his judicial authority. The scroll lying open on his knees bears the acclamation "Probiane floreas."

If Probianus was the prefect of Rome of 416 (Chastagnol, *Les Fastes de la Préfecture de Rome au Bas-Empire,* pp. 275–76), then he held the vicariate in the very late fourth or in the first decade of the fifth century, either before 402 or after 408, given that two and not three emperors are depicted on the inkstand (R. Delbrück, *Die Consulardiptychen und verwandte Denkmäler* [Berlin and Leipzig, 1929], plate 65).

of the rescripts preserved from the late third century by the lawyers Gregorius and Hermogenianus, who assembled the codes that bear their names, clearly show that a legal system was in operation for the handling of these petitions.[12] It is perhaps stretching matters a little to call the system a "free legal advice service,"[13] but even the most fervent supporters of the idea that emperors did the daily work of government themselves could hardly deny that these rescripts were the work of jurists.

Whereas thousands of examples are recorded from the second and third centuries, little is known about the use of rescripts in the fourth century. That they continued to be used is shown by a late treatise that cites three rescripts among a group of seven texts from a single year, 365, but since fourth- and fifth-century rescripts were not systematically codified, this evidence lacks the context of supporting material.[14] Something of the sort may be implied by Ammianus Marcellinus' description of the argument that the praetorian prefect Modestus used to dissuade the emperor Valens from giving his personal attention to private lawsuits: the activity was below his dignity—one almost designed, as Modestus put it, for the very purpose of humbling his loftiness.[15] As this passage and many others imply, a vast amount of jurisdiction affecting individuals was exercised in the emperors' names, whether by rescript or in some other way, by the praetorian prefects and other officials at the imperial court. Whether or not rescripts possessed the quality of *generalitas,* that is whether they not only resolved points of law in particular cases but, in doing so, made law for others in the future, was an issue that was always problematic and remained so at the time of the composition of the Theodosian Code.[16]

The second way in which the emperors "made law" was through positive pronouncements intended for general observance and directed to the public in the

12. Tony Honoré, *Emperors and Lawyers* (2nd ed., 1994), chap. 2 (pp. 33–48).

13. Ibid., p. 33.

14. The seven texts are preserved in the so-called *Consultatio veteris cuiusdam iurisconsulti,* 9.1–7; Riccobono, vol. 2, pp. 610–11. Their ascription to the Codex Hermogenianus indicates a later revision of the Diocletianic text. The three rescripts among them are nos. 2 (to Pompeius Favonius), 5 (to Aelia Bavonia), and 6 (to Ampelia). Apart from its references to rescripts, the Theodosian Code contains at least one text that should be classified as such: 8.15.1, a pronouncement of Constantine in favor of Codia(s) and Agrippina. For Constantinian and later examples preserved in the Codex Justinianus and other sources, see Corcoran, *Empire of the Tetrarchs,* pp. 35–37, 301–2.

15. Amm. Marc. 30.4.2: "causarum minutiae privatarum." In the Tetrarchic period the emperor would normally have given his reply by rescript. To judge by the Notitia Dignitatum, later practice may have been to handle them in the administrative bureaus, or *scrinia* (see Chapter 7).

16. See Chapter 4.

form of edicts, or sent to their officials and provincial governors in the form of letters (*epistulae*), which it was their duty to make public under the authority of their own edicts.[17] These texts were made known by being read out and then displayed in the public places of the communities to which they were sent, usually in the form of paper notices, sometimes on linen sheets or wooden placards; occasionally, when permanency was desired, on stone or bronze inscriptions.[18] Unlike rescripts and decrees, which were essentially concerned with resolving legal questions, edicts and letters might be on any subject to which the emperor had occasion, for whatever reason, to turn his mind.

It is imperial pronouncements of this second category that our juristic sources of the late empire mean when they use the term *leges,* or laws. The use of the word in this sense is a departure for those accustomed to a more Classical usage. What is not in question are the leges of the republic and early empire, the equivalent of the modern idea of statute law, passed by the sovereign assemblies of the Roman people. Such laws, like some *senatusconsulta* of the early Empire, still underlay significant areas of the law of the later empire; their traces can be found in the Theodosian Code.[19] So too, very extensively in its earlier books, can the traces of the Praetor's Edict, formerly the publication by the urban praetor as he entered his year of office, of the manner in which he intended to conduct his legal administration. Roman praetors had long ceased to publish the edict in this way, but its cumulative contents, edited in the early second century and discussed by Gaius and in massive works by Paul and Ulpian, among others, continued to influence the procedures of Roman private law and the manner in which it was studied.[20] In the terminology of the late empire, leges might refer to any primary texts with the force of law, whether *lex populi* or senatusconsultum, magisterial edict, or—by several magnitudes the largest category—pronouncements made by the emperors in any of the forms just described.

If leges in this broader sense, otherwise called *constitutiones,*[21] are to be defined as the pronouncements of emperors considered as primary texts, this raises a second order of difficulties. Not all imperial pronouncements were of the same status, and they took varied forms, whether as edicts to the people, letters to magistrates, decrees, or (a category not mentioned earlier) legal interventions (*interlocutiones*) made in the course of proceedings in court. Were all such pronouncements,

17. Millar, *The Emperor in the Roman World,* pp. 566–84.

18. See the composite description of these procedures in Chapter 7.

19. Gaius, *Inst.* 1.4, raised the question whether senatusconsulta had the force of a lex; Gaius believed so, though others doubted it. The situation was probably that they did if the emperor endorsed them; Brunt, "Lex de Imperio Vespasiani," p. 112.

20. See Chapter 5.

21. As by Gaius, *Inst.* 1.5 (see n. 9).

which might have been made in specific circumstances or in response to specific inquiries, intended to have general validity, and was it possible to be sure that no others contradicted or superseded them? General applicability in the law might be defined formally so as to exclude rescripts; as we saw, these were not supposed to be valid in any case other than that for which they had been issued. But even this principle was difficult to apply in practice.[22] The emperors often gave general reasons for resolving cases as they did, the resulting judgment was displayed in public, and it might be difficult for a court confronted with any document emanating from the emperor to set aside its authority. That rescripts could make good law was shown by the Gregorian and Hermogenian Codes, which for the most part contained precisely such responses made to individuals in particular cases.[23] What was contentious about them, as with other individual pronouncements that might be adduced in court by advocates who happened to know about them, was doubt, not so much about their legal quality as about the integrity of the processes of petition and reply that had caused them to be issued; the sources are full of references to rescripts given "contra ius," or elicited in dubious circumstances or by improper means of influence.[24]

Given its scale and complexity, and the vast amount of juristic writing about it, the collection, analysis, and classification of this material was a scholarly challenge of massive proportions, and it was not fully accomplished until the publication of the Digest, representing in its monumental fifty books a reduction of the original material to about one-twentieth of its original bulk. The result, that the abbreviation seemed longer than the original, came as a paradox to its authors, though they had an answer for it. Lawyers and judges had been taking short cuts: "One remarkable fact has come to light from these books: that the mass of old work gives the appearance of being smaller in compass than the present work for all its brevity. The fact is that the men who conducted legal action in days gone by, in spite of the large number of laws that had been laid down, nevertheless made use of only a few of them in litigation, either because of a lack of books, which it was impossible for them to procure, or because of their own ignorance; and lawsuits were decided according to the will of the judges rather than by legal authority."[25] To put the matter

22. On *generalitas* see further Chapter 3. Cf. Honoré, *Emperors and Lawyers,* 2nd ed. (n. 12), p. 41: rescripts "did not purport to make law, though in practice they could hardly avoid doing so."

23. Honoré, *Emperors and Lawyers,* 2nd ed., pp. 29, 139–42.

24. Cf. the acclamations in the Gesta Senatus discussed in Chapter 3.

25. Const. "Tanta" (trans. G. E. M. de Ste. Croix), §17; Kunkel, *An Introduction,* p. 169. On the scale of the reduction, cf. Honoré, *Tribonian,* 147; well over two hundred legal works were excerpted, comprising about fifteen hundred "libri" of around ten thousand words each. The Digest itself claimed that two thousand books were read, a total of three million lines of

more sympathetically—it is the great Tribonian speaking, and it is a hard day for lawyers and judges when his standards are prescribed for everyone—in consequence of the sheer scale of the law of the jurists, the courts had operated with a selection of the Classical texts, and with abbreviated versions prepared by later writers; examples of this simplified application of ius are such texts as Paul's *Sententiae,* the *Regularum liber singularis* of Ulpian, and the *Epitomae* of Hermogenian.[26]

In circumstances where, through the combined efforts of emperors and jurists, the law had so proliferated both in quantity and in form, a case for its systematic codification could have been made at any time; in a sense, what is most surprising is the belatedness with which it was in fact undertaken. Mommsen expressed this surprise, in pointing out at the very beginning of the Prolegomena to his edition, that the Theodosian Code was the first occasion since the Twelve Tables on which a Roman government had attempted by public authority to collect and publish its leges.[27] In so saying, Mommsen no doubt underestimated the official status of the Gregorian and Hermogenian Codes under Diocletian,[28] but his judgment still deserves consideration. We do find complaints in fourth-century sources on the confusion in the state of the law and the opportunities for abuse and corruption to which this gave rise. In a satirical passage, Ammianus Marcellinus describes lawyers fleecing their clients by adducing recondite allusions to long-forgotten jurists and obscure legal precedents, in order to enrich themselves by prolonging lawsuits.[29] A near-contemporary of Ammianus, the anonymous writer of the tract *De rebus bellicis,* ends his work by requesting a revision of the law to eliminate its obscurities and contradictions: "One remedy designed to cure our civilian woes awaits your Serene Majesty: throw light upon the confused and contradictory

---

text; see the list of works read, pp. lxvi–xix Mommsen/Krüger—a claim repeated in Const. "Tanta," §1.

26. Cf. Honoré, *Tribonian,* p. 139. On Hermogenian, see Detlef Liebs, *Hermogenians Iuris Epitomae: Zum Stand der römischen Jurisprudenz im Zeitalter Diocletians* (1964).

27. Mommsen, Prolegomena, p. xi: "Per longa saecula, quibus stetit res publica Romana, bis tantum leges publico iussu collectae sunt et promulgatae, tempore antiquissimo Romae per decemviros legibus scribendis, collabente imperio Constantinopoli per Theodosium secundum."

28. Liebs, *Hermogenians Iuris Epitomae,* p. 25f.; J. D. Harries, "How to Make a Law-Code," in M. Austin, J. D. Harries, C. Smith (eds.), *Modus Operandi: Essays in Honour of Geoffrey Rickman* (1998), pp. 63–78, at 65–66.

29. Amm. Marc. 30.4.11f.; cf. my "Ammianus on Roman Law and Lawyers," in *Cognitio Gestorum: The Historiographic Art of Ammianus Marcellinus* (1992), pp. 47–57, at 48–50. At 30.4.11 Ammianus presents the relationship between ius and leges as one of conflict caused by contradictory leges: "Qui iuris professi scientiam, quam repugnantium sibi legum abolevere discidia." A different picture is given at 27.6.14: "Constans semper legumque similis [the magister memoriae and quaestor Eupraxius], quas omnibus una eademque voce loqui in multiplicibus advertimus causis," but this is an ideal, reflecting Cicero, *De officiis* 2.12.41f.

rulings of the laws by a pronouncement of Your August Dignity and put a stop to dishonest litigation. For what is so alien to decent conduct as to give vent to one's passion for strife in the very place where the decisions of Justice distinguish the merits of individuals?"[30]

One remark by a satirically inclined historian and another by an unknown commentator of generally acknowledged eccentricity, do not add up to a program of reform. But an awareness of the need for reform runs closer to home than this. Constantine, confirming in 333 rights of jurisdiction earlier given to bishops, adduced in support of his grant the "long and almost endless toils of litigation" in which petitioners might be "entangled" in the regular courts.[31] The eastern law of 15 February 438, by which the Theodosian Code received authority in the east, referred in equally expressive language to the "thick cloud of obscurity" by which the mass of imperial constitutions had been "shut off from human ingenuity." The emperor, by contrast, claimed to have "dispelled the darkness and given the light of brevity to the laws," to have "cleared away the cloud of volumes on which have been wasted away the lives of many persons."[32] He was referring to another feature of the Theodosian Code, not so much the act of codification itself, but the clearing away by its editors of the exhortatory rhetoric in which imperial pronouncements were regularly clothed.

The question why, given the general case for it, codification should be undertaken at any particular time relates in part to the juristic and general intellectual culture of an age, and also to the political climate. The attitude of lawyers, if we take at face value the comments of Constantine and the remarks of Ammianus, might be expected to be in favor of a carefully tended obscurity in the law, to give them the opportunity to profit from the "endless toils of litigation" and the naivety of their clients. Such suspicions have been expressed at all times and in all societies in which the law and its interpreters have any role to play. Against such self-interested obscurantism, we should set those "lawyerly" types described with such sympathy in the writings of Tony Honoré; intellectual lawyers seeking elegance, clarity, and consistency in the formulation of the law. For such men, sufficient complexity lay in the substance of the law to justify the existence of the legal profession. The law could not meet the ever-complex needs of society without being complex in itself, as was appreciated in another intriguing passage of the Emperor Justinian—again expressed on his behalf by Tribonian. "Things divine," wrote Tribonian, "are perfect,"

30. *De rebus bellicis,* 21; trans. E. A. Thompson, *A Roman Reformer and Inventor* (1952), p. 123.

31. *Sirm.* 1 (ed. Mommsen, p. 908).

32. *Nov. Th.* 1, §§1,3.

> but the character of human law is always to hasten onward, and there is nothing in it which can abide forever, since nature is eager to produce new forms. We therefore do not cease to expect that matters will henceforth arise that are not secured in legal ties ["quae adhuc legum laqueis non sunt innodata"]. Consequently, if any such case arises, let a remedy be sought from the Augustus, since in truth God has set the imperial function over human affairs, so that it should be able, whenever a new contingency arises, to correct and settle it and to subject it to suitable procedures and regulations. We are not the first to say this.[33]

This being so, all the greater is the need for consistency and clarity in the expression of the law, and the greater the intellectual satisfaction experienced in the achievement of these qualities.

To return to the age of Theodosius, apart from its practical usefulness, the intellectual resources surely existed for a work of codification. There is no question about the vigor and high profile of legal studies in the generations preceding the commissioning of the Theodosian Code, and indeed throughout the fourth century. Examples of a continuing interest in the law and legal texts include compilations such as the so-called *Fragmenta Vaticana,* possibly compiled in the early fourth century and expanded later, and the *Collatio legum Mosaicarum et Romanarum,* incorporating a text of 390 also included, from a different original version, in the Theodosian Code.[34] From the fourth century too come the Sentences of Paul and the Epitomes of Ulpian and Hermogenian mentioned earlier—all evidence of a sustained interest in Classical Roman law and of a perceived need for manageable statements of the writings of the jurists.[35] An eastern law of 396 cited an opinion of the Antonine jurist (Q. Cervidius) Scaevola, describing him as the "most learned of jurisconsults," a reference to a once famous jurist that has been taken to indicate a "new depth of research into past legal authorities."[36] One

33. Digest, Constitutio "Tanta," §18 (the quoted metaphor is the same as that of *Const. Sirm.* 1, but in a very different spirit). A similar sentiment is expressed in *Nov. Just.* 60 pr. (of 537): "Quosdam namque veri simile est multitudinem legum quae per singula a nobis adiciantur, non considerantes, quia opere semper vocante consonas causis ponere leges compellimur, cum semper inopinabile emerget at ab his quae iam posita sunt mederi non valent." The precedent cited by Tribonian is that of Salvius Julianus, the second-century redactor of the Praetor's Edict.

34. Riccobono, vol. 2, pp. 463–540, 539–89. The *Collatio* text is discussed in Chapter 9, "Theodosius on a Moral Scandal."

35. Honoré, *Tribonian,* p. 139.

36. *CTh* 4.4.3, "prudentissimum iuris consultorum"; cf. J. D. Harries, "Sozomen and Eusebius: The Lawyer as Church Historian in the Fifth Century," in C. Holdsworth and T. P. Wiseman (eds.), *The Inheritance of Historiography, 350–900* (1986), pp. 45–52, at 50; also at *JRS* 78 (1988), p. 169. For his full name, *PIR,* 2nd ed., C 681. Digest 27.1.13, §2, cites

may even detect the same survival, or indeed resurgence of interest in the Classical jurists, in the late fourth-century biographies of earlier emperors known as the Historia Augusta. In this text, not only are the political activities of Ulpian and Papinian exaggerated and idealized; fictitious dynasties of politically active lawyers are invented, ostensibly rising to prominence under the Severan emperors.[37] Tony Honoré presents the author of the Historia Augusta as an official or bureaucrat familiar with the requirements of legal documentation and even, specifically, with works of Gaius and Ulpian, and with the Gregorian and Hermogenian Codes.[38] Whether this is so or not, it would appear that legal studies were in the later fourth century enjoying the same scholarly (and scholastic) attention that can be demonstrated in the same period for other branches of literature and learning.

As many cases show, legal studies provided access to public careers in government and administration. Augustine described in his *Confessions* how his friend Alypius moved from a legal training at Rome to the post of assessor to the Italian branch of the *comes sacrarum largitionum;*[39] and Ammianus Marcellinus produces the case of Maximinus, the son of a government official, who rose to his infamous vicariate of Rome and then the praetorian prefecture of Gaul, having earlier practiced as a mediocre pleader of cases. The epigraphic evidence provides analogies, such as Sextilius Agesilaus Aedesius, known in his retirement as an initiate into various mystery cults at Rome. Aedesius, who also makes a passing appearance in Ammianus, described himself as a "not undistinguished orator [that is, barrister] at the African bar and in the imperial consistory," qualifications which led him successively to the offices of *magister libellorum et cognitionum sacrarum, magister epistolarum,* and *magister memoriae*. The career, and its combination of legal and bureaucratic experience, anticipate the professional qualifications of the fifth-century compilers of the Theodosian Code.[40]

---

him along with Paul and Ulpian as "leaders among the jurists" (in Greek, *koryphaioi tōn nomikōn*).

37. Harries, p. 50; cf. R. Syme, "Fiction About Jurists," *ZSS* 97 (1980), pp. 78–104 [= *Roman Papers* 3, pp. 1393–1414].

38. Tony Honoré, "Scriptor Historiae Augustae," *JRS* 77 (1987), pp. 156–76, at 166–68; developed in his *Law in the Crisis of Empire, 370–455 A.D.: The Theodosian Dynasty and Its Quaestors* (1998), chap. 9.

39. *Conf.* 6.8.13; 10.16; Detlef Liebs, "Nichtliterarische römische Juristen der Kaiserzeit," in K. Luig and D. Liebs (eds.), *Das Profil der Juristen in der europäischen Tradition* (1980), pp. 123–98 (Alypius at 189–91). The department in which Alypius was a legal *assessor* (cf. Augustine's "adsedebat") is listed at Notitia Dignitatum, Occ. 11.7, "comes largitionum Italicianarum," cf. 29 (Rome).

40. Maximinus, Amm. Marc. 28.1.6: "Post mediocre studium liberalium doctrinarum defensionemque causarum ignobilem." Aedesius, Amm. Marc. 15.5.4, 15; *ILS* 4152; *PLRE* I, p. 15f. (Aedesius 7). Regarding the career pattern, see Chapter 4.

These examples come from the later fourth-century west, but this is merely a matter of selection of the evidence. Law and the teaching of law had long enjoyed high standing in the east, notably in the development of the schools of law of Berytus (Beirut); it is significant that this took place in a Roman *colonia,* where the Latin language and Roman legal procedures were more in evidence than in a regular Greek city. The jurists Gaius (possibly) and Ulpian (certainly) came from the Roman Levant—the latter from the ancient city of Tyre, an origin of which he was extremely proud.[41] In the fourth century many letters and speeches of Libanius, however reluctantly—because they offered a serious challenge to the literary education provided by Libanius and his colleagues—attest the prestige of the schools of Berytus and of the Latin language in which Roman law was taught there. In one particularly venomous passage among many in which he expressed his view of legal studies, Libanius characterized students of law as having a dullness of intellect matched only by the weight of the great fat tomes that bore them down to their knees.[42]

Most modern writers see in such passages the recognition of a real and significant shift from the old literary to the new professional studies.[43] In describing how in 370, in order to justify the executions that were taking place at Antioch and in other eastern cities, the emperor's agents publicly burned the libraries of men accused of magic arts and conspiracy, Ammianus claimed that the supposedly incriminating books were harmless scholarly works of literature and law, "liberalium disciplinarum indices variarum et iuris."[44] The same author's satirical description of the behavior of members of the legal profession twice refers to their abuses as particularly rampant in the eastern provinces (30.4.4,8). It does not matter whether the allegation is true or not; it expresses an authentic perception of the prevalence of Roman law in the cities of the east. We have already seen, in an

41. Cf. for Gaius, Honoré, *Gaius* (1962), p. 85 (speculative), for Ulpian, Dig. 50.15.1 pr., *PIR,* 2nd ed., D 169; Honoré, *Ulpian* (1982), pp. 8–10. Tyre achieved colonial status in the Severan period; Berytus was an Augustan colony. See the general characterization of eastern legal culture by Honoré, *Law in the Crisis of Empire,* p. 24.

42. *Or.* 4.18 Foerster. I owe this particularly enjoyable reference to Raffaella Cribiore of Columbia University.

43. Jones, *Later Roman Empire,* pp. 512f., 753, 989f.; J. H. W. G. Liebeschuetz, *Antioch: City and Imperial Administration in the Later Roman Empire* (1972), pp. 242–55 ("The Rival Studies"); Honoré, *Law in the Crisis of Empire,* pp. 9–10. A classic study of the schools of Berytus is P. Collinet, *Histoire de l'école de droit de Beyrouth* (Etudes historiques sur le droit de Justinien, 1925).

44. Amm. Marc. 29.1.41. The passage also distinguishes, no doubt for stylistic reasons only, between texts written in codex and those written in roll form: "Congesti innumeri codices, et acervi voluminum multi." Ammianus can hardly mean that either specific branch of literature was by preference consigned to *volumina* or codices.

eastern law of 396, the citation of an opinion of that "most learned of jurisconsults," Scaevola.[45] There is no suggestion that the eastern empire was in any way deficient in legal expertise; rather, from Ulpian through Hermogenian to the Digest,[46] it led the field. It is just what one would expect, given the progressive shift of political power to the east, confirmed in the time of Constantine, which had continued through the fourth into the early fifth centuries. Also relevant in the broader context is the increased franchise of the Latin language in the Greek east, promoted by the move of the emperors and their government apparatus to eastern capital cities.[47]

The fourth century was as much a time of litigation and lawyers as any other period of the Roman Empire; how should it be otherwise? A question still attaches to the quality of the product, and some observers have perceived a serious decline in the quality of late Roman jurisprudence. A particularly telling example has been seen in the law addressed in the form of an imperial oration to the Senate of Rome on 7 November 426, which can be recovered in various extracts from the Theodosian Code and the Codex Justinianus. This law confirmed as valid the writings of five Classical lawyers, Papinian, Paul, Gaius, Ulpian, and Modestinus, giving Gaius the same authority as the others and allowing the citation of any passage of his writings.[48] It also allowed the validity of other authorities cited by these five, naming as examples Scaevola—presumably the Q. Cervidius Scaevola already mentioned—Sabinus, Julianus, Marcellus, and "any others whom they may cite," provided that the texts of the citations were confirmed. Conflicting views were to be resolved by a counting of opinions among the five, and where this left the matter unsettled, the decisive opinion was to be that of Papinian, a man of genius "superior to any other, though inferior to two." In any case where the authorities were equally divided (presumably in the absence of a ruling from Papinian), the discretion would lie with the presiding judge.

This, the so-called Law of Citations, has been described as the "low-water mark of Roman jurisprudence," for the unsophistication of its critical principles.[49] It is at

45. The Q. Cervidius Scaevola mentioned earlier.

46. The origin of Hermogenian is not known, but he pursued his work under Diocletian, hence in the east.

47. *The Roman Empire of Ammianus,* pp. 71f., 80, 467f.

48. *CTh* 1.4.3. The same authorities provided the basis also for the Digest (but without the weight of authority given to Papinian); Honoré, *Tribonian,* p. 146. The law of 426 also allowed the authority of the *Sententiae* of Paul, but it disallowed that of the *notae* of Paul and Ulpian on Papinian. This last point had been long established—cf. *CTh* 1.4.1, 9.43.1 (21 and 28 September, 324).

49. Jones, *Later Roman Empire,* p. 471; Schulz, *Roman Legal Science,* pp. 281f.—though neither writer recognizes the complexity of the entire text as recovered from the Codes. For a more positive view, see J. D. Harries, "'Sacra generalitas': The Administrative Background to

first sight remarkable that the authority of legal opinions could be determined by a counting of heads. But it is not obvious that the method set out here is any less sophisticated or any more arbitrary than that described nearly three centuries earlier by Gaius. According to that writer, if the *prudentes* (the jurists) were in agreement, then their collective view had the force of law, but if they did not agree, then the judge was "at liberty to follow whichever decision he pleases."[50] And if that view is oversimplified (it does not seem likely that Gaius is actually mistaken), then so may be the impression given by the Law of Citations. The extract here summarized is part of a much more extensive constitution covering, in excerpts preserved elsewhere in the Theodosian Code and in the Codex Justinianus, some complex questions in testamentary law and the law of property relating to gifts and transfers through *emancipatio*. None of this marks a "low-water mark"; it is difficult legislation requiring a high level of legal comprehension. The further excerpts of the law, lost from the Theodosian Code but preserved in the Codex Justinianus, reveal a different emphasis.[51] Here we find definitions of the categories of imperial pronouncements that constituted "leges generales" (*CJ* 1.14.2–3), rescripts given "contra ius" (1.19.7), questions relating to fraudulent petitions (1.22.5), and replies given by the consistorium in response to reports and consultations of judicial authorities in particular cases (1.14.2).

The combination of topics covered by the imperial *oratio* of 426 is a mystery, since one would expect its comprehensive statements about the sources and authority of law to be matched by a broader set of applications than the one substantive issue that seems to be addressed.[52] Whatever the explanation of the asymmetry between form and substance in the law, one thing is clear: it by no means betokens a decline in the science of jurisprudence.

---

the Theodosian Code," in *Estudios de Historia da Derecho Europeo* (1994), pp. 34–35; the purpose of the law was to guide judges on which legal authorities could and could not be cited in their courts. Similarly Tony Honoré, *Law in the Crisis of Empire,* p. 250, considers that the provision "does not deserve the disesteem into which it has fallen" and points out that it was necessary to put some limits on the application of Gaius, *Inst.* 1.7. It must be remembered that the law had not yet been codified, a situation that greatly enhanced the difficulties facing courts of law.

50. *Inst.* 1.7: "Quorum omnium si in unum sententiae concurrunt, id quod sentiunt legis vicem optinet; si vero dissentiunt, iudici licet quam velit sententiam sequi." There is a body of opinion that takes this to be a fourth or fifth century interpolation, but there really are no grounds for this—de Zulueta, vol. 2, p. 21.

51. These extracts were included in the Theodosian Code and are absent from it only because of the incomplete preservation of its early books (see Chapter 5).

52. Honoré, *Law in the Crisis of Empire,* pp. 249–51, describing the law as a mini-code, attributes the initiative to Galla Placidia and, p. 255, the authorship to Antiochus, later chairman of the first Theodosian Code commission, but I think this too heavy an inference. What we have is an imperial *oratio* covering two subjects.

The law suggests a further possibility. Because of its broader aspects as they relate to the definition and restriction of the notion of "general law," and because it precedes by less than three years the initiation of work on the Theodosian Code, it is natural to wonder whether it may have some bearing on the origins of the Code itself. If so, the connection is indirect. The law originated in the west, as an address of Valentinian III to the Senate at Rome, of which there is, or at least there survives, no eastern counterpart; short of evidence, it cannot simply be assumed that either the legislation itself or the initiative for it came from the east.[53] That the editors were aware of the law when they addressed their work on the Theodosian Code is beyond doubt, but its relevance to the origins of the Code cannot be taken for granted.

We are closer to the actual working environment in which the Theodosian Code was conceived in an eastern law, of 27 February 425, regulating the practice of higher education at Constantinople; it survives in two extracts included at separate places in the Theodosian Code (14.9.3; 15.1.53). The main terms of the law were to establish three orators and ten grammarians in the Latin language and five "sophists" and ten grammarians in Greek. In addition, since these studies were to lead to "a more profound knowledge and learning," there were to be one professor of philosophy and two "who shall expound the formulas of the law and statutes."[54]

One possible misconception can be cleared up at once. The law does not indicate a vast expansion of higher education at the eastern capital; its more obvious aim is a tightening of state control, expressed particularly in the separation of public from private teaching, and in its restrictions upon the latter. It withdrew the right to practice from freelance professors who had gathered around them bands of students in public or private places, and although it permitted professors employed by private households to continue teaching in them, this was the only teaching they were allowed to do. Conversely, approved professors were debarred from teaching in private houses. Another law issued less than a month later enhanced the status of the public teaching profession; in this law, professors who had attained twenty years of service were granted the rank of *comes primi ordinis* with equivalent status to ex-*vicarii*.[55] This provision, assimilating the status of professors of law to that of senior governors and civil servants, has a bearing upon the successive commissions established to supervise the editorial work on the Theodosian Code.[56]

A special feature of the law of 425 is its emphasis on the physical premises in

53. It is sometimes argued that the western law was issued in response to an eastern initiative, but there is no proof of this.

54. "Iuris ac legum formulas"—note again the distinction between *ius* and *leges*.

55. *CTh* 6.21.1 (15 March 425). The six first beneficiaries in the various branches of learning are listed; the jurist was Leontius (*PLRE* 2, p. 669; Leontius 7).

56. See Chapter 4.

which the teaching was to be conducted. One does not usually encounter in ancient sources such an image of higher education in a form resembling that of a medieval or modern university, that is to say in a specific location with dedicated buildings and an established professorate. The teaching was conducted at the so-called Capitolium; this was a location, named after though not much resembling its Roman original, situated at the end of the porticoes of the Mesê, the main avenue leading from the Hippodrome through the Forum of Theodosius I and on to the Golden Gate.[57] The law stated the need for the auditorium assigned to each teacher to be separate from others, "in order that the teachers may not drown out each other, and the mingled confusion of tongues may not divert the ears or the minds of any from the study of letters." The second excerpt, preserved as *CTh* 15.1.53, shows that substantial building or conversion work was planned. This excerpt speaks of *exedrae* (conference halls) adjoining the "north portico," which could form rooms of sufficient size and elegance for the use of teachers (whose modern successors would often welcome this criterion). The rooms on the east and west sides should be assigned for use by the old *popinae* or snack bars (extending the modern parallel, one thinks of student cafeterias); with no ready access to the streets, these halls could not readily be used for teaching. The law also authorizes the taking over of smaller rooms adjoining lecture rooms and the removal of dividing walls to create larger teaching spaces, with the provision that any current occupants who owned the requisitioned accommodation by imperial or other gift or by legal purchase were to be compensated from public funds. Whether the exedrae and portico referred to in this excerpt are the same as, or in some part of, the Capitolium of 14.9.3 is not entirely clear, but that is the natural reading of the text of the law. John the Lydian, writing in the sixth century, still refers to his legal education as having been received "at the Capitolium"; it was only later that any other location is connected with the teaching of law.[58]

As already suggested, ancient universities were usually rather loose organizations of individual and often rival teachers, operating in favored cities with followings of students in public spaces and gardens, in libraries, and in private or rented accommodation rather than in purpose-built or dedicated premises or anything resembling a modern faculty.[59] This is certainly the impression gained, for the fourth century, from the writings of Libanius, Eunapius, and Augustine. But it must

57. *CTh* 14.9.3; cf. Cyril Mango, *Le développement urbain de Constantinople, IVe–VIIe siècles* (1985), p. 30, with nn. 44–46; P. Lemerle, *Le premier humanisme byzantin* (1971), pp. 63ff., with n. 58.

58. John Lydus 3.29; R. Janin, *Constantinople byzantine* (2nd ed., 1964), pp. 174–76; Mango, p. 30 n. 44. The Capitolium is distinct from the Basilica in which the study of the law was conducted at a later time.

59. Cf. Jones, *Later Roman Empire,* p. 998; and esp. Alan Cameron, "The End of the Ancient Universities," *Journal of World History* 10.4 (1967), pp. 653–73, at 653–56.

always have been truer of some subjects than of others. Philosophy can no doubt be studied while walking round a garden or sitting under a tree, but this was not true of the more technical and empirical subjects, for which reference books and commentaries were in constant use. One can hardly imagine that the specialized schools of Alexandria in mathematics, astronomy, and medicine lacked dedicated premises to house their resources. Least of all would one suppose that schools of law, with their needs for libraries and archives (think of the fifteen hundred *libri* summarized in the Digest, not to mention the students mentioned by Libanius, weighed down by their load of books), could have managed without premises adapted to the nature of their work. It may in the end be the case that, far from representing a new image of an ancient university, the schools of Constantinople were being organized like some existing ones, with the emperor providing appropriate facilities, in prominent buildings that would enable the schools to express their newly enhanced public role, and to rival older and more famous institutions.

One obvious feature connects the Theodosian Code with the old world of the Roman Empire: the Latin language. Not for another century would Greek take its definitive place as the language of government and administration in the east, as it was and always had been the language of its culture.[60] The adoption of Greek by the eastern administration in the 530s was deplored by the conservative bureaucrat John the Lydian as a reprehensible break with the past perpetrated by his bête noire, the infamous John the Cappadocian.[61] A precedent was assigned by John the Lydian to the Empress Eudocia's protégé the praetorian prefect Cyrus, who is said to have issued edicts in Greek. The outrage prompted John, in two almost identical passages, to cite an oracle predicting the decline of the Roman Tychê, or Fortune.[62]

We must not exaggerate the practical effects of such initiatives. The question is largely one of ideology rather than practice; insofar as it is one of practice, it affects mainly the central administration and certain formal transactions in law. In private transactions, the essential concessions to social experience had been made long ago, and not only in relation to Latin and Greek. Ulpian had in the early third century allowed the validity of *fideicommissa* made not only in Latin or Greek but in Punic, Gallic (that is, Celtic), "or any other language," and in another passage discussed the force of verbal agreements made between parties who used different languages. He endorsed the view that contracts might be made in any language, provided that both parties understood what was being said, through an interpreter

60. G. Dagron, "Aux origines de la civilisation byzantine: Langue de culture et langue d'état," *Revue Historique* 241 (1969), pp. 23–56.

61. Michael Maas, *John Lydus and the Roman Past* (1992), esp. pp. 25, 32, 87.

62. Joh. Lyd. 2.12, cf. 3.42; Cyrus "proclaimed decrees" (*psêphous*) in Greek; Dagron, p. 41.

if necessary.[63] Legal texts of the late fourth and mid-fifth centuries show that formal judgments and the wills of Roman citizens were no longer required to be written in Latin, according to the old custom. Both rulings were concessions to existing practice, and the second of them, in a text of 439, extended an established right.[64] If the inspiration for this law may be assigned to the prefect Cyrus, then it is worth emphasizing that despite his predilection for Greek, the law was actually promulgated in Latin. The rationale for the law might even lie in the publication of the Theodosian Code itself, if this might have been thought to reinforce the position of Latin against the tendency of practical use. Lawyers might have begun to challenge the validity of wills made in Greek, thereby forcing a restatement of the position that this language might be used.

The issue is not whether, or to what extent, Greek was used in the cities of the east and in legal transactions conducted there—practical considerations ensured, and the evidence makes clear, that this always had been so—but whether Latin should remain the official language of an administration now concerned only with Greek-speaking provinces. The evidence of the Theodosian Code conforms with that of the vast bulk of the codification initiated by Justinian, where the Digest, Institutes, and Codex Justinianus still show Latin as the official language of the central administration.[65] Only partway through the Novellae, say from about 535, does the Greek language assert itself over the conservatism of John the Lydian.[66] For practical purposes, indeed, the Justinianic codification was translated into Greek immediately upon its publication. From then on, as A. H. M. Jones remarked, Latin ceased to be essential even for the academic lawyer.[67] At the time of publication of the Theodosian Code, that was very far from being the case. Latin was still the language of law and the central administration, and the sense of imperial unity, itself the conscious focus of imperial policy, would ensure that this remained so.

For Mommsen, as we saw, the Theodosian Code offered a double paradox: that Roman law was compiled by public order only twice, at the very beginning of the history of Rome and in the days of its decline; and that the second of these

63. Digest 32.11 pr.; 45.1.1 (Latin, Greek, Punic, "Assyrian," i.e., Syriac).

64. *CJ* 7.45.12 (of 397); *Nov. Theod.* 16.8 (of 439). The old legal custom is set out by Gaius, *Inst.* 2.281: "Legata graece scripta non valent, fideicommissa vero valent."

65. For a Latin papyrus of the Theodosian Code from the late fifth/early sixth century, see Chapter 3.

66. Honoré, *Tribonian,* chap. 4; cf. the figures nn. 1–3 to p. 124: between the years 529 and 535, 257 surviving texts were issued in Latin, 33 in Greek; by contrast, between 535 and 541 only 21 were issued in Latin, 115 in Greek.

67. Jones, *Later Roman Empire,* pp. 989f. and n. 7.

initiatives was brought about not at Rome but at Constantinople after the end of the Roman state.[68] I have been attempting an explanation in cultural terms of why the project was undertaken at this late hour in Roman history, and in the east, and have proposed as the context the perceived need for a simplification of the law, and the prominence of the eastern provinces in the study of Roman law, while denying the claim that late Roman law was an art in decline.

In considering this question, however, it is not only juristic criteria that we have to take into account. The presence of interested individuals, the necessary stimulus and organization, these things speak for themselves but do not necessarily explain why a project of codification should go forward at any particular moment. For this, we may also have to reckon with a historical perception of the role and importance of law. The law is not just a facility for resolving problems and attributing responsibility in a peaceful and publicly accountable fashion; it stands for something significant in the ideology of the state, which may be felt much more acutely at some times than at others. With the Theodosian Code, as later with the work of Justinian, we find ourselves at such a moment, when a need is felt to make this clear, to sum up an achievement because it forms a part of the perceived aims of a state or because these aims are threatened. This perspective, self-evident in the case of Justinian, with the reconquest of the west taking shape as an idea within the government at the same time as the codification of the law,[69] is also relevant to our understanding of the Theodosian Code.

As will be clear from the first chapter of this book, the Theodosian Code was published at a time when the unity of eastern and western partes imperii was a matter of very public emphasis, in terms both of practical politics and of ceremonial promotion. We are now going to see how the Code, received by the western delegate Faustus at Constantinople, was presented by him to the Roman Senate for publication in the western empire. Its acceptance by the Senate was a foregone conclusion, for the vote followed more than ten months after its validation in the east, by the constitution of 15 February 438, addressed to the praetorian prefect of the east (*Nov. Th.* 1). The circumstances of acceptance in the west are nevertheless of great interest, both in themselves and as providing neglected evidence on the historical development of the late Roman Senate. In going from the new Rome to the old, we move into a world of ceremonious formality that could serve as a model for anything Byzantine.

68. Prolegomena, p. xi (quoted in n. 27). For Mommsen, the codification of Justinian clearly fell outside the "longa saecula, quibus stetit res publica Romana."

69. Honoré, *Tribonian,* esp. pp. 17–19; Kunkel, *Introduction to Roman Legal and Constitutional History,* pp. 163–64; cf. Digest, Const. "Tanta," §23, where the completion of the Digest is connected with victory over Persia and the recovery of the west.

# 3

## "Senatus Amplissimi Gesta"

Conveyed to the west by Faustus, the Theodosian Code was promulgated there at a meeting of the Roman Senate held on 25 December 438. The record of the proceedings, as published by Fl. Laurentius, "exceptor amplissimi senatus," whose subscription with this title appears at the end of the document, is preserved in a single eleventh-century manuscript in the Ambrosian Library at Milan.[1] The manuscript also preserves a law of 23 December 443, from which it appears that the record of the meeting, described as "senatus amplissimi gesta," had been sent to the government at Ravenna by the praetorian prefect Faustus, then holding that office for the second time.[2] Faustus had appended the Gesta Senatus to support his request for confirmation that exclusive rights in the preparation of copies of the Code be vested in the *constitutionarii* Flavius Anastasius and Hilarius Martinus; it was to them that the emperor's reply, the law of 443, was addressed. On pain of a fine, no persons other than the constitutionarii were to engage in the publication or manufacture of copies for sale: "nec habeant [that is to say, unauthorized persons] vel de editione vel de confectione commercium."

The situation revealed by the law is an interesting one and is evidence for an

1. See Chapter 5. The manuscript of the Breviarium of Alaric is that known as *A*. The epitaph of Laurentius, describing him as "scriba senatus," survives as *CIL* 6.33721. He was buried on 12 March 451; *PLRE* 2, p. 659 (Laurentius 11).

2. Cf. *Nov. Val.* 2.2 (13 August 442); *PLRE* 2, p. 454.

early demand for texts of the Code. It appears that the need for copies already outstripped the rate of official production, so that even competent authorities were forced to seek pirate copies.[3] The law also recalled how the measures devised by Theodosius for the protection of the Code had been further supported by the diligence of the Senate.[4] This is a reference to the Gesta of 438, in which the Senate's "diligence" had been expressed, in the series of acclamations to be discussed below. The Senate was very specific on the question of protecting the text of the Code and supporting the authority of the constitutionarii; it was possibly the latter who ensured that this confirmation of their rights would be preserved, by appending both the Gesta and the law of 443 to copies of the Code subsequently produced by them, one of which descended to the manuscript in the Ambrosian Library. If so, it is to the constitutionarii, and their champion the praetorian prefect Faustus, that we owe the survival of a fascinating document, unique evidence for the conduct of a meeting of the late Roman Senate.

The Gesta Senatus begin with the consuls of 438, the Emperor Theodosius (for the sixteenth time) and Anicius Acilius Glabrio Faustus. Then follows an interesting detail. It was at Faustus' residence "quae est ad Palmam," and not in the Curia Senatus or any other public building which might be used for the purpose, that the Senate assembled to hear his address.[5] The place referred to here and in sources of the early sixth century as "ad Palmam" or Palma Aurea was apparently situated in the district known as Carinae ("the Keels"), at the foot of Mons Oppius, between the baths of Trajan and the Subura.[6] To the south were the Colosseum, the Templum Urbis and the basilica of Constantine, to the west and north-west the impe-

3. This may be inferred from the text of the law: "Sacrilegii poena constringi *tam cognitionale officium quam eos* qui nostris minime paruerunt constitutis" (the words italicized here refer to judicial officials and their departments).

4. "A senatu diligentia maiore munitum." The Senate is not claiming diligence superior to the emperor's. The meaning is that the emperor's diligence was further enhanced by that of the Senate.

5. Richard Talbert, *The Senate of Imperial Rome* (1984), pp. 113–20, shows that in the earlier period several locations were used, including (for the emperor's convenience) the Palatine, and various temples. These particular locations were not appropriate in 438, but this is not to say that no choice of venue existed.

6. Platner-Ashby, *Topographical Dictionary of Ancient Rome* (1929), p. 382; an alternative location suggested for the domus of Faustus is the place known as domus Palmata mentioned by Cassiodorus (*Variae* 4.30) as situated by the porticus Curva of the Forum of Trajan (Platner-Ashby, p. 187). Jordan, *Topographie der Stadt Rom,* 1.2, pp. 257–59 and n. 91, identified the two locations domus Palmata and Palma Aurea, connecting both with the apsed *secretarium senatus* restored by the prefect of Rome in A.D. 412 after a fire (*CIL* 6.1718 = *ILS* 5522). Whether this is so or not, the most natural understanding of the texts is to locate the domus of Faustus in the Old Forum area near the Curia Senatus.

rial fora. Close by was the temple of Tellus and the tribunal and *secretarium,* or departmental office, of the urban prefecture. The *domus* of Faustus thus stood near the administrative quarter of fourth- and fifth-century Rome. It was here, "ad Palmam," that king Theoderic began his visit to Rome in 517 by addressing the people,[7] and other sources bear out the character of the location as a place of official and public assembly.

The holding of a meeting of the Roman Senate in a private house is in part to be explained by the continuing habit of the praetorian prefects of conducting business in their own premises.[8] This practice, attested at Constantinople into the later fifth century, is still more likely to be true of Rome, since the praetorian prefecture, unlike the *praefectura urbis,* was not a local function and did not possess official accommodation in the city. The praetorian prefect could, if he wished, have requested the senators to assemble at one of their normal venues and gone there to present to them the business entrusted to him by the emperor; that he did not do so was perhaps designed to emphasize his initiative in what was not after all a regular meeting of the Senate.

To this "constitutional" point we must add a practical sense of the social realities of fifth-century Rome, in which Faustus was not only praetorian prefect but a leading member of one of the greatest senatorial families. For all his official regalia as praetorian prefect and consul, he was still the senator they knew, his prestige established beyond all question by the three urban prefectures he had already held. As for the "domus," we should think of a substantial mansion, equipped with a ceremonial audience hall such as the brilliantly decorated basilica known from the Esquiline house of the Constantinian prefect Junius Bassus, later converted into the church of S. Andrea in Catabarbara.[9] Though a private property, the domus of Faustus will, in design and decor as well as in its location, have conveyed much of the public ambience befitting a meeting of the Roman Senate. Faustus is also known from inscriptions to have set up statues of his father, Acilius Glabrio Sibidius Spedius, and of his father-in-law, Tarrutenius Maximilianus, in the *forum* of which his father was the "founder and first builder."[10] Whether it is connected with

7. Anonymus Valesianus 2.66; cf. *Vita Fulgentii* 13.

8. John Lydus, *De Mag.* 2.20; cited by A. H. M. Jones, *JRS* 54 (1964), p. 79.

9. Otherwise "cata Barbara Patricia"; the church was dedicated by the Goth Fl. Valila (qui et) Theodovius (*PLRE* 2, p. 1147) in 471/83, cf. *Liber pontificalis,* ed. Duchesne (2nd ed., Paris, 1955), vol. 1, p. 250; Raymond Davis, *The Book of Pontiffs (Liber pontificalis)* (1989), pp. xxxii, 41. For the location and history of the basilica, see Platner-Ashby, *Topographical Dictionary,* pp. 80–81; Ernest Nash, *A Pictorial Dictionary of Ancient Rome* (1961), pp. 190–95, with plates 213–20. The building was in ruins by the fifteenth century and its remains were finally destroyed in 1930.

10. "Fori huiusce inventori et conditori primo," *ILS* 1281 = *CIL* 6.1678, cf. *ILS* 1282 = *CIL* 6.1767.

the house "ad Palmam" or with some other property of the family of Faustus, the building of such a private forum expresses the social and economic pre-eminence of the senatorial class of Rome at a time when many parts of the city were in disrepair; other sources of the same period mention the forum of Apronianus, and that of Petronius Maximus.[11] The situation is typical of that underpinning of public office by private prestige and wealth which had characterized the role of the senatorial class of the fourth century and was still more important in the fifth.[12]

The full title of Faustus, "tertio expraefecto urbi, praefectus praetorio et consul ordinarius," also heads the names of the three high officials present at the meeting of the Senate: the others, mentioned in order of seniority, are Fl. Paulus, "v.c. et inl(ustris) urbis praefectus," and Iunius Pomponius Publianus, "vir spectabilis vicarius urbis aeternae." Then come "proceres amplissimusque ordo senatus." The senators, having assembled, had some discussion among themselves, the nature of which is not recorded but which one can guess was procedural. Then the constitutionarii Anastasius and Martinus were invited to join the meeting; these are the Fl. Anastasius and Hilarius Martinus, to whom, still at their work five years later, the law of 23 December 443 was addressed. The constitutionarii were not senators; despite the unusual circumstances of this meeting, the ancient convention of formally inviting them to join the deliberations was observed.

With all relevant parties present, Faustus was ready to address the meeting. He began by reminding his listeners of the circumstances. Recalling his attendance the previous year at the marriage of Valentinian and Eudoxia, he told how, after the wedding ceremonies, the Emperor Theodosius had announced his desire to present to the world a compendium of imperial law, to be called after himself.

Having thus mentioned the emperor, Faustus paused, while his words were greeted with acclamations of approval, somewhat generous, on the evidence he had provided so far, of the eloquence of his presentation: "nove diserte, vere diserte." When the acclamations were over, he described how the emperor had summoned to his presence Faustus and the praetorian prefect of the east, and had ordered a copy of the new codex to be conveyed to each of them from his "divine hand." Faustus concluded his statement by acknowledging the presence in the Senate of the constitutionarii and proposing the reading out of the law by which the emperor had brought all this about. (Faustus actually says "leges" in the plural, but only one was read.)

Again acclamations followed, this time of assent—"aequum est, placet, placet"—and Faustus, presumably taking the copy from the constitutionarii, proceeded to read out the law of 26 March 429, addressed to the senate of Con-

11. Respectively, *CTh* 13.5.19, of 400; *CIL* 6.1197, of 443/5.

12. Matthews, *Western Aristocracies and Imperial Court,* chaps. 1.1 and 14, pp. 355–62.

stantinople, by which the project had been initiated. The law, cited by Faustus "ex codice Theodosiano, libro primo, sub titulo 'de constitutionibus principum et edictis,'" is *CTh* 1.1.5 in the edition of Mommsen and is the fundamental evidence for the manner in which the Theodosian Code was compiled, and for its purpose. The contents of the law are described in the Chapter Four. For the moment, however, we turn our attention to the acclamations that followed Faustus' reading of the law, which were such a distinctive feature of the senatorial proceedings.

Acclamations have been defined as "the expression, in unison, of wish, opinion or belief, by large gatherings of people, often employing conventional rhythms and turns of phrase."[13] Among the many religious, social, and political contexts in which they are found, acclamations by urban crowds gathered at places of assembly such as theaters and hippodromes had long been a feature of the life of Hellenistic and Roman cities. A well-known example is the slogan "Great is Artemis of the Ephesians!" chanted for "about two hours" in the theater at Ephesus during the visit there of the apostle Paul and his traveling companions; this particular demonstration was organized by the silversmiths of Ephesus, anxious about the loss in trade they would incur if the great goddess Artemis and her temple, one of the Seven Wonders of the World, should go out of business.[14]

For Rome itself, sources of the later republican and early imperial periods provide vivid examples of the range and variety of sentiments that might be uttered by a well-informed—or well-guided—populace, and there are instances of even the most overbearing emperors' being forced to yield to popular demands expressed in this way.[15] In acclamations at the theater the people forced Tiberius to restore a well-loved statue to its place in the baths of Agrippa, from where he had removed it to his house (Pliny, *Hist. Nat.* 34.62); according to Suetonius (*Tib.* 47), the same emperor was unwilling to attend public shows after he was forced by acclamations to manumit a popular comic actor. Tiberius' successor Caligula had to cancel

13. This is the definition offered at the outset of Charlotte Roueché's wide-ranging "Acclamations in the Later Roman Empire: New Evidence from Aphrodisias," *JRS* 74 (1984), pp. 181–99; see also T. Klauser, "Akklamation," *Reallexikon für Antike und Christentum*, vol. 1 (1950), cols. 213–33.

14. Acts 19.23ff.; A. N. Sherwin-White, *Roman Society and Roman Law in the New Testament* (1963, repr. 1965), pp. 83–92; Roueché, "Acclamations in the Later Roman Empire," p. 181, noting Louis Robert's suggestion that the slogan was a ritual cry addressed to the goddess. For a particularly interesting later (third-century) sequence of acclamations, see Charlotte Roueché, "'Floreat Perge,'" in M. M. Mackenzie and C. Roueché (eds.), *Images of Authority: Papers Presented to Joyce Reynolds on the Occasion of her 70th Birthday* (1989), pp. 204–27.

15. Z. Yavetz, *Plebs and Princeps* (1969), at pp. 18–24 and in many later passages.

unpopular new taxes, and on one occasion to withdraw from Rome to Campania in the face of popular demands that he outlaw informers (Dio 59.28.11; 13.7). It is not surprising that he should wish, in a famous remark, that the people of Rome had a single neck, given that they were so capable of speaking with a single, and hostile, voice (Suetonius, *Cal.* 30.2)! The historian Josephus, appreciating the situation as a general one, wrote of the Circus at Rome that "the Romans are particularly enthusiastic about this spectacle. They are accustomed to gather there and to make requests of the emperor, and the emperors gain popularity by yielding" (*Ant. Iud.* 19.25).

The demonstrations, which might be more or less spontaneous, were organized into rhythmic, sometimes also antiphonal, chants by cheerleaders, behind whom might lurk senatorial or other pressure groups. A common soldier who led a military mutiny in A.D. 14 had learned his skill as a theatrical cheerleader at Rome: "dux theatralium operarum . . . miscere coetus histrionali studio doctus."[16] Or the people could demonstrate against unpopular local masters, as when Julian was greeted at Antioch in 362 by the chant "Everything plentiful, everything dear," directed to the emperor in the theater against the producers and shopkeepers whom the people believed responsible for the high price of food. At least as an expression of opinion it was successful. Julian responded by instructing the local council to sort the matter out within three months and, when this failed, by imposing a price freeze.[17]

The more formal acclamations acquired status as the legitimate expression of the people's will. Constantine encouraged the utterance of acclamations in praise and censure of governors, instructing that praetorian prefects and their deputies should refer to "Our Knowledge" the "voices" of the provincials, so that the emperor might reward or criticize governors as appropriate: "We grant to all persons the privilege of praising by public acclamation the most just and vigilant judges, so that We may grant increased accessions of honor to them. On the contrary, the unjust and the evildoers must be accused by cries of complaints, in order that the force of Our censure may destroy them. For we shall investigate whether such utterances are truthful and not poured forth effusively and wantonly by clients. The praetorian prefects and the counts who are stationed throughout the provinces shall refer to Our wisdom the utterances of Our provincials."[18] The acclamations of the people of Rome, like those of provincials, were conveyed to the emperor by the *cursus publicus,* it being the urban prefect's duty to transmit

16. Tacitus, *Ann.* 1.16.4; the soldier's name was Percennius. He had perhaps been recruited to the legions in the urban levies conducted after the defeat of Varus in A.D. 9.

17. *Misopogon,* 368C. That Julian's own measures were not successful is a different story: Matthews, *The Roman Empire of Ammianus,* pp. 409–13.

18. *CTh* 1.16.6; 1 Nov. 331.

them to the court as the *acta populi.*[19] An example of this is Symmachus' referral to the emperor of the acclamations of grief expressed by the people of Rome upon the death of the great senator Praetextatus: "When the bitter rumour of his death spread through the city, the people renounced their customary pleasures of the theatre and with many an acclamation bore witness to his illustrious memory" (*Relatio* 10.2, trans. R. H. Barrow).

Acclamations are found not only among popular gatherings in the cities but among other groups of people with the opportunity to assemble and make them, notably the church and the army.[20] A fascinating example preserved in the Theodosian Code records the acclamations of army veterans making representations to Constantine in 320;[21] the text, given here in Pharr's translation, distinguishes between individual utterances and those made in unison by the veterans:

> When [Constantine] had entered the imperial headquarters of the army and had been saluted by the military prefects and tribunes, and by the Most Eminent men, the acclamation arose: "Augustus Constantine! The gods preserve you for us! Your salvation is our salvation. In truth we speak, on our oath we speak!"
>
> The assembled veterans[22] cried out: "Constantine Augustus! To what purpose have we been made veterans if we have no special grant of imperial privileges?"
>
> Constantine Augustus replied: "It is My duty the more and more to increase the happiness of My fellow veterans rather than to diminish it."
>
> Victorinus, a veteran, then said, "We pray that you do not allow us to be compelled by law to perform compulsory public services and to bear grievous burdens in all places."
>
> Constantine Augustus replied: "Indicate more plainly. What are the compulsory public services especially that most persistently oppress you?"
>
> All the veterans said: "Surely, you yourself fully understand."
>
> Constantine Augustus then proclaimed: "Be it known that it has now just been conceded to all veterans by My munificence that no one of them shall be compelled by law to the performance of a compulsory municipal service."

19. *CTh* 8.5.32; cf. A. Chastagnol, *La préfecture urbaine à Rome sous le Bas-Empire* (1960), pp. 81–83 (with discussion of the connected issue, not relevant here, of the circus factions).

20. Some examples of ecclesiastical acclamations will be discussed later.

21. *CTh* 7.20.2. The date and place of issue of the text present some difficulty. The transmitted consular date is 320, but in that case the place of issue, "civitas Velovocorum," has to be understood, not as Beauvais (civ. Bellovacorum) but, in order to suit Constantine's movements at the time, as an unknown place near Serdica. Barnes, *New Empire,* p. 69 n. 102, tentatively suggests the year 307, when Constantine could have been at Beauvais, but at considerable disturbance to the transmitted consular date. The reference to "the gods" in the text of the acclamations is in itself no argument for an early date.

22. "Adunati veterani exclamaverunt"—perhaps *adunati* means "in unison" rather than "assembled."

In an episode narrated by Ammianus Marcellinus, we see the actual genesis of an acclamation and its aftermath. When, in 367, Valentinian I promoted his young son Gratian to the rank of Augustus, he ended his speech to the army by asking for its confirmation of his choice (27.6.13). The magister memoriae Eupraxius responded with "Familia Gratiani hoc meretur" (The house of Gratian is worthy of this), clearly the text of an acclamation. Eupraxius was at once promoted to quaestor (in which capacity he is of further interest for students of the Theodosian Code).[23] To see the incident merely as opportunistic behavior on the part of Eupraxius is to miss the point of the occasion. He was filling a prearranged ceremonial role. The form of words chosen is characteristic of known acclamations: crisp and rhythmic, easy to pick up and repeat; and it contains an unexpected but relevant detail, the name of Valentinian's father and the new Augustus' grandfather, in order to give added dynastic gloss to the choice of the young Gratian. Eupraxius' instant promotion to quaestor was also prearranged, but it enacted the pretense that he had spontaneously performed a political service to the regime in critical circumstances. It is a perfect example of the genre.

Acclamations had thus for centuries been an important aspect of the political communications in Roman society, acquiring as time passed an increasingly ceremonial function. As part of senatorial procedure they are mentioned, without any detail, in the younger Pliny's panegyric of Trajan in A.D. 100 and, more than a century later, in the Roman History of Cassius Dio.[24] It does not look as if in this earlier period the utterances were more than brief concerted expressions of sentiment, more or less spontaneous; neither verbatim text nor any organized sequence of acclamations is recorded.[25] In the late fourth-century *Historia Augusta* we find for the first time sequences of acclamations purportedly addressed by the Senate to Marcus Aurelius, Commodus and several other emperors of the second and third centuries, all fictitious but no doubt reflecting the senatorial procedures of the

23. Tony Honoré, "The Making of the Theodosian Code," *ZSS* 103 (1986), pp. 190–203; Chapter 7.

24. Talbert, *The Senate of Imperial Rome,* pp. 297–302, discusses the evidence for this earlier period; cf. O. Hirschfeld, "Die römische Staatszeitung und die Akklamationen im Senat," *Kleine Schriften,* pp. 682–702, and Barry Baldwin, "Acclamations in the *Historia Augusta,*" *Athenaeum,* n.s. 59 (1981), pp. 138–49.

25. With the possible exception of *Epitome de Caesaribus* 18.6, a late fourth-century source on the accession of Pertinax. There is no obvious reason for which the more extensive acclamations known from the later period *could* not have been devised in the earlier, but they appear not to have been. Talbert concludes (p. 302) that the recorded examples incorporate "merely brief greetings and praises reserved for the emperor"; cf. also, on the lack of early texts, Baldwin, p. 144. The change might be connected with an increase in the practice of recording them: Roueché, "Acclamations in the Later Roman Empire," pp. 184f.

author's day.[26] To take an example: "'Antonine pie, di te servent. Antonine clemens, di te servent. Tu voluisti quod licebat, nos fecimus quod decebat. Commodo imperium iustum rogamus. Progeniem tuam robora. Fac securi sint liberi nostri. bonum imperium nulla vis laedit. Commodo Antonino tribuniciam potestatem rogamus, praesentiam tuam rogamus. philosophiae tuae, patientiae tuae, doctrinae tuae, nobilitati tuae, innocentiae tuae. vincis inimicos, hostes exuperas, di te tuentur.' et reliqua" (*Av. Cass.* 13.2–5). Two later lives in the *Historia Augusta* introduce another feature relevant to the Theodosian Gesta Senatus, the number of repetitions accorded to each acclamation.[27] In the *Vita Claudii* these are characteristically exaggerated (the allusions to third-century history in the later part of the passage do not concern us here): " 'Auguste Claudi, dii te praestent.' Dictum sexagies. 'Claudi Auguste, te principem aut qualis tu es, semper optavimus.' Dictum quadragies. 'Claudi Auguste, te res p. requirebat.' Dictum quadragies. 'Claudi Auguste, tu frater, tu pater, tu amicus, tu bonus senator, tu vere princeps.' Dictum octogies. 'Claudi Auguste, tu nos ab Aureolo vindica.' Dictum quinquies. 'Claudi Auguste, tu nos a Palmyrenis vindica.' Dictum quinquies. 'Claudi Auguste, tu nos a Zenobia et a Vitruvia libera.' Dictum septies. 'Claudi Auguste, Tetricus nihil fecit.' Dictum septies" (*Claud.* 4.3f.).

The form and to a certain extent the language of these acclamations, and of others in the *Historia Augusta,* resemble quite closely some of those preserved in the Gesta Senatus of 438, although the fictitious acclamations in the *Historia Augusta,* while they may exceed them in extravagance, in no way match the authentic ones of the Gesta in cumulative logic or coherence of subject.[28] The latter are of unique significance, not only as evidence for the way in which the Theodosian Code was received and published in the west, but for the history of the late Roman Senate and the development of its protocol.

The acclamations recorded in the Gesta Senatus occur at five points in the proceedings, by far the most extensive and complex group being the third and central group.[29] As we saw, Faustus' initial address to the Senate was twice punctuated by acclamations, given, respectively, as "nove diserte, vere diserte" and "aequum est, placet, placet" (the first two of the five groups here defined). The number of

26. Talbert, p. 298 and n. 57.

27. Baldwin, "Acclamations in the *Historia Augusta,*" 143f. Apart from the passage of the *Vita Claudii* cited here, the number of repetitions accorded to the acclamations is recorded only in *Tacitus* 5.1f.

28. Baldwin, "Acclamations in the *Historia Augusta,*" pp. 147f., draws parallels between the authentic acclamations of the Gesta Senatus and the fictitious ones of the *Historia Augusta.*

29. See now, with a somewhat different emphasis, Jill Harries, *Law and Empire in Late Antiquity* (1999), pp. 65–69.

repetitions of these acclamations is not stated, and it seems likely that they represent, not highly organized acclamations such as follow in the central and later sections of the series, but more spontaneous shouts of approval, whose general tenor rather than necessarily precise wording may be preserved in the Gesta; in that respect they are comparable to acclamations recorded in the earlier period of the Roman Empire. The main body of acclamations, forty-three in number, repeated between eight and twenty-eight times, for a total of 748 separate utterances, follows Faustus' reading to the Senate of the law of 26 March 429. The series is completed by two additional groups of three honorific acclamations, repeated between ten and sixteen times; these greeted further remarks by Faustus, in which he recalled his own role in conveying the emperors' wishes to the Senate, and then proposed the arrangements, relating to the preparation and distribution of texts of the Code.

It is the central group of forty-three acclamations that is, from a historical point of view, the most interesting, and it well repays analysis. Far from being random or spontaneous effusions of sentiment, the acclamations move logically from point to point and are balanced by an internal symmetry that is clearly the result of planning. The text as here printed is set out in sections indicating the subdivisions according to which it is discussed here. One line, enclosed in ⟨ ⟩, is transferred, as I argue, from its position at the end of the series in the text.

Adclamatum est:

I.a. Augusti Augustorum, maximi Augustorum. Dictum VIII.
Deus vos nobis dedit, deus vos nobis servet. Dictum XXVII.
Romani imperatores et pii felices, multis annis imperetis. Dictum XXII.
Bono generis humani, bono senatus, bono rei publicae, bono omnium. Dictum XXIIII.
Spes in vobis, salus in nobis. Dictum XXVI.
Ut vivere delectet Augustos nostros semper. Dictum XXII.
Orbe placato praesentes triumphetis. Dictum XXIIII.
Haec sunt vota senatus, haec sunt vota populi Romani. Dictum X.

b. Liberis cariores, parentibus cariores. Dictum XVI.
Extinctores delatorum, extinctores calumniarum. Dictum XXVIII.
Per vos honores, per vos patrimonia, per vos omnia. Dictum XXVIII.
Per vos arma, per vos iura. Dictum XX.

c. Dispositioni vestrae gratias agimus. Dictum XXIII.
Constitutionum ambiguum removistis. Dictum XXIII.
Pii imperatores sic consulunt. Dictum XXVI.
Causis consulitis, quieti consulitis. Dictum XXV.

Plures codices fiant habendi officiis. Dictum X.
In scriniis publicis sub signaculis habeantur. Dictum XX.
Ne interpolentur constituta, plures codices fiant. Dictum XXV.
Ne constituta interpolentur, omnes codices litteris conscribantur. Dictum XVIII.
Huic codici, qui faciendus a constitutionariis, notae iuris non adscribantur. Dictum XII.
Codices in scriniis habendi sumptu publico fiant, rogamus. Dictum XVI.

II.a. Fauste, aveas. Dictum XVII.
Bis consulem te. Dictum XV.
Omnia explicas, neminem laedis. Dictum XIII.
Codices conscripti ad provincias dirigantur. Dictum XI.
Tantorum beneficiorum dignus perlator. Dictum X.

b. Paule, aveas. Dictum XII.
Consulem te. Dictum XI.
Ut in scriniis publicis habeantur, rogamus. Dictum XV.
Ad curam pertineat praefecturae. Dictum XII.

c. Singuli praefecti signacula sua adhibeant. Dictum XV.
In officiis suis singulos codices habeant. Dictum XII.
Ut ad preces nullae leges promulgentur, rogamus. Dictum XXI.
⟨His subreptionibus possessorum ius omne confunditur. Dictum XVII.⟩

III. Aeti, aveas. Dictum XV.
Ter consulem te. Dictum XIII.
Excubiis tuis salvi et securi sumus. Dictum XII.
Excubiis tuis, laboribus tuis. Dictum XV.

IV. Fauste, aveas. Dictum XIII.
Bis consulem te. Dictum X.
Desideria senatus ut suggeras, rogamus. Dictum XX.
Conṣervator legum, conservator decretorum. Dictum XVI.

At the head of the series stand twenty-two acclamations addressed to the Augusti, shown here in three groups. The first eight acclamations (I.a) evoke the emperors' virtues, express the esteem of the Senate, *res publica,* and mankind for them and offer prayers for many years of benevolent rule. We then move, in a group of four syntactically distinct acclamations (they have no verbs), to the role of the emperors as the opponents of injustice and champions of honors, property, arms, and the law (I.b). These form a transition to the third group, comprising four acclamations on the emperors' general services to the law, and then six on the practical subjects of the making of further copies of the Code, their safekeeping, and their protection from interpolation and annotation (I.c). The content and significance of these acclamations will be discussed later.[30]

The Senate now turns its attention from the emperors, with five acclamations to the praetorian prefect Faustus (II.a). Hopes are expressed that he may receive a second consulship; he is praised as a humane interpreter of the law ("omnia explicas, neminem laedis") and, in a function specifically appropriate to the praetorian prefect, is asked to have copies of the Code sent to the provinces. The fifth acclamation to Faustus alludes to his role as the worthy bringer of such benefits—to wit, the Code itself—to the Senate. It is now the turn of the prefect of Rome Fl. Paulus, to whom the Senate expresses in four acclamations (II.b) the hope that he will be made consul and requests that as one of the duties of his prefecture he maintain copies of the Code in the *scrinia publica*. In a further four acclamations (II.c), the prefects are together requested to apply their seals to the Code and to maintain copies in their respective offices and are asked to ensure that no laws are promulgated in response to *preces*, or petitions. The final acclamation in this section, transposed here from the very end of the series, explains that by such "surreptitious acts" the integrity of all law is undermined.

The next four acclamations (III) are addressed to the *magister militum* Fl. Aetius. They express the desire that he receive a third consulship (he had held this office in 432 and 437) and otherwise refer to the military labors by which the safety of the Senate (and the Roman world in general) was achieved. No actual request is made of Aetius; he stands for the *arma* rather than the *iura* of a previous acclamation to the emperors (cf. I.b.4).

A final sequence of four acclamations (IV), reasserting his eminence in the proceedings, is addressed once again to the praetorian prefect Faustus; repeated wishes are expressed for a second consulship, he is asked to convey the wishes of the Senate—that is, the entire sequence of acclamations—to the emperor,[31] and is once more, and in conclusion, praised as the guardian of leges and decreta.

The total of four acclamations in this last group to Faustus was achieved by transferring the last acclamation in the transmitted text, "His subreptionibus possessorum ius omne confunditur," from this place to the end of the sequence addressed jointly to the praetorian and urban prefects. There is however little doubt that this is where it belongs. Allowed to stand at the very end of the series, it is isolated in sense and bears no obvious relation to what has preceded, whereas it

30. Another syntactical and stylistic point will be noted, that in the last acclamation of the twenty-two addressed directly to the emperors, the sequence of subjunctives in the last six acclamations ends firmly with the indicative verb *rogamus*.

31. On the regular duty of the *praefectus urbi* in this respect, cf. A. Chastagnol, *Préfecture urbaine,* esp. p. 67.

follows perfectly from the last of the series of acclamations addressed in common to the two prefects: "Ut *ad preces* nullae leges promulgentur, rogamus" is answered by "*his subreptionibus* . . . ius omne confunditur."

To move the acclamation from its transmitted place at the end of the text has the further effect of enhancing the symmetry of the whole series, by raising the number of acclamations addressed to the two prefects jointly from three to four, and reducing from five to four the concluding group of acclamations to Faustus. Balance is achieved, and the sequence to Faustus, and the whole set of acclamations, conclude with renewed emphasis on the purpose of the proceedings, and indeed of the Theodosian Code itself: "Conservator legum, conservator decretorum." The only other asymmetry in the whole series is the first group of five acclamations to Faustus, but this is explained by the last of the group, "tantorum beneficiorum dignus perlator." This expresses the specific role of Faustus, one not shared by his colleague the prefect of Rome, in personally conveying the completed Code to the west after his visit to Constantinople in 437. Faustus had alluded to this visit in his introductory remarks to the Senate, and would again do so in his intervention following the main series of acclamations. The additional acclamation in his favor is relevant to the circumstances, alludes to remarks which he himself made, and reflects Faustus' extra distinction in relation to his colleague.

The symmetry in the series of acclamations as a whole is shown in the following summary of its organization, arranged by recipients or honorands (the numbers that would result from not transposing the final acclamation are shown in square brackets under sections II.c and IV):

I. The Augusti:
   (a) 8 acclamations on the emperors, Senate, and people;
   (b) 4 transitional acclamations, leading to:
   (c) 10 acclamations or, broken down:
      4 on the emperors and general concern for law;
      6 on the maintenance and preservation of Code.

II. The praefecti:
   (a) Faustus, praefectus praetorio: 5 acclamations (2 + 3), including request to send copies of the Code to provinces;
   (b) Paulus, praefectus urbi: 4 acclamations (2 + 2), including request to keep the Code in the scrinia publica;
   (c) both praefecti: 4 [3] acclamations (2 + 2) on responsibilities of "singuli praefecti" for maintaining the Code and deprecating the issuing of laws in response to preces.

III. Aetius, magister militum:
   4 acclamations on his military prowess.

IV. Faustus, praetorian prefect:
 4 [5] acclamations, the first two repeated from II(a), adding the request to convey the Senate's wishes to the emperor and praising him as the preserver of the law.

It will be obvious from both the content and the ordering of the acclamations, that they were no spontaneous effusion of sentiment.[32] They are rigorously controlled. The acclamations to the Augusti move logically from the general to the particular, from the love of the Senate and human race for them, to their concern for the preservation of law and its clarification, and from there to the practical arrangements for the safekeeping of the Code and the maintenance of its text. The acclamations to the praetorian and urban prefects, and to the magister militum, are balanced in number and distinguish the specific duties of each of these functionaries. The praetorian prefect is enjoined to send copies to the provinces, the urban prefect to maintain copies in the public archives as part of the *cura praefecturae* entrusted to him. Aetius is praised for his military services and no request is made of him in respect of the Code. Every acclamation is in its proper context and matched to its recipient.

Two further points may be added. First, the role of Faustus in the transportation of the Code to the west and in its publication there is not only reflected in the additional acclamation commemorating his role and in the extra sequence of four acclamations at the end of the series; it is further emphasized in two further groups of three acclamations which greet his later interventions in the proceedings of the Senate. Second, within the main groups of acclamations the number addressed to the emperors, 22 in all (here divided 8 + 4 + (4 + 6)), exceeds by one the total of acclamations allowed to everyone else, that is the praetorian and urban prefects and the magister militum collectively (5 + 4 + 4 + 4 + 4). This may be coincidental, but given the planning inherent in the entire sequence, one suspects that it is not.

The acclamations, part honorific, part practical, progressing by logical stages and divided with a sure sense of protocol and relevance among their various recipients, correspond to what would in earlier times have been set out as a continuous senatusconsultum proposed in a *sententia,* no doubt in response to an imperial letter or *oratio,* and approved by vote.[33] If we were to rewrite the acclamations in the form of a senatusconsultum of the earlier period, we would need to alter the

32. In this I would allow still less spontaneity than does Harries, *Law and Empire,* p. 66. Even the competitive "shouts of support" for Faustus, Paulus, and Aetius are contained by the controlled symmetry of the sequence.

33. Cf. Talbert, *The Senate of Imperial Rome,* chap. 8, pp. 290–97, on legislation in response to imperial *orationes*.

balance between formality and substance, but not the logical order of the sentiments. The difference is one of ceremonial presentation.

As to how the performance was achieved in practice, and what precise form it took, these are questions best answered by conjecture and analogy. It is obvious that the regularity and symmetry of the acclamations preclude a completely, or even a largely, spontaneous performance. The acclamations and their order must have been decided in advance, each pronouncement being called out and answered in response by the assembled senators, perhaps (though this does not seem necessary) with the help of prepared scripts: or perhaps they were rehearsed in advance of the meeting. One can then imagine various possibilities. The simplest is also the most laborious: that each acclamation was repeated in full by the entire assembled company between the eight and twenty-eight times recorded in the Gesta. Alternatively, the acclamations were greeted by concerted shouts of assent ("Aye!," "Hear! Hear!") which were counted as repetitions; or possibly the number of repetitions represents the number of individual senators repeating each acclamation in turn.

The question is settled in favor of the first of these alternatives by the weight of comparative evidence, both secular and ecclesiastical.[34] Church councils held at Rome at the turn of the fifth and sixth centuries provide particularly close parallels, the most striking being the council held at Rome in 499 under pope Symmachus. The following sequence occurs near the beginning of the proceedings:[35]

> Acclamatum ab omnibus episcopis et presbyteris:
> Exaudi, Christe! Symmacho vita! Dictum decies.
> Cuius sedem et annos. Dictum octies.
> Ut facias rogamus. Dictum decies.

followed a little later by:

> Universi episcopi vel presbyteri dixerunt:
> Ut fiat rogamus. Dictum decies.
> Ut scandala amputentur, rogamus. Dictum novies.
> Ut ambitus extinguatur, rogamus. Dictum duodecies.

34. Hirschfeld, "Die römische Staatszeitung," pp. 692f.

35. Mommsen, *MGH auct. ant.* 12, pp. 402–3 (= *PL* 130.993f.), amending the presentation to bring out the similarities with senatorial procedure. Similar acclamations may be found at other Roman church councils, e.g., *PL* 59.186 (under Pope Gelasius); *PL* 130.1024, 1029–30 (also under Symmachus). A much earlier example is preserved by Augustine, recording the acta of the meeting of clergy and congregation at Hippo in 426 which accepted the election of Eraclius as his coadjutor and eventual successor, *Ep.* 213 "Gesta ecclesiastica" (*CSEL* 57.372–79; on ecclesiastical acclamations in general, cf. Roueché, "Acclamations in the Later Roman Empire," pp. 184, 186–88). Particularly interesting in this series is the division of sense and syntax sometimes carried over between successive acclamations. Again, the planning is obvious.

Exaudi, Christe! Symmacho vita! Dictum sexies.
Cuius sedem et annos. Dictum quinquies.
Ut de praesenti fiat. Dictum decies.

It would be equally interesting to know how the acclamations were brought to an end — whether this was done through concerted guidance, or whether they were allowed to peter out more spontaneously (like standing ovations at party conferences, brought to an end by party managers immediately, or preferably just before, the enthusiasm shows signs of waning);[36] in either case, it presumably fell to the exceptor senatus Fl. Laurentius to count the repetitions accorded to the separate acclamations, as well as to record their content.[37] If each acclamation were repeated verbatim, the specified number of times and if we allow, say, five seconds per acclamation, the grand total of 748 acclamations would have consumed well over an hour of almost continuous acclaiming. This is not such a long time if one considers the time spent to deliver a panegyric, the length of applause given in modern times to political leaders at party rallies (or indeed the endless rigmarole of certain university ceremonies). In such cases, a sense of participation and peer pressure, not to mention reluctance to withhold enthusiasm from the powers that be, may help alleviate the monotony.

There is no obvious pattern in the number of repetitions assigned to each individual acclamation, except that those addressed to the emperors each received more repetitions than those addressed to the prefects and magister militum; the average number of repetitions of the first twenty-two acclamations is 20.6 per acclamation, of the next twenty-one acclamations, 14.1 repetitions per acclamation. A glance back at the printed text will also show that the individual acclamations in favor of emperors were appreciably longer than the others, and for this reason, too, will have consumed proportionately more time in the acclaiming. Apart from this change of level between the "imperial" and the "nonimperial" acclamations, there is no significant decrease in the number of repetitions toward the end of the series; it does not look as if the decline in the number of repetitions for emperors and other recipients has anything to do with tiredness or boredom on the part of the acclaimers. The actual figures, counted by the sections of acclamations as described earlier, are as follows:

36. At *PL* 130.1029 the text continues after the acclamations: "Et paulo post cum resedissent, *facto silentio* universus synodus dixit," and "*facto silentio,* Symmachus episcopus ecclesiae catholicae urbis Romae dixit," etc.

37. Cf. Roueché, "Acclamations in the Later Roman Empire," pp. 184f., 186 on the role of *notarii*. The acclamations of 499 already cited were ordered to be entered into the record (Mommsen, p. 405; *PL* 130.995): "Adclamationes vestras synodique iudicium praesentia gesta suscipiet."

| | No. of acclamations | Total no. of repetitions | Min./max. | Average per acclamation |
|---|---|---|---|---|
| I. The Emperors | | | | |
| (a) | 8 | 163 | 8/27 | 20.4 |
| (b) | 4 | 92 | 16/28 | 23.0 |
| (c) | 10 | 198 | 10/26 | 19.8 |
| II(a). Faustus | 5 | 66 | 10/17 | 13.2 |
| II(b). Paulus | 4 | 50 | 11/15 | 12.5 |
| (c). joint | 4 | 65 | 12/21 | 16.25 |
| III. Aetius | 4 | 55 | 12/15 | 13.75 |
| IV. Faustus | 4 | 59 | 10/20 | 14.75 |

It is natural to wonder who the author of the series of acclamations was, and how, and by what authority, they were planned and executed. Were they in general the product of "imperial" or "senatorial" initiative? The full answer to these questions is no doubt beyond reach, but it is worth lingering on those acclamations in which a senatorial rather than an imperial interest or point of view can be detected.

In no fewer than four separate acclamations—two inside the main series just discussed, two more outside it—the Senate requested a second consulship for the praetorian prefect Faustus. Faustus had become consul for the first time in that very year, 438. He was praetorian prefect again in 442/43, but no further tenure of the consulship was ever given. The Senate also requested the consulship for the praefectus urbi Paulus, but he never held one. The third consulship requested for the magister militum Fl. Aetius was forthcoming, but only in 446, and it is out of the question that this tenure of the office had anything to do with a request made by the Senate in 438.

On these matters we can say only that the Senate was not simply making requests that it already knew would be granted by the emperor, for none of them was so granted. We should not conclude that the Senate was exposing itself to rebuff, or that its failure to gain its requests was in any real sense a humiliation. The emperors were constantly receiving petitions of this sort—indeed, this was just how consulships and other high offices were frequently awarded. To make such requests was in itself a way of paying a compliment, not only to the intended beneficiary but to an emperor, by putting him in a position in which, precisely, he might decline without giving offense. It is a glimpse of a future that Tacitus would have understood: deliberately to give advice that one knows may not be accepted represents the ultimate affectation of senatorial liberty and the practice of adulation. This is perhaps too sensitive an interpretation for the later period: both *libertas* and *adulatio* will have, by then, achieved the bland and benign status of pure ceremony. The underlying logic is, however, the same.

The request that no laws be issued in response to preces, if connected, as argued above, with the response "His subreptionibus possessorum ius omne confunditur," may express either an imperial or a senatorial view, depending on whether one groups the word *possessorum* with what precedes or with what follows it. Was it the improper influence of landowners ("his subreptionibus possessorum") that undermined the law, or did the improper influence of others undermine the rights of landowners ("possessorum ius omne")? The proposition that the rule of law was undermined by corrupt practice was one that both parties could subscribe to; the interests of the "possessores" in the preservation of law, it might be claimed, were not divergent from but identical with those of the emperors. Despite differences between them on matters of taxation, Senate and emperor shared an interest in the maintenance of private property. It is, however, a better interpretation of the situation to suppose that it is here not the landowners' but the emperors' interests, or rather those of the law itself, that are being defended; it is the "possessores" who are here, as so often in the Theodosian Code itself, being accused of improper influence ("subreptio"), to the detriment of legal principles ("ius").[38] If so, it was a clever move to get the senators of Rome to denounce (seventeen times!) as prejudicial to the integrity of the law the improper influence of their own landowning class.

If we think of the acclamations as a communication from Senate to imperial government in a spirit inspired by or acceptable to the latter, it might have occurred to either party to praise the emperors as the initiators or preservers of *honores* and *patrimonia,* particularly since they are connected, in the next acclamation, with arma and iura; the two acclamations are part of the transitional sequence (I.b) leading to the specific provisions for the safe maintenance of the Code. As for these provisions, remarkable as they are in their ceremonial context, they are part of the official procedures for publishing the Code and must be seen as imperial instructions conveyed along with its text: similar provisions must have been applied in the east. The responsibility for conveying the instructions, as well as the text which they protected, can again be assigned to Faustus. In an acclamation in the main series (II.a.5) he is praised as the dispenser (*perlator*) of these great benefits, and at a later point declared himself honored to convey to the Senate what the emperors had decided with regard to their laws: "quae pro legibus suis statuere dignati sunt."[39] This intervention, in which Faustus also proposed that the law as read out

38. Both Honoré, *Law in the Crisis of Empire,* p. 128, and Harries, *Law and Empire,* p. 66, take the opposite view, but I find the opposition between "subreptiones" and "ius" a compelling argument in favor of the view presented here.

39. For the text at this point ("et adiecit: hanc quoque partem inter beneficia aeternorum

by himself be entered into the Gesta, was greeted by a group of three acclamations directed to Faustus himself; after which he made a final contribution relating to the instructions of the emperors on the preparation of texts of the Code. To this we now turn.

In his final contribution, Faustus—senator, envoy, praetorian prefect, and orator—shines as publisher and textual scholar. He proposed to the Senate that, according to the instructions of the emperors and the wish of the Senate, copies of the Code should be prepared in three *corpora,* or classes. This was to be done under the supervision of the vir spectabilis Veronicianus, chosen by common consent of Faustus and the Senate (how or when is not recorded),[40] and the constitutionarii Anastasius and Martinus. The last two, it will be recalled, had been invited into the Senate at the opening of the proceedings; their role was technical and professional, to do with the physical preparation of copies of the code. The otherwise unknown Veronicianus, as a vir spectabilis, was no doubt present in his own right. If he had gained the rank according to the provisions of the law of 425 establishing the law school of Constantinople (see Chapter 2), then we might see him as an eastern lawyer sent to the west with the constitutionarii to exercise a supervisory role in the preparation of copies of the Code. The suggestion is conjectural, but not implausible.[41]

The three classes of manuscripts now described by Faustus were the codex received by him from Theodosius' "divine hand," and two copies to be made from it. The original and authoritative copy received by Faustus was to remain in the office of the praetorian prefect;[42] this manuscript was unique in its corpus, or class. Of the two further classes of manuscripts to be transcribed from it, one exemplar was to reside in the archives of the praefectus urbi; this, again, was unique in its class. The other would be retained by the constitutionarii for publication to the people; no further texts were permitted to be published unless transcribed from this third copy by the constitutionarii in their own hand. Faustus himself would

principum numero," etc., for the meaningless manuscript reading "et ad inter," etc.), see Theresa S. Davidson, "A Problem of Senate Procedure in the Later Roman Empire," *American Journal of Philology* 67 (1946), pp. 168–83. The decisive parallels, from ecclesiastical and other sources, are registered by her at pp. 179ff.

40. Possibly as part of the preliminaries referred to earlier; Gesta Senatus, §1.

41. He is Veronicianus 1 of *PLRE* 2 (p. 1156). The two other Veroniciani listed in *PLRE* 2 are both eastern (one of them a translator who also edited the *acta* of the Council of Chalcedon); so also the two Veroniciani listed in *PLRE* 1 (p. 952)—a vicarius Asiae, and a philosopher from the pages of Eunapius.

42. This would mean that when the praetorian prefecture was again attached, as was normal, to the imperial court, the Code would migrate with the prefect's *officium* to Ravenna. A copy would stay at Rome in the archives of the urban prefect.

accept the responsibility of transmitting a copy prepared in this way to the province of Africa. In this he was satisfying one of the requests addressed to him by the Senate in the main series of acclamations (II.a.4), that copies of the Code be sent to the provinces.

Faustus' final contribution receives three more acclamations, largely repeating those of the previous group of three, and the Gesta come to an end with the certification *alia manu* of Laurentius, and the date, "sub d(ie) VIII k. Ian."[43]

Although at first sight confusing in its use of the terms *codex, corpora* and *exemplaria,* Faustus' intervention is clear if the terms are interpreted consistently. Indeed, his words are a working guide to the basic principles of textual criticism. Together with his colleague the *praefectus praetorio Orientis,* Faustus had received from the emperor's hands a copy of the Codex Theodosianus. These two copies, directed to the eastern and western empires respectively, were to be the authoritative sources of all others. A textual critic might call them twin archetypes in the manuscript history, equally authoritative and in theory simultaneously produced, but with separate lines of descent. If their delivery to the hands of the praetorian prefects constitutes initial "publication," then they were, literally, published simultaneously. The copy brought by Faustus to the west and presented to the Senate was to be the source of the other two copies mentioned in his speech, those held, respectively, by the praefectus urbi and the constitutionarii.

The first phase of transmission in the west thus consisted in the preparation of three master copies of the code, the second and third of which were direct copies of the first. The three corpora referred to by Faustus are the classes of manuscripts which might in theory be derived from each of these master copies. In looking at the transmission of the official text of the Theodosian Code we need concern ourselves only with the further exemplaria made by the constitutionarii from the copy entrusted to their keeping, the third of those discussed here. It was not proposed that any copies would be made from either of the other two corpora; each manuscript here was unique in its class. Faustus' words make clear that it was from the copy held by the constitutionarii, and not even from that held in his own *officium* as praetorian prefect, that he proposed to prepare the copy of the Code to be sent to the province of Africa.

The earliest stages in the preparation and transmission of the text of the Code in the west can therefore be represented as follows (and a similar scheme of transmission postulated for the east):

43. See n. 1. The formula *alia manu* is used for representing a signature when a document is transcribed for distribution or filing, or for public display, for example on an inscription; in this case it shows that Fl. Laurentius had endorsed by his personal signature a record of proceedings actually taken by someone else.

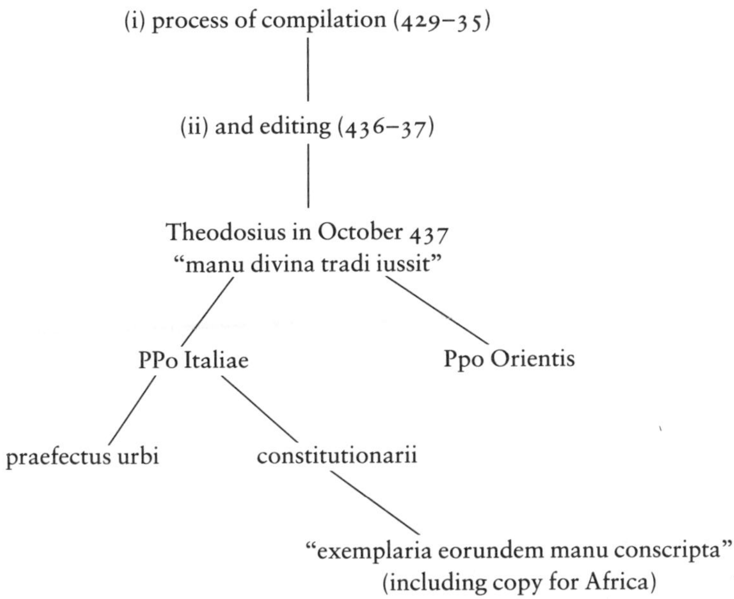


It was presumably from the copy sent to Africa or from a transcript of it that the Arian bishop Maximinus cited two laws from the Code in his so-called *dissertatio* written in the 440s into the margins of a manuscript of Ambrose's work *De fide*.[44] Writing in the same period, the church historian Sozomen cited several laws from the Theodosian Code. Some of these he may possibly have derived from his knowledge of the work of compilation rather than from the published text itself, but others, because of the way in which Sozomen refers to them and the argument they are used to support, should come from the completed Code. Sozomen was able to refute the argument that Constantine embraced Christianity as the only religion that would offer forgiveness for the murders of his son Crispus and his wife Fausta (Crispus' stepmother), by pointing to laws in favor of Christianity issued in the joint names of Constantine and Crispus. This conclusion, wrote Sozomen, could be drawn from the dates affixed to these laws, and to the lists of the legislators.[45]

44. E. Gilson, *Scolies ariennes sur le Concile d'Aquilée* (Sources Chrétiennes, 267: 1980), pp. 97–100; the laws are 16.4.2 and 16.4.1 (in that order); cf. Peter Heather and John Matthews, *The Goths in the Fourth Century* (1991), pp. 145f. See further Chapter 8, n. 118, for the significance of Maximinus' citation.

45. See *Hist. Eccl.* 1.5, 2.3, for evidence that Sozomen was a practicing advocate at Constantinople during the years in which the Theodosian Code was being compiled; Jill Harries, "Sozomen and Eusebius: The Lawyer as Church Historian in the Fifth Century," in Christopher Holdsworth and T. P. Wiseman (eds.), *The Inheritance of Historiography, 350–900*

An extract of Book 7 of the Code preserved in a parchment fragment from Oxyrhynchus perhaps derives from the copy sent to the province of Egypt by the praetorian prefect of the east.[46] Similarly, the copies known to the southern Gallic scholars who collaborated in the production of the Breviarium of Alaric, and of the Lex Romana Burgundionum in which the Theodosian Code is cited, should derive from exemplaria made by the constitutionarii for dispatch to the provinces.

Whether these citations and copies derived from the authorized transcripts of the Code produced by the constitutionarii or from less official sources must remain an open question. It is obvious that it was in the production by the constitutionarii of multiple copies, and more especially of "pirated" versions by unauthorized copyists in uncontrolled conditions, that the emperors' efforts to protect the integrity of the text were most at risk. Their anxiety is already apparent in the law addressed to the constitutionarii with which this chapter began, in which unauthorized persons are prohibited from having any traffic in the production of copies. The concluding remark in this law, that all illegitimate activity must *cease* ("omni obreptione *cessante*"), and the allusion to "those who *have* not obeyed our laws" ("qui nostris minime *paruerunt* constitutis"), imply that such abuse had already begun by 443 and had been reported to the emperor by Faustus, then praetorian prefect for the second time.[47]

In addition to this control over the production of copies, the integrity of the text of the Code was secured by the implementation of a group of six consecutive acclamations uttered in the senatorial meeting of December 438 (I.c.5–10):

(i) Plures codices fiant habendi officiis.
(ii) In scriniis publicis sub signaculis habeantur.
(iii) Ne interpolentur constituta, plures codices fiant.
(iv) Ne constituta interpolentur, omnes codices litteris conscribantur.
(v) Huic codici, qui faciendus a constitutionariis, notae iuris non adscribantur.
(vi) Codices in scriniis habendi sumptu publico fiant, rogamus.

It is not clear in every detail how these acclamations relate to each other, but their general bearing is intelligible. (i) Multiple copies of the book were to be made, and held in the officia. No doubt these were the officia of the praetorian and urban prefects and other high officials at Rome, Ravenna, and other places, such as the seat of the praetorian prefecture of the Gauls at Arles, but it is not clear whether

(1986), pp. 45–52, esp. 48. Sozomen knew of three laws on manumission in churches, where the Theodosian Code has only one; but this is a reflection of the incomplete transmission of the early books of the Code (this title was *CTh* 4.7).

46. *P.Oxy.* 1813; E. A. Lowe, *Codices Latini Antiquiores,* vol. 2, no. 211.

47. See n. 2. Given his role in the enterprise, Faustus may be forgiven for having a proprietorial interest in its outcome.

these copies are the same as or different from those held, according to the next acclamation (ii), "sub signaculis" in public archives. The distinction is perhaps between administrative departments that retained texts of the Code for their own use, and the maintenance of copies for public access. The phrase *sub signaculis* means not that these copies were to be kept permanently under lock and key, but that they were released only under strict controls to those who wished with good authority to read or consult them; the purpose of the provisions is to prevent contamination of the text of the Code, not to prevent its use altogether.

That the copies in the public archives should be kept there at public expense (vi) is self-explanatory. It is not however self-evident that (iii) the preparation of multiple copies would prevent interpolation of the *constituta.* Most textual critics would assume that the possibilities of corruption increase rather than diminish with the number of copies of a work that are made, but the emperors were no doubt hoping that multiple copies of the text, produced under controlled conditions, would be enough to outweigh the corruptions that might occur in one or a small number of manuscripts. It is a reasonable precaution (iv) that to prevent interpolation, all copies of the Code should be written out "litteris"—that is, in full, without the use of abbreviations and signs, common causes of corruption in the transmission of a text. The provision (v) that legal abbreviations were not to be written into the copy of the Code prepared by the constitutionarii is also clear in principle and in intention.[48] The copy to which this provision applies, "qui faciendus a constitutionariis," is evidently the third of the three master-copies discussed above: this is the text from which all further copies were to be made. It may be a corollary that in subsequent exemplaria derived from this copy legal abbreviations *were* anticipated. This was in practical terms inevitable if the Code were to succeed in its intention to be of use to the *scholastica intentio* of lawyers (Chapter 4). Neither emperors, prefects, nor the Senate had power to prevent "contamination" in the Code once it had left the primary stage of preparation and entered general circulation.

It is obvious that the publication of the Theodosian Code offered occasions for corruption and error of many different kinds. Theodosius' advisers must, however, be given the credit for taking what measures were possible. The needs both to prepare sufficient copies for actual use and to preserve authoritative copies of the original text presented contradictory requirements. The authorities could not prevent interested parties from making personal copies of the Code or of particular sections and laws that were of concern to them. Much imperial legislation of the fourth and early fifth centuries was preserved for the compilers of the Code by

48. On "notae iuris," see Honoré, "The Making of the Theodosian Code," p. 160—also interpreting "litteris conscribantur" as meaning "to be written in letters, not numbers."

individuals who had done precisely this,[49] a practice which would certainly not come to an end. Nor would lawyers, whose understanding of their subject advanced by the complementary processes of the compilation of individual enactments (leges) and the pursuit and refinement of juristic principles (ius), be deterred from continuing their research. The emperors could however attempt to ensure that the copies of the Code held by the chief officers of state, and those issued under official license by the constitutionarii, remained free from contamination at source. In their somewhat unusual form—it must be unique to find the basic rules of textual criticism shouted out in public between eighteen and twenty-five times—the Gesta Senatus provide evidence on how this was done. Alone among ancient texts (and entirely neglected by modern scholars), they offer a working model, operating in controlled conditions, of the principles of manuscript transmission and textual criticism.

49. See Chapters 7 and 10.

# 4

# *Editing the Code*

Discussion of the editorial procedures that were applied to the work of compilation of the Theodosian Code, and of the editorial panels that undertook it, is best approached through the full text of the constitution of 26 March 429, by means of which, almost ten years after the fact, the project was described to the Senate by Faustus. It is here given in Pharr's translation, with the replacement of the designations of late Roman offices of state with their Latin originals:

> *Our Lords, Emperors Theodosius Augustus and Valentinian Augustus to the Senate.*
>
> We decree that, after the pattern of the Gregorian and Hermogenian Codes, a collection shall be made of all the constitutions that were issued by the renowned Constantine, by the sainted Emperors after him, and by Us, and which rest upon the force of edicts or sacred imperial law of general force.
>
> First, the titles, which are the definite designations of the various matters therein shall be so divided that, when the various headings have been expressed, if one constitution should pertain to several titles, the materials shall be assembled wherever each is fitting. Second, if any diversity should cause anything to be stated in two ways, it shall be tested by the order of the readings, and not only shall the year of the consulship be considered, and the time of the reign be investigated, but also the arrangement of the work itself shall show that the laws which are later are more valid.

Furthermore, the very words themselves of the constitutions, in so far as they pertain to the essential matter, shall be preserved, but those words which were added not from the very necessity of sanctioning the law shall be omitted.

Although it would be simpler and more in accordance with law to omit those constitutions which were invalidated by later constitutions and to set forth only those which must be valid, let us recognize that this code and the previous ones were composed for more diligent men, to whose scholarly efforts it is granted to know those laws also which have been consigned to silence and have passed into desuetude, since they were destined to be valid for the cases of their own time only.

Moreover, from these three codes and from the treatises and responses of the jurists which are attached to each of the titles, through the services of the same men who shall arrange the third code, there shall be produced another code of Ours. This code shall permit no error, no ambiguities; it shall be called by Our name and shall show what must be followed and what must be avoided by all.

For the consummation of so great a work and for the composition of the codes—the first of which shall collect all the diversity of general constitutions, shall omit none outside itself which are now permitted to be cited in court, and shall reject only an empty copiousness of words, the other shall exclude every contradiction of the law and shall undertake the guidance of life—men must be chosen of singular trustworthiness, of the most brilliant genius. When they have presented the first Code to Our Wisdom and to the public authority, they shall undertake the other, which must be worked over until it is worthy of publication. Let Your Magnificence acknowledge the men who have been selected; We have selected Antiochus, vir inlustris, exquaestore et praefecto, Antiochus, vir inlustris, quaestor sacri palatii, Theodorus, vir spectabilis, comes, et magister memoriae, Eudicius and Eusebius, viri spectabiles, exmagistri scriniorum, Iohannes, vir spectabilis, excomite nostri sacrarii, Comazon and Eubulus, viri spectabiles, exmagistri scriniorum, and Apelles, vir disertus scholasticus. We are confident that these men who have been selected by Our Eternity will employ every exceptionally learned man, in order that by their common study a reasonable plan of life may be apprehended and fallacious laws may be excluded.

Furthermore, if in the future it should be Our pleasure to promulgate any law in one part of this very closely united Empire, it shall be valid in the other part on condition that it does not rest upon doubtful trustworthiness or upon a private assertion; but from that part of the Empire in which it will be established, it shall be transmitted with the sacred imperial letters, it shall be received in the bureaus of the other part of the Empire also, and it shall be published with the due formality of edicts. For a law that has been sent must be accepted and must undoubtedly be valid, and the power to emend and to revoke shall be reserved to Our Clemency. Moreover, the laws must be mutually announced, and they must not be admitted otherwise. Et cetera.

*Given on the seventh day before the kalends of April at Constantinople in the year of the consulship of Florentius and Dionysius.* (Gesta Senatus §4 = *CTh* 1.1.5)

## *Editorial Policy*

As the emperor explained through Faustus, the Theodosian Code was to be a successor to the earlier codes of Gregorius and Hermogenianus and would be composed in their likeness.[1] In summary, it would include all imperial constitutions possessing the force of edicts or of general application issued by Constantine and his successors down to the present day: "Cunctas constitutiones, quas Constantinus inclitus et post eum divi principes nosque tulimus edictorum viribus aut sacra generalitate subnixas." The laws were to be disposed under titles (or subjects), with the proviso that extended texts containing material relevant to more than one subject were to be divided, and the separate parts classified under the respective titles to which they applied. Then, because of the inconsistencies that would arise between individual laws,[2] they were to be set out in the order of their date of issue. In this way the arrangement of the material would itself make clear which constitutions on any particular subject were the later and therefore the more valid: "Ipsius etiam compositione operis validiora esse, quae sunt posteriora, monstrante." The actual wording of the laws was to be preserved, and extraneous matter not relevant to the point of substance in a law was to be omitted. This no doubt refers (though other views have been held) to the rhetorical embellishment habitually used to enhance the force of late Roman legislation;[3] and the Code was to be complete, even to the extent that earlier laws superseded by later were still to be included.[4] It would be simpler and more in accordance with justice, the emperor admitted, if only currently relevant law were included, but the Theodosian Code, like its predecessors, was to be as complete a compilation as could be made. It was to be a work for *diligentiores* — specialist scholars and practitioners, whose professional interest (*scholastica intentio*) would wish to know even of laws valid only in an earlier time and now obsolete; as in the case of Sozomen, discussed in the previous chapter, the term *scholasticus* indicates not just an academic, but an

1. For what follows see especially Honoré, "The Making of the Theodosian Code," *ZSS* 103 (1986), pp. 133–222, at 161–68, and *Law in the Crisis of Empire,* chap. 6; Harries, *Law and Empire in Late Antiquity,* pp. 59–64.

2. "Quod in utramque dici partem faciet varietas."

3. W. Turpin, "The Purpose of the Roman Law Codes," *ZSS* 104 (1987), pp. 620–30, p. 628, writes of the elimination of extraneous matter as intended "to cut down on the talking which went on in the law courts," but it is better understood as referring to extraneous words in the written laws.

4. Ibid., pp. 621f. The idea that old law may still be valid "in affairs [i.e., in outstanding cases] dating back to the time when the obsolete legislation had been issued" ("pro sui tantum temporis negotiis valitura") is only naturally relevant to the more recent superseded law and cannot provide a general explanation of this provision. It is better to think of a legal historian's interest in older cases and their solutions.

advocate or pleader at law.[5] The emperor's point here was perfectly valid, if it is true that the understanding of law is made more profound by an insight into its development. It is however important to register the point that the editors of the Code were precluded from making substantive decisions on points of law in the texts that came into their hands. Their role was one of collection and compilation of the primary texts in the form of imperial constitutions, and that was all.

The emperor now turned to his longer-term ambitions. He offered the prospect of a further volume in which the Gregorian, Hermogenian, and new Theodosian Codes, together—a most important enlargement of scope—with the opinions of jurists on the subjects in question, would contribute to a compilation of law free of error and ambiguity, which would reveal definitively for all what was to be followed and what avoided: "sequenda omnibus vitandaque monstrabit."[6] Although this volume would also be published by Theodosius and would bear his name, it was a project for the future. The law of 429 looked forward to it, and indeed envisaged that the same panel of experts would be responsible for its implementation,[7] but it did not set out at the present moment to encompass it. Indeed, it could hardly do so. The further project would involve quite different editorial and critical procedures and could not be undertaken until the Theodosian Code itself was complete. Without such an authoritative compilation of imperial constitutions as was represented by the Code, juristic opinion had no way of knowing to which texts it should address its expertise.

The law of 429 went on to nominate an editorial panel of nine persons with powers to coopt experts and concluded with a provision, in effect a limiting clause, on the relevance in either part of the empire of laws issued in the other. Such laws were to be valid only if they were officially directed to, and accepted and published in, the part in which they were received.[8]

With these instructions, we may suppose that the editorial panel of nine, with

5. Cf. ibid., pp. 621–22, where Turpin argues convincingly that the codes were not just scholastic enterprises but were intended to clarify the law for practical use. For Sozomen, see Chapter 3, n. 45.

6. This was to be done under the same titles as those under which the imperial constitutions were classified: "per singulos titulos cohaerentibus prudentium tractatibus et responsis."

7. *CTh* 1.1.5: "*eorundem opera,* qui tertium [that is, the Theodosian Code] ordinabunt"; later I shall discuss their identification.

8. On the issue of validity in the east and west of individual laws, and of the Theodosian Code itself, see A. J. B. Sirks, "From the Theodosian to the Justinian Code," *Atti dell'Accademia Romanistica Costantiniana: VI Convegno Internazionale* (1986), pp. 265–302, and his "Observations sur le Code Théodosien," *Subseciva Groningana* 2 (1985), pp. 21–34, at 28. Paradoxically, laws previously published only in eastern or western "partes imperii" acquired theoretical authority in both, simply by their inclusion in the Theodosian Code.

their coopted assistants, had enough guidance for the task, on which they now embarked. After a space of more than six and a half years, however, the emperors returned to the subject in a law issued at Constantinople on 20 December 435, which again, with some repetition, defined editorial procedures (*CTh* 1.1.6). We find in this law the same instructions to collect all general laws issued by Constantine and his successors up to the present day, to arrange by titles, dividing laws where necessary, and to omit material not relevant to the substantive point at issue. A new editorial panel is appointed, this time of sixteen persons, only three of whom are carried over from the previous panel.

It is often argued that the arrangements set out in the law of 435 represent a substantial amendment, or even a cancellation, of those of 429. Mommsen thought that the law of 435 indicated an abandonment of an earlier plan that had turned out unsuccessful, and his opinion had considerable influence on later writers. It was expressed also by Gaudemet, and by Jolowicz, who wrote of "a new commission with different instructions" set up by the law of 435.[9] Wolfgang Kunkel supposed that "the commission appointed by the emperor [in 429, that is] . . . evidently produced nothing," and that a "second commission called into being six years later" completed in two years a modified version of the initial project of Theodosius.[10] A similar view was expressed by A. H. M. Jones.[11] Archi, whose discussion of the relevant evidence is both detailed and perceptive, still wrote of an "old" and a "new" program, and of "saving what could be saved of the project of 429."[12] The same opinion, though with some change of emphasis, is expressed in a series of articles by Boudewijn Sirks.[13]

As far as concerns cancellation or abandonment of an original plan, these inter-

9. Mommsen, Prolegomena, p. ix; J. Gaudemet, *Institutions de l'Antiquité* (2nd ed., 1982), p. 738; H. F. Jolowicz, *Historical Introduction to the Study of Roman Law* (1952), p. 483. See also L. Wenger, *Die Quellen des römischen Rechts* (1953), p. 536.

10. *Introduction to Roman Legal and Constitutional History,* p. 158; cf. Schulz, *History of Roman Legal Science,* pp. 288 ("the plan failed") and 315 ("more ambitious plans having come to naught").

11. A. H. M. Jones, *Later Roman Empire,* vol. 1, p. 475: "They apparently failed to complete even their first task" (namely, the collection of imperial constitutions, the second task being the collection of the opinions of jurists); cf. *PLRE* 2, pp. 102–3 (Antiochus 6 and 7).

12. G. G. Archi, *Teodosio II e la sua codificazione* (1976), pp. 33, 37.

13. Compare Sirks's view expressed in his article of 1986, "From the Theodosian to the Justinian Code," p. 271, "Whatever goals Theodosius had in mind when he ordered his first Code in 429 (see CTh. 1.1.5), it is certain that the Code as we have it is the result of CTh. 1.1.6" (cf. his "Observations sur le Code Théodosien," at p. 34: "Nous ne savons pas ce que ce projet [of 429] est devenu. Il a dû échouer," etc.), with his apparently modified view in "The Sources of the Code," in Harries and Wood (eds.), *The Theodosian Code,* pp. 56–59 (discussed later).

pretations are surely based upon a misreading of the evidence.[14] That the instructions given in 429 were repeated in 435 does not show that the earlier project was a failure, only that it was an extensive project that took some time (it will be suggested below that the law of 435 responded to queries raised by the editors themselves, still working in accordance with their original instructions). Jolowicz's further observation, again echoed by Jones, that "the project of including juristic writings was abandoned" in 435 is also a misunderstanding. Only at a later stage was it envisaged that the jurists would be included, to produce a definitive compendium of Roman law, both leges and ius. The constitution of 429 deferred for the future the project of a critical digest containing only currently relevant law. It is true that this further project never came to fruition, but the constitution of 435 does not express this failure. We may add that, by the mere fact that the law of 429 was read out, the senatorial meeting of 25 December 438 was invited to view the earlier law as initiating a process brought successfully through to completion. Unless, as is unlikely, something is wrong with the text of the Gesta Senatus, the law of 435 was not read to the Senate.[15]

If the law of 435 does not represent an abandonment of the project launched in 429, can we nevertheless see in it evidence of amendments to the original plan? The idea that amendments were introduced is inherently quite plausible, if we concede that, like the rest of us, the editors of the Code gained experience and began to see their work in a different light as it progressed. The arguments that this did indeed happen are based partly on the interpretation of the laws of 429 and 435, partly on more general judgments regarding the manner in which the work on the Code was pursued in the period between them. Detailed discussion of the arguments will come later, but it will be helpful now to outline the main general considerations that have been advanced.

The first consideration relates to the nature of the work of compilation done by the editors of the Code between 429 and 435. According to one view, they were engaged in assembling scattered texts from wherever they were to be found; both from archival sources readily accessible to them and from more distant sources—especially in the western empire, from which, at least in the earlier period, the majority of the texts assembled in the Code originate. The work involved research and travel, in what must often have been difficult and, when we think of what was happening in the west in the early 430s, even dangerous circumstances, and it took

14. See also, agreeing with the view expressed here, Honoré, "The Making of the Theodosian Code," at pp. 166–67; Honoré, *Law in the Crisis of Empire,* pp. 142–49.

15. Cf., on the (non)reading to the Senate of *CTh* 1.1.6, Honoré, "The Making of the Theodosian Code," p. 16; Honoré, *Law in the Crisis of Empire,* pp. 126–27; Sirks, "From the Theodosian to the Justinian Code," p. 277, and "The Sources of the Code," p. 59.

time. This argument is supported by the texts published in the Code that have in their protocols the details of the place and time of their receipt—sometimes in addition to the date and time of issue, sometimes instead of them. Such details can hardly have been recovered in this form from central archives; they must derive, at least by way of intermediate sources, from their places of reception, where the relevant details ("posted at Carthage," "received at Hispalis," "read at Capua," "recited in the Senate," and so on) were added to the protocols and recorded by those who copied down the laws. The nature of these "intermediate sources" is equally a matter of debate; but according to this view, the compilers had plenty to occupy them between 429 and 435 without any need to justify the six years taken over this stage.

The counterargument maintains that the bulk of the material recovered by the compilers lay not in distant archives and scattered locations, but readily accessible in central files or registers maintained at Constantinople and, in the west, at Rome or Ravenna, and in a few "reliable private collections."[16] This view emphasizes the relatively small number of published laws with annotations recording their place and time of reception[17] and points to the great majority of texts that are simply annotated by place and date of issue; this would be the form in which they would have been entered into registers or daybooks kept by the central administration. According to this view, the compilers had relatively little to do in collecting the primary material for the Code. That the first stage of their work should have taken as long as six years is then explained by a suggested change in the nature of the work performed by the editors, from the mere compilation of texts to the consideration of wider issues. So, in the opinion of Boudewijn Sirks, the actual collection of the texts was "a relatively simple task, soon finished, and the delay was due to other factors."[18] According to Sirks, these other factors were inherent in a change of editorial policy between 429 and 435. The editors broadened their activities from the compilation and editing of texts to substantive matters of legal judgment; in particular, to distinguishing between rules of law that were currently valid and those which were obsolete.

The first consideration therefore relates to the character of the sources of the Theodosian Code, and the manner of its primary compilation, and it leads to a second, the character of the work performed by the editors. A further question

16. Sirks, "The Sources of the Code," p. 56. An obvious question attaches to the nature of such western sources, especially as one goes back into the earlier fourth century; how complete or systematic were they? The question of the private collections is like that of the intermediate sources mentioned earlier. Their scale and character can be hypothesized to support either side of the argument. The question is further discussed in Chapters 8–10.

17. Sirks, "The Sources of the Code," p. 50: "Merely c. 200 out of more than 2,300"; cf. his "Observations," pp. 23–24.

18. Sirks, "The Sources of the Code," p. 56.

arises from these two: the number of recovered texts that were rejected by the editors. If they kept within their original instructions, they would have included in the Code all the texts that fulfilled the formal criteria laid down and would have rejected relatively few. If, however, they went beyond the instructions given them in 429 and applied themselves to the elimination of obsolete rules that were no longer in force, then they would have rejected a much larger proportion of the texts that passed before their eyes. This is an important question for those for whom the primary use of the Theodosian Code is as a source of documentary evidence for conditions in the Roman Empire. Whether the Code contains a relatively large or a relatively small proportion of the laws that were originally issued makes a great difference to the way in which the historian may exploit it.

Since our conclusions on these matters involve the interpretation of the law of 435 in relation to that of 429, it is with the original texts of these laws that we should begin. Their relevant paragraphs are here given in full but are set out for clarity with their common elements identified as clauses (a)–(e). The new elements in the law of 435 are shown in bold in angle brackets. The question is whether the new elements add up to a change of policy or emphasis, either as first agreed in this law or as reflecting a change in editorial policy that had already been initiated.

1. Law of 429:

> *DD.NN. Impp. Theodos(ius) et Valentinianus AA. ad senatum.*
> Ad similitudinem Gregoriani atque Hermogeniani codicis
> (a) cunctas colligi constitutiones decernimus, quos Constantinus inclitus et post eum divi principes nosque tulimus edictorum viribus aut sacra generalitate subnixas.
> (b) Et primum tituli, quae negotiorum sunt certa vocabula,
> (c) separandi ita sunt ut, si capitulis diversis expressis ad plures titulos constitutio una pertineat, quod ubique aptum est, collocetur;
> (d) dein, quod in utramque partem dici partem faciet varietas, lectionum probetur ordine, non solum reputatis consulibus et tempore quaesito imperii, sed ipsius etiam compositione operis validiora esse, quae sunt posteriora, monstrante,
> (e) post haec ut constitutionum ipsa etiam verba, quae ad rem pertinent, reserventur, praetermissis illis, quae sanciendae rei non ex ipsa necessitate adiuncta sunt.
>
> Sed cum simplicius iustiusque sit praetermissis illis, quas posteriores infirmant, explicari solas, quas valere conveniet, hunc quidem codicem et priores diligentioribus conpositos cognoscamus, quorum scholasticae intentioni tribuitur nosse etiam illa, quae mandata silentio in desuetudinem abierunt, pro sui tantum temporis negotiis valitura.
>
> Ex his autem tribus codicibus, et per singulos titulos cohaerentibus prudentium tractatibus et responsis, eorundem opera, qui tertium ordinabunt, noster erit alius, qui nullum errorem, nullas patietur ambages, quo nostro nomine nuncupatus

sequenda omnibus vitandaque monstrabit. Ad tanti consummationem operis et contexendos codices—quorum primus, omni generalium constitutionum diversitate collecta nullaque extra se, quam iam proferre liceat, praetermissa, inanem verborum copia recusabit; alter omni iuris diversitate exclusa magisterium vitae suscipiet—deligendi sunt viri singularis fidei, limatioris ingenii, qui, cum primum codicem nostrae scientiae et publicae auctoritati obtulerint, adgredientur alium, donec dignus editione erit, pertractandum. . . .
*Dat. VII k. April. Constantinopoli Florentio et Dionysio conss.*

2. Law of 435:

> *Idem AA.*
> (a) Omnes edictales generalesque constitutiones ⟨**vel in certis provinciis seu locis valere aut proponi iussae**⟩, quas divus Constantinus posterioresque principes ac nos tulimus,
> (b) indicibus rerum titulis distinguantur,
> (d) ita ut non solum consulum dierumque supputatione, sed etiam ordine conpositionis apparere possint novissimae.
> (c) Ac si qua earum in plura sit divisa capita, unumquodque eorum, diiunctum a ceteris apto subiciatur titulo
> (e) et circumcisis ex quaque constitutione ad vim sanctionis non pertinentibus solum ius relinquatur.
> (f) Quod ut brevitate constrictum claritate luceat, ⟨**adgressuris hoc opus**⟩ et demendi supervacanea verba ⟨**et adiciendi necessaria et demutandi ambigua et emendandi incongrua tribuimus potestatem**⟩, scilicet ut his modis unaquaeque inlustrata constitutio emineat. Erunt contextores huius Theodosiani codicis, etc.
> *Dat. XIII k. Ian. Constp., DD.NN. Theod(osio) A. XV et Val(entini)ano IIII A. conss.*

We can now see how the law of 435 looks back to that of 429. The similarities are clearly deliberate. Phrases are varied, and some matters are stated more concisely in the later law, but there is an almost complete overlap of content and expression. There seem to be just three points of difference in the law of 435. The first two relate to editorial considerations of a relatively technical character and can be considered briefly; the third is somewhat more complicated.

First (clause (e) in the texts), the editors were empowered not merely, as in 429, to abbreviate laws by omitting extraneous matter but, in order to ensure the clarity of the published texts, to expand where necessary, to alter what was unclear and to "emend"—that is to say, correct—what did not make sense: "et *adiciendi* necessaria et *demutandi* ambigua et *emendandi* incongrua tribuimus potestatem."[19]

19. Cf. Honoré, "The Making of the Theodosian Code," pp. 165f., and *Law in the Crisis of Empire,* pp. 142–49, on these powers and their restrained use by the editors. Turpin, "The

This clause can be seen as the response to a request from the editors, based on inspection of the material they had collected, that they be given specific powers to exercise their judgment in correcting texts, where the state in which they were transmitted to the editors, or the editorial process itself, had left them unclear. The law of 429 had only spoken of abbreviation and omission, but it must in time have become apparent that this provided insufficient freedom; even while respecting the original wording of imperial laws, the editorial methods employed would sometimes create the need for more positive intervention. Expressions would need to be added, syntax adjusted, clarifications introduced, mistakes eliminated.[20] Sometimes there would be obscurities in the original texts, which did not always reach the editors in perfect shape. It was prudent to settle this point of editorial principle, for even the most obscure words of the emperors issued from their divine mouth (which is, indeed, sometimes called an oracle). As Symmachus learned as prefect of Rome in 384, to question the emperor's judgment in making appointments was an act of sacrilege, which might cost the offender ten pounds, and his officium five pounds of gold in fines.[21] To amend the emperor's utterances might be no less hazardous than to question his judgment, or, indeed, than to deface the text of his laws; it was impossible to be too careful.

Second (clause (f) in the law of 435), the new powers are assigned to those "*about to begin* this work": "*adgressuris* hoc opus." We can understand this phrase as referring to the stage of production that had now been reached, that of editorial ordering, in the manner described in the constitutions both of 429 and 435, of the material that had been assembled. The enlargement of the editorial panel from nine to sixteen members was another appropriate step to take at this stage: a recognition, not of failure, but of the fact that the project had reached a point at which the nature of the work had changed from one of collection to one of editing, at which the true extent of its scale and variety was beginning to be realized, and it was convenient to review the size and composition of the panel that would now be required to undertake a rather different kind of work.

If the law of 435 did no more than reassert with amendments the terms of the

---

Purpose," p. 622 n. 7, regards this clarification of the meaning of texts by altering their wording as the "principal difference" in the law of 435 as compared with that of 429. The procedures closely resemble those described by Quintilian, *Inst. Or.* 10.4.1: "Sequitur emendatio, pars studiorum longe utilissima. . . . Huius autem operis est adicere detrahere mutare."

20. Some examples of these procedures are given in Chapter 6, on the Sirmondian Constitutions.

21. *CTh* 1.6.9 (28 December 384), taken with Symmachus, *Relatio* 17; see my "Symmachus and His Enemies," in *Colloque Genevois sur Symmaque* (1986), at pp. 165–66.

law of 429, it would help resolve one of the questions just raised concerning the scope of the work performed by the editors of the Theodosian Code. Did they attempt to determine substantive issues of law, to the extent of distinguishing currently valid from obsolete rules? This was argued by Boudewijn Sirks, partly on the basis of a phrase in the law of 435, specifying that the editors are to eliminate matter not relevant to the point of law raised in a text: "circumcisis ex quaque constitutione ad vim sanctionis non pertinentibus solum ius relinquatur." Sirks took as the meaning of this provision that "a rule, no longer in use, has no force any more" and concluded that "therefore this prescription implies that obsolete rules have to be omitted."[22] But it seems more natural to read this phrase in the law of 435 as a reiteration of the slightly more expansive statement of the same point in 429 (clause (e) in both texts). In that law, the editors were a few lines later told to do no more than eliminate the "inanem verborum copiam" of imperial rhetoric. With that clarification, it does not seem possible that clause (e) in the law of 435, repeated in almost identical terms to its predecessor's, instructed them to apply themselves to the adjudication and elimination of obsolete rules. The removal of this criterion for the omission of laws by the editors yields a further inference. The editors were to include *any law that met the stated criteria, obsolete or not.* If a law of whose existence we know from another source was not included in the Code, it was not because the editors had found but rejected it, but because they had not found it in the first place.

The third new point raised by the law of 435 therefore involves the more complex and broader issue of the criteria for the inclusion of laws (clause (a) in both texts). The constitution of 429 defined the laws to be collected as those "with edictal force or of general application": "constitutiones . . . *edictorum viribus aut sacra generalitate* subnixas."[23] That of 435 echoes this definition in the phrase "omnes *edictales generalesque* constitutiones," with the new provision that laws valid or published in particular provinces or places were also to be included: "*vel in certis provinciis seu locis valere aut proponi iussae.*"

This at first sight radical amendment in the law of 435 should be understood in the context of what is meant by a "general law."

The most detailed and authoritative definition of *generalitas* is given in Codex Justinianus 1.14.2–3, parts of a long constitution addressed to the Roman Senate on 7 (or 6) November 426. These particular extracts do not survive in our present,

22. Sirks, "The Sources of the Code," p. 57.

23. The phrases *edictorum viribus* and *sacra generalitate* are not mutually exclusive; the conjunction *aut* is not adversative in that sense. Perhaps one could say "with edictal force or (in other ways) of general application."

incomplete text of the Theodosian Code; it is clear however that they once stood there.[24] According to this constitution, which was certainly known to the editors of the Code, the quality of generalitas was inherent in a number of specific formal categories of imperial pronouncements.

In first place are pronouncements sent to the Senate, like this very constitution, in the form of imperial *orationes,* or issued by the emperors as edicts, however they had arisen—whether the emperor's own initiative—his *spontaneus motus*—had called for the making of a law, or whether a petition, report, or piece of litigation had provided the occasion for it. In the second place, generalitas was also possessed by imperial constitutions sent to provincial governors or other officials and published by them under the authority of a governor's edict. This category, defined by the additional point raised in the law of 435, covers the vast bulk of the texts assembled in the Theodosian Code, which take the form of letters addressed to governors and other officials. Finally, also falling under the heading were imperial decisions relating to individual cases, which were specifically said to be applicable to others; and any law whose own text actually called it a general law, or which contained the instruction that it should apply universally, possessed the force of an edict and thereby acquired generalitas.[25]

The definition thus covers all pronouncements made public by decree, letter, or edict, which were intended to cover similar cases in future, whatever the specific situation that had occasioned them. Excluded were rescripts given to individual petitioners, *interlocutiones,* or legal rulings made in the course of specific proceedings without the intention that they should be applied more generally;[26] and grants of privilege made as special favors to individual cities, provinces, or corporations.

All this seems comprehensible, and certainly should have been so to the editors of the Theodosian Code, with their combination of administrative and juristic

24. See, on this very important issue, Chapter 5. On the exact date of the constitution (not relevant here), see Seeck, *Regesten,* p. 352.

25. For the presence of such instructions in the Sirmondian Constitutions and other texts, see Chapter 6. The definition of *generalitas* adopted here is more emphatically formal than those of Honoré, *Law in the Crisis of Empire,* pp. 128–29, or Harries, *Law and Empire in Late Antiquity,* pp. 62–63; see, too, N. van der Wal, "*Edictum* und *lex generalis:* Form und Inhalt der Kaisergesetze im spätrömischen Reich," *Revue Internationale des Droits de l'Antiquité* 28 (1981), pp. 277–313.

26. *CJ* 1.14.2. A statement of Arcadius restricting the validity of "rescripta ad consultationem emissa vel emittenda" to the matters in respect of which they were issued survives as *CTh* 1.2.11, 6 December 398. Three rescripts to private individuals are among texts of the year 365 preserved by the *Consultatio veteris cuiusdam iurisconsulti* (see Chapter 2, n. 14).

expertise. Why should they ever have raised the question? Their difficulty was of two kinds: in part pertaining to formal definition, in part arising from the the notion of generalitas, which was not intuitively consistent with the actual nature of late Roman legislation. A large proportion of the legislation was, according to a commonsense view, not defined by its general relevance; rather it covered any subject, large or small, upon which the emperors had made pronouncements. It is important also to remember that the constitution of 426 preceded the compilation of the Theodosian Code and did not have before it the comprehensive view that the Code itself provided, of the character of late Roman legislation. It is possible that, without the Theodosian Code and its editors' experience to inform it, the constitution expressed an over-optimistic view of the formal clarity of that legislation. In any event, the editors would have to treat the text of 426 as a retrospective definition and apply it to texts that had been drafted without its provisions in mind.

If the editors of the Code began their work by applying the formal understanding of generalitas as set out in the constitution of 426—that is, by excluding rescripts, interlocutory rulings, and individual grants of privilege—they must still have found much of their material difficult to classify. Of the texts recovered by the editors and published in the Theodosian Code, the vast majority were *epistulae,* letters sent by emperors to public officials and corporations. Only a relatively small proportion actually recorded the fact that they had been formally posted by provincial governors under the authority of their own edicts. There is nothing surprising in this, since before the law of 426 it would not have occurred to anyone transcribing the law that this element was essential for a constitution to possess general validity. This derived from its having been issued by an emperor with a certain intention, not on the contingent circumstance of its having been posted by a governor according to the normal procedures; those interested in the substance rather than the form of published laws might see no need to transcribe also the formalities of promulgation. In the light of the law of 426, the editors would have to decide whether epistulae not formally recorded as having been posted as edicts by a governor (even if there was no reason to doubt that they had been so posted) fell under the category of general laws or not.[27]

Given that the members of the editorial commissions were men with experience of how laws were made and distributed, they would also be aware of the different procedures that lay behind the drafting of imperial legislation at first instance (that is, by recommendation and discussion in the consistorium) and the epistulae by

27. Possibly this is the explanation of the phrase "valere aut proponi iussae" in the law of 435. Editors could assume that a law sent in the form of a letter to a provincial governor was "ordered to be valid," even if there were no specific record of its promulgation by posting.

which the legislation was communicated to the departments of the administration and to local audiences.[28] They will certainly have realized that many of the texts recovered were versions, addressed to particular officials and with limited territorial application, of laws expressed in more general terms which had *not* been recovered.[29] They would know too that the distribution of late Roman legislation could be a very complicated process. As texts embodying imperial pronouncements passed down from emperor to praetorian prefect to provincial governor to local community, they underwent changes in form and acquired commentary by intermediate authorities; a law brought to the attention of the compilers of the Code might in principle have been intercepted in any of its various phases, and might not be directly from an emperor at all. *CTh* 7.13.11, issued on 15 May 382 "at Tyre the metropolis" and posted at Beirut, cannot derive from an imperial letter but must be part of an edict of the praetorian prefect of the Orient sent on to a provincial governor, and there are other such cases.[30]

The Gregorian and Hermogenian Codes, cited as precedents in the law of 429, might further confuse the issue. If they observed the terms of the constitution of 426, the editors of the Theodosian Code worked under the assumption that rescripts did not partake of generalitas, but the Gregorian and Hermogenian Codes, though in many ways more "juristic" in character than the texts which now lay before the editors, consisted mainly of rescripts issued to private individuals in specific cases rather than of imperial letters, edicts, or communications with public officials.[31] Roman communities had long been accustomed to regarding *any* imperial pronouncement as possessing general validity; indeed, Ulpian, on the specific matter of burial regulations, had said that rescripts overrode any municipal law

28. J. D. Harries, " 'Sacra Generalitas': The Administrative Background to the Theodosian Code," in *Estudios de Historia da Derecho Europeo* (1994), at pp. 39ff.

29. Harries, " 'Sacra Generalitas,' " p. 35, and in Harries and Wood (eds.), *The Theodosian Code,* pp. 5f.

30. See Mommsen in his edition, ad loc. (p. 339), Seeck, *Regesten,* p. 11; the other cases include *CTh* 5.14.34; 8.1.8, 4.6; 16.2.12, 15. An excellent example of documentary proliferation in legislation is provided by the edict of toleration issued by Galerius at the end of the Great Persecution (Stephen Mitchell, *JRS* 78 [1988] pp. 105–24, at 113). Galerius' edict was posted at Nicomedia on 30 April 311. It was followed by a letter to the rest of the empire, and itself refers to other letters to provincial governors about the rules to be applied, presumably in the restoration of property to Christians. However, Maximinus, who occupied Asia Minor after Galerius' death, did not wish to end the persecution, and he merely issued verbal instructions to his praetorian prefect Sabinus to send out letters to governors. These letters (Eusebius, *Hist. Eccl.* 9.1.3–6) "enjoined on governors the task of writing to *logistai, strategoi,* and those who had charge of the *pagi* of each city to ignore 'that letter' " (that is, the instructions of Galerius) and implement the new policy.

31. Honoré, *Emperors and Lawyers* (1981), esp. pp. 33–41 and 104–106.

because they were "generalia."[32] Ulpian perhaps had in mind replies sent to provincial governors in response to inquiries from them, rather than the rescripts to private petitioners that largely compose the Gregorian and Hermogenian Codes; but no one can (or could) claim that the situation was entirely clear.

Apart fom these formal considerations, assumptions made by the editors about the character of general laws must also repeatedly have clashed in common sense with the very specific nature, and often the sheer oddity, of the situations in which their ever-conscientious emperors had expressed themselves. Considering such a law as that which appears as *CTh* 7.1.13, instructing that horses be washed downstream, out of sight of military camps, so that drinking water was not polluted by mud and sweat (and worse), nor the eyes of beholders by the sight of naked grooms splashing about in the river, the editors might have inferred a general principle relating to public health and propriety. The law stated a comprehensible benefit, and one could see why it should always be observed. A more elusive principle lay in such a provision as that expressed in a law of 355 addressed to the praetorian prefect: "Henceforth, whenever cured pork, or perhaps fresh meat, is issued to soldiers stationed in Africa, We command that only the hoofs and tips of the noses of the animals shall be cut off and removed, so that all the pork shall not be separated but shall serve in the issue of the food supplies" (7.4.2, trans. Pharr). The generalitas of this regulation lay not in its wide reference to all sorts of situations, or in any statement of principle, but merely in the assertion that it was applicable to any similar situation in the future.[33] The well-known law of 397, posted at Rome in the Forum of Trajan and, on pain of exile and confiscation of property, banning the wearing of Oriental and Germanic pantaloons in the streets of the venerable city, derives its generalitas from the categorical nature of the ban and from its proclamation to the people, rather than from the universality of the situation envisaged; it could only, by definition, affect the city of Rome.[34] The whole of Book 14 of the Code contained provisions relating specifically to the cities of Rome, Constantinople, Alexandria, and Carthage, but they were all general laws.

As these examples show, it is important not to misunderstand the nature of generalitas in the law. Indeed, part of the problem may be that it is so easy to fall

32. Digest 47.12.3.5 (Ulpian); cf. Harries, "'Sacra generalitas,' p. 36.

33. Pharr's "Henceforth, whenever," translating the Latin "cum . . . deinceps," makes it clear that, however specific the situation, the rule that applied to it was always to be observed. The law is addressed to Taurus without designation of office, but he is known to have been praetorian prefect of Italy in 355–61, *PLRE* 1, pp. 879–80 (the law refers to the military *annona* in Africa, a matter concerning the praetorian prefect).

34. *CTh* 14.10.2. Does the phrasing "usum tzangarum adque bracarum . . . nemini liceat *usurpare*" imply that some (bona fide Oriental visitors, perhaps) had the *right* to wear this garb? The text is discussed at no. 10 under "'Palingenesia': Laws Reconstituted," Chapter 8.

victim to a simple logical fallacy. "General laws" are not like categorical moral imperatives ("Do your duty," "Conduct yourself in a civilized manner," "Be kind to your neighbor"), precepts to be observed by all at every time and in every place, but enactments on specific subjects, large or small, *to be obeyed in all relevant circumstances;* it is in this last phrase that generalitas is to be sought. But many laws are *so* specific that any such concept seems inappropriate in considering them. Indeed, it might be dangerous to do so, as in the case of those laws that deal with the aftermath of usurpation or revolution. The fall of the generalissimo Stilicho in August 408 was followed by a sequence of laws confiscating his property and that of his supporters, and denouncing his policies towards the barbarians. One would not wish to subscribe too openly to the idea that such circumstances could recur.[35] We have to imagine our editors, confronted with cases like these, constantly attempting to reconcile the abstract notion of generalitas with the actual content of the laws which they discovered. Were they really to suppose that the washing of horses, the snouts and hoofs of slaughtered pigs, or the wearing of trousers at Rome were issues of general law, just because the emperors had pronounced upon them in letters to public officials?

I suggest therefore that we see in the phrase "vel in certis provinciis seu locis valere aut proponi iussae" not an amendment of their original instructions but a clarification to help the editors of the material as they contemplated their task. Like the other new points raised in the law of 435, it responds to queries raised by the editors as they began their work of excerpting and arranging the material they had collected. It does, however, go to the heart of the Theodosian Code. Whether or not they were specifically known to have been posted as magisterial edicts, imperial epistulae sent to public officials were to be treated as general laws. The effect of the definition, which covered the vast bulk of the material they had collected, would be to confirm that the editors should treat it, often against the apparent implications of its actual content, as falling within the definition of generalitas as set out in 426. Without its guidance, the editors might well have been tempted to omit the snouts of slaughtered pigs, an omission which the modern historian would justly regret.[36]

If these arguments are valid, and the law of 435 represents not the initiation of a new project but a stage in the development of the original one, then we have here

35. Matthews, *Western Aristocracies and Imperial Court,* p. 285. The laws are *CTh* 9.42.20–22, of 24 September–22 November 408.

36. It is again worth emphasizing that the problems outlined here confronted the editors at the outset of their work, when the full range of imperial conscientiousness had become apparent to them but before they had had much time to digest it.

important information on the progress of work on the Code. The period from March 429 to December 435 was that in which the work of assembling the primary material for the compilation was taking place; the recovery of the texts of imperial constitutions. By late 435 the compilers had done enough preliminary work to pose the further questions of editorial policy discussed here. It would be unrealistic to suppose that it had not begun at all, but the editorial process proper—the division of the material under titles, the amendment of texts where necessary, the extrapolation of points of substance and the elimination of superfluous matter, the arrangement in chronological order, and so on—all this could now take place in earnest, and it occupied the much shorter period until the late summer or early autumn of 437. As we saw, the completed Code was put into the hands of the praetorian prefects of east and west after the marriage of Valentinian and Eudoxia on 29 October of that year. From inception to completion, the whole project had taken eight and a half years.[37]

## *The Editorial Commissions*

The main stages of work on the Theodosian Code were marked by the appointment, in 429 and 435, of successive editorial committees, with some limited overlap between their personnel. Further, the law of 15 February 438 that gave authority to the Code in the east ended with an eloquent statement of thanks to those men of high rank who were connected with the work at its final stage of publication.[38] The second part of this chapter examines these individuals who are named as connected with the preparation of the Theodosian Code in its various phases. In most cases they are no more than names, but sometimes it is possible to say a little more about them; and since we can usually identify the offices held by the members of the commissions, we should be able to locate the work on the Theodosian Code within the scheme of duties and promotions at the eastern court. The results of the investigations might also enable us to draw some provisional conclusions concerning the nature of the work and how it was organized.

1. The Commission of 429. The members of the commission initially entrusted with the task of preparing the Theodosian Code appear as follows, with their offices or ranks, in the law of 26 March 429 (the names in bold type are of members also of the second commission of 435):

37. As Honoré remarks, *Law in the Crisis of Empire*, p. 141, "Modern experts, with the aid of advanced technology, might well take longer."

38. *Nov. Th.* 1, §§7–8. The emperor thanked only those involved in the work at this final stage; he did not mention those who had been involved earlier but had for some reason disappeared from the record.

Antiochus (1), vir inlustris, ex quaestore et praefecto
**Antiochus** (2), vir inlustris, quaestor sacri palatii
**Theodorus,** vir spectabilis, magister memoriae
Eudicius et Eusebius, viri spectabiles, magistri scriniorum
Iohannes, vir spectabilis, excomite nostri sacrarii
Comazon et **Eubulus,** viri spectabiles, exmagistris scriniorum
Apelles, vir disertissimus scholasticus

This is a comprehensible list of names, and a number of inferences can be drawn from it. Of the panel of nine, seven were present and past imperial officials drawn from what may be broadly described as the legal and secretarial (as against the financial and administrative) side of the service: quaestors, magistri memoriae, and magistri of the other scrinia to be discussed below.[39] It is difficult to differentiate to the last detail the respective duties of these officials, but they generally involved the hearing of consultations, the drafting of annotations and of replies to petitions from individuals and communities. In particular, one can distinguish between the duties of the quaestor and those of the magister memoriae by saying that it was the quaestor's duty to draft imperial constitutions at the instance of and for consideration by the consistorium; it was that of the magister memoriae to compose the letters sent by the emperor to his public officials. All the officials mentioned had experience relevant to the work of compilation of imperial constitutions now initiated.[40]

The first two members of the panel, both called Antiochus, are respectively described as "exquaestore et praefecto" and as "quaestor sacri palatii." Presumably they had held the quaestorship in succession, or near succession, Antiochus (1) having then been promoted to the praetorian prefecture from which he had also now retired (he was "expraefecto" as well as "exquaestore"), and Antiochus (2) being the current holder of the quaestorship.[41] If it is correct to attribute to the quaestors responsibility for the drafting of imperial legislation, then it was Antiochus (2) whom we may assume to have drafted the law of 429. Having so launched the project, he saw it through to the end, and in 438 he was foremost among those thanked for his work.

After the two quaestors, past and present, is named the magister memoriae The-

39. A scrinium is a case or chest for keeping books and documents. The plural *scrinia* is the generic term for the bureaucratic offices listed here.

40. Jones, *Later Roman Empire,* vol. 1, pp. 367f., 504.

41. *PLRE* 2, pp. 102–4 (Antiochus 6 and 7). The first Antiochus was *PPo Illyrici* by 14 October 427, but it is not known exactly when the second Antiochus (Chuzon) became quaestor. Honoré, *ZSS* 103 (1986), p. 187 (cf. his *Law in the Crisis of Empire,* pp. 112–18), says "not later than 16 March 427," by inference from stylistic analysis.

odorus. Then, separated in the list by Iohannes, vir spectabilis, come Eudicius and Eusebius, magistri scriniorum and Comazon and Eubulus, ex magistris scriniorum.

According to the relevant section of the eastern Notitia Dignitatum (Or. XIX), the scrinia consisted, in descending order of precedence, of the departments of the magistri memoriae, epistolarum, libellorum, and epistularum Graecarum. We have just accounted for the first of these officials, the magister memoriae Theodorus, in the law of 429, and the last of them, the magister epistolarum Graecarum, is not relevant to the work in hand. Indeed, his post is omitted from the western section of the Notitia Dignitatum, his duties in the east being to draft letters issued in Greek, or to translate into Greek letters dictated in Latin.[42] The stage of work on the Theodosian Code now being planned involved the collection for publication, in Latin, of imperial constitutions written in Latin, for which the services of this official were not required. The magister epistolarum Graecarum can therefore be set aside for the time being, and we are left with the magistri and exmagistri epistolarum and libellorum. Following the order of precedence in the Notitia Dignitatum, we may conclude that in 429 Eudicius had recently succeeded Comazon as magister epistolarum, and that Eusebius had succeeded Eubulus as magister libellorum. All, whether current or retired officials, were retained for work on the Code.

In order of precedence between the currently serving and the recent magistri scriniorum is Iohannes, who is described as "vir spectabilis, excomite nostri sacrarii," an undefined title which tells us only that he was a former comes consistorianus, without further specification of his duties or professional interests.[43] His relationship with the magistri epistolarum and libellorum with whom he shares the rank of spectabilis, and the extent of his legal expertise, if any, are unknown.

This is not so of the ninth and last member of the commission. Apelles, vir disertissimus, scholasticus, is differently characterized from the others: not by office or rank but by intellectual character and profession. As mentioned above, the most natural inference is that Apelles was a practicing lawyer, possibly detailed to the work from the school of law of Constantinople.

The extent to which specialist legal expertise was relevant to the conduct of any of the official posts whose representatives were included in the panel of 429 is a matter for debate. This is so even of the quaestors, who were primarily responsible for the drafting of the laws required by the consistory but who, to judge by the available evidence, were men of varying degrees of legal experience. Although they might need to know some law, and might indeed show distinct personal preferences

42. Not. Dig., Or. 19: "Magister epistularum eas epistulas quae graece solent emitti aut ipse dictat aut latine dictas transtulit in graecum." The magister epistularum Graecarum nevertheless appears as a member of the commission of 435.

43. *PLRE* 2, p. 595 (Iohannes 7).

in the way they conceived and expressed it, it does not look as if a professional legal expertise was a consistent criterion for the selection of these officials.[44] More often a high level of *literary* expertise is the obvious qualification. Indeed, it better suited the actual duties of the office, which had more to do with drafting texts (including those of a broader literary character such as imperial orationes to the Senate) than with formulating the law.[45] Nor would the editing of the Theodosian Code be a predominantly "juristic" operation. The Code would contain much material relating to jurisprudence and legal procedure (appearing mainly in the early books), but this was only one set of topics among many. The bulk of the texts to be assembled were administrative documents of a much broader character.

It would certainly be a mistake to regard the members of the panel of 429 as amateurs without qualifications for the work in hand. Of the nine members of the panel of 429, seven—past and present quaestors, magistri memoriae, epistolarum, and libellorum—were men who knew from personal experience in government how laws were conceived, revised, drafted, and issued. Another member was a comes consistorianus of unknown qualifications but no doubt with some knowledge of government (one did not get this rank for nothing). The panel also included a professional lawyer. Moreover, in a most important clause it was empowered to coopt, or at least to consult, learned advisers, for the elimination of legal errors: "hos [that is, the editors] . . . *eruditissimum quemque adhibituros* esse confidimus, ut communi studio vitae ratione deprehensa iura excludantur fallacia."[46] These advisers, like the vir disertissimus scholasticus himself, were presumably found in the legal profession or the newly reformed law school of Constantinople, or else in the ranks of legally qualified civil servants. Indeed, one would not expect the named members of the commission themselves to have undertaken the prolonged and laborious research in the physical collection of texts, which was involved in the earlier stages of work on the Theodosian Code. Most of them had other duties and might expect to be promoted, as some were, to higher office while the project was in progress.

44. For the office of quaestor and its evolution, see the fuller discussion in Chapter 7.

45. Harries, *JRS* 78 (1988), pp. 159ff., pointing (at 169f.) to an apparent increase in the legal expertise of quaestors in the 420s and 430s. This impression may to some extent be exaggerated because of the composition of the Theodosian Code itself. In his law of 15 February 438, the emperor referred elegantly to the double functions of the quaestorship; he described Maximinus as "eminens omni genere litterarum," and his successor Martyrius as "nostrae clementiae fidus interpres."

46. *CTh* 1.1.5 (Mommsen, p. 29, lines 1–2). Note that the text refers to iura, not leges. The word *adhibituros* does not imply that these experts were permanently engaged in work on the project, although this may have been its practical effect; *adhibituros* is used of formal consultation, as in a Roman *consilium*—cf. the letter of Domitian to the Falerienses (*CIL* 9.5420; Bruns, no. 82, Riccobono, no. 75), "adhibitis utriusque ordinis splendidis viris cognita causa," etc.

The conclusion implied by the membership of the commission of 429 is that the emperor mobilized the most relevant departments of the imperial bureaucracy, the present holders of the offices in question—the quaestor and the magistri scriniorum—being afforced by their recent predecessors.[47] The extent to which the serving court officials involved could give their own time to the project is an open question, but their retired predecessors would have been able to, and those in office were presumably able to assign to it members of their staffs. The quaestor, in particular, could use the discretion assigned to him in the Notitia Dignitatum to recruit assistants elsewhere in the bureaucracy; given his commitment to the project, there is no doubt that Antiochus would have been willing to do this.[48] Many of the working decisions must have rested (and were best left) with the learned assistants ("eruditissimum quemque") who were to be consulted. Taking all this into account, and assuming the effective delegation of the practical tasks and the recruitment of qualified assistants, the balance of political authority, departmental experience, and legal expertise visible in the choice of its members seems to have been well adapted for the work in hand.

We can support this impression from the relatively short period in which the original documents from which the Code was edited, were collected. The Code contains, in Mommsen's edition, just over 2,500 entries, a figure that understates both the number of texts it originally contained and the number of texts that were recovered. Some of these texts can be shown to have been parts of the same law, classified under different titles according to the instructions given to the editors, and therefore representing a smaller number of original constitutions; at the same time, the Code does not survive complete, and it is certain that some laws were discarded as irrelevant or insufficiently general in application, or as duplicate versions of laws that were included.[49] By the end of 435, the editors were in a position to ask for the further guidance described above on questions of procedure and

47. This was true of all the personnel in question except the magister memoriae, only the current holder of this office, Theodorus, being mentioned. I would guess that Antiochus (2) filled this gap, and that he had been magister memoriae before he was quaestor.

48. Not. Dig., Or. 12.6: "Officium non habet, sed adiutores de scriniis quos voluerit"; cf. Occ. 10.6: "Habet subaudientes adiutores memoriales de scriniis diversis."

49. Mommsen counted 2,509 surviving texts, plus seven fragments, in the published Code; Honoré, "The Making of the Theodosian Code," p. 165 n. 20, has 2,529, "including some tenuous constitutions"; my own count is 2,515 (Chapter 2, n. 2). These raw figures exclude the 233 texts recovered by Krüger from the *Codex Justinianus* and make no allowance for the splitting of original texts into more than one part, or for the rejection of texts by the editors. Sirks, "The Sources of the Code," pp. 64–66, suggests a total of about 2,700 + *y* original texts from which the Code was edited, *y* being the number of recovered texts which were omitted by the editors. Sirks's estimate of *y* is much higher than mine, the discrepancy deriving from a difference of opinion regarding the procedures of the editors.

editorial policy. These questions were resolved in the constitution of 20 December, which also named the members of the second commission.
2. The Commission of 435. Again we may begin by setting out the names of the members of the commission, as they appear in the law of 20 December 435 (*CTh* 1.1.6). The names shown here in bold type are those of the eight members who were thanked for their services in the law of 15 February 438 giving authority to the Theodosian Code in the east (*Nov. Th.* 1,§7):

**Antiochus** (2), amplissimus adque gloriosissimus praefectorius et consularis
Eubulus, inlustris et magnificus comes et quaestor
Maximinus (1), vir inlustris, insignibus quaestoriae dignitatis ornatus
**Sperantius,** ⟨vir⟩ spectabilis comes consistorianus
**Martyrius** "
Alypius "
Sebastianus "
**Apollodorus** "
**Theodorus** "
Eron "
**Maximinus** (2), ⟨vir⟩ spectabilis comes et magister scrinii
**Epigenes** "
Diodorus "
**Procopius** "
Erotius, vir spectabilis, ex vicariis iuris doctor
Neoterius, vir spectabilis ex [. . . . ].

At most three members of the commission of 429 were also included in the enlarged panel now set up to begin the work of editing and codification. The most important of these was Antiochus 2 (also known as Chuzon), quaestor sacri palatii in 429 and six very distinguished years later "vir amplissimus adque gloriosissimus praefectorius et consularis" (he was eastern consul in 431). Antiochus Chuzon is emerging as a man with a particularly deep commitment to the project of the Theodosian Code. His was the hand that drafted the constitution of 429 initiating the entire project. He is mentioned in pride of place at all three stages of planning and preparation, and he carried his interest far into his official "retirement" from public office; he has rightly been seen as one of the great men of his age, a precursor of Justinian's great jurist, Tribonian.[50] The other members of the commission of 435 who had also been named in 429 were Eubulus, in 429 exmagister libellorum

50. Honoré, "The Making of the Theodosian Code," pp. 165, and esp. 183–89 (Tribonian is mentioned at 189): "Some Quaestors of the Reign of Theodosius II," in Harries and Wood (eds.), *The Theodosian Code,* pp. 84–89; Honoré, *Law in the Crisis of Empire,* pp. 112–18.

and in 435 "vir inlustris et magnificus comes et quaestor noster"; and, if the same man is indicated on the membership lists of both commissions, Theodorus. Previously magister memoriae, Theodorus was now "vir spectabilis, comes consistorianus," but we have no further definition of his functions or responsibilities.[51]

What had happened to the other six members of the first commission between 429 and 435 is unknown. Death or physical impediment may account for some disappearances, but six (or seven) out of nine seems a high rate of loss, and other possibilities exist, such as promotion or retirement, not to mention unsuitability or distaste for the work. Not everyone would find the work congenial, and there were many opportunities for distraction as the attentions of the government were diverted elsewhere. One such diversion was theological politics, notably in the council of Ephesus of 431 and its aftermath, precisely coinciding with the years in which the essential work of collecting material for the Theodosian Code was being performed. Nor did the real world go away. Interest and support, undoubtedly involving active diplomatic contact, had to be extended to the troubled regime of Valentinian III in the west. An unsuccessful campaign was conducted against the Vandals in 431, and trouble also arose with the Huns. This too was settled by diplomacy, which means educated manpower. There was no shortage of distraction for those originally appointed to supervise the work on the Code. In the meantime, once initiated, that work could be left to continue, in the hands of the scholars and lesser officials to whom it was in practice delegated.

The new members of the commission established in 435 begin with Maximinus (1), vir inlustris, who had received the honorary insignia of the quaestorship. He is followed by seven men who are described without further definition as "spectabiles comites consistoriani"; Sperantius, Martyrius, Alypius, Sebastianus, Apollodorus, Theodorus, Eron. Nothing is said of any court posts held by these seven, though if Theodorus is the same man as the Theodorus named on the first commission, he had been magister memoriae.

The next four names are of men who were the current holders of office; another Maximinus — Maximinus (2) — Epigenes, Diodorus, Procopius. Together they are designated "viri spectabiles comites et magistri sacrorum scriniorum." Again inferring the offices of these four from the order of precedence given in the Notitia Dignitatum, we can say that Maximinus (2) was magister memoriae and that Epigenes, Diodorus, and Procopius were magistri, respectively, epistolarum,

51. *PLRE* 2, p. 1090 (Theodorus 24); he was later quaestor, possibly an honorary title. Assuming the identity, only he and Antiochus are attested at all three stages of the preparation of the Code, from 429 to 438. Theodorus is an extremely common name (*PLRE* has sixty-three entries, plus one who also occurs in vol. 1); it will also be noted that the first commission included two men called Antiochus, the second two men called Maximinus.

libellorum, and epistolarum Graecarum. The last of these officials is a newcomer on the commission since that of 429. Like the first commission with its "scholasticus" Apelles, the second also had a professional lawyer in Erotius, "vir spectabilis ex vicariis iuris doctor," and the list concludes with Neoterius, also vir spectabilis, another past officeholder — or possibly another *iuris doctor* — whose office or position does not survive in the preserved text of the constitution of 435.[52]

One key to understanding how the commissions of 429 and 435 actually addressed their work lies, of course, in the amount of time their members were able to devote to it. This was not the same in each case, nor did the emperor expect that to be so, at least if he considered the competing duties of the members of the commissions. That of 429 included the currently serving quaestor and magister memoriae and the men whom we have identified as the heads of the other two main eastern bureaus, the magistri epistolarum and libellorum. The role of these men as current officeholders with other duties to perform cannot have been identical with that of the ex-quaestor, of the ex-magistris scriniorum also included, or with that of the professor of law who was invited to serve. Whatever one's doubts about the efficiency of the late Roman administration and the workload of its officials, it must make *some* difference to the disposal of one's time whether one is actually in office or not. We have just seen that the years 429–35 offered no lack of possible distractions.

The same observation is relevant to the commission of 435. Again, below Antiochus Chuzon, it included Eubulus, "inlustris ac magnificus comes et quaestor noster" and four "spectabiles comites et magistri sacrorum scriniorum": Maximinus (2), Epigenes, Diodorus, and Procopius. Now, Eubulus, a member of both the first and the second commission, is not among those thanked for their services in the law of 15 February 438 conveying authority on the Code. The reason is clear. By 3 April 436, Eubulus is recorded as praetorian prefect of Illyricum, his office being known from two laws referring to him in this office and included in the Theodosian Code.[53] The law of 435, as we shall see, allowed for the possibility that members of the commission might be prevented from serving by public office or natural circumstance, and Eubulus is a case in point. His promotion as praetorian prefect would remove him, within a few months of appointment, from the commission, and so he is not among the eight persons thanked in the law of 15 Febru-

52. See Chapter 2. Erotius' titles would surely have come to him in this fashion. It might be that Neoterius was a similar case, though the incompleteness of the text makes it impossible to be sure. He is *PLRE* 2, Neoterius 2 (p. 776), where the identification with the *comes* Neoterius 1, not suggested by *PLRE*, seems possible; he was involved in the aftermath of the council of Ephesus.

53. *CTh* 8.4.30; 12.1.187. There is some editorial significance in this — see Chapter 8.

ary 438. In his place as quaestor we find, presumably in succession, Maximinus (2) and Martyrius, both by promotion from offices or ranks they had held in 435.[54]

By comparing the laws of 435 and 438, we can see that two more of the officials thanked in 438 then held offices to which they had been promoted from those they had held in 435: Epigenes from epistolae to memoria and Procopius from epistolae Graecae to libelli. These were both cases of regular promotion through the scrinia. The third of the four magistri scriniorum listed in 435, Diodorus, is not mentioned in the law of 438, having been replaced as magister libellorum by Procopius. Like Eubulus, Diodorus had left office, and his work on the commission had come to an end: whether in his case too by promotion to higher office outside the scrinia or whether through death, illness, or some other cause we do not know.[55] Lastly Martyrius, comes consistorianus in 435, was by 438 quaestor sacri palatii, in which office he must have succeeded Maximinus (2).[56]

The results of these changes between 435 and 438 can be shown as follows. The members of the commission of 435 who were not thanked in 438 are given in square brackets:

| Law of 435 | Thanked in 438 |
|---|---|
| Antiochus | ex praefecto et consule |
| [Eubulus, QSP] | [→PPo Illyrici] |
| [Maximinus (1) "honorary" QSP] | |
| Maximinus (2), magister (memoriae) | →(ex-)QSP |
| Sperantius, comes consistorianus | comites sacri |
| Apollodorus, " " | nostri con- |
| Theodorus, " " | sistorii |
| Epigenes, magister (epistolarum) | →memoriae |
| [Diodorus, magister (libellorum)] | |
| Procopius, magister (epist. Graecarum) | →libellorum |
| Martyrius, comes consistorianus | →QSP |

54. Maximinus (2) was ex-quaestor in 438, having evidently held the office in the intervening period, 435/8. This is more likely than that Maximinus (1), "honorary quaestor" in 435, subsequently held the substantive office.

55. If the normal sequence of promotions had applied, Diodorus would be expected to have become magister epistolarum, but no official of this rank is named in 438. I suspect that Diodorus was promoted to this office but that he either died or was promoted elsewhere shortly before the publication of *Nov. Th.* 1.

56. Martyrius was therefore the official who drafted *Nov. Th.* 1, thanking himself and his colleagues for their work on the Code. Depending on his rank in 435, he may have leapfrogged Epigenes and Procopius in his advancement to the quaestorship.

Of the three "viri spectabiles comites consistoriani" on the commission of 435 who were thanked in 438, Apollodorus and Theodorus later appear, in the same order of precedence, with the rank of ex-quaestor in the records of the council of Chalcedon of 451. Whether they held the quaestorship between 438 and 451 or whether their rank in 451 was honorary is not known, nor is it relevant here; the former has been adjudged the more likely.[57] Further to emphasize the variety of concerns that pressed upon the government and its supporters in these years, Epigenes, magister epistolarum in 435 and magister memoriae on 15 February 438, was promoted quaestor soon after (no doubt in succession to Martyrius), and figures in the narrative of Priscus of Panium as a man of distinction, chosen to serve as an envoy to Attila the Hun.[58]

These arguments are unavoidably complicated and are not helped by the unmemorable character of fifth-century personal names. A general conclusion does however seem well founded. In the period of up to 1¾ years (December 435–October 437) during which the work of editing, classification, and preparation of the final version of the Theodosian Code was being pursued, promotion of the higher personnel mentioned in December 435 was going on in the usual way, sometimes allowing officials to remain attached to the project to be thanked in 438, sometimes not. The roles played by each member of the commission of 435 cannot, given their widely different qualifications and status, have been identical, nor can their devotion to the project have been equally time-consuming.

If the arguments given in the first part of this chapter are accepted, the persons actively involved in the work between 429 and 435, who anticipated that its nature would now change and had certain questions of editorial policy to be confirmed or refined, must have reported in this sense to the emperor. The response, in the law of 20 December 435, gave to the editors the advice that they requested and renewed the government's commitment to the project by establishing the second and larger commission just described, to supervise the work.

Since the period from December 435 until the autumn of 437 was that in which the actual editing and arranging of the texts was being performed, it is natural to ask whether the sixteen members of the commission of 435 correspond to the sixteen books in which the Theodosian Code was ultimately published. The question is worth putting at this stage, since it allows us to address, if only to eliminate, some possible ways in which the work of the editors might have been organized. On the hypothesis that each member of the commission was entrusted with the preparation of a particular book, we might then be able to study the body of texts prepared by individual editors in the respective books assigned to them and to

57. *PLRE* 2, pp. 120 (Apollodorus 5), 1090 (Theodorus 24); cf. 754 (Menas 2).
58. *PLRE* 2, p. 396.

speculate, in certain circumstances, about their attitudes toward their subject matter and about the working relations between the editors. We might even be able to assign certain books to particular editors. Such a mode of analysis is a fundamental element in modern interpretations of the composition of Justinian's Digest.[59]

For reasons already suggested, in the case of the Theodosian Code the hypothesis is unlikely to be correct. Apart from the question whether it could be known at this stage that the Code would in fact be published in sixteen books, it would require that the editorial role of each of the sixteen members, all working in parallel, was similar in character. But this can hardly be how the work was organized, given the diversity in the different types of text, with different legal characteristics, that would be contained in the various books of the Code, the markedly different lengths of the books themselves,[60] and the differences in character and qualification between the members of the commission; at the one extreme, Antiochus Chuzon, quaestor sacri palatii in 429, "amplissimus adque gloriosissimus praefectorius ac consularis" in 435, and first of those thanked by the emperor in February 438, and, at the other extreme, Erotius, "vir spectabilis ex vicariis iuris doctor" on the commission of 435, succeeding Apelles, "vir disertissimus, scholasticus," on that of 429. Apelles and Erotius were academic lawyers whose role was surely different in kind from that of Antiochus, and also from that of the magistri scriniorum on the commissions of 429 and 435. One imagines them as devoting particular attention, say, to what ultimately appeared as Books 2–5 of the Theodosian Code, texts on private law following the arrangement of the Praetor's Edict, and otherwise as supplying their juristic advice wherever it was needed. It was not a sensible approach, to set them to work on one book, while a grandee like Antiochus Chuzon worked on another. The value of their contributions lay in a more general, coordinating role, and the same argument must extend to the other members of the commission.

The modus operandi of 435 was therefore not that of one book of the Code for each of the sixteen members of the commission. Some other working structure must have been devised. In considering this, three points seem worthy of emphasis: first, the particularly prominent role of those individuals mentioned in all three, or at least two, of the laws of 429, 435, and 438—notably, of course, Antiochus Chuzon and possibly Theodorus, who were there from the beginning to the end of

59. Schulz, *History of Roman Legal Science*, pp. 318–22; Honoré, *Tribonian*, chap. 5, esp. pp. 146ff. Apart from the arguments that will be presented, we should consider the very different types of material represented in the two collections. The Theodosian Code was a compilation of primary, the Digest of secondary sources.

60. The number of titles in the fully preserved books ranges between 11 (Books 13 and 16) and 45 (Book 9), and the number of individual laws between 99 (Book 14) and 304 (Book 11).

the project; and second, the presence on both commissions of a "legal specialist," with a general advisory role covering all aspects of the commissioners' work where their expertise was required. In third place, there is the role of the unattached comites consistoriani on the commission of 435, who were not actively involved in the care of departments of state. This point will bear a moment's expansion.

One feature of the commissions both of 429 and 435 was the proportion of men—five out of nine on the first, ten out of sixteen on the second commission, including professional lawyers and a member of the second commission whose status is unknown—who possessed official titles but were not the current holders of court office. Eight of the ten members of the second commission who fall into this category are placed in order of precedence immediately below the praetorian prefect and quaestor of the time, and above the serving magistri scriniorum. The only member of this group of eight who was promoted to a substantive court office in this period was Martyrius, who had become quaestor by 15 February 438; but this seems to have been a very recent appointment, probably made after work on the Code was complete. Neither he nor any of the other unattached comites consistoriani or legal experts mentioned in 435 was prevented by any other commitment in the imperial service from working full-time on the Code. It is natural to suppose that these were the men, rather than those actively involved in the duties of court office, who devoted the greater part of their time to work on the Code.

It is also worth paying attention to the language in which the emperor expressed his thanks to those responsible for the Code in 438. The guiding genius of the project, Antiochus Chuzon, received the most fulsome expressions of praise for his endless hard work (*vigiliis*) in bringing the work to completion; this is no more than a true acknowledgment of his role in the enterprise. Then, addressed to the past and present quaestors, Maximinus and Martyrius, we find expressions that convey complementary aspects of that official's duties. The ex-quaestor Maximinus is "eminent in all forms of literature" ("eminens omni genere litterarum"), while Martyrius, who by then held the quaestor's office, is "the faithful mouthpiece of our Clemency" ("nostrae clementiae fidus interpres")—an elegant combination of expressions that does some credit to Martyrius, who presumably composed it.

One final point is of some interest. The commissioners of 435 were empowered to replace by cooptation any of their number who were prevented by public business or any other cause from continuing to take part in the project: "Si quis aut humano praepeditus casu aut aliqua rei publicae sollicitudine ab iniuncto fuerit abstractus negotio" (*CTh* 1.1.6, §3). Now, the law of 15 February 438 mentions only eight of the sixteen. The absence of Eubulus is explained by his promotion to the prefecture of Illyricum; that, if anything, might be described as "rei publicae sollicitudo." We have noted also the disappearance of Diodorus, whose apparently predictable promotion from magister libellorum to magister epistolarum is not recorded, either because it did not take place or because Diodorus did not survive or otherwise qualify to be thanked for his contribution. That still leaves six members of the commission of 435 who are absent from the list of those thanked in 438. Some of the same questions can be asked about these as were asked about the six members of the first commission who disappeared from view between 429 and 435. Many contingencies, predictable and otherwise, are allowed for in the phrases "humano praepeditus casu" and "rei publicae sollicitudo." Equally interesting, however, is the fact that, despite the powers of the commissioners to draft replacements, no *new* names are recorded in 438. The simplest explanation of this is that no cooptations were made, because none were found necessary for the continuance of the project.[61]

It does not look as if each of the sixteen commissioners, many of whom had other work to do and some of whom were promoted to higher office while the preparation of the Code was under way, was equally indispensable for the actual work of preparing the texts for publication. Much of this work was done by adjutants of lesser seniority—whether of greater specialist expertise remains open to conjecture, though one recalls the possible involvement of the advocate and later church historian Sozomen, mentioned in Chapter 3. Given the presence of law professors on the commissions, it would be perverse to ignore the role of the law school of Constantinople. Just as its influence is relevant in understanding how the Code came to be conceived, so its products must surely have provided much of the technical support required for the project.

The detailed study of the sources that produced, in the Theodosian Code, more than 2,500 surviving texts (and in addition, as we shall see in the next chapter, 233 texts recovered from the Codex Justinianus), is a complicated and uncertain process. But the framework within which the work was conducted is remarkably well documented. We know the editorial policies that were proposed, in the laws of 429 and 435. We know when the work was begun and finished, how it was published and distributed, even how it proceeded in its successive phases. We know the names of the successive editorial commissions appointed to perform the work, and we have a list of those who, on 15 February 438, were thanked for their contribution to the now completed Code. We know the measures taken to promulgate the text, and to ensure that sufficient authoritative copies were made for distribution to the provinces. As with any Classical text, however, and particularly in the case

61. Possibly the emperor did not thank those who had worked on the project for less than two years. But this seems out of keeping.

of the Theodosian Code, there is a wide gap between the condition of the text as it was left by its ancient author or editor and that in which it is presented to the modern reader. We now turn to the published text itself, in the first place to describe its manuscript and other sources and then to account for the condition in which it has been transmitted to us.

# 5

## *The Text of the Code*

It will be obvious from a glance at the apparatus criticus to Mommsen's edition of the Theodosian Code that the story of its descent from the original copies commissioned by Theodosius is a far from simple one. Only two-thirds of the Code—namely, Books 6–16—has good manuscript support; for these books the restoration of the text, leaving aside many individual points of difficulty, is relatively unproblematic. The first five books, by contrast, which are based only two very incomplete manuscripts, must be reconstructed from a variety of sources, not merely for the reading of particular passages, but with regard to the entire question of the contents and structure of the original text. The most important of these sources is the selection of laws from the Theodosian Code in the Breviarium of Alaric, better called Lex Romana Wisigothorum, compiled in the early sixth century to provide a summary of Roman law as then seemed relevant for the Roman populations living under the Visigoths. It is the purpose of this chapter to describe the status of the text of the Theodosian Code and some of the critical problems that attend its reconstruction. No novelty is claimed, for an account that derives necessarily from Mommsen's exhaustive Prolegomena. Readers may nevertheless welcome something more accessible than that formidably stern treatment, and, as will be seen, it is possible to take issue with one important aspect of Mommsen's reconstruction of the text.

To begin with the less problematic section of the text, Books 6–16 of the Theodosian Code rest on two manuscript sources, both of Gallic origin.[1] Books 6–8 are preserved in Parisinus 9643 (known as *R*), in the Bibliothèque Nationale. An excellently written uncial manuscript of the sixth century, it was in 1559 in the possession of Etienne Charpin, a priest of Lyons; it was later owned by Franciscus Pithoeus (Pithou), who in 1620 gave it to his nephew Petrus Pithoeus.[2] This manuscript was used by both Cuiacius (Cujas) in his editions of 1566 and 1586, and by Gothofredus (Godefroy) in his great commentary published in 1665; the printed texts of both editors may sometimes be used to recover readings in this manuscript which have been lost or damaged since those times. Its most notable lacunae are at the beginning of Book 6 and at the end of Book 8 of the text. In Mommsen's edition, it preserves from the last lines of 6.2.12 to the middle of the penultimate title of Book 8.[3]

The chief source for Books 9–16 of the Code is a manuscript now in the Vatican Library (Vat. Reg. 886 = *V*), again expressing a tradition running through libraries in early medieval France.[4] It contains a complete text from the beginning of Book 9 to near the end of Book 16. From the middle of 16.10.12 in Mommsen's edition to the end of the text at 16.11.13, the laws are supplied from manuscripts from a different tradition of descent, either preserving separately the laws affecting the Christian Church in Book 16, or in the form of manuscripts of the Breviarium expanded for the same purpose.[5] Books 6–16 are not free of textual problems, but these are specific to certain laws and do not affect our understanding of the general character of these books. For all intents and purposes, they are transmitted complete.

For Books 1–5 the situation is quite different. Calculating from the proportions of the surviving to the lost parts of *R* and of a manuscript from Turin (*T*) to be discussed below, Mommsen estimated that of Books 1–5 of the original Code only

1. In Mommsen's words, "Servavit nobis Theodosianum Gallia" (Prolegomena, p. xxxviii); cf. Ian Wood, "The Code in Merovingian Gaul," in Harries and Wood (eds.), *The Theodosian Code,* esp. pp. 164–66, with references to E. A. Lowe's *Codices Latini Antiquiores* but unfortunately not directly identifying the individual manuscripts.

2. Prolegomena, pp. xlii–xliv; Lowe, *CLA* 5, no. 591. The third main, though fragmentary, source, a lost manuscript at Turin (*T*—see n. 7), appears to have been at Bobbio and was no doubt of Italian origin: Mommsen, Prolegomena, pp. xxxix–xlii, depending, as he often did, on the report of Krüger.

3. The missing first title of Book 6, "De dignitatibus," together with a few missing lines at the end of Book 6, are supplied from the Codex Justinianus. The missing portion of Book 8—namely, 8.18.9–10 and 19.1—is in part supplied by the Breviarium and the Codex Justinianus.

4. Mommsen, Prolegomena, p. xxxvii, xliv–xlvi, cf. lxxxviii–lxxxix.

5. Prolegomena, pp. xc–xcii; cf. Mark Vessey, "The Origins of the *Collectio Sirmondiana:* A New Look at the Evidence," in Harries and Wood (eds.), *The Theodosian Code,* pp. 182–83.

about one-third has survived.[6] The reconstruction of this part of the text as we now read it involves a variety of sources and methods that raise a number of still debatable points of editorial policy.

The first contribution to the text of Books 1–5, though not the most important in terms of the quantity of text involved, is made by two manuscripts. One of these, the Turin manuscript just mentioned (*T*), preserves on forty-three largely discontinuous folios laws from all except two of the sixteen books of the Theodosian Code; its first sixteen folios contain sections of Books 1–5 of the Code.[7] The other, a manuscript in the Ambrosian Library at Milan (C. 29 inf. = *A*), is, strictly speaking, a manuscript of the Breviarium, but for part of Book 1 of the Breviarium it follows the full text of the Theodosian Code (from 1.4.1 to 1.16.6 of Mommsen's text). It was this manuscript, as we saw in Chapter 3, that alone preserves the Gesta Senatus by which the Theodosian Code was promulgated in the west, together with the law of Valentinian of 443 arising from the Gesta. It also contains the first Novel of Theodosius of 15 February 438, "De Theodosiani codicis auctoritate"; this law is of course otherwise attested.[8] These manuscripts, *T* and *A*, have a certain value in relation to the texts of specific laws and supply a number of laws omitted by the Breviarium. In other ways too, in the pages which survive, they offer controlled information about the original nature of the text of the Code in these early books. They may show how many laws stood in the original titles, and on occasions they provide the original numbers assigned to titles and to individual laws. Among lesser contributors, a further manuscript in the Bibliothèque Nationale (Cod. Par. 4413) preserves after an abbreviated text of the Breviarium the names of the rubrics of sixteen of the titles contained in Book 1 of the Theodosian Code.[9] These again provide a control, confirming and extending the rubrics otherwise attested for this book of the Code.[10] Even when its text is missing or curtailed, therefore, the original scope and contents of Book 1 are quite well known.

The Breviarium, the source for the great majority of laws preserved from these books of the Theodosian Code, was published by the Visigothic king Alaric II in 506, the year before his defeat by Clovis at the battle of Vouillé and the reduction of the Visigothic kingdom to its Spanish domains.[11] Endorsed by an assembly of Gallo-Roman nobles and clergy and prepared by learned men, or "prudentes," it

6. Prolegomena, p. xxxviii.

7. Mommsen, Prolegomena, pp. xxxix–xliii, where he again acknowledges the (published) contribution of Krüger to its reading and accepts Krüger's analysis of the structure of the manuscript (which was destroyed in a fire in the library at Turin in 1904).

8. Prolegomena, pp. lxxxiii–lxxxv.

9. Prolegomena, p. lxxxv.

10. Notably by the index of *A*, which lists the names of many of its titles.

11. See esp. J. Gaudemet, *Le Bréviaire d'Alaric et les Epitome* (1965).

comprised selections from the Theodosian and also from the Gregorian and Hermogenian Codes, and from the Novellae of Theodosius II, Valentinian III, and Majorian issued after the Theodosian Code was published. Also included were summaries of juristic writings—the Institutes of Gaius, the Sentences of Paul, and a fragment of Papinian. These were the jurists to whom the late empire had also given special authority, especially in the so-called Law of Citations of 426, which was itself included in the Breviarium.[12] Appended to the selected texts, with the exception of Gaius, were *interpretationes*, explanatory notes added according to their instructions by the compilers of the Breviarium.[13] The proportion of texts from the Theodosian Code chosen for inclusion in the Breviarium varies according to the perceived relevance of the legislation of the Code to the conditions of the early sixth century. Given the deficiencies in the manuscript evidence for this part of the text, it is fortunate that Alaric's epitomators, for reasons that will be explained below, had a special interest in the first five books of the Code.

The Breviarium was itself supplemented by later scholars who retained access to the full text of the Code, and their additions sometimes allow us to supply texts omitted by the epitomators of Alaric. The most significant example of this for the early books is the Ambrosian manuscript of the Breviarium (*A*) which, as we have just seen, for a considerable part of Book 1 of that text actually followed a full text of the Theodosian Code and added more material besides. Another case, to be discussed later, is the so-called Appendix Legis Romanae Wisigothorum, which in the course of supplementing the Breviarium contributes a number of otherwise lost texts to Books 1 and 4 of the Theodosian Code.

The Breviarium closely conforms to the structure and sequence of contents of the Theodosian Code. It too was arranged in sixteen books—or rather, given the scope of some of them, under sixteen headings—in the same order of subjects; within each "book" the selected titles, and within each title the selected laws, are presented in the same order as in the Theodosian Code. Because of the large number of omitted titles, the Breviarium does not keep step with the Code, but it moves along with it. In the first five books of the Code, for which the manuscript evidence is so fragmentary, it is by far our best and usually our only guide to its original contents. Sometimes, as in Books 4 and 5 of the Code, its text as edited by Mommsen is little more than the text of the Breviarium with occasional insertions from other sources.

Although their sequence is identical, the proportion of titles from the Theodosian Code included in the Breviarium varies very widely between books. Of the 417 (plus) titles included in Mommsen's edition of the Code (the precise number of

12. *Brev.* 1.4.1 (Mommsen, pp. 34–35).
13. Gaudemet, *Le Bréviaire*, pp. 37–41.

original titles cannot be established, but it was significantly higher than this) the Breviarium contains 180,[14] but this number masks the very different percentage of titles chosen, respectively, from Books 1–5 and from Books 6–16 of the Code. From Books 1–5, of the 143 (plus) titles of Mommsen's edition, 96 are represented in the Breviarium; from Books 6–16, of a total of 263 titles in Mommsen, only 84 have been chosen. The disproportion is still greater when one looks at the number of individual laws, rather than of titles, included in the Breviarium. For Books 7 and 14 of the Code only 1 title from each is included in the Breviarium, and from Book 13 only 2 titles; but the numbers of individual laws chosen from these titles were one, onc, and three, respectively — that is to say a total of five laws from three entire books of the Theodosian Code.[15] In some cases, as Gaudemet observes, it appears as if the epitomators were choosing a single representative law, a "constitution témoin," simply to ensure that a title did not disappear altogether.[16]

The disproportion in the representation of Books 1–5 and 6–16 of the Code in the Breviarium reflects the preference of the sixth-century epitomators for the contents of the first part of Theodosius' compilation. They were interested neither in the everyday realities of the Roman empire of the fourth and early fifth centuries nor in the detail of its political institutions. One can see this in Book 1, where they selected just eleven of the original thirty-four (?) titles (for the number of titles see below), including laws relating to forms of legislation and jurisdiction, but omitting whole sequences of titles relating to the duties of late Roman imperial and civic officials that were of no concern to the Visigothic regime. Nor were they much concerned with the privileges of the senatorial class and palace officials (Book 6), military affairs and minor administrative matters (Books 7–8), legislation about *navicularii* and other matters to do with Roman taxation (Books 10 and 13), or the administration of Rome, Alexandria, and other large cities (Book 14), and so on. What mainly interested them was the private law of the Romans with its sources, and it was this that was set out in the first five books of the Theodosian Code.

From time to time other fifth- and sixth-century writers, jurists, and others who

14. See Mommsen's tables, pp. 5–26 of his edition. Gaudemet, *Le Bréviaire,* p. 23, has 162 titles for the Breviarium, but his numbers for the individual "books" (that is to say, sections of the Breviarium corresponding to books of the Theodosian Code) give 180, and this is the correct total. I emphasize that the figures relate to *titles,* not individual laws; the discrepancies are increased if one looks at the relative numbers of laws taken even from those titles selected for representation.

15. From Book 6, only two laws appear in the Breviarium (6.1.1–2), but these are both the laws from *CTh* 6.5, *Ut dignitatum ordo servetur,* where *R* gives the full contents of the title.

16. Gaudemet, *Le Bréviaire,* p. 27. This is not as pointless as it may seem, since the constitutions, as some of the interpretationes state, were to be supplemented by the ius, or juristic opinion, also included in the Breviarium.

had access to the Theodosian Code, gave citations from it in their works and occasionally included the texts of otherwise lost laws. We saw that the Breviarium was itself supplemented by later writers, the most notable of these being the author of the Appendix Legis Romanae Wisigothorum, citing (with references) no fewer than fourteen constitutions from the Theodosian Code, for many of which it is the only evidence.[17] A more specialized contribution comes from the collection of writers on land measurement known as the Gromatici (from the *groma*, an instrument used in surveying); this text provides the fullest—indeed, probably a complete—version of a title of five laws in Book 2 of the Theodosian Code.[18]

The last and most important of these supplementary sources for the first five books of the Theodosian Code, and the one that raises the most important questions about editorial policy, is the Codex Justinianus. This work, the first installment in the program of codification implemented by Justinian and his quaestor Tribonian, was published in its first edition in 529. This first edition is, however, lost, and what is now referred to as the Codex Justinianus is a second edition published in 534. The loss of the first edition complicates the study of the work undertaken by Justinian's editors but has a less serious effect on the question of its sources.[19] The Codex Justinianus, unlike the Theodosian Code and its predecessors, was based not on raw material but on texts already codified—namely, the codes of Gregorius and Hermogenianus, incorporating laws of the third century, and the Theodosian Code for texts of the fourth and early fifth. For the time after the publication of the Theodosian Code, it drew on the Novellae of Theodosius II and his successors down to Anthemius, together with some laws of the first years of the reign of Justinian himself.

It has never been doubted that the Theodosian Code was the source for the laws included in the Codex Justinianus for the period 312–437; nor has it been claimed that any other source apart from the Theodosian Code was involved. A study of the footnotes to Krüger's edition of the Codex Justinianus would confirm that, where the Theodosian Code is complete, the laws of this period cited in the Codex Justinianus can invariably be found there. It should follow that the Codex Justinianus can be used as a source for laws missing from the *incomplete* books of the Theodosian Code. If a law is found in the Codex Justinianus but not in the Theodosian Code, it should be possible to assume that that was its source, and efforts be made to restore it to its appropriate title in the earlier books.

17. Riccobono, vol. 2, pp. 670–79 (again, Krüger's text); the texts cited are on pp. 673–76.

18. *CTh* 2.26.1–5, *De finium regundorum.*

19. Tony Honoré, *Tribonian* (1978), chap. 7 (pp. 212–22). The main implication is that texts appearing there in a different form from that in *CTh* may have been adapted either in their transmission from *CTh* to *CJ* or between the two editions of *CJ* itself.

Despite his acceptance of the principle that it had no other source, Mommsen declined to use the Codex Justinianus as a quarry from which to supply — or, as he put it, to "repeat" (*repetere*) — texts lost from the incomplete books of the Theodosian Code.[20] He was far from ignoring it, for he entered references to the Codex Justinianus in the lists of dates, names, and places included in the Prolegomena to his edition; and in his annotations to his established text of the Theodosian Code he gave parallel references to the Codex Justinianus for the hundreds of laws which also appeared there. These annotations are a complement to Krüger's dense footnotes, which refer the reader from the Codex Justinianus to its predecessor.

One can understand why Mommsen was reluctant to embark upon a process of reconstruction that would in its detail involve uncertainty; it would not always be possible to be sure to which title of the Theodosian Code to restore a law found in the Codex Justinianus, or in what form it had appeared there. Nevertheless, considered in general, Mommsen's decision not to include in his edition of the Theodosian Code unsupported texts from the Codex Justinianus, even when he knew it to be their source, was not logical. If the purpose in editing the Theodosian Code was to present it in a form as close as possible to the original, it would not matter if laws were "repeated" there from the Codex Justinianus; while any assumption that interested readers should be willing to find the reference and look up the text for themselves (as they have to do) seems an unduly reserved attitude for the editor of a reconstructed text.

With respect to laws not preserved in the full manuscript tradition of the Theodosian Code or in the Breviarium, Mommsen applied very rigid criteria on what he would accept for inclusion in his printed text of the Code. Only if a positive attribution of a law could be made to a specific place in the Theodosian Code would he accept it. In the absence of such attribution, he declined to use inferential grounds for including texts, even if, as he himself believed in the case of the Codex Justinianus, there could be no other source for them than the Theodosian Code. These texts he treated as authentic but unattached ("Extravaganten"), and they do not appear in his edition.

The following paragraphs give examples of the arbitrary nature of this procedure. The cases chosen are examples only, but they are among the most important, and the approaches they illustrate could certainly be applied more widely. The arguments are somewhat involved, those in the first paragraph particularly so. The essential points, however, are conveyed by the second to fifth paragraphs.

1. The Appendix Legis Romanae Wisigothorum referred to earlier (Riccobono, vol. 2, pp. 670–79) preserves with references to book and title the whole or part of

20. Prolegomena, pp. lix–lx. As will be explained, in adopting this approach, Mommsen differed substantially from his collaborator Krüger.

the texts of fourteen laws from the Theodosian Code. Twelve of the citations are from the early books, where the text of the Code is incomplete.

(i) The first citation, App. 1.20, with its reference to "lib. IIII de re iudicata," is included by Mommsen as the first of two laws under this title in the Theodosian Code (4.16.1); the second law in the title is supplied from the Breviarium (4.14.1 = *CTh* 4.16.2). Both laws are also included, under separate titles, in the Codex Justinianus (7.50.3 and 7.48.2). Without the attribution in the Appendix, Mommsen's criteria would not have permitted the inclusion under this title of *CTh* 4.16.1, even though it occurs, clearly from this source, in the Codex Justinianus.

(ii) App. 1.21–23 provides three laws in the following title of the Theodosian Code, 4.17, *De sententiis ex periculo recitandis.*[21] The title consists of five laws in the edition of Mommsen, including the three supplied by the Appendix. The first is from App. 1.21, supported by *CJ* 7.44.3; the second from App. 1.22; the third from the Breviarium (4.15.1); the fourth from App. 1.23; and the fifth again from the Breviarium (4.15.2). None of the four texts 4.17.2–5 has further support apart from the Appendix or the Breviarium. If it had not been for the attestation of App. 1.21, Mommsen could not have cited *CJ* 7.44.3 as a text from the Theodosian Code. In this he would have been mistaken. Where he is not simply mistaken but actually illogical is that *CJ* 7.44.2, which not only is on the same subject but is addressed to the same recipient as 7.44.3, is not included in his text of the Code. The only distinction between the two laws is that one happens to have been cited in the Appendix, the other not—but from the point of view of the text of the Theodosian Code this is purely a matter of later circumstance and has nothing to do with their inherent nature. If one text is accepted into the Theodosian Code, then so should the other be.

(iii) App. 1.24–25 preserves, with reference to the title and in both cases unsupported, the final two texts of *CTh* 1.2.11–12, *De diversis rescriptis.* The first three laws in this title of the Theodosian Code are preserved in *T;* seven, including one of the first three, in the Breviarium (1.2.1–7 = *CTh* 1.2.2, 4–8, 10); and one (*CTh* 1.2.9) in another supplement to the Breviarium by a later writer.[22] Of the twelve laws in the title so reconstructed from its diverse sources, five (nos. 3, 5, 6, 8, 10) are also found distributed among different titles of the Codex Justinianus, most of them with new and more precise designations than those used in the Theodosian Code; they are *CJ* 1.14.1, under the title *De legibus et constitutionibus principum et edictis;* 1.19.2 and 4, *De precibus imperatori offerendis et de quibus rebus*

21. The name of the title is cited by App. 1.21, the number of the book being the same as in 1.20.

22. Viz., other than the Appendix. The source is a lost manuscript known to Pithou and used by Cujas in 1566; Mommsen, p. 32, and Prolegomena, p. lxxxv.

*supplicare liceat vel non;* 1.20.1, *Quando libellus principi datus litis contestationem facit;* and 1.22.4, *Si contra ius utilitatemque publicam vel per mendaciam fuerit aliquid postulatum vel impetratum.*

Following this guide, it should be possible to find distributed among these titles of the Codex Justinianus other laws whose source was title 1.2 of the Theodosian Code. The search reveals some notable absentees from Mommsen's text. Of the laws in *CJ* 1.14, *De legibus,* the first is found in the Theodosian Code (1.2.3), but none of the other three laws relevant to the period covered by the Code is found there. The absentees include *CJ* 1.14.2–3, extremely important parts of a constitution of 426, of which other extracts do appear in the Theodosian Code; the text was clearly known to its editors, as I shall discuss. From *CJ* 1.19, *De precibus,* only two of seven laws from the relevant period can be found in the Theodosian Code (one of them in Book 8, where the text is complete), and the missing laws again include part of the important constitution of 426. Nothing relevant is missing in the Code from the short title *CJ* 1.20, *Quando libellus* (1.20.1 = *CTh* 1.2.10, from *Brev.* 1.2.7), but from *CJ* 1.22, *Si contra ius,* there are two missing texts (3 and 5), including yet another extract from the constitution of 426. We should add the title in the Codex Justinianus that corresponds directly in name to that in the Theodosian Code, *CJ* 1.23, *De diversis rescriptis et pragmaticis sanctionibus.* This includes one law that is preserved elsewhere in the Theodosian Code (1.23.4 = *CTh* 1.1.1, *De constitutionibus principum et edictis*), but another (*CJ* 1.23.5) that is not found there.

It will be seen from these examples that between the Theodosian Code and the second edition of the Codex Justinianus an increase in the number and some reclassification of the content of titles took place, but it should still be possible to suggest from a range of alternatives the titles of the Theodosian Code to which the missing laws should be attributed.

(iv) Another title in Book 1 of the Theodosian Code, title 22, *De officio iudicum omnium,* contains four laws, of which three (nos. 1, 2, and 4) are from the Breviarium (1.9.1–3).[23] Two of these three are also included in the Codex Justinianus (1.48.1 and 3.14.1). The fourth law (the third in the title) is again provided by the Appendix (1.27) without further support. Of the titles in the Codex Justinianus referred to, 3.14 (*Quando imperator inter pupillos vel viduas vel miserabiles personas cognoscat et ne exhibeatur*) contains only this one law. The other title, however, *CJ* 1.48, *De officio diversorum iudicum,* contains three laws; the first is the one under discussion from the Theodosian Code (1.22.1), and the second is not

23. Mommsen's edition, pp. 61–62. The number of the title is not positively recorded but can be inferred from the Paris Index and the titles of the Breviarium in the sequence beginning from *CTh* 1.16 (= *Brev.* 1.6).

found in the Theodosian Code and should clearly be restored to it. The third (*CJ* 1.48.3) is found in the Theodosian Code, but in a variant and slightly longer version, and in a part of the text (6.26.5) where the manuscripts give full support. This version, however, has its derivative in the corresponding title at *CJ* 12.19.2. If one compares the two texts in the Codex Justinianus, it becomes clear that the version at 1.48.3 is unlikely to derive from that at 12.19.2, or hence from *CTh* 6.26.5. If so, the version of the law found at *CJ* 1.48.3 is not accounted for in the Theodosian Code and should be restored to it. It is not uncommon for the Theodosian Code to include two, and even two variant, versions of the same law under different titles.

2. The second example is in a way the converse of the first. Book 2 of the Theodosian Code contains a title, 2.26, *De finium regundorum,* for which there is no direct manuscript support, but in which all five laws are cited by an independent source, the so-called Gromatici. Of the five laws, the first is also cited in two parts by the Codex Justinianus (3.39.3, 8.4.5), the second by the Breviarium (2.26.1, the only law in this title) as well as by the Codex Justinianus (3.39.4),[24] and the fourth and fifth by the Codex Justinianus (3.39.5–6). Only the third law is preserved by the Gromatici alone. The important point here is that, as opposed to the cases previously discussed, no law from the corresponding title in the Codex Justinianus is unaccounted for in the Theodosian Code. This is because the Gromatici have transcribed the whole title in the Theodosian Code, and have thereby preserved intact the source of the Codex Justinianus. Without the land surveyors' contribution, only the second law in the title, that preserved by the Breviarium, would have been explicitly attested as deriving from the Theodosian Code. Applying his own principles, Mommsen could not have included the first, fourth, and fifth laws on the sole basis of their citation in the Codex Justinianus, even in a title named identically to that in the Theodosian Code. The third law being attested only by the Gromatici, the title would have been reduced to the one law chosen from it for inclusion in the Breviarium. The others would have remained "Extravaganten"—that is to say, not in their proper place.

3. A similar situation, again affecting a single title of the Code, is presented by two laws on episcopal jurisdiction surviving among the Sirmondian Constitutions discussed in the next chapter. The laws in question, nos. 17 and 18, stand outside the main series of texts in the Sirmondian collection. Unlike *Sirm.* 1–16, which are independent of it, they derive from the Theodosian Code, to which they are attributed in an annotation assigning them to title 27, *De episcopali definitione.*[25] The book to which the title belonged is not named, but it has always, and correctly,

24. Also by the Lex Romana Burgundionum (39.3).

25. See Mommsen's edition, p. 63n.

been identified as Book 1 of the Theodosian Code, and it is from this source in the Sirmondian Constitutions that Mommsen supplied the two laws that now stand in his edition under this title. Now, the text of the second law lacks a few words at the end, which Mommsen duly supplied, together with the protocol giving the date 13 December and the names of the consuls of 408, from the version of the law to be found in the Codex Justinianus; it is 1.4.8 in the corresponding if somewhat more comprehensive title, *De episcopali audientia et de diversis capitulis, quae ad ius curamque et reverentiam pontificalem pertinent*. Mommsen did not, however, include its predecessor in the same title, *CJ* 1.4.7, in his text of the Theodosian Code. The only difference between this and the two laws that he did include is that they were cited by the Sirmondian Constitutions, and that the third law was not so cited. This is a purely accidental circumstance. The law should clearly be added to the title (where it will stand between the two laws in Mommsen's edition).[26]

4. Book 6 of the Theodosian Code is the first for which there is manuscript support for the full text in Parisinus 9643 (*R*). The beginning and end of the book are nevertheless missing from this manuscript, and it is interesting to see how Mommsen dealt with this situation. Of the first two titles in his edition, the name (but not the text) of title 2, *De senatoria dignitate*, is provided by *A*, which does not make it clear whether this was the first or the second title of the book. For the actual laws of the title, *R* provides a text beginning in the middle of a law dated by the consuls of 377 and continuous (though far from perfect) thereafter. Whether this law is the seventh or the twelfth of the title is uncertain, as is indicated by Mommsen.[27] The text of the law is also found at *CJ* 12.1.11 under the title *De dignitatibus* (the Codex Justinianus has no title *De senatoria dignitate*), from where Mommsen adduced it to supplement the incomplete version in the Theodosian Code. Now, the title of *CJ* 12.1 was used by Mommsen to supply conjecturally the name of a missing title 1, *De dignitatibus*, in Book 6 of the Theodosian Code; the argument is a good one, since the presence of a title before *De senatoria dignitate* is implied by the numbering by *R* of the fourth title in the book. Titles 1–4 of Book 6 are strictly represented as follows, with what has to be supplied shown in square brackets:

[I. De dignitatibus]
[II.] De senatoria dignitate
[III.] De praediis senatorum
IV. De praetoribus et quaestoribus

26. As it does in Krüger's (pp. 44–45).

27. He shows it as 6.1.12 (? = 7). The numbers of the surviving laws in the title depend on a marginal mark found at Mommsen's 6.2.17 (= 12) — see his note, p. 245.

Despite this, having used the Codex Justinianus to supply the name of title 1 of this book of the Theodosian Code, Mommsen did not extend the argument to the actual texts in *CJ* 12.1. Here are no fewer than six laws not found in the Theodosian Code but which should have stood in *CTh* 6.1 or the missing part (before 377) of 6.2.[28]

As at its beginning, so too at the end of Book 6 of the Theodosian Code: Mommsen adduced the Codex Justinianus (12.32.1) to complete the text of *CTh* 6.38.1, where *R* fails to preserve the last lines of a law of Constantine.[29] It is especially revealing of the connections between *CJ* 12.1.11 and 12.32.1 and the first and last surviving laws of Book 6 of the Theodosian Code that the texts share deficiencies in date and place of issue. In the first case, both versions lack the day and month of issue, though they preserve the year (377) and the place (Hierapolis). In the second, the Codex Justinianus is unable to supply the date and place of issue of a law of which it otherwise completes the text. This should mean that in both cases the Theodosian Code already lacked these details when the editors of the Codex Justinianus consulted it. It is a general rule in textual criticism that an error or omission shared between two texts indicates either the descent of one from the other or the descent of both from a common source that already possessed the fault. In the case before us now, only the first alternative is in question.

5. The next example pursues further a question raised more than once in previous chapters. The Theodosian Code contains a number of extracts from a substantial imperial oration to the Senate of Rome dated 7 November 426, of which other extracts, not preserved in the Theodosian Code, are recovered from the Codex Justinianus.[30] The best-known part of the law is the so-called Law of Citations referred to earlier, confirming the writings of Papinian, Paul, Gaius, Ulpian, and Modestinus and allowing the validity of other authorities cited by these five, provided that the texts of the citations were confirmed (*CTh* 1.4.3). For all its individual renown, this extract is part of a much more extensive constitution covering, in lengthy excerpts preserved elsewhere in the Theodosian Code, some highly complex questions in testamentary and property law. The majority (four out of seven) of these texts occur in a well-preserved part of the text of the Theodosian Code (Book 8), and all are included in the Breviarium, since they covered just the sorts of issues in private law that were of interest to its compilers.

28. The laws to be restored to *CTh* are *CJ* 12.1.2 (of 313/5), 4 (346/9), 5 (n.d.), 6 (357/60), 9 (364/5), 14 (426); cf. Krüger, pp. 188–89. From the point of view of date, 12.1.14 could come only in *CTh* 6.1 (since 6.2 was complete at that point); the other five laws would fit either title but could be assigned to one or the other depending on the judgment about their content.

29. Mommsen, p. 308. An entire page (q. 38 f. 6) is missing from *R*.

30. For the full register of twelve extracts, see Mommsen, Prolegomena, p. ccci; Seeck, *Regesten*, p. 352; Honoré, *Law in the Crisis of Empire*, pp. 249–51.

The excerpts of the law not now found in the Theodosian Code but preserved in the Codex Justinianus show a different emphasis. Here we find definitions of the categories of imperial pronouncements that constituted "leges generales" (*CJ* 1.14.2–3), questions relating to rescripts (1.19.7) and fraudulent petitions (1.22.5), and replies given by the consistorium in response to reports and consultations of judicial authorities in particular cases (1.14.2).

Apart from the general principle that the Theodosian Code was the only source of the Codex Justinianus, it is obvious that all these citations once appeared in the former. It can be seen from the extracts that do appear there that the editors of the Code knew the *oratio* of 426, and it is simply not possible that they included some parts of this constitution but not those most directly relevant to the work upon which they were engaged. In particular, the propositions about leges generales and rescripts preserved in *CJ* 1.14.2–3 provided essential commentary on the instructions to the editors of the Code that they were to collect all constitutions "edictorum viribus aut sacra generalitate subnixas" (*CTh* 1.1.5 and 6; see Chapter 4). If ever there were overwhelming grounds to restore to the text of the Theodosian Code laws lost from it in transmission, this example provides them. There can be no serious doubt either that they once belonged there or from which titles they came.

The name of Paul Krüger, which has been mentioned from time to time in this discussion, is one that is intimately linked with the history of Roman law, particularly with the great period of the scientific editing of its texts in the last decades of the nineteenth century and the first years of the twentieth. Krüger's edition of the Codex Justinianus, first published in 1877 and subsequently reprinted, is still the one in use, and his name also stands, alone or with others, on the title pages of the other volumes of the Corpus Iuris Civilis—namely, the colossal Digest of the Roman jurists and the Institutes of Justinian. His contribution to the editing of the Theodosian Code was described by Mommsen as that of a colleague and was repeatedly acknowledged—for example, in Krüger's reading and analysis of the Turin manuscript, *T*, which were accepted without change in Mommsen's edition.[31] Indeed, Krüger's name stands with Mommsen's on the title page of the edition, as responsible for the apparatus criticus, together with that of Paul Meyer, who was responsible for editing the Novellae of Theodosius and his successors.

Mommsen's (and Krüger and Meyer's) edition is an astonishing achievement, for

31. Prolegomena, p. xxxix, "operis nostri socio"; and for Krüger's work on *T*, pp. xxxix–xlii. For this and what follows, see the perceptive and humane paper of Brian Croke, "Mommsen's Encounter with the Code," in Harries and Wood) (eds.), *The Theodosian Code*, pp. 217–39; on Mommsen and Krüger, pp. 224–25 and 237–38, and Fritz Schulz's obituary of Krüger, *ZSS* 47 (1927), pp. ix–xxxi.

its editors' command of the material, for the work of multiple collaboration that it represents, and of course for Mommsen's extraordinary powers of organization. From its moment of publication it conveyed an unmistakable aura of definitiveness, and all later discussion has been conducted in reference to it. Behind its publication, however, lies a still vivid story of academic discord and resentment.[32]

When in 1898 Mommsen announced his intention to prepare a new edition of the Theodosian Code to replace the antiquated version of G. Haenel, published in 1842, he was speaking of a text on which, as he well knew, Krüger had been working, in the hope of producing the standard text to complement the edition of the Codex Justinianus he had published twenty years before. The sequel is a classic illustration of the tensions between different academic personalities, and one can understand it from both points of view. Approaching the end of his life, with this great project before him, Mommsen was determined to proceed rapidly, even at some cost to the sensitivities of others; indeed, it was only with the help of the efforts of others, working on Mommsen's terms, that the project could be completed with the speed exacted — and achieved — by him. Krüger's work on the Code had not progressed rapidly; he worked alone and lacked the resources to undertake the travel that he thought necessary for a proper evaluation of the manuscript evidence. It must furthermore have been obvious to Mommsen, as it is now to anyone who uses it, that the presentation and descriptive quality of Krüger's edition of the Codex Justinianus could be greatly improved upon in an edition of its predecessor.

Nevertheless, the depth of Krüger's hurt in the face of Mommsen's proposal is equally understandable. It can still be read in Mommsen's replies to his complaints, as Krüger saw his own work annexed by the old man's demands, and his rights in it ignored. "Dear friend," replied Mommsen to Krüger on 14 October 1898, with what one can only call Caesarean decisiveness, "Iacta alea est. I will try to see the thing through to the end. Send to me what you have."[33] Krüger did collaborate, but his resentment remained, and there followed in early 1903 a discussion over the extent and type of acknowledgment that Krüger's very considerable contribution deserved. His appearance on the title page as the author of the apparatus criticus was a compromise proposed by Mommsen that some may think inadequate for the nature of the contribution.

The expressions of warmth with which Krüger greeted the publication of the Theodosian Code in 1905 (Mommsen had died on 1 November 1903) did not express his true feelings. It is all the more telling, therefore, that, between then and

32. For what follows, see Schulz's obituary, just cited, pp. ix–xxxi, followed by a bibliography of Krüger's writings.

33. Quoted by Schulz, obituary, p. xxv.

his own death in 1926, Krüger held to his intention to prepare a new edition of his own. After a number of preparatory articles published between 1913 and 1921,[34] part of his edition appeared in two installments, published by the same house, Weidmann of Berlin, that had brought out Mommsen's edition twenty years earlier.

It was not a success. By the time he came to prepare his edition for publication, Krüger was in his eighties, unwell, and depressed; he did not enjoy the help of collaborators, and it implies no lack of respect to a great scholar to say that he did not possess Mommsen's supreme, indeed—as Krüger had reason to know—ruthless powers of intellect and concentration.[35] The two volumes that appeared contained Books 1–6 (published in 1923) and 7–8 (1926).[36] The edition took for granted the extensive Prolegomena of Mommsen but lacked the explanation that one would have expected about why Krüger thought that a new text was necessary. One reads in Krüger's brief preface merely a list of manuscripts and the abbreviations used to refer to them, not a word about dissatisfaction with Mommsen's edition, nor any account of how Krüger's methods differed—which, in one important respect, they did. In any event Books 9–16 never appeared, and the portion that was published has never been reprinted.[37] Krüger's edition has not entered standard use, and it is clear that it never will.

Yet it should be taken into account. That the edition is incomplete does not negate its usefulness. From the beginning of Book 9, as we saw, the text of the Theodosian Code, with the support of the Vatican manuscript (*V*), is less problematic than in the earlier books. The most problematic of all are Books 1–5, which were contained in Krüger's first volume of 1923. The value of his judgment therefore rests where it is most needed.

In one respect in particular, Krüger's editorial policy differed explicitly from Mommsen's. Mommsen had from the start, and against Krüger's advice, declined to use texts from the Codex Justinianus to supply texts missing from the Theodosian Code; as we saw, he preferred to treat them as unattached ("Extravaganten") rather than assign them to specific contexts in a way that could, to an extent, only

34. Published in *ZSS* under the general title "Beiträge zum Codex Theodosianus"; see esp. "Zur Wiederherstellung der Titelfolge im fünften Buch des Codex Theodosianus," *ZSS* 34 (1913) pp. 1–12; "Über Ergänzung des Theodosianus aus dem Justinianus," *ZSS* 38 (1917), pp. 20–28; "Versuch einer Wiederherstellung der Titelfolge des 4. und 5. Buchs," *ZSS* 38 (1917), pp. 28–34.

35. Croke, "Mommsen's Encounter with the Code," pp. 237–38, with n. 101, acknowledging material provided by Boudewijn Sirks.

36. Schulz describes it as "ein Torso" (p. xxxi).

37. Schulz in the obituary, p. xxxi, with n. 2. According to Croke, p. 238 n. 101, the edition of Books 9–16 was finished but destroyed by bombing in the Second World War. In any event, Weidmann had evidently decided not to publish this installment.

be conjectural.[38] In his edition Krüger—the editor of the Codex Justinianus almost half a century earlier—included them, distinguished by italics, in the printed text of the Code.[39] It makes a great difference. In the first titles of the Code, for example, one can read in Krüger's text all the surviving fragments of the imperial oration of 426 in the places to which they belong (*CTh* 1.1.4a, b; 1.2.13–14).[40] The definition of general law appears under the year 426, immediately before the editors of the Code were told, in 429, to apply it. It is true that some texts have undergone editorial amendment in their citations in the Codex Justinianus, and because the editors of the Codex Justinianus transferred laws between titles and devised many new titles, it cannot always be certain to which title in the Theodosian Code they should rightly be restored; it should be remembered that what we possess in the Codex Justinianus is a revision of a lost earlier edition, and it is likely that some questions of the distribution of texts will reflect differences between its two editions rather than its relationship with the Theodosian Code. The disposition of the second edition of the Codex Justinianus may also reflect the publication of the Digest, but if this is so, then the parallels of organization with the Theodosian Code will be the more telling. In a sense, such problems repeat the experience of the original, fifth-century editors and can be solved by a similar exercise of judgment regarding where a text should be inserted. Whatever the difficulties, there is no doubt that Krüger's method in these books produces a text that is closer than Mommsen's to the original Theodosian Code.

Despite its inaccessibility, therefore, Krüger's edition has a serious contribution to offer to those interested in restoring as far as possible the original appearance of Books 1–5 of the Theodosian Code. One of the main purposes of the second part of this chapter is to justify the restoration to the Theodosian Code of laws and titles from the Codex Justinianus that were not included by Mommsen. If this amounts to a rehabilitation of Krüger's reconstruction of its first five books, then it may be read as an overdue tribute to his judgment about how this task should be performed. A second and more particular aim, for Books 2–5 of the Theodosian Code, is to show in detail what was naturally perceived by Mommsen and Krüger, how in their arrangement of topics the editors followed the traditional order of the

38. Cf. Mommsen's remarks to Krüger in a letter of 10 October 1898, cited by Schulz in the obituary, p. xxiv, pointing out (n. 3) that this was a significant difference of policy from that of Krüger.

39. See esp. his "Über Ergänzung des Theodosianus aus dem Justinianus," *ZSS* 38 (1917), pp. 20–28.

40. Where his insertions interrupt Mommsen's text, Krüger has his numbering conform to it, hence 1.1.4 a, b between Mommsen's 1.1.4 and 5. Where laws are added to the end of a title, Krüger extends the numbering, hence *CTh* 1.2.8 a, b between Mommsen's 1.2.8 and 9, but 1.2.13–15 where Mommsen's title stops at 12.

Praetor's Edict. The argument permits more general conclusions to be drawn about the criteria adopted by the editors of the Code in arranging their work, and these conclusions are briefly stated in the third part of this chapter.

## Books 1–5

Our discussion will take the form of a series of introductions to the manuscript and other sources of the first five books of the Theodosian Code, with a brief indication of their structure and contents. Detailed arguments relating to individual laws are reserved for the specialist literature, the discussion here being confined to the level of titles; it does not address individual cases unless they are relevant to this broader question.

### BOOK 1

The first book of the Theodosian Code presents what might well be called the juridical foundations of the late Roman state. It is arranged in two unequal sections. The first four titles concern the sources of law, in the form, respectively, of constitutions and edicts of emperors, various kinds of rescripts, imperial *mandata,* or directions given by emperors to their officials, and the *responsa* of jurists—their opinions on points of law expressed in replies to questions put to them for consultation. The sequence of titles preserves the distinction between primary and secondary sources of law (leges and ius), and the sources of general law precede rescripts and other instructions of more limited scope. The remaining titles of the book concern the duties of imperial officials, from the praetorian prefects and prefects of the city down through the four "illustrious" court offices, proconsuls and vicarii, provincial governors, and civil and military authorities in general (including bishops and *defensores senatus* and *civitatum*), lesser officials such as procurators and *primicerii,* and concluding with *assessores, domestici,* and *cancellarii.*

The arrangement of topics closely resembles that of the first chapters of Gaius' Institutes (and later the first book of the Digest), where imperial constitutions, whether in the form of decrees, edicts, or letters, and "responsa prudentum," are listed among the sources of law, together with the traditional forms of legislation no longer in use—namely, leges, plebiscita, and senatusconsulta, and edicts issued by magistrates competent to issue them.[41] The second and major portion of Book 1 of the Theodosian Code thus expressed in its register of the duties of imperial officials the recognition that the emperor, and those operating under his sovereignty, were now the sole authorities responsible for the administration of the law.

41. Gaius, *Inst.* 1.2–7; de Zulueta, vol. 1, pp. 2–5, with vol. 1, pp. 13–23.

A glance at Mommsen's edition seems to show that the book consists of thirty-four numbered titles. This may be close to the true number, but not all the original titles are represented in Mommsen's sequence. From its manuscript and other sources, *CTh* 1.1–16 preserves a full register of titles (and in most cases their full complement of individual laws), but in the second half of the book five titles, 17–19, 30, and 33 in Mommsen, consist only of their headings, without texts, surviving in an index of titles in the Paris manuscript described below. Even the numbers, as well as the contents, of four other titles, 23–26, are missing from Mommsen's edition; this is because after what stands as 22, the number and name of title 27, *De episcopali definitione,* as well as the two laws that it comprises, are given by an external source. Except for 27, the numbers of all titles above 16 are only hypothetical in Mommsen's edition, where they are shown in brackets.[42]

The reconstruction of the contents of Book 1 involves contributions from various sources. The result is a patchwork with many lacunae, but, in the end, not the worst preserved of the incomplete books of the Code.

An important contribution is made by manuscript sources, in the first instance by *A,* the manuscript of the Breviarium mentioned earlier as the source of the Gesta Senatus. For a considerable part of Book 1, *A* followed a full text of the Theodosian Code, producing a sound though not a complete text for titles 4.1–16.6; that it is not complete is shown by title 5, from which *A* certainly omitted two laws, and by title 6, from which it probably omitted two more. A particular benefit of the contribution of *A* is that many of these titles (namely, 6–15) were omitted altogether by the Breviarium in its main tradition, while in titles 4, 5, and 16, which it did include, the relative number of laws excerpted was very small—only 1:4, 1:14, and 5:14, respectively. For the rest of the book, *A* rejoins the manuscript tradition of the Breviarium, and possesses no distinct importance.

A second manuscript source, the lost Turin manuscript, *T,* preserves discontinuous sequences of texts from Book 1: 1.5–2.3; 5.4–14; 28.1–29.5 and 31.1–32.7. For a few laws in title 5 (4–5 and 7–11) we possess the double attestation of *A* and *T.*[43] In a few cases *T* also preserves the numbers of laws within titles as well as the names of the titles. It does not preserve the numbers of titles, but it shows that what we now read as title 28 is continuous with 29, and 31 with 32. Mommsen's numbering of title 28 follows from the enumeration of 27 attested by an external source, as mentioned above.

An unusual contribution to the structure, though not to the textual contents of

42. Cf. Mommsen's note in his edition, p. 6 (on title 17). Later I shall discuss titles and texts added by Krüger from *CJ.*

43. 1.5.6 is omitted by *A.* References given here to laws extant in *A* and *T* include texts for which any part survives.

the book, comes from the Paris manuscript referred to above (Bibl. Nat. cod. lat. 4413). This is an abbreviated manuscript of the Breviarium from the ninth century,[44] which contains on its last page the names of sixteen titles from Book 1 of the Theodosian Code "de nomina officialium qui curam gerebant antiquo iure in Romam" (*sic*), adding a few words on the office in question, and sometimes alluding to the content of individual laws. In some cases this is enough to identify the law, but never in such a way as to contribute to establishing its text. It does seem, however, that the writer of the index had access to a copy of the full text of the Theodosian Code. The titles in question are Mommsen's titles 6–8, 10–11, 13–15, 17–19, 28, 30–31, and 33–34.[45] Even if it is not a complete series, the order of titles agrees with that attested in the sections of Book 1 for which there is manuscript evidence, and the list is therefore a guide to the sequence and naming of titles where there is no such evidence. We saw that Mommsen's titles 17–19, 30, and 33 appear as headings without text on the evidence of the Paris Index.

The Breviarium of Alaric preserves excerpts from eleven titles: 1–5, 16, 20–22, 29, and 34. Much though the historian may regret them, the omissions in the Breviarium are intelligible. Its editors had no interest in the duties of defunct or irrelevant Roman officials. What survives is material relating to the sources of Roman law (titles 1–4), followed by a selection of the titles concerned with the duties of officials that could still be thought relevant in the Visigothic period; the praetorian prefect (title 5), provincial and military governors (16, 20–22), defensores civitatis (29), and assessores, domestici, and cancellarii (34). With these exceptions, what is omitted is in effect an account from a juristic point of view of the late Roman administrative system.

Among the various sources that supplement these from time to time to provide the rest of the contents of Book 1, special note should be taken of the group of laws (six in all) preserved in the Appendix Legis Romanae Wisigothorum edited by Krüger and the two laws of title 27, *De episcopali definitione,* which are provided, with the number as well as the name of the title, by the manuscript that also contains the Sirmondian Constitutions (Chapter 6).

The final text from which laws can be supplied to incomplete titles of the Theodosian Code, as well as the names of some missing titles, is of course the Codex Justinianus, from which, in Book 1 alone, Krüger recovered forty-eight texts not

44. Mommsen, Prolegomena, p. xcvvvi, reports it as written at Bayeux in 832, but on p. lxxxv calls it a manuscript of the tenth century. I assume the more precise attribution to be correct.

45. Mommsen, Prolegomena, p. lxxxv. The separate annotations in the Paris Index were published (after Krüger) by Mommsen in his list of titles to the Code (pp. 5–8), and as continuous text as Additamenta at the beginning of Krüger's edition.

included in Mommsen's edition, disposed them among Mommsen's titles, and added five titles himself.[46]

As to the names and numbers of titles of Book 1, a comparison of the editions of Mommsen and Krüger shows agreement between them as far as the sixteenth title. This as it should be, for as we have seen, the manuscript and other evidence preserves the titles of this portion of the book, with a fair proportion of their contents. After title 16, Krüger added a title (XVII) consisting of a single law, derived from one book of *CJ* (9.29.3), and the title from another (1.41, *Ut nulli patriae suae administratio sine speciali permissu principis permittatur*). This is an unusually hazardous example of Krüger's method (unfortunately, since it is the first to occur in his text of the Code), and it may be that this text should be absorbed into the previous title 16, *De officio rectoris provinciae*.[47] With better reason, Krüger inserted after Mommsen's title 18 (Kr. XIX) a title XX *De officio praefecti annonae,* again with a single law derived, with its title, from *CJ* (1.44).[48] Krüger also inserted after Mommsen's title 22 (Kr. XXIV) two titles on aspects of the duties of provincial governors, XXV, *De officio eius, qui vicem alicuius iudicis obtinet* (*CJ* 1.50) and XXVI, *De modo multarum quae ab iudicibus infliguntur* (*CJ* 1.54). If the former possesses only one text, the latter has three, and there is a strong case for the restoration at least of this title as well as its texts.[49] Here and elsewhere, whatever doubt may attend Krüger's restoration of missing titles, it cannot be too strongly emphasized that if they are not accepted, then room must be found in the relevant sections of the Theodosian Code for the texts assigned to them.

## BOOK 2

Book 2 of the Theodosian Code consists of thirty-three titles in Mommsen's edition, both the titles and what remains of their contents being mainly recovered from the Breviarium; two further titles were, with good reason, added by Krüger.

46. One of which is a clear error, as we shall see. Here as in Books 2–5, the exact number of laws to be restored to *CTh* is impossible to know, since the editors of *CJ* may have divided texts and entered them under different titles in their own work.

47. Its title would then be an innovation in *CJ*. For the text itself, part of a long law addressed to Eutropius in 381, see Chapter 8, " 'Palingenesia': Laws Reconstituted," no. 7.

48. Krüger is, however, mistaken (ad loc., p. 41) in referring to this title as among those listed by the Paris Index; both Mommsen and Krüger's own text of the Index make clear that this is not so.

49. Krüger's restoration of a title XXXII, *De curatoribus civitatum,* is an unfortunate error, since his own title XXX (Mommsen 30) also bears this name; it is included in the Paris Index, as Krüger observes in both places. The Index shows that XXX, *De curatoribus civitatis,* precedes XXXI, *De administratiunculis intra urbem,* while Krüger's repetition of the former title at XXXII also contradicts the sequence of titles guaranteed by *T*. The two brief texts included under these titles from *CJ* (10.32.30 and 1.56.2, respectively) should be included under a single title or disposed elsewhere.

Parts of three titles—namely, the sequence of laws 8.18–10.3, together with the numbers of all three titles and the names of titles 9 and 10—are preserved by *T*, and isolated contributions are made by external sources, such as the Lex Romana Burgundionum and the Appendix Legis Romanae Wisigothorum. In particular, the Gromatici preserve what looks like an entire title on the subject of boundaries. This title is printed by Mommsen as *CTh* 2.26, but a note in a Paris manuscript of the Breviarium, in which one law from the title was excerpted, indicates that its original number was 27.[50] This means that the register of titles in the book is nearly complete, since titles 8–10, so numbered in *T*, correspond with those of the Breviarium and Mommsen's edition; while if the note in the Paris manuscript is right, only one further title has disappeared between title 10 and the original title 27. The sequential character of titles 31 and 32 is supported by their correspondence with the rubrics of the Praetor's Edict, as we shall see.[51] The authors of the Breviarium may have felt the need to give a full representation of the range of contents of a book of the Theodosian Code that concerned such fundamental issues in Roman jurisprudence.

The proportion of individual texts surviving in Book 2 of the Code is a different matter. The majority of titles preserve only one or a few texts recovered from the Breviarium, the rate of loss being readily visible from title 8, *De feriis*, where *T* presents a sequence of laws numbered 18 through 26 (the end of the title). The Breviarium has just three laws from the title, the second and third of them present in the sequence surviving in *T* (19, 26); the first, a law of 321, is printed as the first text in the title. That is to say, sixteen texts have been lost from the first seventeen that once stood there. The following title, 9, *De pactis et transactionibus*, which is essentially complete in *T*, contains three texts, of which only the third was excerpted in the Breviarium. The first text is referred to (without attribution) in the Lex Romana Burgundionum (33.5); the second was excerpted in *CJ* (2.4.40), from which Mommsen was able to fill out deficiencies in the text as preserved in *T*. In title 10, *De postulando*, only the first three texts survive in *T*, the last of which is incomplete but can again be supplemented from *CJ* (2.6.5). The three texts are laws of 319 (two laws) and 325 (the year being recovered from *CJ*). For the remainder of the title we have another three texts, excerpted in the Breviarium. They are laws of 326,[52] 370, and 422. This is unlikely to represent the actual distribution of texts on such an important subject; it seems clear that after the end

50. Paris, 12445, f. 210: "in libro secundo legis Theodosianae cap. XXVII de finium regendorum." The law is *CTh* 2.26.2 (*Brev.* 2.26.1), ed. Mommsen, p. 116.

51. Krüger added titles XVIIIa, *De ordine iudiciorum* (*CJ* 3.8), and XXXIII *Mandati* (*CJ* 4.35), each with one law. This conforms with the numbering of titles as described earlier; XVIIIa will be the missing title from the sequence 10 through 27.

52. Correcting the office of the recipient, Bassus, from *p*[*raefectus*] *u*[*rbi*] to *p*[*raefectus*] *p*[*raetori*]*o*.

of this manuscript page of *T,* a few words into 10.3, many texts from this title are missing. In general, Book 2 allows less scope than its predecessor for the restoration of missing texts from the Codex Justinianus, but Krüger's edition still adds thirty-four laws to those printed by Mommsen—disposed among Mommsen's titles and two new ones.[53]

Book 2 is the first of the three books of the Code in which the arrangement of topics conforms to that set out in the Praetor's Edict.[54] Its contents fall into two parts, corresponding to the essential distinction in the Edict between issues of jurisdiction (*De jurisdictione,* titles 1–17, cf. Edict II–XIII), and the conduct of cases in the courts (*De iudiciis,* titles 18–32; cf. Edict XIV–XVIII). To make this clear, a few words are needed about the development of the Praetor's Edict.

The Praetor's Edict, codified by the great jurist Salvius Julianus in the time of Hadrian,[55] evolved during that long period of time after the Twelve Tables (450 B.C.) in which Roman jurisprudence progressed not so much by deliberative changes in the law as by the procedural interventions of magistrates with powers of jurisdiction.[56] It was the practice of such magistrates—usually praetors but also provincial governors (acting "pro praetore"), aediles, and quaestors—to publish an edict when they entered office, in which they announced what their policy would be in matters of jurisdiction. They would set out what legal actions they would (and would not) allow, and in what conditions and circumstances, and which claims, defenses, and exceptions they would (and would not) admit. This power they would exercise in the legal preliminaries to a case, known as the proceedings *in iure,* in which, at the request of the parties, the magistrate appointed a judge and agreed to the "formula," the statement of rules under which the case would be heard. The formula was in effect a series of questions expressed as conditional clauses, as for instance in a case of debt: "It being stated that Y received an amount

53. See n. 51 for Krüger's titles XVIIIa and XXXIII.

54. Cf. the tabular presentation of rubrics set out in Mommsen's Prolegomena, pp. xiii–xviii. The edict was reconstructed in the classic work of O. Lenel, *Das Edictum Perpetuum* (3rd ed., 1927), from which is derived the text set out in Riccobono, vol. 1, pp. 335–91; see also Bruns, pp. 211–37. Mommsen's demonstration is picked up by J. D. Harries, "How to Make a Law-Code," in M. Austin, J. Harries, C. Smith, *Modus Operandi: Essays in Honour of Geoffrey Rickman* (1998), pp. 71–77, but the case can be more powerfully made with reference to *CJ* and Krüger.

55. On Salvius Julianus, whom later sources tend to conflate with his nephew or grandnephew the emperor Didius Julianus, *PIR* S 102, see A. M. Honoré, in *Oxford Classical Dictionary,* 3rd ed. (1996), p. 778, dating the approval of his codification by senatus consultum to A.D. 131 (the evidence is Jerome's *Chronicle*).

56. See esp. Alan Watson, "The Development of the Praetor's Edict," *JRS* 60 (1970), pp. 105–19 = *Law Making in the Later Roman Republic* (1974), chap. 3.

of money from X, if it was a loan and not a gift, and if X has allowed no extension of time (or, if an extension was granted by X but was extracted by deception), then the judge must condemn according to the sum claimed; if not [that is, if any one of these conditions is not satisfied], he must absolve."[57] It was for the judge, in the second stage of proceedings *apud iudicem,* to decide the relevant facts within this framework of conditions. The formula instructed the judge to condemn or absolve as appropriate, though the praetor might enforce his decision by executive decree, or interdict; and there was no right of appeal. This could in any case not have been on legal grounds, for the parties had agreed on both the formula and the naming of the judge in advance of the hearing.

Magistrates influenced the development of law in various ways: by a more sensitive view of the circumstances in which they would admit actions; by adducing considerations of equity where the law seemed inadequate, or lacking in some necessary provision; by enlarging the classes of persons to whom they would allow actions (a *peregrinus,* for example, might be plaintiff or defendant in an action against a Roman citizen by virtue of a "legal fiction" that he possessed the requisite citizenship);[58] by their definitions of the arguments they would admit as relevant; and so on. It was their policy in such matters, as they devised it themselves or inherited it from their predecessors, that they announced in their edict. Some edicts, issued for one set of circumstances only, later lapsed, but others of more general bearing, known as *edicta perpetua,* remained in force throughout a magistracy and, if found satisfactory, would be adopted by successive magistrates. In the course of time, as the principles set out in successive jurisdictions were tried, tested, and refined, the Perpetual Edict became an authoritative statement of practice and procedure across the whole domain of private law.

Under the principate, a new form of jurisdiction, combining proceedings in iure and apud iudicem in hearings in which a single judge heard the case and (with legal advice) both defined the legal issues and determined matters of fact by simple inquiry or *cognitio,* rapidly superseded the "formulary system" administered by praetors and other magistrates. The chief exponent of the new system was the emperor himself, whose role both as judge and as primary legislator came to supersede all others. Salvius Julianus had written that if any imperfection were now to be found in the law, it should be remedied by imperial sanction—that is to say, not by procedural intervention but by primary legislation, a provision that was taken as axiomatic by the time of Justinian's Digest.[59] Like the formulary system

57. This is to recast the presentation of Schulz, *Classical Roman Law,* pp. 20–21, based on Gaius, *Inst.* 4.30ff.; de Zulueta, vol. 1, pp. 245ff., and vol. 2, pp. 250ff.

58. Gaius, *Inst.* 4.37.

59. Constitutio "Tanta," §18: "Ipse Iulianus legum et edicti perpetui subtilissimus conditor

itself, the Praetor's Edict fell into disuse as an instrument of jurisdiction, but it remained an authoritative statement of the principles of private law, and it was as such that it was codified by Salvius Julianus. Commentaries on the Edict or parts of it, especially those by Paul and Ulpian, in eighty and eighty-three books, respectively, written in the early third century and extensively preserved in the Digest, were in practice commentaries on Roman private law.[60] As the Digest explained, the Edict also canonized the order in which topics in private law were taught and studied, and it is this order that was adopted by the editors of the Theodosian Code for its early books on the private law.[61]

The Edict itself is not extant, either in its "evolutionary" stage or as codified by Salvius Julianus, but it was reconstructed by Lenel on the basis of the references to it in the Digest, notably by Paul and Ulpian, and in other sources. It may seem hazardous to collate a reconstructed text with the incomplete books of the Theodosian Code; but neither the Theodosian Code nor the Codex Justinianus was among the texts used by Lenel, while the references of Paul and Ulpian to the Edict are very numerous, and concordant in their sequence.[62] Conforming as closely as it does to the order of topics found in the Praetor's Edict, the Theodosian Code corroborates Lenel's reconstruction.

### BOOK 3

The third book of the Theodosian Code concerns three topics in private law: 1) contracts for sale (*Empti venditi,* titles 1–3); 2) marriage (*De re uxoria,* titles 5–16), divided into matters preceding the marriage (titles 5–6), the marriage itself (titles 7–15, including titles on dowries), and divorce (title 16); and 3) tutelage and the property of minors (*De tutelis,* titles 17–18 and 30–32).[63] The corresponding

---

in suis libris hoc rettulit, ut, si quid inperfectum inveniatur, ab imperiali sanctione hoc repleatur" (cf. Chapter 2, n. 33).

60. Digest, list of authors excerpted; pp. lxvi–lxvii in Mommsen/Krüger. Gaius also is there said to have written thirty-two books on the Provincial Edict, and a work on the Urban (that is, the Praetor's) Edict, of which only ten books could be found. The earliest commentary of any substance was by Aulus Ofilius, a friend of Julius Caesar; his contemporary Servius Sulpicius wrote "two brief books" on the Edict, which he dedicated to Brutus: Digest, 1.2.2.44.

61. Const., "Deo auctore," §5, on the organization of the Digest: "Totum ius digerere, tam secundum nostri constitutionum codicis [to wit, the Codex Justinianus] quam edicti perpetui imitationem"; cf. Const. "Omnem," §1, where Tribonian complains that first-year students were not being taught the law "secundum edicti perpetui ordinem," but in a disorderly fashion.

62. See the tables of references in Lenel's *Edictum,* pp. xvi–xxiv. The Digest cites texts by author, title, and book number, so that reconstruction of the order of references is quite straightforward.

63. See the later discussion on the numbering of these titles.

books of the Codex Justinianus are 4 and 5, where these topics occur in the same general order, including the title not listed above: this is *CTh* 3.4, *De aediliciis actionibus,* which occurs at *CJ* 4.58, among the titles relevant to the law of sale.[64]

The incompleteness of this book of the Theodosian Code is evident from a glance at Mommsen's text and emphasized (though not proven) by the far greater number of titles in the corresponding sections of the Codex Justinianus.[65] The main source is the Breviarium, with some help from *T* in the fifth and in the last three titles of the book, and one or two individual insertions from other sources. Mommsen's edition follows the numbering of the titles of the Breviarium as far as title 18. That this is an entirely notional numbering is shown by a later scholion referring to a law, of which the text is not extant, from Book 3 of the Code. If the reading of the scholion is correct, the law originally stood as the fifteenth law of title 15 of the third book of the Code; the reference was inserted by Mommsen at the end of his title 5 (as 5.14).[66] That the scholion so nearly corresponds with Mommsen's numbering of the individual laws in the title derives from the large proportion of its text that is extant in *T* (5.3–10) and the Breviarium, which selects eight laws from it, five of them not from the sequence preserved by *T*.[67]

This reconstruction means that already by the fifth title of Mommsen's edition no fewer than ten titles have been lost from the original text of the Code, from the first two of the three subjects mentioned earlier (*CTh* 3.5 being the first of the surviving titles on marriage law). Several of the lost titles are supplied by Krüger, with a high level of likelihood, from the corresponding sequence of titles in the Codex Justinianus.[68] One other title was certainly lost after the original title 15, since Mommsen's edition advances from title 18, not to 29 (to allow for the ten missing titles in the earlier part of the book), but to 30.[69] This is because *T,* which

64. "Aediliciae actiones" were covered by the edict of the curule aediles, whose duties included the supervision of markets. As relevant here, they concerned the sale of slaves and animals; cf. Riccobono, vol. 1, pp. 389–91; Bruns, pp. 237–38.

65. Not proven, since *CJ* in any case involves an increase of titles over those in *CTh*. Krüger's additions of titles to Mommsen's edition will be discussed later.

66. That is, the *Scholia Sinaitica;* cf. Mommsen, *CTh,* pp. 132, 139 (on 3.5.14).

67. In fact, *T* preserves only part of the opening protocol of 3.5.10, the text being provided by *CJ* 5.1.3. Since the text preceding the scholion reference, 3.5.13, is a law of 428, it looks as if only one text is completely missing from the title.

68. After the first title of Book 3 Krüger inserts IA, *Quae res venire non possunt et qui vendere vel emere vetantur* (*CJ* 4.40 — 6 texts), IB, *Quae res exportari non debeant* (*CJ* 4.41 — one text), IC, *De commerciis et mercatoribus* (*CJ* 4.63 — one text), ID, *De eunuchis* (*CJ* 4.42 — one text), and IE, *De veteris numismatis potestate* (*CJ* 11.11 — one text). He also places title IVA, *De nundinis* (one text), after Mommsen's title 4.

69. Krüger inserts XVIA, *De concubinis* (*CJ* 5.26 — one text), after Mommsen's title 16.

preserves the full text of the Code from near the end of 30.2 to the end of the book at 32.2, gives the numbers as well as the names of titles 31–32, and by implication, since the transition to title 31 from its predecessor is intact in *T*, the number also of title 30. In any case the break in the numbering of titles 18 and 30 is misleading, these two titles forming part of a continuous, or nearly continuous, series.

A corollary is that relatively little in the way of titles (not, of course, of individual laws) has been lost from the third of the subjects mentioned, the law of tutelage. This may seem surprising, especially given the very large number of titles in the Codex Justinianus covering the subject, and the considerable length of some of them. Examination of these titles shows, however, that in many cases the Theodosian Code did not provide useful material for the Codex Justinianus, the main bulk of the latter's titles being composed of extracts from the Gregorian and Hermogenian Codes, and of legislation of the later fifth century and of Justinian himself. Krüger's harvest from the Codex Justinianus yielded thirty-one texts, of which sixteen belong to the new titles added by him to the first ten titles of the book. It was here, as we have seen, that the transmitted text of the Code suffered most of its losses.

### BOOK 4

The fourth book of the Theodosian Code contains twenty-four titles in Mommsen's edition, of which the last is attested in a single reference in an outside source, while the position of one other, the eleventh, is doubtful. The sequence of titles 1–10 and 13–23 is supported by the Breviarium, while the continuity of 12 and 13 is shown by *T*, which attests the run of texts 12.3–13.9. The original numbering of Mommsen's title 12 is indicated as 13 or 14 by *T*, and there is an argument, as we shall see, for transposing his title 11 to stand after 13; in either case, the evidence of *T* would suggest that at most three titles have been lost from the first part of the book.[70] One additional title is supplied to this early sequence by Krüger, and a second to a later part of the book, from the Codex Justinianus; in all, Krüger supplied to Book 4 from this source a total of thirty-eight texts, only four of them to these two titles.[71] Five topics are covered: 1) title to property under inheritance and the status of property under litigation (titles 1–5); 2) questions of personal status, especially as regards the acquisition of property under gift and succession by acknowledged but illegitimate children, and by freedmen and freedwomen

70. Three titles are lost, if title 11 is moved to stand after 13 and the numbering of Mommsen's title 12 (now 11) was 14 in *T*. Only one title is lost if title 11 is left where it is and the original numbering of title 12 was 13 in *T*.

71. Namely, VII, *De vindicta libertate et apud consilium manumissione* (*CJ* 7.1 — one text), and XVA, *Ne rei dominicae vel templorum vindicatio temporis exceptione submoveatur* (*CJ* 7.38 — three texts).

(titles 6–10, 12); 3) *vectigalia,* or indirect taxation (title 13); 4) time limits relevant to litigation concerning property ownership (titles 11, 14–15); and 5) the administration of disputed property after litigation is concluded, including the enforcement of the outcome by the interdicts of magistrates (titles 16–22).[72]

An impression of discontinuity in subject matter, under the general rubric of the law of property, is no doubt aggravated by the incomplete nature of the text, and by the intrinsic nature of the Code, consisting of extracts from leges, without such juristic comment as might have made clear their connections with each other. Its true explanation rests, however, on the fact that, as with previous books, Book 4 follows the order of topics covered by the Praetor's Edict. The most striking illustration relates to title 13, *De vectigalibus et commissis.* At first sight this title seems out of place, until we realize that it relates to indirect taxation collected by subcontractors and that it therefore represents the section *De publicanis,* which occurs at the corresponding point in the edict.[73]

As mentioned, there is some uncertainty about the position of the eleventh title. This arises from the contribution to the text of the Code made by two unconnected leaves of a Vatican manuscript, Vat. Reg. 520, ff. 94–95.[74] On f. 94 appear, in this order but with no reference or indication of their position, the five texts that stand in Mommsen's edition as *CTh* 4.8.8, 10.2–3, and 11.1–2; on f. 95 appear the six texts that stand as 4.12.1–3 and 5–7. To all but one of the texts (4.11.2 on f. 94) is appended a short *interpretatio.* In the exceptional case the interpretatio is all that survives, apart from the dating formula, which is written in the margin, of the missing text. None of the texts appears in the Breviarium, from which the style of the interpretationes also differs, in their greater simplicity. The copyist apparently had before him a full text of this part of the Code, from which he took the laws in question and commented on them in the manner of the Breviarium, but at a more elementary level, offering brief summaries of the texts without explanation.

The texts from Vat. Reg. 520 were first included in the Theodosian Code by Cujas in 1566, and since those from f. 95 standing in Mommsen's text as *CTh* 4.12.3 and 5–7 are also supported by *T,* no serious question arises regarding their

72. On the character of interdicts as expressions of executive authority giving effect to legal decisions, see Gaius, *Inst.* 4.138–142; de Zulueta, vol. 2, pp. 288–98. The traces of this section of the edict in the Theodosian Code are unmistakable and are reinforced by the similar sequence in *CJ.*

73. In Riccobono, XXXII.185. By exception, this point was not taken by Mommsen—Prolegomena, p. xvii.

74. Mommsen, Prolegomena, p. lxxxvi–lxxxvii. The two folio pages, from the eleventh and twelfth centuries, are from different manuscripts but seem to derive from the same collection of texts.

authenticity. These six texts can be assumed to be in their correct place; although only the last four of them occur in *T,* the first two are in the correct dating sequence and clearly belong to the same title, *Ad senatusconsultum Claudianum.* Indeed, the interpretatio of the missing text, 4.12.2 (f. 95.2), makes explicit reference to the senatusconsultum.

As for the five texts of f. 94, Mommsen, following Cujas, edited nos. 2–5 in sequence though under successive titles, as *CTh* 4.10.2–3 and 11.1–2. There can be little doubt that the second and third of the laws, 4.10.2–3, are in their correct place; in subject matter they belong to the title *De libertis et eorum liberis* given by the Breviarium, and in sequence of time they follow the single law preserved there under that title. The situation regarding the other three texts of f. 94 (nos. 1, 4, and 5) is more uncertain. As far as its transmitted date is concerned, the first of the laws could stand immediately before the second and third and in the same title: that is to say, between 4.10.1 and 2 in Mommsen—a law of 26 October 332 following that transmitted by the Breviarium with the editorial date 27 July 332, though in fact from an earlier time.[75] On grounds of subject matter, however, Mommsen separated the law from its partners on f. 94 and inserted it at an earlier point, in its chronological position in title 8, *De liberali causa* (hence 4.8.8). He then printed the fourth and fifth texts from f. 94 as an entire and separate title 11, *De longi temporis praescriptione,* the name of the title being imported from *CJ* 7.33. If, however, these two texts are not continuous with their predecessors, then it may be that the title should be transposed to stand after 12 and 13 (which may then be numbered *11 and *12). This would give a much better sequence, new title *13, *De longi temporis praescriptione,* standing before 14, *De actionibus certo tempore finiendis,* and 15, *De quinquennii praescriptione,* all to do with the effect of the passing of time on legal claims; the preceding sequence of titles, *De causa liberali,* is also now uninterrupted as 4.6–*11. This is where the title was located by Mommsen's predecessor Haenel, and there is a good case for reverting to his order.[76] It is also supported by the order of titles in the relevant section of the Codex Justinianus, where corresponding titles appear at 7.33–40.

As mentioned, the concluding titles of Book 4 (21–24 in Mommsen) represent the interdicts, or executive decrees whereby the praetor implemented decisions made by a iudex to whom they had been referred; their rather arcane names,

75. *CTh* 4.10.1 bears the consular date 332 but was issued at Colonia Agrippinensis (Cologne) and is therefore much earlier, before Constantine's conquest of the east in 324. It may indeed be as early as 313—cf. *CTh* 11.3.1 (1 July 319, corr. 313). The editors of the Code may still have treated it as a law of 332; cf. Chapter 8, "A Selected Title," nos. C.1–5.

76. Krüger's sequence of titles is here the same as Mommsen's.

"Quorum bonorum," "Unde vi," and "Utrubi" (missing from the sequence is "Uti possidetis"), are the first words of the pronouncement in question.[77] The fourth of these titles, the somewhat surprising 24, *De aedificiis publicis et privatis,* contains in Mommsen one text, known only from a reference in the Lex Romana Burgundionum, summarizing a law attributed to Book 4 under a title of this name.[78] The reference does not give the number of the title, but a location at this point is supported by the sequence of titles in *CJ* 8.1–10, which follow the same order as those extant in *CTh.* The title, to which Krüger added five more texts derived from *CJ* 8.10, *De aedificiis privatis,* seems in its content and location to express a relatively unknown praetorian interdict, "Ne quid in loco publico." In the Digest, the late republican jurist Alfenus[79] discusses the legal situation arising from the piling up of a midden-heap against a wall, causing it to become damp. According to Alfenus, the remedy differed, according to whether the wall was on public or private property. In the former case, enforcement could be by interdict: "Si in loco publico id fecisset, per interdictum cogi posse, sed si in privato, de servitute agere oportere."[80] In Alfenus' pronouncement we surely have the explanation for the appearance of a title *De aedificiis publicis et privatis* among the titles derived from praetorian interdicts.[81]

In Book 4 as in its predecessors, the sequence of titles in the Theodosian Code generally corresponds to those of the Codex Justinianus and of the Praetor's Edict. Titles 1–4 correspond to *CJ* 6.9–36, while the content, and no doubt also the title, of *CJ* 6.37, *De legatis,* should be restored to this sequence in *CTh.*[82] Titles 8–9 are *CJ* 7.6 and 10, respectively; title *11 (12 Mommsen) is *CJ* 7.24, and titles *13 (11

77. Cf. Gaius, *Inst.* 4.48–53 and 160 on the interdicts "Utrubi" and "Uti possidetis," used, respectively, for movable and immovable property. The case considered in *CTh* 4.23.1 involves *coloni* in flight from their masters; they are considered movable property.

78. Lex Romana Burgundionum 17.6; cf. Mommsen, p. 210): "De servitute luminis vel aeris similiter constitutum: ut inter privatorum fabricas decem pedes, inter publicas quindecim dimittantur, secundum legem Theodosiani libri IIII sub titulo: De edificiis privatis et publicis." *Servitus,* in modern parlance a servitude or easement, refers to rights of access and usage enjoyed in respect of the property of others.

79. Alfenus Varus, a friend of the Servius Sulpicius mentioned in n. 60.

80. Dig. 8.5.17.2; cf. Alan Watson, *JRS* 60 (1970), p. 110. Reference to the interdict "Ne quid in loco publico" is found at Edict 43.237.

81. The counterpart and source of the complementary title in *CJ* 8.11, *De operibus publicis,* is found at a different point in *CTh,* as 15.1. Most of the succeeding titles of *CTh* 15 recur at *CJ* 11.41–47; it appears that in this particular respect *CJ* has reverted to an order closer to that of the Praetor's Edict.

82. It does not appear in Krüger. Nothing relevant to the Theodosian Code occurs in *CJ* 6.38–54, while the last titles of the book (55–62) appear at the beginning of Book 5 of *CTh.*

Mommsen) and 14–24—that is to say the entire series *13–24 in the amended numeration—are found in the same order in *CJ* 7.33–8.10.

Of the titles of *CTh* 4 that do not recur in the same sequence in *CJ*, title 5 appears at *CJ* 8.36, title 6 at 5.27, title 7 at 1.13, title 10 at 6.7, and title *12 (13 Mommsen) at 4.61. Most of these changes represent a displacement of texts from their sequence in the edict, to contexts influenced by a different view of the substance of the laws, and in one case, that of episcopal jurisdiction (*CTh* 4.7 to *CJ* 1.13), by a change in the political ideology of the government. The implications are discussed in the concluding part of this chapter.

### BOOK 5

Of the first five books of the Code, Book 5 offers some of the most acute difficulties of reconstruction, and the widest discrepancies between the presentations of Mommsen and Krüger.[83] It consists of eighteen titles in Mommsen's edition, not numbered continuously, of which the first eight and the last four are documented by the Breviarium with some support from *T*, while titles 11–16 are recovered solely from some damaged and discontinuous pages of that manuscript. The sequence of titles 1–10 in Mommsen is not complete, titles 4 and 5 being absent from his numeration. This is to allow for the fact that the number of the title in *T* corresponding to Breviarium 5.6, *De ingenuis qui tempore tyranni servierunt*, was with some hesitation read by Krüger, to whom Mommsen owed his information, as 8.[84] If so, then two of the first ten titles have been lost, it being merely a matter of convenience that the missing titles are counted as 4 and 5. What is really lost is any two titles between Mommsen's 2 and 5, inclusive, since the sequence of laws 6.2–8.1 survives in *T* and there is no assurance that the Breviarium made its selections from continuous titles. The two missing titles were supplied by Krüger from the Codex Justinianus as II, *De bonis libertorum* (*CJ* 6.4, *De bonis libertorum et de iure patronatus*), and IV, *De naviculariorum et cohortalium* (*CJ* 6.62), with one and two texts, respectively. Although the first of these titles seems out of place in relation to its position in *CJ*, this may be a misleading impression,[85] while

83. See esp. Krüger, "Zur Wiederherstellung der Titelfolge im fünften Buch des Codex Theodosianus," *ZSS* 34 (1913), pp. 1–5. Krüger's supplement of laws from *CJ* is the largest of any of Books 1–5: seventy-five texts.

84. Mommsen, *CTh*, p. 224: "uiii (*sic dubitans Krueger*)." At *ZSS* 34 (1913), p. 2, Krüger says that the number viii stood before the rubric of the *preceding* title, *De postliminio*, in which case not two but three titles would be missing. However, in his edition he retains without comment Mommsen's numbering of titles 7 and 8.

85. Its position in *CJ* corresponds to *CTh* 4.8ff. However, as will be explained, it may be that the title came in Book 5 of the Theodosian Code because its subject did not fall under the Praetor's Edict but under the *ius civile*.

the second clearly belongs to this part of the Theodosian Code.[86] In addition, since *CTh* 5.6.2 and 3 are laws of 409 following one of 347 recovered from the Breviarium, it is likely that some earlier texts were missing from that title, while the single text of 314 preserved from the Breviarium, and incompletely from *T*, as *CTh* 5.8.1 is most unlikely to represent the complete contents of that title. The subject matter, *De ingenuis, qui tempore tyranni servierunt,* certainly offered scope for repetition in the course of the fourth and early fifth centuries. The three texts of title 7, *De postliminio* attested by *T* could however represent the complete title.

At the end of the book, titles 17–20 are derived almost entirely from the Breviarium with the support, in two cases only, of references from the Lex Romana Burgundionum; they are therefore very incomplete. One of these references, however, to what stands as 17.3, makes clear that this was the last law in this title of the Theodosian Code, and the other, to 19.2, points to a law in the Codex Justinianus, from which the Theodosian Code text can be restored.[87] Between Mommsen's titles 19 and 20 (the last in the book) Krüger supplied from the Codex Justinianus no fewer than nine titles, numbered XVIII–XXVI. Of these titles, XXI, XXII, and XXIV, with five, three and five texts, respectively, and all on significant subjects, seem secure restorations,[88] but it must be open to question whether the Theodosian Code anticipated its successor with separate titles *De colonis Palaestinis, De colonis Thracensibus,* and *De colonis Illyricianis* (Krüger XVII–XIX; CJ 11.51–53). Whether or not Krüger is right in his restorations of all these titles, however, it does seem certain that the texts contained in them belong in this part of the Theodosian Code.

The uncertainties regarding the order of contents of Book 5 otherwise fall on the middle section of titles, 11–16 in Mommsen, which are preserved by *T* in discontinuous sequences with no support from the Breviarium. As usual, a number of texts are preserved in the Codex Justinianus, from which they may be restored to the Theodosian Code; to which titles they should be assigned is however a difficult problem, this being the section of the Code in which Mommsen's and Krüger's

86. *CJ* 6.62.2 occurs at *CTh* 5.6.1, while 6.62.3 should clearly be restored to the same title (*De bonis militum*) and 6.62.4 to *CTh* 5.2, *De decurionum.* It seems clear that *CJ* 6.62.1 belonged to an original *CTh* title *De naviculariorum et cohortalium.*

87. *CJ* 11.50.2; see Mommsen's edition, pp. 239, 241.

88. Respectively, XXI, *De agricolis et mancipiis dominicis vel fiscalibus sive rei privatae* (*CJ* 11.68), XXIII, *De diversis praediis urbanis et rusticis templorum et civitatum* (*CJ* 11.70), and XXIV, *De locatione praediorum civilium vel fiscalium sive templorum sive rei privatae vel dominicae* (*CJ* 11.71). Possibly more doubtful are XXV, *De palatiis et domibus dominicis* (*CJ* 11.77—one text), and XXVI, *De cupressis ex luco Daphensi vel Perseis per Aegyptum non excidendis vel vendendis* (*CJ* 11.78—two texts).

editions differ most markedly. The following are the contents of the relevant pages of *T*, with references to Mommsen's numbering of titles:[89]

| | |
|---|---|
| f. 12*r* | first half missing, then 11.7–9 |
| f. 12*v* | first half missing, then 11.11–12 |
| f. 13 | 12.1–13.4 |
| f. 14 | 14.30–36 |
| f. 15 | 15.14–21 |
| f. 16*r* | first half missing, then 16.29–32 |
| f. 16*v* | first half missing, then 16.33–35 |

The continuity of Mommsen's titles 12 and 13 is clear from *T*, where they are found on the recto and verso of f.13; while in the top right corner of f. 13*r* is a note, "t. XII.," indicating the presence on this page of title 12, and on f. 14*r* a similar note, "t. XIII[I?]," permitting the identification of title 13 or 14, and certainly excluding 15. It is thus likely that folios 13 and 14 were continuous, and that 12–14 were the correct numbers of the titles written on them. *T* does not however show the divisions between titles, nor their names.

Mommsen's title 11, its individual texts numbered 7–12 but omitting 10, is based on f. 12, recto and verso, allowing space for one notional law in the missing part on each side of the manuscript page. So too is Krüger's, with the difference that he accepted the title heading derived from *CJ* 11.59, *De omni agro deserto et quando steriles fertilibus imponantur,* where, despite the explicit contents of the title, Mommsen had left it without name; Mommsen employed this name instead for his title 15, to which it seems as inappropriate as it is appropriate for title 11. Krüger's judgment on this point is clearly superior.[90]

Krüger followed with his title XII, in which he combined Mommsen's now unnamed title 15 with 12 (in that order) under the name *De fundis patrimonialibus et saltuensibus et enfyteuticis et eorum conductoribus* (= *CJ* 11.62), which Mommsen had assigned to his title 12. Krüger's reconstruction is chronologically coherent, gathering together, in a still incomplete title, laws of 364–67/9 (Mommsen's title 15) and 409–34 (Mommsen's title 12). It expresses the substantive contents of the texts, and resolves Mommsen's inappropriate choice of heading for his title 15 by its absorption into another. The solution involves the transposition of f. 15 of *T* to stand before f. 13, but weight must be given to Krüger's decision in this matter. His was the latest and most careful reading of *T* before its destruction by fire, and Mommsen's own account of the manuscript is by explicit acknowledgment based

89. Mommsen, Prolegomena, p. xli; cf. Krüger, "Beiträge zum Codex Theodosianus," pp. 3–4.

90. "Beiträge zum Codex Theodosianus," p. 5: "Die Ergänzung [of Mommsen] . . . ist nicht haltbar; sie passt nicht zu dem Inhalt der übrigen Konstitutionen."

on the material provided by Krüger.[91] Mommsen himself had indicated that the order of leaves in *T* as well as the structure of this part of the manuscript was extremely uncertain.[92]

The remainder of Mommsen's titles in this part of the Code, 13, 14, and 16, Krüger consolidated into his title XIII, *De fundis rei privatae et saltibus divinae domus,* the name assigned by Mommsen, from *CJ* 11.66, to his title 13.[93] This maintains the order of folio pages 13, 14, and 16 (f. 15 being transposed) and again gives a consistent chronological order, with laws of 341–64/9 followed by texts of 386–97/405[94] and 399–426/9. It seems from the annotations in *T* of the last two texts in this sequence that the resulting composite title contained at least thirty-five laws,[95] of which eighteen are extant.

The contents of Book 5 seem at first glance to overlap with those of Books 2–4 and to be difficult to understand as a set of coherent topics. The first title, *De hereditatibus,* might seem, for instance, to belong with the sections on testamentary law in Books 2 and 4, or with the interdicts concerning possession of property covered in the last titles of Book 4. The reason for the separate treatment of this and the succeeding topics in Book 5 is a formal one, deriving from the Praetor's Edict in the negative sense that the book gathered issues in private law that were historically not covered by the Edict and were therefore not treated under this rubric in juristic writing; they were dealt with as an addition or appendix to the Edict.[96] The first title, in full, *De hereditatibus legitimis,* may help to make this clear. It refers to rights of succession determined not by the praetor but by ius civile, that is to say under rules deriving, in Papinian's words, "from statutes,

91. See n. 31.

92. Cf. his note, p. 227: "Omnino in hac parte neque collocatio foliorum superstitum codicis T evidenter constituta est neque separatio titulorum certa ratione perfici potuit."

93. Krüger, "Beiträge zum Codex Theodosianus," p. 4n. 2, reports Vesme's confident claim ("V. sagt, er habe . . . ganz sicher gelesen") to have seen in the rubric of this title the letters "..]atrimonia[.."; cf. Mommsen, ad loc. (p. 229: "de c. . . . patrimonia"). This would suggest the title of *CJ* 11.65 *De collatione fundorum patrimonialium et emphyteuticorum,* but Mommsen takes no account of Vesme's report, and in his edition (p. 174) Krüger rules it out on grounds of content.

94. Mommsen here noted, on his title 14, that its surviving laws were numbered 30–36, "per leges quae sequuntur" (p. 231). This would be a difficulty for Krüger's reconstruction, but Mommsen gives no grounds for his statement.

95. Mommsen, *CTh,* p. 237, again based on Krüger.

96. On this see Krüger, "Beiträge zum Codex Theodosianus," pp. 1–2, referring to the sequence of topics in Salvius Julianus' *Digesta,* where the subjects of titles 1–5 of the Breviarium (*CTh* 5.1–7) were covered in Books 59–62, titles 6–10 (*CTh* 7–18) in Books 63–65, and title 12 (*CTh* 5.?20 = Kr. XXVII) in Book 84. This seems to offer a formal resolution of the observations of Harries, "How to Make a Law-Code," pp. 77–78.

plebiscites, senatusconsulta, imperial enactments, and the authority of the jurists" (Dig. 1.1.7). The distinction is made explicitly in the very first extant text of Book 5, declaring that a petition for "bonorum possessio" was not required in the circumstances considered, since the benefit rested on the law and not on praetorian action: "Quoniam huius legis, non praetoris est beneficium" (*CTh* 5.1.1).[97] The same is true, at a glance, of the other topics considered in Book 5: property of decurions, clerics, soldiers and other groups, *postliminium* (property rights of those captured in warfare), free persons enslaved under tyrants or usurpers, ownership of abandoned land, imperial and public properties, runaway slaves, and imperial and other agricultural tenants. These were issues in private law not historically falling under praetorian jurisdiction; indeed, most of them had arisen in the period following the disappearance of this jurisdiction in favor of that of the emperor and officials deriving their powers of jurisdiction from him.

## *Books 6–16: The Structure of the Code*

In summary, Book 1 of the Theodosian Code addresses the nature and authority of the law and the duties of public officials who held their authority from the emperor; Books 2–4, on private law, follow the order of the Praetor's Edict, while Book 5 covers matters of private law not falling under the Edict but under the ius civile—the law as determined by legislative pronouncement and by the authority of jurists. These five books are seriously incomplete, deriving from the selections of material in the domain of private law made by the compilers of the Breviarium, and from the discontinuous manuscript sources of the Code itself, but permitting supplementation from the Codex Justinianus.

This situation continues into Book 6 of the Code, where the first title, *De dignitatibus,* with what remains of its contents, and part of the second, *De senatoria dignitate,* are supplied from the Codex Justinianus.[98] From this point until the end of the Code at Book 16, however, we possess the manuscript authority of *R* and *V,* which by extraordinary good fortune make a nearly perfect join at the end of Book 8. For the end of the penultimate and for the whole of the last title of Book 8 (in all, three surviving texts) we are again beholden to the Breviarium, which otherwise, for reasons stated earlier, makes a much more limited contribution to the text of Books 6–16 than it does to Books 1–5 of the Code.

In its concern with questions of dignity and status in public life and administration, Book 6 in a way presents the obverse of the theme of imperial authority

97. The same distinction is made in *Sirm.* 1 (on episcopal jurisdiction): "Omnes itaque causae, quae vel praetorio iure vel civili tractantur," etc.

98. With seven additional texts in Krüger.

discussed in the later part of Book 1. The contents of Book 6 and its successor conform to the names of their first titles, *De dignitatibus* ("dignities" are public offices and the ranks assigned to them) and *De re militari*. Continuing the theme of government and administration, the bulk of Book 8 is on administrative practice, a long title of fifty-five texts (8.5) being devoted to the imperial transport service, the *cursus publicus*. The last eight titles of Book 8 (12–19) are concerned with a different and unrelated subject: gifts and their revocation, gifts made to or extracted by those in public office, rights accruing to parents by virtue of their children, and property acquired by maternal inheritance and through marriage by sons and daughters in patria potestas. After this rather awkward (and difficult) combination of topics, Book 9 is devoted to the criminal law, and Book 10 to the law affecting the imperial *fiscus*, this term covering those institutions and services under the immediate control of the emperor, from purple-dyeing and arms factories and mines to the properties of the imperial household. Again, the first titles of each book, *De accusationibus et inscribtionibus* and *De iure fisci*, respectively, define the subject matter of what follows. Book 11, *De annona et tributis*, is about taxation, with a group of eleven titles at the end of the book on legal procedures, appeals, and the law of evidence (11.29–39); this section might follow from Book 9, its connection with the earlier part of Book 10 being not at all clear.

Books 12–15 are logically organized, and they form a coherent development of subject matter. Book 12 is entirely about the position and duties of decurions and city councils, and Book 13 begins with the *lustralis collatio*, a tax on trades and professions, then discusses the liabilities or exemptions of some of those who pursued them—namely, doctors and professors, artists and craftsmen, shipowners and their estates (two titles containing 48 texts in all); then follow cargoes and shipwrecks, and tax assessors and inspectors. Book 14 concerns the cities of Rome and Constantinople (including bakers and the corn supply, swine and cattle dealers, woodmen, lime-burners, porters, and trade guilds in general), with titles also on Carthage and Alexandria; and 15, beginning with the generic title *De operibus publicis*,[99] is about public services and civic amenities, from roads and aqueducts to the staging of games and spectacles, and the status of actors and actresses. The penultimate title, one of fourteen texts, is, however, on the authority of legal decisions made under "usurpers or barbarians" (15.14). The title has no clear connection with the rest of Book 15 and would more obviously have appeared earlier, for instance among the legal titles at the end of Book 11.[100] It is by an

99. See n. 81 for the position of this title in *CJ*.

100. It would not occur in Book 9, which is about the criminal law; the question in *CTh* 15.14 concerns decisions in private law, many of them routine transactions to do with such things as inheritance and transfers of property, by authorities later declared unlawful.

interesting exception to their generally logical and lucid arrangement of topics throughout the Theodosian Code that in these three later books, 8, 11, and 15, the editors appended titles involving law and legal procedures to material to which they are not obviously relevant. The explanation for this is not known but may reflect adaptations to an already decided structure that the editors had to accommodate at a relatively late stage of their work.

Book 16, beginning with its two titles *De fide catholica* and *De episcopis, ecclesiis et clericis* (the latter a title of forty-seven laws), is devoted to the subject of religious practice and belief, and correctness and incorrectness in the same; heretics (sixty-six laws) and apostates, Jews, and pagans are disciplined and punished in titles of depressing thoroughness.

It is a natural and certainly a widely held assumption that this final book was intended as the culmination of the entire Theodosian Code; the moment at which the ideology and inheritance of Constantine's Christian empire were laid out for all to see. It is, however, a relevant observation that the Codex Justinianus of a century later took just the opposite approach, assembling at the very opening of the work the texts on the subject collected in the Theodosian Code together with those issued at later times; the titles on religion and religious belief, on bishops and monks, Jews, heretics and pagans, and the privileges of churches precede even those on the sources and authority of the law placed at the beginning of the Theodosian Code. In the Codex Justinianus there is no mistaking the ideological significance of the change in the organization of the text, the authority of God being placed, in a book of Roman law, before that of the emperors. The situation regarding the Theodosian Code is different. Here, the sources and authority of law stand first, because these, and not religion, were still the primary issue.[101] After its sources, the Theodosian Code moves straight on to the law itself, beginning in the traditional way with the order of topics inherited from the Praetor's Edict, and after that to the sequence of topics as described earlier, conceived and designed with their inherent logic. The subject of religious authority and religious belief did not belong to a traditional sequence of topics in Roman law, being itself a new topic in that domain. Its presence at the end of the Theodosian Code is simply a consequence of its not being at the beginning. The all-important shift of emphasis had taken place by the time of composition of the Codex Justinianus but does not occur in its predecessor.

101. In a book of law (so in Gaius, in the Digest, and in Justinian's Institutes), it is the definition of law that stands first; see also Harries, "How to Make a Law-Code," p. 78.

# 6

## *The Sirmondian Constitutions*

The Sirmondian Constitutions are named after the Jesuit scholar Jacques Sirmond, who in 1631 published what he called an appendix to the Theodosian Code, consisting of twenty-one constitutions of the fourth and early fifth centuries on various matters affecting the privileges and discipline of the Christian Church;[1] among the subjects covered are episcopal jurisdiction as both exercised and claimed by the clergy, the exemption of churches from taxation, sanctuary in churches, the expulsion of bishops from their sees by church councils, Easter amnesties for petty criminals, the recovery of those captured by barbarians at a time of invasion (an issue in which the Church was much involved), and the suppression of heretics and pagans and the sequestration of their property.

Of the twenty-one texts published by Sirmond, the last three, which he added from other sources he knew, are not relevant here. For the main body of the Constitutions (nos. 1–18) his source was a manuscript from Lyons containing a variety of conciliar and other ecclesiastical material from the period from the early fourth to the late sixth century; the texts in question are found at the end of the

1. For what follows, see esp. Mark Vessey, "The Origins of the *Collectio Sirmondiana:* A New Look at the Evidence," in Harries and Wood (eds.), *The Theodosian Code,* pp. 187–99 — a fine paper, with a full account of earlier discussion. The most detailed descriptions of the individual manuscripts are to be found in Mommsen's Prolegomena.

compilation.[2] The manuscript, which Sirmond had borrowed but evidently never returned to its owners (the chapter library of Lyons Cathedral), was still in the library of the Jesuit Collège de Clermont in Paris, to which Sirmond had belonged, when the Collège was suppressed and its library dispersed in 1764.[3] Its first two sections, comprising 186 folios, were later acquired by a Russian collector and in due course given by him to the imperial library at St. Petersburg. The third section of 120 folios, the part of the manuscript that includes the Sirmondian Constitutions, was acquired by a Dutch collector and then by the famous English bibliophile Sir Thomas Phillipps. After Phillipps' death it was bought by the Deutsche Staatsbibliothek at Berlin; and there, referred to as Berol. Phillipps 1745 (= *Z*), it was used by Mommsen to prepare the text of the Sirmondian Constitutions which he appended to his edition of the Theodosian Code.

Paleographical study of the Lyons manuscript in which Sirmondian Constitutions 1–18 are preserved has shown that it was written by two scribes working in concert, with the occasional help of a third and possibly a fourth, at some time in the second half of the seventh century.[4] Its contents, as we saw, include conciliar material of the fourth to sixth centuries, the latest referring to the first council of Mâcon, held between 581 and 583. It further appears that the Sirmondian Constitutions were written by the same hand as that responsible for the material relevant to that council.[5] It has also been noted that the acts of that council and of the second council of Mâcon of 585 refer to secular legislation on topics covered in the Sirmondian Constitutions—namely, the privileges of ecclesiastical courts and the possession by Jews of Christian slaves. It is reasonable to conclude that the Sirmondian Constitutions, as they are found in the Lyons manuscript, have to do with attempts to ally secular with ecclesiastical law, and in particular to show that privileges claimed by the Church under barbarian rulers were based on preroga-

2. The source of the last two of the eighteen texts was the Theodosian Code itself, nos. 1–16 being independent of it.

3. Mommsen, Prolegomena, p. ccclxxx. For the vicissitudes in the manuscript's history, see Vessey, "The Origins of the *Collectio Sirmondiana,*" pp. 183–88.

4. C. H. Turner, "Chapters in the History of Latin MSS.," *Journal of Theological Studies* 1 (1900), pp. 435–41; and "Chapters in the History of Latin MSS., vol. 3, The Lyons–St. Petersburg MS of Councils," Ibid. 4 (1903), pp. 426–34. Mommsen's brief report is in Prolegomena, p. ccclxxviii, with lxii.

5. Vessey, "The Origins of the *Collectio Sirmondiana,*" 192f., relying partly on reports of E. A. Lowe, *Codices Lugdunenses Antiquissimi* (1924), p. 45, and *Codices Latini Antiquiores* 8 (1959), no. 1061, and 11 (1966), no. **1061. In addition, an early seventh-century annotation to a Corbie manuscript, now at Paris (Par. lat. 12097), refers to the thirteenth (not fourteenth, as Vessey states, p. 198 n. 58) Sirmondian Constitution, with the error xliii for xiii; Mommsen, *CTh,* p. 917n, and Prolegomena, pp. ccclxxix, ccclxxx.

tives given by the legislation of Roman emperors.[6] Another text included in the Lyons manuscript, the so-called Notitia Galliarum, is likewise a secular text of the late Roman period put to ecclesiastical use in the sixth century.[7]

These observations may show how the Sirmondian Constitutions came to be associated with the conciliar material, ending with the two councils held at Mâcon in the 580s, contained in the Lyons manuscript. They do not show whether the late sixth century was the first time that the texts had been assembled as a collection or whether they had been put together by an earlier compiler; nor, in the latter case, do they suggest when this might have been. Since thirteen of the eighteen texts published by Sirmond fall after 400 and no text is as late as the appearance of the Theodosian Code (the latest is a law of 425), it has often been assumed that the collection already existed in an original form in the years immediately preceding the publication of the Code. Because of the contents and protocols of certain of the texts contained in it, relating in particular to Gaul and Africa, the collection is supposed to have originated in one or the other of these provinces, of which Gaul is then favored because of the provenance of *Z* and the other manuscripts attesting it (to be discussed). It is argued that the publication of the Theodosian Code, and the particularly careful preservation of Book 16 in the transmission of its text, would render superfluous such private initiatives. The same argument would also explain why no laws later than 425 appear in it.

This argument is persuasive, but it prejudges the question of the relation between the Theodosian Code and the Sirmondian Constitutions. Mommsen's belief that a version of the collection was used by the editors of the Code is unconvincing, for it sets aside the fact that six of the sixteen constitutions which are independent of the Theodosian Code do not occur in edited form at places in the Code where one would expect them, and that others, which do occur, appear in significantly different versions. The situation cannot be properly assessed without a closer description of the manuscript evidence for the Constitutions in relation to that of the Theodosian Code.

Only the Lyons manuscript used by Sirmond, and a Paris manuscript directly copied from it,[8] contain the text of all eighteen constitutions published by him (the three texts added by Sirmond from other sources are here left out of account). There also exists, however, what is usually called a short recension of the texts, preserved in a group of manuscripts of the Breviarium of Alaric, in a form which

6. Vessey, "The Origins of the *Collectio Sirmondiana*," p. 197.

7. J. D. Harries, "Church and State in the *Notitia Galliarum*," *JRS* 68 (1978), pp. 26–43. The point is explicitly made in the sixth-century rubric to the text.

8. Paris, lat. 1452; Mommsen, Prolegomena, p. ccclxxix. This manuscript makes no independent contribution, but it is of use in restoring readings of *Z* when its readings are damaged.

included Book 16 as supplemented from the full text of the Theodosian Code. Of these sources three, manuscripts from Berlin, Paris, and Oxford collectively known as *YDO,* contain Sirmondian Constitutions 1–7 in the same order as the Lyons manuscript.[9] Another manuscript of the Breviarium, *E* (from Ivrea), and one copied from it, contain only Constitutions 1–3, but this is a truncated version of *YDO* and does not represent a third, still shorter, recension of the collection as a whole.[10] It is therefore classified with *YDO*. This group of texts, *EYDO,* is of much later date than Sirmond's Lyons manuscript of about 650/700, but it is of course possible that it derives from a predecessor or an earlier version of that manuscript. It cannot, in its present associations, precede the Breviarium itself, but the Breviarium is much earlier than the Lyons manuscript, and leaves open the possibility that an original version of the Constitutions belongs to the same period as the majority of the texts.

Of the eighteen laws edited by Sirmond from the Lyons manuscript, the last two were inserted there from the Theodosian Code itself, with an attribution to "titulus xxvii de episcopali definitione"; it is from this source that editors have provided what remains of title 27 in the incomplete text of Book 1 of the Theodosian Code (Krüger correctly adding a third text from the Codex Justinianus to the two supplied by Mommsen from the Sirmondian Constitutions).[11] Added to the second of these two constitutions is an annotation to the effect that, since it is later than all other laws on the subject, it is for that reason more valid.[12] This remark echoes the instruction given to the editors of the Theodosian Code, in a law which does not occur in the Breviarium but was evidently known to the author of this annotation, to set out the texts in chronological order. The tendency of the instruction should have been to encourage the ordering of the Sirmondian Constitutions in chronological sequence, but there is no sign that this was ever attempted. The implication that, as they are set out in the Lyons manuscript, the texts imported from the Theodosian Code stand outside the main series of Constitutions, is borne out by the fact that Constitutions 13–16 are numbered, but not these two. The Lyons

9. In detail: *Y* = Berol. Phillipps 1741; *D* = Paris, Bibl. Nat. 12445 (both Mommsen, p. lxxxviii); *O* = Oxford, Bodleian Library, Selden B.16 (Mommsen, lxv–lxvii). Listed at Mommsen, p. vi.

10. Ivrea (Eporediensis) 35 (Mommsen, pp. lxvii–lxviii). Cujas edited the first three constitutions from this source in 1566 and 1586: Mommsen, p. ccclxxx.

11. See Chapter 5.

12. Mommsen, *CTh,* p. 63n.: "Item alia lex de Theodosiano sub titulo XXVII de episcopali definitione, et hoc validior, quia omnibus posterior." The note is placed at the head of the law, the text of which ends with the Lyons manuscript at the word *cognitio.* The few remaining words of the Constitution are supplied from *CJ* 1.4.8.

manuscript evidently had a precursor in which all the first sixteen constitutions were numbered, in a way that was independent of the Theodosian Code itself.[13]

That the connection of the Sirmondian Constitutions with the Theodosian Code is with the later history of the published Code and not with the period of its original compilation is also apparent in *EYDO*, where the first text, a law of Constantine securely dated to the year 333 (and correctly attributed by the Lyons manuscript), is wrongly assigned to the emperors Arcadius, Honorius, and Theodosius. That is to say, it is meant to be read in sequence with the last laws in the Theodosian Code, which carry the names of these emperors. Indeed, one manuscript, *O*, leaves out the names of the emperors altogether and simply enters, in editorial fashion, "Idem Augusti." The error may belong to a late stage of the tradition, but it emphasizes that the writers of *EYDO*, like the writer of the Lyons manuscript, connected their texts with the Theodosian Code. This was in a version independent of the Breviarium, which includes only the first law of Book 16 title 11, the final title in the Code. This law carries the names of Arcadius and Honorius, and cannot have provided that of Theodosius to the mistaken attribution of *Sirm.* 1.[14]

Despite the connections of both with the manuscript history of the Theodosian Code, the relationship between *EYDO* (or their source) and the Lyons manuscript (or its source) is unclear. Does the "short recension" of *EYDO* represent an abbreviation of an already existing longer one, or does it represent an early collection later extended to form the collection of constitutions represented by the Lyons manuscript?[15] There is more than enough time between the dates of the latest Sirmondian Constitution and of the conciliar and other material of the late sixth century collected in a manuscript of the later seventh to permit either alternative. The second is inherently the more interesting (which does not make it the more likely), for if *EYDO* represents a shorter collection later expanded, then it will show the constitutions at an earlier stage of development than does the Lyons manuscript. Without knowing anything about the sources of the two families of manuscripts, however, we shall still be unable to say how early the collection began to develop in this way.

What has perhaps not been sufficiently emphasized in discussion of the problem

13. For the numbering of *Sirm.* 13 in the early Corbie manuscript, see Mommsen, *CTh*, p. 917n., and n. 5 to this chapter.

14. The last law of *CTh*, 16.11.3 is a law of 410 of Honorius and Theodosius (Arcadius had died in 408). Its predecessor, a law of 405, has the names of all three Augusti; *CTh* 16.11.1, included in the Breviarium, cannot itself have provided the "Idem Augusti" of O.

15. For these alternatives, Vessey, "The Origins of the *Collectio Sirmondiana*," p. 182f.

is the common features between the traditions represented by the Lyons manuscript and *EYDO*. In the first place, Constitutions 1–7 (in the case of *E*, nos. 1–3) occur in the same order in both families of manuscripts. This is not the chronological order.[16] It is true that the earliest four of the constitutions occur, in imperfect sequence (in order of date nos. 1, 4, 7, 3), in *YDO* and in the first seven texts preserved in the Lyons manuscript,[17] but these first seven texts also include two of the latest laws (nos. 5 and 6, of 419 and 425), and the texts are otherwise transcribed in an apparently random order. It should then be significant that all our manuscripts share it.

Another feature common to both manuscript traditions is that they lack the closing protocol of *Sirm.* 7, an Easter amnesty granted in 380/81 by an imperial college alleged inaccurately to be Valentinian, Theodosius, and Arcadius. The law is addressed to Eutropius as praetorian prefect, and since we know that this prefecture was of Illyricum, which at this time fell under the control of the eastern emperor, Theodosius I, we can deduce from this emperor's movements that the law must have been issued at or just before Easter, at either Thessalonica (if in 380) or Constantinople (if in 381).[18] None of this, however, survives in its usual place at the end of the text, a deficiency that must be taken seriously, given that this is the only Constitution to have suffered this form of damage. Since *Sirm.* 7 is the last text to survive in *YDO* (*E*, it will be recalled, only contained nos. 1–3), the most natural inference takes one of two forms. Either the protocol has disappeared at the end of a common source of *YDO* that had ended at this point, or it was lost along with whatever followed it in the common source. The latter supposition is unlikely, for if what was lost from the source of *EYDO* was the rest of the "long recension" represented by the Lyons manuscript, the question would at once arise, how this manuscript also lost the protocol of *Sirm.* 7 but was able to continue with *Sirm.* 8–16. The situation is a complicated one, but its most natural interpretation seems to be that the part of the Lyons manuscript represented by the Sirmondian Constitutions possessed a common ancestor with (*E*)*YDO* for *Sirm.* 1–7, from which both it and they inherited the loss of the protocol of *Sirm.* 7.[19] The Lyons manuscript or

16. The chronological order of the texts is as follows; 1, 4, 7, 3, 8, 2, 12, 9, 16, 14, 11, 15, 5, 13, 10, 6. Not even the three pairs of texts belonging to the same year (9 and 16, 11 and 15, and 5 and 13—the first two pairs to the same two officials) are put together or in chronological order.

17. The fifth earliest, absent from (*E*)*YDO*, is Constitution 8 in the Lyons manuscript. The first text is an especially complicated case, since *EYDO* mistakenly reports it as a text of Arcadius, Honorius, and Theodosius rather than of Constantine.

18. *PLRE* 1, p. 317 (Eutropius 2).

19. Mommsen, Prolegomena, p. ccclxxx, notes the irregularity of protocols in *Z* (the Lyons manuscript). As far as I can tell from Mommsen's reports of the manuscript readings, apart

an antecedent then gathered *Sirm.* 8–16 from a different source not known to *EYDO,* adding 17 and 18 from the Theodosian Code itself. In terms of the alternatives set out earlier, despite their later date as manuscripts, *EYDO* represents an earlier stage of the Sirmondian Constitutions, supplemented at a later stage by the Lyons manuscript or its source. That is to say, the collection came into existence progressively.

Apart from their intrinsic interest, the Sirmondian Constitutions claim the historian's attention because they preserve in their original form, or in something very close to it, constitutions that appear in edited form in the Theodosian Code.[20] They thus allow an examination of the editorial procedures used in the Code in relation to an extant body of primary material. This does not apply to every one of the sixteen texts in the main series preserved in the Lyons manuscript. Of the sixteen, ten offer fuller versions of laws abbreviated and edited by the editors of the Theodosian Code, according to the instructions they received in 429 and 435. The other six texts do not occur in the Theodosian Code, either because they were not recovered by the editors or because they were rejected by them (or possibly, in two cases, because the text of the Code is deficient where they would have been found). The six absent texts are *Sirm.* 1, a letter written in 333 by Constantine to his praetorian prefect Ablabius confirming the emperor's policy on episcopal jurisdiction; 3, a law of Theodosius I of (?)384 on a related topic, the rights of clergy to be heard by ecclesiastical courts; 5, a law of Honorius and Theodosius of 419 on the recovery by their owners of slaves and dependents supported by others during a time of famine; 7 and 8, Easter amnesties relating to the years 380/81 and 386, respectively; and 13, a law, also of 419, extending church sanctuary to a distance of fifty paces from the door of the church and granting to bishops the right to enter prisons to support the sick and needy and to intervene with provincial governors in cases where they discovered that innocent people were being held without trial.

As to whether these laws were not found, or were found but rejected, by the editors of the Code, the first alternative is by far the more likely. The law of Constantine to Ablabius should perhaps stand outside the argument. Not that it lacks significance. It instructs the praetorian prefect to observe the ruling himself and make it known to others. The matter is one of substance: Constantine's ruling referred to earlier legislation and was intended to be definitive; and we have seen that title 27 in Book 1 of the Code, *De definitione episcopali,* supplied from nos.

---

from the closing protocol of 7, Constitution 10 lacks an opening protocol, while the text of 15 is incomplete.

20. To be quite clear, I do not believe that the editors of the Theodosian Code knew of *Sirm.* or any version of it, but rather that they found in their own sources between ten and thirteen texts that were also included, sometimes in different forms, in *Sirm.*

17–18 of the Sirmondian Constitutions and supported in Krüger's edition by a third text from the Codex Justinianus, concerned precisely this subject. The law is exempted from the argument because it is just possible that its text was included in this now mainly lost title in Book 1 of the Code but escaped the interest of the compilers of the Codex Justinianus as well as of the Breviarium.[21] The same provisional exemption applies to *Sirm.* 3, on the rights of clergy to ecclesiastical jurisdiction. A version of this law might have existed in the same incomplete title of the Theodosian Code and have escaped the interest of the compilers both of the Breviarium and of the Codex Justinianus.

The same exemption does not however apply to *Sirm.* 7 and 8, for they would form part of a natural sequence in a title of the Code that survives entire. This title, *CTh* 9.38, *De indulgentiis criminum,* contains eleven laws, of which five are Easter amnesties. All are western laws (the two Sirmondian Constitutions are both, as it happens, eastern) and include amnesties of (?)367, 368, 381, 384, and 385, of which the last was included, with *interpretatio,* in the Breviarium. An obvious home for *Sirm.* 5, the recovery of slaves and dependents after a time of famine, would have been *CTh* 5.7, *De postliminio,* where the complete text of the title is preserved in *T;* indeed, an edited form of *Sirm.* 16 does appear there.[22] Similarly, *Sirm.* 13, on church sanctuary, would fit naturally into Theodosian Code 9.45, *De his, qui ad ecclesias confugiunt,* containing texts of 392, 397, 398, and 431.

All these texts, being addressed to public officials, take the form of general legislation. There is no prima facie reason why any should have been rejected by the editors of the Theodosian Code—on the contrary, every reason to include them. At least as regards the four of these six texts that would fall under titles of the Code which are preserved complete, we should conclude that the editors failed to recover them.

We now turn to the ten texts, of which edited versions appear under one or more titles in the Theodosian Code. Mommsen's edition of the Sirmondian Constitutions registers very carefully the variations between the Constitutions and their edited versions, but not in such a way as to make the comparisons very easy. In what follows, the Sirmondian and relevant Theodosian Code texts are set out in full, with the points of differences highlighted. In the Sirmondian texts, printed in the first column, passages taken over by the editors of the Code are printed in

21. One might think that such a law would be of interest to the authors of the Breviarium, but the entire title in the Theodosian Code is unrepresented there. The absence of the law from *CJ* title 1.4, *De episcopali audientia et de diversis capitulis,* etc., would however be surprising if it had ever been included in the Theodosian Code.

22. See Chapter 5 and text no. 3 in this chapter. The *CTh* title contains two laws, both from the Breviarium, the second also supported by *CJ* and *Sirm.* 16.

bold characters. This represents the beginning of the editorial process, the point at which matters of substance were selected from the original texts. Words and phrases not shown in bold within these selected passages were omitted by the editors of the Code. Changes made in the process of editing are then shown in the second column as they appear in the Theodosian Code, additions and variations being given in italics. Divergencies in manuscript readings are noted only selectively, when they bear upon some point of substance or general interest. Minor differences in punctuation and syntax are not indicated, nor are most discrepancies in the protocols, which can occur through abbreviation at any stage of the transmission of a text. Contradictions between protocols, however, are noted, for they may be relevant to the process of editing. The comparison of texts can only sensibly be carried out in the original Latin, but each Sirmondian text is accompanied by a summary of its contents; this can also be used as a guide to the edited texts in the Theodosian Code.

The texts are arranged in ascending order of complexity. This arrangement will offer an opportunity to gain a progressive understanding of the methods employed by the editors of the Code. It will be recalled that in the law of 429 they were instructed to excerpt points of substance in the texts of laws, to classify the excerpts under relevant titles, dividing texts between titles where appropriate, and to abbreviate texts by omitting superfluous wording not relevant to the point of law in question. In the law of 435, they were given authority to make additions where necessary, to clarify ambiguous passages, and to emend texts to remove incongruities. In what follows we shall see how they interpreted these instructions in practice. We begin with texts edited under only one title in the Theodosian Code.

## CONSTITUTIONS EDITED UNDER ONE TITLE

### *Sirm.* 9; *CTh* 16.2.39, *De Episcopis, Ecclesiis et Clericis*

Bishops removed from or resigning their office must be claimed by curial orders to perform fiscal duties appropriate to their personal standing and the level of their wealth. A fine of two pounds of gold is imposed on *decemprimi* (leaders of curial orders) who by connivance help them to evade this provision, and the former bishops are barred all access to service in the imperial *militia*.

> *Impp. Arcadius et Honorius Augg. Theodoro iterum praef. praetorii.* Utinam quidem ii tantum clericorum nomen induerent, quorum in deteriorem partem relabi vita non possit. Esset laetitia communis et facile pios ritus cultusque divinos veneratio humana sequeretur. Sed facile vitia subrepunt, ut illuc etiam error inrepat, ubi esse nisi pura non possunt. Et si censura iudicii sacerdotalis in specula provideat, ut inter bonos non sint, qui boni esse non possunt, ne tamen

crimina deprehensa luxurient et sit libera peccantibus pertinacia, placet, ut, **quemcumque clericum indignum officio suo episcopus iudicarit et ab ecclesiae ministerio segregaverit, aut qui professum sacrae religionis** obsequium **sponte dereliquerit, continuo eum curia sibi vindicet, ut liber illi ultra ad ecclesiam recursus esse non possit et pro hominum qualitate vel quantitate patrimonii vel ordini suo vel collegio civitatis adiungat, modo ut quibuscumque apti erunt publicis necessitatibus obligentur, ita ut conludio quoque locus non sit; ut per singulos binae librae auri inferendae aerario nostro a decem primis curialibus exigantur, si alicui inlicitam coniventiam et conludia foeda praestiterint,** omnisque **hominibus inprobissimis ab omnibus officiis militiae aditus obstruatur.** Nusquam enim fidi esse non summo ecclesia refuteraverit, deo summo ecclesia refuteraverit, Theodore parens carissime adque amantissime. Quod inlustris magnificentia tua in omnium notitiam datis ad singularum iudices provinciarum litteris faciet pervenire, ut universis id proposita sollemniter edicta declarent. *Data V kal. Decemb. Ravennae Basso et Filippo vv. cc. conss.*

*Idem AA. Theodoro ppo II.* Quemcumque clericum indignum officio suo episcopus iudicaverit et ab ecclesiae ministerio segregaverit, aut *si* (1) qui professum sacrae religionis sponte dereliquerit, continuo eum curia sibi vindicet, ut liber illi ultra ad ecclesiam recursus esse non possit et pro hominum qualitate *et* (2) quantitate patrimonii vel ordini suo vel collegio civitatis adiunga*tur:* modo ut quibuscumque apti erunt publicis necessitatibus obligentur, ita ut conludio quoque locus non sit. Per singulos *igitur* binae librae auri inferendae aerario nostro a decem primis curialibus exigantur, si ali*quibus* inlicitam coniventiam et colludia foeda praestiterint hominibusque (3) inprobissimis ab omnibus officiis militiae aditus obstruatur. *Dat. V kal. Dec. Rav. Basso et Philippo conss.*

(1) The omission of *si* in *Sirm.* is of no real importance but makes for a more pungent Latin.

(2) *Et* is used as a synonym for *vel;* it is in a way more precise, since the phrase cannot then be read disjunctively.

(3) *CTh* drops the double emphasis of *Sirm.*'s "omnis [sc. aditus] ab omnibus officiis obstruatur."

This is a straightforward example of editorial methods. The editors have omitted the reflective and rhetorical opening sentences of *Sirm.* 9, containing also the emperor's reason for making the law, the address to the praetorian prefect Theodorus, and the instructions to him to send the law to provincial governors under his jurisdiction for publication by them. The text is one of several illustrations in this dossier of the abstract language with which the emperor addressed his officials by rank, together with the phrase "parens carissime et amantissime" with which he greeted them personally. The substance of the text is reproduced in a single extract and is identical with *Sirm.* 9, except for amendments of wording and syntax, none of them of any real significance. There is no contradiction or difficulty in the protocols of the respective versions. *CTh* 16.2.39 is particularly well attested, since it was one of the few texts from Book 16 to be included in the Breviarium.

*Sirm.* 2; *CTh* 16.2.35, *De Episcopis*

The emperor has learned that some bishops expelled by church councils have been rejecting these verdicts and reclaiming their sees, stirring up support in their cities and getting laws and rescripts in their favor from the imperial court. In future, clergy who defy decisions to remove them taken at councils and reclaim their sees are according to a (lost) law of the emperor Gratian to be expelled one hundred miles from their cities and forbidden access to the imperial court, and all privileges so gained by them are invalidated. Any who protect them are threatened with imperial, in case they imagine they will escape divine, retribution.

> *Imppp. Arcad., Honor. et Theod. AAA. Hadriano ppo.* Ut veneratio sacerdotibus debetur innoxiis, ita et poena moderata inquietis adque deiectis. Quemadmodum enim deo servientes et divini sacerdotii integritate lucentes non solum vitam suam proprio praestant ornamento, sed etiam subiectae plebis atque oboedientis exemplo, ita hi, quorum indigniora sunt sub integritatis professione peccata, si exclusi degradatique ab episcopiis (1) conprobentur, qui resupinos spiritus adversum definita rettulerint, separati ab his urbibus, quas errore proprio tenuerunt, et sibi debent esse reperti (2) et aliis constituta ablegatione terrori. Plurimos enim bonos faciunt et veneratio optimorum sacerdotum et notabilis reprehensio pessimorum. Suggerentibus episcopis didicimus quosdam sacerdotes Christianae legis, quorum delicta coetu episcopali et deprehensa fuerint et eorum sententia vindicata, in sinu earum urbium, in quibus talia commissa sunt, permanere et quaerere turbas populi, convocare turbatores quietis, exsistere tumultus popularis auctores, innocentes se post iudicium dicere, plebem colligere et velut adhuc

episcopos salutari, comitatum sacrum petere, mereri mendaciis oracula et furtiva rescripta. Sancimus itaque hac lege, ut **quicumque residentibus sacerdotibus fuerit episcopali loco detrusus et nomine, si aliquid vel contra sententiam vel contra quietem moliri fuerit deprehensus rursusque sacerdotium petere, a quo videtur exclusus, procul ab ea urbe, quam** indignus **infecit, secundum legem divae memoriae Gratiani centum milibus vitam agat. Sit ab eorum coetibus separatus, a quorum est societate discretus;** careat urbe, quam tenuit, segregetur a plebe, quam mentitus vitae praeceptor infecit. **Sit huiusmodi personis tenore** huius legis **inlicitum sacra nostra adire secreta et inpetrare rescripta; omnia abiectis per culpam sacerdotio personis quae impetrata sunt** vel quae impetrata fuerint (3) **infecta permaneant; scituris his, quorum defensione nituntur, absque sui reprehensione non futurum, si hoc eis polliceantur suffragium, qui divinum non videntur meruisse iudicium,** Hadriane parens carissime atque amantissime. Hanc igitur legem sublimis magnificentia tua cunctas per dioceses sibi creditas publicabit edictis, ut id, quod pro quiete repertum, pro iudicii episcopalis confirmatione constitutum, pro

Idem AA. Hadriano ppo. Quicumque residentibus sacerdotibus fuerit episcopali loco detrusus et nomine, si aliquid vel contra *custodiam* (5) vel contra quietem *publicam* moliri fuerit deprehensus rursusque sacerdotium petere, a quo videtur *expulsus,* procul ab ea urbe, quam infecit secundum legem divae memoriae Gratiani centum milibus vitam agat. Sit ab eorum coetibus separatus, a quorum est societate discretus,

sitque huiusmodi personis inlicitum tenore (6) sacra nostra adire secreta et inpetrare rescripta. Omn*ibus* (7) abiectis per culpam sacerdotio personis quae impetrata sunt infecta permaneant, scituris his, quorum defensione nituntur, absque sui reprehensione non futurum, si hoc eis pollic*entur* suffragium, qui divinum non videntur meruisse iudicium. *Dat. prid. non. Feb. Rav. Stilichone et Aureliano cons.*

reprimendis culpis inventum est,
ab omnibus excolatur, a
sacerdotibus reservetur. *Data
pridie nonas Februarias Ravennae
Stilichone II cons.* (4)

(1) *Episcopiis,* Mommsen; *episcopis,* manuscripts.
(2) *Reperti* (Z) is difficult; other manuscripts have *perti, periti; O,* cutting the knot, tries *dampnationi.* As Mommsen points out, what is needed is something like *reprobationi;* guilty bishops will be a reproach to themselves and a deterrent to others.
(3) *Fuerint* is Mommsen's suggestion against the manuscripts' *fuerant,* the law then referring to present and future, rather than present and past acquisition of improper rescripts. The phrase is omitted in *CTh.*
(4) *Stillicone secundo* (written in full) *Z.*
(5) *Custodiam,* manuscripts, except *O,* which restores *sententiam* from the text of *Sirm.*
(6) To judge by its manuscripts (*VL,* followed by Mommsen), the editors of the Code omitted *huius legis* from the *Sirm.* version but left *tenore*—intentionally, since the word order is changed to accommodate it. The effect is to leave *tenore* unattached. Again, O restored "tenore huius legis" ("huius legis tenore" *YD*) from the text of *Sirm.*
(7) The reading *omnibus* is an error. The editors presumably took the word with "abiectis . . . personis," but the construction is "omnia . . . quae impetrata sunt infecta permaneant."

*Sirm.* 2 is composed in four sections: 1) the emperor's introductory reflections; 2) the explanation of how he came to know about it, where the words following "suggerentibus episcopis" are presumably a summary of the *suggestio* itself; 3) the substance of the law, which follows after "sancimus itaque hac lege"; and 4) the instruction to the prefect Hadrianus to ensure the publication of the law in the dioceses under his jurisdiction (Italy and Africa). This was done by sending the law to provincial governors with the instruction to display it under the authority of their own edicts. This part of the law also offers another example of the emperor's forms of address to his official, as "magnificentia tua" and "parens carissime et amantissime"; see earlier remarks on *Sirm.* 9. The version in *CTh* 16.2.35 picks up the text after "sancimus itaque hac lege" and includes only 3) the substance, as just described, with the omission of a line, evidently thought superfluous, in the middle. Among the lesser changes, the editors omitted the reference to past (or future, n. 3 above) benefits illegitimately gained by members of the clergy in question. In two other cases, the editors seem to have misunderstood, or to have ill adapted, the Latin of the original version (nn. 6 and 7).

There is a problem of dating. The closing protocols of *Sirm.* 2 give Stilicho as "cos. II" (405), without mentioning his eastern colleague of that year, Anthemius. The manuscripts of *CTh* give "Stilicone et Aureliano coss.," that is to say 400; but the place of issue, Ravenna, is not compatible with that date, and 405 should certainly be accepted. Other laws to Hadrianus demonstrate the same or a similar confusion between the two consulships of Stilicho and those of his colleagues in 400 and 405, Aurelianus and Anthemius.[23]

*Sirm.* 16; *CTh* 5.7.2, *De Postliminio*

After the defeat of barbarian invaders by force of arms, the emperors order that no persons of whatever sex, status, or age taken captive by barbarians are to be prevented from returning home freely; any expenditure on their restoration to health or on their clothing or support is to be put down as charity and not compensated, except for persons purchased from the barbarians. In such cases the individual in question is to repay the price paid, or perform labor or other services for his or her purchaser for a period of five years—adequate compensation, explains the emperor, given that some will not live that long to enjoy the benefit of the law. Those free by birth will retain this status. Any resistance to the order by the agent of a landowner is to be punished by condemnation to the mines or deportation, or, if by a landowner, by confiscation of property and deportation. Bishops and town councils are to assist the implementation of the law by bringing cases to the attention of governors. Governors and their staffs who yield to pressure to neglect the law are to be fined ten pounds of gold, since the duty to implement it rests mainly on them.

*Imp. Honorius ad Theod(oro) II praef. praet.* Punitis auctoribus mali publici laesorum quidem dolori dedimus ultionem, sed provincialibus nostris libertatis restituendae festinatione sentimus uno eodemque tempore armis et legibus consulendum. Hinc denique bellorum curis mixta ratio et salubris constitutio admonuit faciendum, ut **diversarum homines provinciarum cuiuslibet sexus condicionis aetatis, quos barbaricae feritatis** discursus **captiva necessitate transduxerat, invitos nemo retineat, sed ad**

*Impp. Hon. et Theod. AA. Theodoro ppo.* Diversarum homines provinciarum cuiuslibet sexus condicionis aetatis, quos barbarica feritas captiva necessitate transduxerat, invitos nemo retineat, sed ad

23. See Mommsen's note, p. 89, on 2.8.24, addressed to Hadrianus on the same date as the present constitution, but evidently distinct from it.

| | |
|---|---|
| **propria redire cupientibus libera sit facultas. Quibus si quicquam in usum** recuperandarum virium **vestium vel alimoniae** dicatur **inpensum, humanitati sit praestitum, nec** maculet boni facti gloriam avara **victualis sumptus repetitio,** cum forsitan alimoniae istius mercedes operarum reddiderit conpensatio. Quod in examen venire non patimur, ne ad propria redire cupientes indecoris contentionibus retardentur; | propria redire cupientibus libera sit facultas. Quibus si quicquam in usum vestium vel alimoniae inpensum *est,* humanitati sit praestitum, nec *maneat* victualis sumptus repetitio: |
| **exceptis his, quos quis barbaris vendentibus** emisse **docebitur, a quibus status sui pretium propter utilitatem publicam emptoribus aequum est redhiberi:** ne ingentis **damni consideratio in tali necessitate positis negari faciat emptionem,** et inveniamur, quorum libertati consuli voluimus, saluti potius obfuisse. | exceptis his, quos quis barbaris vendentibus *emptos esse* docebitur, a quibus status sui pretium propter utilitatem publicam emptoribus aequum est redhiberi: ne *quando enim* damni consideratio in tali necessitate positis negari faciat emptionem, |
| Hos **decet aut datum pro se pretium emptoribus restituere, aut labore, obsequio vel opere quinquennii vicem referre beneficii, habituros incolumem, si in ea nati sunt, libertatem.** Nec honestas emptoribus quinquennii tempus ad conpensationem maioris forsitan pretii datum ingemiscat exiguum, quia humanae vitae fragilitas forte intra metas potest temporis constituti deficere nec ad legis beneficium pervenire. Credant saltim perditum casibus, quod humanitate detulerint, licet humana misericordia deo iudice quod alteri tribuit, sibi praestet. Quapropter servata | decet *redemptos* aut datum pro se pretium emptoribus restituere, aut labore, obsequio vel opere quinquennii vicem referre beneficii, habituros incolumem, si in ea nati sunt, libertatem. |

definitione legis, cuius moderationem placere non dubium est, **reddantur sedibus propriis, quibus iure postliminii et veterum responsis** prudentium **incolumia cuncta servata sunt.** Quam sanctionem adeo volumus custodiri, ut, si **quisquam** temeritate sacrilega **praeceptis fuerit conatus obsistere, actor** et **conductor procuratorque,** qui ad tuendam absentis domini possessionem esse detegitur, **dari se metallo** aut poenam **deportationis non ambigat subiturum. Si vero possessionis dominus** contra mansuetudinis nostrae salubre constitutum venire temptaverit, **rem suam fisco noverit vindicandam seque** per rectoris provinciae sententiam **deportandum. Et ut facilis exsecutio proveniat imperatis,** Christianae ⟨religionis⟩ sacerdotes, vicinorum et **proximorum locorum** ecclesias retinentes, quorum moribus congruit effectus talium praeceptorum, **curiales quoque proximarum civitatum placuit admoneri, ut emergentibus** talium necessitatum **causis** adeant iudices **legis nostrae auxilium** petituri. Et ne quis contumaciae suae culpam praecepti ignoratione tueatur, Theodore parens carissime adque amantissime, inlustris magnificentia tua legis tenorem litteris suis edictisque propositis ad omnium iudicum et provincialium notitiam faciet

Reddantur *igitur* sedibus propriis *sub moderatione qua iussimus,* quibus iure postliminii et veterum responsis incolumia cuncta servata sunt.

Si quis *itaque huic* praecepto fuerit conatus obsistere, actor conductor procuratorque,

dari se metall*is cum poena* (1) deportationis non ambigat subiturum. Si vero possessionis dominus,

rem suam fisco noverit vindicandam seque deportandum. Et ut facilis exsecutio proveniat imperatis, *Christianos* proximorum locorum *volumus huius rei sollicitudinem gerere.*

Curiales quoque proximarum civitatum placuit admoneri, ut emergentibus tal*ibus* causis *sciant* legis nostrae auxilium *deferendum,*

| | |
|---|---|
| pervenire, **ita ut noverint rectores universi decem libras auri a se et tantundem ponderis a suis apparitoribus exigendum, si** quod **praeceptum** est, in gratiam cuiuspiam **neglectum** esse doceatur: cum saluberrimae sanctionis exsecutionem deferri ab omnibus quidem, sed iudicum maxime et officiorum cura obsequioque iubemus. *Data III non. Decemb. Ravennae Basso et Filippo vv. cc. conss., accepta XVI kal. Ianuarias.* | ita ut noverint rectores universi decem libr*arum* auri a se et tantundem ponderis a suis apparitoribus exigendum, si praeceptum negl*exerint*. (2) *Dat. IIII id. Dec. Rav. Hon. VIII et Theod. III AA. conss.* |

(1) "Aut poenam"/"cum poena": it is not clear whether *CTh* means to add deportation to condemnation to the mines, rather than treating them as alternative penalties.

(2) These three words are a heavy abbreviation from *Sirm.* In particular, the allusion to improper influence (*gratia*) is absent from *CTh*.

With numerous small changes of wording and syntax, *CTh* offers a faithful version of *Sirm.* 16, omitting four substantial sections of two lines or more and several shorter clauses. Among the more important omissions are the opening reference to a recent defeat of barbarians that provides the circumstances of the law, some remarks on the shortness on human life (which in *Sirm.* does in a callous way bear upon the argument), the moral benefits of charity and the passing reference to improper influence (*gratia*), and, as usual, the address to the praetorian prefect and his instruction to ensure the circulation of the regulation. The text of *CTh* 5.7.2 is well supported, since it occurs in the Breviarium (with a long interpretatio) as well as in *T,* but it still contains an error in the protocol; to conform with the office of Theodorus and for other reasons, the law must be from late 408, as *Sirm.*, not 409; the barbarian defeat referred to would be the first withdrawal from Italy of Alaric at the end of 408. The explanation for the discrepancy is probably that the Theodosian Code text represents a version sent on by the prefect for publishing in another place and that the consular year expresses the date of acceptance in that place rather than that of issue at Ravenna; as in many other cases, the details in the protocol that would make this clear have dropped out of the text.[24] The divergence

24. R. Delmaire, "Etude sur les souscriptions de quelques lois du Code Théodosien," in M. Christol and others (eds.), *Institutions, société et vie politique* (1992), pp. 316–28. The phenomenon can be found elsewhere in the Theodosian Code, and must sometimes have occurred where there is no means of detecting it.

between the dates of issue of 3 December (*Sirm.*) and 10 December (*CTh*) should perhaps be explained in the same way; as we shall see (in the discussion of *Sirm.* 6), such variations are inherent in the way in which laws were issued and made public.

*Sirm.* 11; *CTh* 16.2.40, *De Episcopis*

In response to a *suggestio* of the praetorian prefect, it is ordered that Church lands be exempted from all menial fiscal burdens in kind and from all contributions in gold, so that the resources of churches may be entirely devoted to divine service. Anyone attempting to impose such burdens is to be exiled.

*DD. NN. Impp. Honorius et Theodosius Augg. Melitio praefecto praetorii.* Recte clementiam nostram sacrosanctae religionis obsequiis devotis adsiduitatibus servientem ad confirmationem privilegiorum, quae ecclesiis dicavit vetustas, magnificentiae tuae suggestio religiosa commonuit, ut temerariorum hominum conatibus penitus obpressis, quibus studium est Christianam innocentiam

<table>
<tr>
<td>semper appetere, eam nostri formam sanciamus arbitrii, cui deinceps nullus inpune refragator existat. **Placet** igitur **rationabilis consilii tenore perpenso,** quoniam quid remedii . . . . (1) confusa nequissimis ausibus viam relinquunt, **destricta moderatione praescribere, a quibus specialiter necessitatibus ecclesiae urbium singularum habeantur inmunes. Primo quippe illius usurpationis contumelia depellenda est, ne praedia usibus caelestium secretorum dicata sordidorum munerum fasce vexentur. Nulla iugationem talium privilegiorum sorte gratulantem muniendi itineris constringat iniuria; nihil extraordinarium ab hac** vel **superindicticium flagitetur; nulla pontium instauratio, nulla translationum sollicitudo gignatur. Non aurum ceteraque talia poscantur. Postremo nihil,** quod **praeter canonicam**</td>
<td>*Impp. Honor. et Theod. AA. Melitio ppo.* Placet rationabilis consilii tenore perpenso,<br><br>destricta moderatione praescribere, a quibus specialiter necessitatibus ecclesiae urbium singularum habeantur inmunes. Primo quippe illius usurpationis contumelia depellenda est, ne praedia usibus caelestium secretorum dicata sordidorum munerum fasce vexentur. Null*am* iugationem, *quae* talium privilegiorum sorte gratul*atur*, (2) muniendi itineris constringat iniuria; nihil extraordinarium ab hac superindicticium*ve* flagitetur; nulla pontium instauratio, nulla translationum sollicitudo gignatur. Non aurum ceteraque talia poscantur. Postremo nihil, praeter canonicam inlationem,</td>
</tr>
</table>

| | |
|---|---|
| inlationem adventiciae necessitatis sarcina repentina depoposcerit, eius functionibus **adscribatur.** Vacent ecclesiae solis, quibus bene consciae sunt, divinae praedicationis officiis, cuncta in orationibus celebrandis horarum omnium momenta consumant. Gaudeant nostra in perpetuum liberalitate munitae, quarum nos erga cultum pietatis aeternae devotione gaudemus. Quapropter sublimis magnificentia tua religiosis mentibus in huiuscemodi negotio nobiscum decenter adcincta, oraculi praesentis adque in omnem aevum perpeti firmitate duraturi serie conperta, roboratis omnibus, quae sacrosanctae venerationis intuitu huiusce sanctionis auctoritate praescribimus, provinciarum iudices scribtis currentibus admonebit, quo evidenter agnoscant universos, | *quod* adventiciae necessitatis sarcina repentina depoposcerit, eius functionibus adscribatur. |
| qui deinceps temerariae praesumptionis adnisu in iniuriam ecclesiarum nostrique praecepti aliquid fortasse temptaverint, severissima interminatione quatiendos, ita ut in talibus deprehensi contumacia fervente peccati | Si quis contra venerit, |
| **post debitae ultionis acrimoniam, quae erga sacrilegos iure promenda est, exilio perpetuae deportationis utantur.** *Data VIII kal. Iulias Ravennae DD. NN. Theod. Aug. IIII cons.* | post debitae ultionis acrimoniam, quae erga sacrilegos iure promenda est, exilio perpetuae deportationis *uratur.* (3) *Dat. VIII kal. Iun. Rav. Honor. VIIII et Theodosio V AA. Conss.* |

(1) Some words are missing here, in which the emperor seems to have asked what remedy might be sought. Mommsen's "quid remedii ⟨occurrat quaeritur sacerdotumque postulata⟩

confusa" ("We seek whatever remedy may occur and the confused [unanimous?] requests of the priests leaves a way," trans. Pharr) seems unlikely. The entire clause was omitted in *CTh* 16.2.40.

(2) *Sirm.* "Nulla iugationem . . . gratulantem": reading *nulla* with *iniuria* at the end of the clause. *CTh* reads the phrase as *nullam iugationem,* which works well with the following clauses ("nihil . . . nulla . . . nulla . . . ").

(3) *Sirm., utantur:* The change to the singular follows from the omission of the plural subject "qui . . . deprehensi" in *Sirm.* The colorful *uratur* may be an error in transmission for *utatur.*

The *CTh* excerpt offers a faithful reading of the substantive elements of *Sirm.* 11, leaving out the introduction referring to the suggestio of the praetorian prefect, the unusually expansive instruction to the prefect to circulate the law to provincial governors, and an explanatory clause ("quoniam quid remedii . . . relinquunt") not relevant to its substance. The reference to the sanction is heavily abbreviated, with a consequential syntactical change in *CTh* 16.2.40 from singular to plural, and there are other minor changes. The abbreviations lose the effective, even elegant, link made in *Sirm.* 11 between the prefect's "suggestio religiosa" and the emperor's sharing with him the pious duty to enforce the law: "Sublimis magnificentia tua religiosis mentibus . . . nobiscum decenter adcincta." *CTh* retains in its opening words the reference to the "rationabilis consilii tenor" of *Sirm.* 11 without saying anything about its origin, the praetorian prefect. The concluding protocol refers (DD.NN.) to two emperors, but only one is named. Theodosius was in fact cos. IIII without colleague in 411. *CTh* 16.2.40 has instead Honorius VIIII and Theodosius V as consuls (in 412). Melitius is recorded as PPo (Italiae) from 16 November 410 to 15 February 412, and his successor Iohannes is first attested on 6 June 412. Melitius could therefore be addressed on either 24 June 411 (*Sirm.*) or 25 May 412 (*CTh*).[25] Alternatively, the law could have been issued at Ravenna late in 411 and (after some delay) have been received somewhere else, possibly Carthage, on one of these dates in 412.

*Sirm.* 15; *CTh* 16.2.41, *De Episcopis*

By virtue of the reverence due to them, bishops and other members of the clergy, who in respect of their personal conduct are subject to Church discipline, are not to be accused of any criminal offense by any person, whatever his political or social status, except before bishops. Any such accusation must be supported by full proofs and documentation, on pain of *infamia* for the accuser. Bishops are to hear such cases only with many witnesses and in proper written proceedings.

25. Mommsen assigned the law without comment to 25 May or 24 June 412 (Prolegomena, p. ccxcii) and presents *Sirm.* 11 as being from 24 June 412, thus ignoring the overlap with the tenure of Iohannes.

*Impp. Honorius et Theodosius AA. ad Melitium virum inlustrem praefectum praetorii.* (1) Non cassum veterum prudentia constituit quod adpetitam innocentiam solaretur et purgatis repperit ultionem, ne libera calumniantis intentio insontes adfligeret. Terret quidem reum proposita poena criminibus et facit accusatorem vindictae contemplatione cautiorem, ne quisquam solis aliquando inimicitiarum stimulis incitatus ingerat non probanda iudicibus. Quae fori aequitas,

responsis veterum et legum nostrarum aeternitate solidata, cunctis est delata personis, debet **clericis** nunc prodesse, quos **non nisi apud episcopos convenit accusari.** Quibus nihil convenit habere commune, (2) ne cultus venerabilis sacerdos et Christianae legi dicatus minister, quibus intuitu religionis maior quam ceteris talibus reverentia deferenda est, securo calumniantis arbitrio cuiuslibet criminis nondum probata obiectione maculetur et talibus personis, quibus dignum est detulisse pro merito, peccatum iniuria fieri et sine ultione inlicite patiamur. Quapropter placitura omnibus legis aeternitate sancimus, ut, **si episcopus vel presbyter, diaconus et quicumque inferioris loci Christianae legis minister apud episcopos, si quidem alibi non oportet,** (3) **a qualibet persona fuerint accusati, sive ille sublimis vir honoris sive cuiuslibet alterius dignitatis, qui hoc genus miserandae intentionis arripiat,** ut homo peccatis aliquibus vel criminibus pollutus mentiendo probatis obsequio vel locum tenentibus sacerdotii vel divinis servientibus mysteriis

*Idem AA. Melitio ppo.* Clericos non nisi aput episcopos accusari convenit.

*Igitur* si episcopus vel presbyter, diaconus et quicumque inferioris loci Christianae legis minister aput episcopos, si quidem alibi non oportet, a qualibet persona fuerint accusati, sive ille sublimis vir honoris sive *ullius* alterius dignitatis, qui hoc genus *laudabilis* (5) intentionis arripi*et*,

| | |
|---|---|
| delationem ingerat, (4) **noverit** docenda probationibus, monstranda documentis se debere deferre. In quo si est culpa, minister religionis vitae suae pollutione removendus sacris non potest interesse secretis. At si huius est vesaniae, quae nullis fulta probationibus composita criminatione talium virorum adpetisse propositum videatur aut [. . . . ] **si quis** igitur **circa huiusmodi personas** [. . . . | noverit docenda probationibus, monstranda documentis se debere *in*ferre. |
| | Si quis *ergo* circa huiusmodi personas non probanda detulerit, auctoritate huius sanctionis intellegat se iacturae famae propriae subiacere, ut damno pudoris, existimationis dispendio discat sibi alienae verecundiae inpune insidiari saltem de cetero non licere. Nam sicut episcopos presbyteros diaconos ceterosque, si his obiecta conprobari potuerint, maculatos ab ecclesia venerabili aequum est removeri, ut contempti post haec et miserae humilitatis inclinati despectu iniuriarum non habeant actionem, ita similis videri debet iustitiae, quod adpetitae innocentiae moderatam deferri iussimus ultionem. Ideoque huiusmodi dumtaxat causas episcopi sub testificatione multorum actis audire debebunt. *Dat. III id. Dec. Rav. Honor. VIIII et Theod. V AA. conss.* |

(1) *Z* reads here *praefectum* (in full) but omits *praetorii* (also *A.A.* after the names of the emperors). The manuscripts of *CTh* 16.2.41 have the usual abbreviation *ppo*.

(2) Seeck suggested "commune cum saeculo."

(3) The reading "apud episcopos . . . oportet" is supplied from *CTh; Z* has "episcopis solum non ab alio oportet."

(4) "Delationem ingerat": so Mommsen for *Z, dilacerit.*

(5) The surprising variation *laudabilis* (some manuscripts have *inlaudabilis*) for *Sirm. miserandae* implies a different understanding of the sense. Perhaps the idea is that even when an accusation is in principle well founded ("estimable" rather than "deplorable"), the accuser must still ensure that it is properly supported by proof.

*CTh* omits the explanatory introduction on the offense of calumny and other comments on the special position of the clergy but is otherwise a close, although not continuous, version of *Sirm.* 15, with only minor or syntactical changes (on the reading *laudabilis* for *miserandae,* see n. 5). With the loss of manuscript support for the text of *Sirm.* 15, we are in the unusual position of completing it from *CTh*. There is no way of telling how close this brings us to the original text, but it is possible that only formal concluding material has been lost.

### CONSTITUTIONS EDITED UNDER MORE THAN ONE TITLE

#### *Sirm.* 10; *CTh* 16.2.44, *De Episcopis,* + 9.25.3, *De Raptu vel Matrimonio Sanctimonialium Virginum vel Viduarum*

Clerics are not to live with women not connected with them, under the guise of a "sisterly" relationship; this practice encourages scandal. Such relationships must cease, with the exception of daughters and (real) sisters, and wives already married to clergy before they were ordained. Further, anyone who abducts a dedicated virgin will have his property confiscated and suffer exile. Any person may lay an accusation freely and without fear of the penalties of *delatio;* for to lay such information is an act of pious humanity, not betrayal.

| | |
|---|---|
| [*Impp. Honor. et Theod. AA Palladio ppi*].(1) Religiosi sacerdotis fida suggestio exigit **probabilem saeculo disciplinam. Agit** enim bonis moribus, ne clerici sacris ministeriis servientes feminis iungantur | *Idem AA. Palladio ppo. Eum, qui* probabilem saeculo disciplinam agit, |
| externis, quas **decolore consortio sororiae appellationis** excusant. Credimus quidem hanc devotis mentibus dei inesse reverentiam, ut divorsorii huius habitaculum conscientia pravae persuasionis ignoret. Sed hac societate seu amicitia non penetret, (2) fama contaminat, datque sinistris moribus (3) locum alterni sexus adiunctio, cum foris positos ac publico | decolor*ari* consortio sororiae appellationis *non decet*.(4) |

iure viventes ad inlecebram criminis trahit obscaenae suspicionis exemplum. Quae cum ita sint, inlustris et praecelsa magnificentia tua praesentis oraculi sanctionem propositis ubique divulget edictis, ut noverint cuncti, qui **cuiuscumque gradus sacerdotio fulciuntur vel clericatus honore censentur, extranearum sibi mulierum interdicta consortia: hac sibi tantum facultate concessa, ut matres, filias adque germanas intra domorum suarum saepta contineant. In his enim nihil scaevi criminis aestimari foedus naturale permittit. Illas etiam non relinqui castitatis hortatur affectio, quae ante sacerdotium maritorum legitime meruere coniugium. Neque enim clericis inconpetenter adiunctae sunt, quae dignos sacerdotio viros sui conversatione fecerunt.**

*Quicumque igitur* cuiuscumque gradus sacerdotio fulciuntur vel clericatus honore censentur, extranearum sibi mulierum interdicta consortia *cognoscant,* (5) hac *eis* tantum facultate concessa, ut matres, filias adque germanas intra domorum suarum saepta contineant; in his enim nihil scaevi criminis aestimari foedus naturale permittit. Illas etiam non relinqui castitatis hortatur adfectio, quae ante sacerdotium maritorum legitim*um* meruere coniugium. Neque enim clericis incompetenter adiunctae sunt, quae dignos sacerdotio viros sui conversatione fecerunt. *Dat. VIII id. Mai. Rav. D.N. Theod. A. VIIII et Constantio III v.c. conss.*

Illam vero desiderii partem legum quoque praeeuntium scita solidarunt, ut **quisquis dedicatam deo virginem prodigus sui raptor ambierit, publicatis bonis deportatione plectatur, cunctis accusationis huius licentia absque metu delationis indulta. Neque exigi convenit proditorem, quem pro pudicitia religionis invitat humanitas.** *Data VIII id. Mai. Ravennae Domno N. Theodosio Aug. VIIII et Constantio III v.c. conss.*

*Impp. Honor. et Theod. AA. Palladio ppo.* Post alia: Si *quis dicatam* deo virginem prodigus sui raptor ambierit, publicatis bonis deportatione plectatur, cunctis accusationis huius licentia absque metu delationis indulta. Neque *enim* exigi convenit proditorem, quem pro pudicitia religionis invitat humanitas. *Dat. VIII id. Mart. Rav. Theod. A. VIIII et Constantio III v.c. conss.* (6)

(1) The opening protocol, which is not in *Z*, is supplied from *CTh*.
(2) *Non penetret* does not make clear sense; Mommsen suggests something like *non penitus qui abstinet*.
(3) *Moribus* can be understood in the context, but Seeck's suggestion *rumoribus*, reported by Mommsen, is elegant.
(4) The first sentence defining the scope of the law is boldly condensed, while retaining some phrases, from the proposition set out in the first two sentences of *Sirm*. Omitted at the very beginning of the excerpt is the reference to the suggestio of the bishop.
(5) Picking up *Sirm. ut noverint cuncti* in the omitted section.
(6) The law makes only trivial changes to the last two sentences of *Sirm*. Read in the concluding protocol *Mai.* for *Mart.*

*Sirm.* 10, like others, includes an explicit acknowledgment of the motive force behind the legislation. In this case it is the "fida suggestio" of a pious bishop, whose presentation of the situation in need of remedy perhaps lies behind the first few lines of the text, up to the phrase *quae cum ita sint* that introduces the address, in its now familiar form, to the praetorian prefect. He is again instructed to ensure that the law, here as elsewhere called an oraculum, is published (by provincial governors) in the form of edicts. With abbreviation and some slight changes, the edited laws in the Theodosian Code preserve closely the sense and wording of *Sirm.* 10, the points of substance being classified under different titles. The editorial expressions *post alia* and *et cetera* mean not that extraneous matter has been excluded (it would be unnecessary to point this out), but that another extract from the original text appears elsewhere in the Theodosian Code.[26] Consistent with this is the fact that neither annotation is found in any of the constitutions edited under one title only, but that in every constitution edited under more than one title, either or both annotations appear in at least one extract. In most cases *post alia* and *et cetera* reveal the order of the extracts in the original text, although there are a few instances where this is not so.[27]

### *Sirm.* 4; *CTh* 16.9.1, *Ne Christianum Mancipium Iudaeus Habeat,* + 6.8.5, *De Iudaeis, Caelicolis et Samaritanis*

The emperor repeats his earlier legislation prohibiting Jews from circumcising slaves of Christian or any other religious persuasion, on pain of liberty for the slave. Jews who convert to Christianity are to be free of harassment from other Jews.

26. Mommsen, Prolegomena, p. ccix.

27. So *CTh* 16.5.63–64 and 16.8.5 carry *et cetera* at what appears to be the end of the original texts, and 16.2.46 has *post alia* at what appears to be the beginning. It is, however, not clear from what original text 16.2.46 and 16.5.63 derive. In all other cases found here, *post alia* correctly indicates preceding, and *et cetera* indicates succeeding material in the original text, to be found elsewhere in the Theodosian Code.

*Imp. Constantinus ad Felicem praefectum praetorio.* Iam dudum quidem constitutionis nostrae saluberrima sanctio promulgata est, quam nostrae repetitae legis veneratione geminamus, ac volumus, ut, **si quispiam Iudaeorum Christianum mancipium vel cuiuslibet alterius sectae mercatus circumcidere** non perhorruerit, **circumcisis** quidem istius statuti mensura **libertatis** conpos effectus eiusdem **privilegiis potiatur;** non fas Iudaeo sit qui circumciderit mancipium generis memorati in obsequium **servitutis retinere.** Illud etenim hac eadem sanctione praecipimus, ut, **si quispiam Iudaeorum** reserans sibi ianuam vitae perpetuae sanctis se cultibus mancipaverit et **Christianus esse delegerit,** ne quid **a Iudaeis inquietudinis** vel molestiae patiatur. Quod si ex Iudaeo Christianum factum aliquis Iudaeorum **iniuria** putaverit esse **pulsandum,** volumus **istiusmodi contumeliae** machinatorem **pro** criminis **qualitate commissi poenis ultricibus subiugari,** Felix parens carissime. Quare divinitatis affectu confidimus ipsum in omni orbe Romano qui nostri debita veneratione servata: (1) ac volumus, ut excellens sublimitas tua litteris suis per dioecesim sibi creditam commeantibus iudices moneat instantissime huiuscemodi debitam reverentiam custodiri.

*Imp. Constantinus A. ad Felicem ppo.* Si *quis* Iudaeorum Christianum mancipium vel cuiuslibet alterius sectae mercatus circumcid*erit, minime* in servitute retineat *circumcisum, sed* libertatis privilegiis, *qui hoc sustinuerit,* potiatur. (2) Et cetera. *Dat. XII kal. Nov. Constantinp.; Pp. VIII id. Mai. Cartg. Nepotiano et Facundo conss.*

*Idem A. ad Felicem ppo.* Post alia: *Eum, qui ex Iudaeo Christianus factus est,*

inquiet*are* Iudaeos *non liceat*

*vel aliqua* puls*are* iniuria, pro qualitate commissi istiusmodi contumelia *punienda.* (3) Et cetera. *Dat. XI kal. Nov. Constanp., pp. VIII id. Mai. Nepotiano et Facundo conss.*

*Data XII kal. Novemb., proposita*
*VII id. Mart. Carthagine*
*Nepotiano et Facundo conss.*

(1) This sentence is lacking a dependent verb after *confidimus*. Mommsen suggested, for the sake of example, "ipsum in omni orbe Romano ⟨tutum fore⟩, nostri debita veneratione servata": the converted Jew will be safe, and respect for the emperor maintained.
(2) The last clauses are abbreviated but retain some expressions *libertatis, privilegiis potiatur*) from *Sirm.; circumcisis* becomes *qui hoc sustinuerit.*
(3) The text is an abbreviated version of *Sirm.* 4 but retains or adapts words and phrases—*ex Iudaeo Christianus factus, inquietudinis* (*inquietare*), *iniuria esse pulsandum* (*pulsare iniuria*), *pro (criminis) qualitate commissi,* and *contumelia.*

In this case, either the editorial methods are here are more flexible than those seen before, or else the editors worked from a version of the text already showing variations from that preserved as *Sirm.* 4.[28] The law is edited under two titles. Omitted from both versions are the opening reference to previous legislation, some moral reflections in the middle of the text, and the instructions to the praetorian prefect at the end to circulate the law to provincial governors. The reference to the punishment ("Quod si . . . subiugari") is heavily abbreviated. The first *CTh* text partly reproduces *Sirm.* 4 verbatim, then proceeds by summary of its contents, but preserving or adapting phrases from the original, with consequent changes to the grammatical structure. The second *CTh* text is an abbreviated version of the corresponding passage of *Sirm.* 4 but again preserves the sequence of thought and several expressions from the original.

There are discrepancies, and minor contradictions, in the protocols. *Sirm.* 4 and *CTh* 16.2.5 have the date of issue as XII Kal. Nov.; *CTh* 16.8.5 has XI Kal. Nov. All three texts agree on the consular year 336, but only the two *CTh* extracts have the place of issue, Constantinople. *Sirm.* 4 and *CTh* 16.9.1 note the place of publication of the law as Carthage, a detail missing from 16.8.5. By contrast, the *CTh* texts agree on the pp. dating as VIII id. Mai., against the VII id. Mart. of *Sirm.* 4; they were no doubt edited together from a version of the law that had this date. In either case, March or May 336 will be the date of acceptance, the law being issued in October 335. On the phrases *post alia* and *et cetera,* see the comments on *Sirm.* 10.

### *Sirm.* 12; *CTh* 16.5.43, *De Haereticis,* + 16.10.19, *De Paganis, Sacrificiis et Templis*

Despite the best efforts of clergy and emperors, human wickedness still risks the force of law and eternal judgment. It is necessary, therefore, to reiterate laws

28. For similar variations in two versions of a law of Constantine, see Chapter 9.

against Donatists, Manichees, and Priscillianists, pagans, and a new sect, the Caelicolae. The buildings of such groups are appropriated to churches, temple properties to the imperial *annona*. Statues are to be destroyed, temples put to public use. Altars and temples on imperial estates are to be sequestrated, their *domini* (proprietors or tenants) to be responsible for their destruction. The execution of the law is entrusted to three *agentes in rebus,* and cases are to be remitted to the proper legal authorities. Governors who neglect the law are to be fined twenty pounds of gold, as are their officia and negligent town councils. The praetorian prefect is to ensure the transmission of the law to provincial governors (the protocol records its publication at Carthage under the authority of the proconsul).

> *Impp. Honorius et Theodosius Augg. Curtio praefecto praetorii.* Profanos haereticorum spiritus superstitionemque gentilium vel sola quidem religiosorum virorum sacerdotum dei in observandis sollicitudo criminibus, sedulitas in monendo, auctoritas in docendo emendare debuerat. Nec nostrarum tamen legum scita cessarunt, quae in dei omnipotentis cultum poenae etiam terrore proposito reducerent deviantes, ignaros quoque in ministeria divina formarent. Sed nimirum ipsa vis mali humana pariter ac divina permiscens deceptos plerosque persuasionibus pravis tam in praesens quam in futurum inpellit exitium et deo simul ac nobis perdit infelicium vitas, quas et hic legibus dedit et illic cogit ferre iudicium. Conpulsi igitur

> Donatistarum pertinacia, furore gentilium, quae quidem mala desidia iudicum, coniventia officiorum, ordinum contemptus accendit, necessarium putamus iterare quae iussimus. Quapropter **omnia, quae in Donatistas, qui et Montenses vocantur, Manichaeos sive Priscillianistas vel in gentiles a nobis generalium legum auctoritate decreta sunt, non solum manere decernimus, verum in exsecutionem plenissimam effectumque deduci, ita ut aedificia quoque vel horum vel Caelicolarum etiam, qui nescio cuius dogmatis novi conventus habent, ecclesiis vindicentur. Poena vero lege proposita velut convictos tenere debebit eos,**

> *Idem AA. Curtio ppo.* Omnia, quae in Donatistas, qui et Montenses vocantur, Manichaeos sive Priscillianistas vel in gentiles a nobis generalium legum auctoritate decreta sunt, non solum manere decernimus, verum in exsecutionem plenissimam effectumque deduci, ita ut aedificia quoquevel horum vel Caelicolarum etiam, qui nescio cuius dogmatis novi conventus habent, ecclesiis vindicentur. Poena vero lege proposita velut convictos tenere debebit eos,

qui Donatistas se confessi fuerint vel catholicorum sacerdotum **scaevae religionis obtentu communionem refugerint, quamvis Christianos esse se simulent.**

Iam vero **templorum detrahantur annonae et rem annonariam iuvent expensis devotissimorum militum profuturae. Simulacra, si qua etiamnunc in templis fanisque consistunt et quae aliquem ritum vel acceperunt vel accipiunt paganorum, suis sedibus revellantur, cum hoc repetita sciamus saepius sanctione decretum. Aedificia ipsa templorum, quae in civitatibus vel oppidis vel extra oppida sunt, ad usum publicum vindicentur. Arae locis omnibus destruantur omniaque templa in possessionibus nostris ad usus adcommodos transferantur, domini destruere cogantur. Non liceat omnino in honorem sacrilegi ritus funestioribus locis** (1) **exercere convivia vel quicquam sollemnitatis agitare. Episcopis quoque locorum haec ipsa prohibendi ecclesiasticae manus tribuimus facultatem.** Nam et agentum in rebus executionem Maximi, Iuliani, Eutychi, ut ea, quae generalibus legibus contra Donatistas, Manichaeos adque huiuscemodi haereticos vel gentiles statuta sunt, impleantur, indulsimus. Qui

qui Donatistas se confessi fuerint vel catholicorum communionem refugerint scaevae religionis obtentu,(3) quamvis Christianos esse se simulent. Et cetera. *Dat. XVII kal. Dec. Rom. Basso et Filippo conss.*

*Imppp. Arcadius, Honorius et Theod. AAA. Curtio ppo.* Post alia: Templorum detrahantur annonae et rem annonariam iuvent expensis devotissimorum militum profuturae. Simulacra, si qua etiamnunc in templis fanisque consistunt et quae *alicubi* ritum vel acceperunt vel accipiunt paganorum, suis sedibus *e*vellantur, cum hoc repetita sciamus saepius sanctione decretum. Aedificia ipsa templorum, quae in civitatibus vel oppidis vel extra oppida sunt, ad usum publicum vindicentur. Arae locis omnibus destruantur omniaque templa in possessionibus nostris ad usus adcommodos transferantur; domini destruere cogantur. Non liceat omnino in honorem sacrilegi ritus funestioribus locis exercere convivia vel quicquam sollemnitatis agitare. Episcopis quoque locorum haec ipsa prohibendi ecclesiasticae manus tribuimus facultatem;

tamen scient in omnibus modum statutorum esse servandum, ut ea, quae contra vetitum videntur esse commissa, mox **iudicibus** iuxta vim legum deferant vindicanda. Quos quidem **viginti librarum auri poena** statutae dudum multae **constringet, pari** multa **officiis** ordinibusque proposita, si **haec** quae statuimus **eorum fuerint dissimulatione neglecta,** Curti parens carissime adque amantissime. Quod ad continendos hominum mores religionemque provisum et ad rectores provinciarum sublimis magnificentia tua faciet pervenire et digno per omnes iubebit vigore servari. *Data VII kal. Decemb. Romae, proposita Carthagine in foro sub programmate Porfirii proconsulis nonis Iuniis Basso et Filippo vv. cc. conss.*(2)

*iudices autem* viginti librarum auri poena constring*imus et* pari *forma* offic*ia eorum,* si haec eorum fuerint dissimulatione neglecta. *Dat. XVII kal. Dec. Romae Basso et Philippo conss.*

(1) The text here, deficient in *Z,* is restored from *CTh.*

(2) The proconsul was C. Aelius Pompeius Porphyrius Proculus (407–8); *PLRE* II, pp. 900–901 (Porphyrius 3). The form *Porfirius* (cf. *Filippo*), as given by *Z* and a manuscript copied from it, is a characteristic late Roman spelling.

(3) This is the manuscript order of *CTh;* Mommsen reports a different order in his marginal notes to *Sirm.* 12.

The wording of the two laws is extremely close to *Sirm.* 12 in omitting as usual the introductory section, the reference to the enforcement of the law by agentes in rebus, and the concluding instructions to the praetorian prefect to send it to provincial governors; the omission of the reference to city councils (the word *ordinibusque* at the end of *CTh* 16.10.19) is also a matter of substance. Otherwise, variations in wording and in word order are unimportant. There are, however, divergencies in the protocols of the texts.

In its particularly informative protocol, *Sirm.* 12 gives the date of posting at Carthage as 5 June in the consulships of Bassus and Philippus, that is 408. In this case the law was issued at Rome on 25 November 407 (VII kal. Dec.). The *CTh* texts give the date of issue as 15 November (XVII kal. Dec.) with the consuls of

408, but this is inconsistent with the place of issue and with the praetorian prefecture of Curtius. Honorius was at Rome in late 407 but not in 408, and by November 408 Curtius had been replaced, first by Longinianus, who was assassinated on 13 August, then by Theodorus. The more detailed protocol of *Sirm.* 12 is accurate; the law was issued in 407 and received in Africa more than six months later. The *CTh* versions have combined the day and month of issue with the year of acceptance, the day and month of acceptance having dropped from the protocol.[29] A trace of the correct year is however, found in the opening protocol of 16.10.19. Arcadius died on 1 May 408; his name is therefore recorded on a law issued in November 407. News of his death had reached the proconsul of Africa by 5 June, in time for his name to be omitted from the protocol of *Sirm.* 12. The incorrect date of issue of 16.5.43 was already present in the copy used by the editors of the Code, for it appears after a law of 14 November 408 giving the Augusti as Honorius and Theodosius; hence "Idem AA." (not "AAA.") in the protocol. A law of 15 November 407 (16.5.41), also addressed to Porphyrius, covers similar ground to *Sirm.* 12 (it is an amnesty to converts from heresy) and clearly forms part of the same bout of legislation, without quite establishing 15 rather than 25 November as the correct date of the laws discussed here. In this case the annotation *et cetera* of *CTh* 16.5.43 leads directly to *post alia* at the beginning of 16.10.19.

*Sirm.* 14; *CTh* 16.2.31, *De Episcopis,* and 16.5.46, *De Haereticis*

Bishops in Africa have been dragged from their homes and even from their churches, and have been subjected to torture and disfigurement, and to public humiliation—obviously with the connivance of the secular authorities, since the crimes were committed openly and were clearly known about. The victims have not brought complaints, believing that the judges would not hear them. Governors are to prosecute such crimes and punish them by condemnation to the mines or deportation and by confiscation of their property. The praetorian prefect is to effect the prohibition of such acts by publishing an edict, and order their perpetrators to be rounded up and punished. Where there is lack of cooperation from local authorities and landowners, or massed opposition, or where the terrain is inaccessible, armed assistance may be sought from the comes Africae. Donatists, Jews and pagans are reminded of the laws against them. Fines of 20lbs of gold are imposed on officia that fail to prosecute the law, with punishment of their first three members in rank, and members of provincial councils who fail to cooperate are punished by exile and confiscation of property.

> *Impp. Honorius et Theodosius Theodoro viro inl. praefecto praetorii.* Dubium non est coniventia iudicum fieri et culpabili dissimulatione inultum relinqui, quod ad turbandam quietem publicam in contemptum Christianae religionis, quam

29. R. Delmaire, "Etude sur les souscriptions," p. 324.

debito cultu veneramur, sub publica testificatione conmissum addiscimus et pariter non punitum. Vicina peccato in iudice dissimulatio est, quem ignoratio commissi criminis non defendit. Per provinciam Africam tantum quorundam temeritati licuisse conperimus, ut Christianae legis antistites de propriis domibus raptos vel, quod est atrocius, de ecclesiae catholicae penetralibus protractos cruciatibus diversis afficerent, alios vero ad solam divini cultus iniuriam avulsa capillorum parte foedatos vel alio iniuriae genere deformatos concurrentium speculis exhiberent, ut esset circa eos venia gravior, quorum saluti contemptus ignoverat. Tanti sceleris nefas et immane flagitium numquam ante conpertum Africanorum iudiciorum auctoritas nec creditae sibi potestatis iure persequitur nec debita cura referendi in nostram fecit notitiam pervenire. Ignorari ab his potuisse non credimus, quod commissum in civitatibus publice memoratur, quod iugis et magistratuum et ordinum cura, stationarii apparitoris sollicitudo, quae ministra est nuntiorum atque indicium, absentiae exhibet potestatum. licet enim insinuare levia, graviora reticere? non tacuissent, quod propriis innotescere rectoribus per alterum formidarent, nisi intellegerent nolle iudicem vindicare. Expectandum fuit institutis accusationibus contra professionis propriae sanctitatem, ut episcopi suas persequerentur iniurias et reorum nece deposcerent ultionem, quos invitos decet vindicari? Deducitur in hanc necessitatem veniae persuasor alienae, praeceptor indulgentiae, ut de se aut ipse tractasse videatur, quod et petenti alius non negaret, aut praeceptis obsecuturus sacerdotii criminosorum vi impunite subiaceat. Episcopos et alios ecclesiae catholicae ministros nisi aut vigor potestatum aut fides iudicum laudabili auctoritate tueatur, erunt addicti audaciae pessimorum. Quapropter iubemus, ut eos, qui talia commisisse dicuntur, diversorum per Africam iudicum sine innocentum laesione requirat auctoritas, ac proprio exhibitos examini, si convinci manifesta probatione cognoverit, cuiuslibet dignitatis et honoris reos probatos aut metallo tradat aut poenam deportationis subire conpellat, facultatibus eorum fisco nostro sociatis, ut habeant vitam sibi clementiae nostrae more concessam, quae similibus non donabitur tempore futuro criminibus. Si quidem praesentis legis aeternitate cunctis observanda constituimus, Theodore parens carissime adque amantissime, quod inl.

magnificentiae tuae praelatum litteris, proponendum edictis, in omnium volumus notitiam pervenire: ut, **si quisquam in hoc genus sacrilegii proruperit, ut in ecclesias catholicas inruens sacerdotibus et ministris vel ipsi cultui locoque aliquid inportet iniuriae, quod geretur, litteris ordinum, magistratuum et curatoris et notoriis** (1) **apparitorum, quos stationarios**

*Idem AA. Theodoro ppo.* Si *quis* in hoc genus sacrilegii proruperit, ut in ecclesias catholicas inruens sacerdotibus et ministris vel ipsi cultui locoque aliquid inportet iniuriae, quod ger*itur,* litteris ordinum, magistratuum et curator*um* et notoriis apparitorum, quos stationarios

**appellant, deferatur in notitiam potestatum, ita ut vocabula eorum, qui agnosci potuerint, declarentur. Et si per multitudinem commissum dicitur, si non omnes, possunt tamen aliquanti cognosci, quorum confessione sociorum nomina publicentur. Adque ita provinciae moderator, sacerdotum et catholicae ecclesiae ministrorum, loci quoque ipsius et divini cultus iniuriam capitali in convictos vel confessos reos sententia noverit vindicandam nec expectet, ut episcopus iniuriae propriae ultionem deposcat, cui** sacerdotii **sanctitas ignoscendi solam gloriam derelinquit. Sitque cunctis non solum liberum, sed** etiam **laudabile, factas sacerdotibus vel ministris atroces iniurias velut publicum crimen persequi ac de talibus reis ultionem mereri,** ut hac saltem ratione, quod agi adversum se per episcopum non posse confidit, at aliorum accusationibus malorum audacia pertimescat. Et **si multitudo violenta civilis apparitionis exsecutione et adminiculo ordinum possessorumve non potuerit praesentari, quod se armis aut locorum difficultate tueantur, iudices Africani armatae apparitionis praesidium, datis ad virum spectabilem comitem Africae litteris praelato legis istius tenore** deposcent, ut rei talium criminum non evadant.

appellant, deferatur in notitiam potestatum, ita ut vocabula eorum, qui agnosci potuerint, declarentur. Et si per multitudinem commissum dicitur, si non omnes, possunt tamen aliquanti cognosci, quorum confessione sociorum nomina publicentur. Adque ita provinciae moderator, sacerdotum et catholicae ecclesiae ministrorum, loci quoque ipsius et divini cultus iniuriam capitali in convictos *sive* confessos reos sententia noverit vindicandam nec expectet, ut episcopus iniuriae propriae ultionem deposcat, cui sanctitas ignoscendi solam gloriam derelinquit. Sitque cunctis non solum liberum, sed *et* laudabile, factas atroces sacerdotibus aut ministris iniurias veluti publicum crimen persequi ac de talibus reis ultionem mereri.

*Quod* si multitudo violenta civilis apparitionis executione et adminiculo ordinum possessorumve non potuerit praesentari, quod se armis aut locorum difficultate tueatur, iudices Africani armatae apparitionis praesidium, datis ad virum spectabilem com. Afric. litteris, praelato legis istius tenore depos*cant*, ut rei talium criminum non evadant. *Dat. VII kal. Mai. Med. Honorio A. IIII et Eutychiano conss.*

**Et ne Donatistae vel ceterorum vanitas haereticorum aliorumque eorum, quibus catholicae communionis cultus non potest persuaderi, Iudaei adque gentiles, quos vulgo paganos appellant, arbitrentur legum ante adversum se datarum constituta tepuisse, noverint iudices universi praeceptis earum fideli devotione parendum et inter praecipua curarum, quidquid adversus eos decrevimus, exequendum. Si quisquam iudicum peccato coniventiae,** dissimulandi arte, **executionem praesentis legis omiserit, noverit amissa dignitate graviorem motum se nostrae clementiae subiturum, officium quoque suum, quod saluti propriae contempta suggestione defuerit, punitis tribus primatibus condemnationi viginti librarum auri subeundum. Ordinis quoque viri, si in propriis civitatibus vel territoriis commissum tale aliquid siluerint gratia obnoxiorum, deportationis poenam et propriarum amissionem facultatum se noverint subituros.** *Data XVIII kal. Februar. DD. NN. Honorio VIIII et Theodosio V Aug. conss. Ravenna.*

*Idem AA. Theodoro ppo II.* Post alia: Ne Donatistae vel ceterorum vanitas haereticorum aliorumque eorum, (2) quibus catholicae communionis cultus non potest persuaderi, Iudaei adque gentiles, quos vulgo paganos appellant, arbitrentur legum ante adversum se datarum constituta tepuisse, noverint iudices universi praeceptis earum fideli devotione parendum et inter praecipua curarum quidquid adversus eos decrevimus *non ambigant* exsequendum. *Quod* si quisquam iudicum peccato coniventiae exsecutionem praesentis legis omiserit, noverit amissa dignitate graviorem motum se nostrae clementiae subiturum, officium quoque suum, quod saluti propriae contempta suggestione (3) defuerit, punitis tribus primatibus condemnat*ione* (4) viginti librarum auri *plectendum*. Ordinis quoque viri si in propriis civitatibus vel territoriis commissum tale aliquid siluerint *in gratiam noxiorum,* deportationis poenam et propriarum amissionem facultatum se noverint subituros. *Dat. XVIII kal. Feb. Rav. Honor. VIII et Theod. III AA. conss.*

(1) *Z* reads *notariis.*
(2) In his marginal notes on *Sirm.* 14, Mommsen notes *CTh* (*VE*) as reading here *error* for *eorum* but (correctly) prints *eorum* in his text of the law.
(3) Mommsen here prints *suggestioni,* but in the apparatus reports both *Z* and *CTh* as reading *suggestione,* which is preferable.

(4) The change of *Sirm. subeundum* to *CTh plectendum* entails the echange from *condemnationi* to *condemnatione.*

The extracts in *CTh* succinctly draw out the general issues from the evidently specific circumstances of *Sirm.* 14 (of which nothing is known, although comparable situations are not hard to find); these are described at length in the first sentences of *Sirm.,* omitted from the edited texts. Also omitted are the emperor's announcement that he had "discovered" certain things ("comperimus"); what may be an indirect reference, in the word *memoratur,* to a *commonitorium* or memorandum through which he had discovered them; and the emperor's extensive reflections on the situation. The editors have also passed over the section on Donatists, Jews, and pagans, the now familiar address to the praetorian prefect and the specification of penalties. All this comes in the first half of the *Sirm.* text.

As to what is included, the editors have retained the original wording, with only minor changes. There are, however, quite extensive discrepancies in the protocols. *Sirm.* 14 has the consuls of 412, but the law must be of 409 (Honorius VIII and Theodosius III for Honorius VIIII and Theodosius V), because of the known tenure of office of Theodorus. *CTh* 16.5.46 has the right year and correctly names Theodorus as praetorian prefect for the second time; 16.2.31, apparently by confusion with the entire protocols of a law addressed to Theodorus in his first praetorian prefecture, has the consuls of 398, the date of issue as 25 April and the place as Milan.[30]

*Sirm.* 6; *CTh* 16.2.47, *De Episcopis,* + 16.5.62 and 64, *De Haereticis*

Churches and the clergy are to recover privileges taken away by the usurper [Johannes, 423–25], especially the benefit of clergy to the jurisdiction of bishops, for it is not right that those who perform divine service should be subjected to the will of secular powers. In Gaul, followers of Pelagius and Caelestius are to be summoned by bishop Patroclus of Arles and given twenty days to recant and rejoin the Catholic Church or face expulsion from Gaul. Manichees and all heretics and schismatics hostile to the Catholic Church are to be expelled from their cities; Jews and pagans are denied access to courts of law, and the right to serve in the imperial *militia,* and may not own Christian slaves, for fear that they may use their power over them to force them to change their religion.

| | |
|---|---|
| *Impp. Theodosius A. et Valentinianus Caesar Amatio v.i. praef. prtr. Gall.*(1) **Privilegia ecclesiarum** vel clericorum | (*CTh* 16.2.47) *Idem A. et Caes. Basso crp.* Privilegia ecclesiarum omnium, quae saeculo |

30. Cf. *CTh* 14.3.20 with Mommsen's note.

**omnium, quae saeculo nostro tyrannus inviderat, prona devotione revocamus. Scilicet ut quidquid a divis principibus** (2) **singuli quique antistites inpetrarunt, iugi solidata aeternitate serventur** nec cuiusquam audeat titillare praesumptio, in quo nobis magis praestitum confitemur. **Clericos etiam, quos indiscretim ad saeculares iudices debere deduci infaustus praesumptor edixerat, episcopali audientiae reservamus,** his manentibus, quae circa eos sanxit antiquitas. **Fas enim non est, ut divini muneris ministri temporalium potestatum subdantur arbitrio.** Inl. itaque auctoritas tua omni aevo mansura quae iussimus in provinciarum missa notitiam praecipiet etiam sub poena sacrilegii custodiri, specialiter id inlustribus conprehensura praeceptis, ut in omnibus circa ecclesiastica privilegia veterum principum statuta serventur. Diversos vero episcopos nefarium Pelagiani et Caelestiani dogmatis errorem sequentes per Patroclum sacrosanctae legis antistitem praecipimus conveniri: quos quia confidimus emendari, nisi *intra viginti dies ex conventionis tempore, intra quos deliberandi tribuimus facultatem, errata correxerint seseque catholicae fidei reddiderint, Gallicanis regionibus expelli adque in eorum loco sacerdotium fidelius subrogari, quatenus praesentis erroris macula de populorum*

nostro tyrannus inviderat, prona devotione revocamus, scilicet ut quidquid a divis principibus *constitutum est vel quae* singuli quique antistites *pro causis ecclesiasticis* (4) inpetrarunt, *sub poena sacrilegii* iugi solidata aeternitate serventur.

Clericos etiam, quos indiscretim ad saeculares iudices debere deduci infaustus praesumptor edixerat, episcopali audientiae reservamus.

Fas enim non est, ut divini muneris ministri temporalium potestatum subdantur arbitrio. Et cetera. *Dat. VIII id. Octob. Aquil. D.N. Theod. A. XI et Valano C. conss.*

[Cf. *CTh* 16.5.62 below]

animis tergeatur et futurae bonum disciplinae iustioris instituatur. Sane quia religiosos populos nullis decet superstitionibus depravari, **Manichaeos** omnesque **haereticos vel schismaticos sive mathematicos** (3) **omnemque sectam catholicis inimicam ab ipso aspectu urbium diversarum exterminari** debere **praecipimus, ut nec praesentiae** quidem **criminosorum contagione foedentur.** Iudaeis quoque vel paganis causas agendi vel militandi licentiam denegamus; quibus Christianae legis nolumus servire personas, ne occasione dominii sectam venerandae religionis inmutent. **Omnes igitur personas erroris infausti iubemus excludi, nisi his emendatio matura subvenerit.** *Data VII idus Iulias Aquileiae D.N. Theodosio A. XI et Valentiniano conss.*

(*CTh* 16.5.64) *Idem A. et Caes. Basso c.r.p.* Post alia: Manichaeos haereticos sive schismaticos omnemque sectam catholicis inimicam ab ipso aspectu urbium diversarum exterminari praecipimus, ut nec praesentiae criminosorum contagione foedentur.

Omnes igitur personas erroris infausti iubemus excludi, nisi his emendatio matura subvenerit. Et cetera. *Dat VIII id. Aug. Aquil. D.N. Theod. A. XI et Valentiniano Caes. conss.*

(*CTh* 16.5.62) *Imp. Theod. A. et Valanus Caes. ad Faustum pu.* Manichaeos haereticos schismaticos sive mathematicos omnemque sectam catholicis inimicam ab ipso aspectu *urbis Romae* (5) exterminari praecipimus, ut nec praesentiae criminosorum contagione foedetur. *Circa hos autem maxime exercenda commonitio est, qui pravis suasionibus a venerabilis papae sese communione suspendunt, quorum schismate plebs etiam reliqua vitiatur.*(6) *His conventione praemissa viginti dierum condonavimus indutias, intra quos nisi ad communionis redierint unitatem, expulsi usque ad centesimum lapidem solitudine quam eligunt macerentur. Dat. XVI kal. Aug. Aquil. Theod. A. XI et Valano Caes. conss.*

(1) O here reads (in error) *Augusti* (the law precedes Valentinian's promotion as Augustus), and (correctly) expands *v.i.* to *viro illustri.*
(2) From the text of *CTh* 16.2.47, O here adds *constitutum est vel quae* (on the significance of the phrase see n. 4), but not the phrase *pro causis ecclesiasticis.*
(3) The word *mathematicos* is omitted in *CTh* 16.5.64 but included in 16.5.62.
(4) These unobtrusive phrases add a reference to general laws to the specific grants mentioned by *Sirm.*
(5) *Sirm.,* referring to Gaul, has *urbium diversarum.* The present law is specific to Rome. So too *foedetur* (that is *urbs Roma*) for *Sirm. foedentur* (*urbes diversae*) at the end of the sentence.
(6) This too applies to Rome, but it retains the allusion present in *Sirm.* (here italicized) to the threat to congregations. Also retained is the twenty-day period of reflection allowed by *Sirm.*

This is by far the most complicated of the cases discussed here. The three laws in *CTh* derive closely, with the omissions and other changes noted, from a text corresponding to *Sirm.,* but not from this version, which is addressed to the praetorian prefect of Gaul and refers to his jurisdiction. Of the edited versions, *CTh* 16.5.62, to the prefect of Rome,[31] refers in new language (italicized) to Rome and the papacy, and replaces exile from "diverse cities" to exile beyond the hundredth milestone. It clearly derives from a different original than *Sirm.* 6.

The other two texts, *CTh* 16.2.47 and 16.5.64, are addressed to the *comes rei privatae.* The first adds a short but significant phrase extending the reference of *Sirm.* to rescripts to cover also general legislation; it is possible that these words occurred in other versions of *Sirm.* 6. The second text keeps closely to the last section of *Sirm.* 6 but omits the clause excluding Jews and pagans from the militia, as not falling within the competence of the comes rei privatae. Except for the omission of the phrase *sive mathematicos,* its first sentence matches that of 16.2.62 but differs from it in referring, like *Sirm.* 6, to exile from "diverse cities." This excerpt, and no doubt 16.2.47, also addressed to the comes rei privatae, therefore descends from a version addressed to a praetorian prefect, presumably of Italy.

31. (Anicius Acilius Glabrio) Faustus is the later praetorian prefect whose role in transmitting the Theodosian Code to the west was described in Chapters 1 and 3.

Despite the fact that all four texts—even the two addressed to the comes rei privatae—carry different dates of issue, it is not clear that efforts should be made to harmonize them. Since both laws to Bassus are dated "VIII id.," it would however be a relatively small matter to reconcile these two copies by reading either "Aug." or "Octob." in the protocols of both laws.

Two other laws, without being textually identical to these, are part of the same phase of legislation. They are *CTh* 16.2.46 and 16.5.63, edited under the same titles as the laws to Bassus and the urban prefect Faustus:

> *Impp. Theod. A. et Valentinianus Caes. Georgio proc. Afric.* Post alia: Privilegia praeteritarum legum ecclesiae sive clericis delata serventur. Et cetera. *Dat. prid. Non. Iul. Aquil. D.N. Theod. A. XI et Valano Caes. conss.*

This law gives the essence of the first two sentences of *Sirm.* 6 in the manner extended by *CTh* 16.2.47 from rescripts to general legislation, but it was issued on yet another date from the other laws in the sequence and may not derive from the same text. It is probably connected with the following law as part of a separate communication to the proconsul. This text covers the same ground as the other laws discussed here but shows no textual relationship with them, except for the first sentence, which resembles the sentence (in bold) near the end of *Sirm.* 6:

> *Idem A. et Caes. Georgio proc. Afric.* Omnes haereses omnesque perfidias, omnia schismata superstitionesque gentilium, omnes catholicae legi (1) inimicos insectamur errores. Si quos vero . . . (2), haec quoque clementiae nostrae statuta poena comitetur et noverint sacrilegae superstitionis auctores participes conscios proscribtione plectendos, ut ab errore perfidiae, si ratione retrahi nequeunt, saltem terrore revocentur et universo supplicationum aditu in perpetuum denegato criminibus debita severitate plectantur. Et cetera. *Dat. prid. non. Aug. Aquil. D.N. Theod. A. XI et Valano Caes. conss.*

(1) *legi:* Mommsen, for the manuscripts' *legis.*
(2) The manuscripts have a lacuna of unknown length, presumably a few words only, at this point.

The protocols of the two laws to the proconsul Georgius are identical in all respects except for the difference of dating as between "prid. non. Iul." and "prid. non. Aug." There must in this case be an argument for accepting one date or the other for both laws; to adopt the later date would keep the law from being the earliest in the entire sequence presented here.

As the manuscript evidence stands, these six related laws bear six different dates. Some discrepancies, like that just discussed, may be eliminated by emendation, but some remain, and the explanation may be that the laws were actually issued at different times. We have seen reason to suppose that in addition to *Sirm.* 6 to the praetorian prefect of Gaul and *CTh* 16.5.62, part of an analogous text addressed to the prefect of Rome, the two laws addressed to the comes rei privatae, *CTh* 16.2.47 and 16.5.64, must derive ultimately from a law addressed to the praetorian prefect of Italy. It was this official who would also communicate with the proconsul of Africa, as in the last two laws discussed. If the procedure was for the emperor to write to each of his praetorian prefects and to the prefect of Rome, adapting his communication to suit the offices of the recipients, and to instruct the prefects to convey the law to other officials involved in its enforcement, one can appreciate how the texts may have issued from the imperial scrinia to the prefects, and from the prefects to their subordinates, at different times.[32]

Comparison of the Sirmondian Constitutions with the edited versions of the texts as they appear in the Theodosian Code reveals features of the original versions that were normally omitted by the editors. These relate partly to the content and expression of the laws and partly to formal aspects of the legislation and to the manner in which it was circulated to provincial governors and made known to the public. The majority of the Sirmondian texts contain all, or nearly all, of these features. Since they also occur in other unabbreviated texts surviving independently of the Theodosian Code, it may be useful to give an account of them, including in the survey those of the Sirmondian Constitutions which are not found in the Theodosian Code, as well as those which are. Readers familiar with the procedures of Roman government will find little that is new or surprising in what follows. The main purpose is to indicate the sort of material in the original texts that was likely to be omitted by the editors of the Theodosian Code.

In almost all the texts the emperors give some account, whether directly or indirectly, of their reasons for making the legislation.[33] They were often acting in response to information, suggestions, or petitions they had received, or to questions that had been put to them for clarification. So Constantine's law to his praetorian prefect Ablabius on episcopal jurisdiction is presented as a reply to an inquiry from Ablabius on the emperor's intentions in the matter (*Sirm.* 1). Constantine's profession of surprise that he should be asked such a question by a supporter of known Christian piety, when the emperor had (in his own opinion) made the matter perfectly clear in his earlier legislation, is somewhat contrived. As the reply to Ablabius indicated, his office as praetorian prefect gave him authority over the secular courts.[34] The matter affected his jurisdiction, and if he had doubts about Constantine's intentions—and their radical character has also surprised

32. See also J. D. Harries, "'Sacra Generalitas': The Administrative Background to the Theodosian Code," in *Estudios de Historia da Derecho Europeo* (1994), pp. 40–41.

33. For the texts relating to this and the following points discussed in this section, see the appendix to this chapter.

34. In the emperor's words, "apud vos, *qui iudiciorum summa tenetis,* et apud ceteros omnes iudices ad exsecutionem volumus pertinere."

modern observers—then he was quite justified in raising them. Another, much later text (*Sirm.* 11), on the immunity of the church from taxation, was written in response to the "suggestio religiosa" of a praetorian prefect. It flattered the prefect in portraying him as having reminded the emperor of the clemency that served the interests of devout Christian service by maintaining the privileges laid down of old and rather elegantly associated the prefect's with the emperor's own piety in executing the intentions of the law. As in the case of Ablabius, the question, on a matter of taxation, concerned the praetorian prefect in his official capacity.

Three cases respond to approaches made to the emperor by the clergy (a disproportion that reflects the character of the Sirmondian Constitutions themselves). In *Sirm.* 2, on a question of church discipline (members of the clergy living with women under the guise of "sisterhood"), the emperor explains that he had learned of the matter at the prompting of bishops; as we saw in discussion of this text, what follows the words *suggerentibus episcopis* can be read as a summary of their petition, prompting and justifying the emperor's response in the legislation that follows. In *Sirm.* 3, protesting that bishops have been submitted by certain of their colleagues to the rigors of secular jurisdiction, the emperor directly attributes his knowledge of the situation to a petition of bishops, read out in the consistory. *Sirm.* 10 credits its inspiration to the "fida suggestio" of a single bishop, whose description of the situation needing remedy may again lie behind the words of the first part of the text.

In two cases, the emperor refers to information gained in other ways. He knows and has been petitioned "by frequent approaches"—which are no doubt the source of his knowledge—about the wrongful imprisonment of innocent men of low social rank whose cases never come to the courts (*Sirm.* 13). On another occasion he refers to his "discovery" (*comperimus*) of maltreatment of members of the clergy in Africa (*Sirm.* 14). Especially worthy of attention in this text are the emperor's allegations that the abuses have been perpetrated through the negligence or indifference of the governors, courts, city councils, and other agencies whose duty it was to prevent them. The use of the word *memoratur* to refer to the events discovered alludes, no doubt, to the emperor's receipt of a *commonitorium* from some informant in which they were set out.

These texts, in which the emperor refers to information in his possession without saying precisely how he acquired it, lead to a further category in which he attempts to convey the impression of having acted of his own volition. The two constitutions on Easter amnesties offer a variety of justifications, from the inspiration of almighty God (*Sirm.* 7) to the emperor's known humanity and to well-established precedent, which makes an amnesty at this time of year as good as mandatory (*Sirm.* 8). In other laws he appeals to the need to maintain previous legislation, to the opinions of jurists, and to equity (*Sirm.* 4, 15). *Sirm.* 16, composed after the repulse of a barbarian invasion, arises, the emperor would have us believe, from the cares of war and an understanding of the need for beneficial legislation. In *Sirm.* 12, the emperor assigns his action to compulsion by the Donatists and pagans, whose persistent intransigence in ignoring the sanctions of both imperial legislation and the judgment of God has left him no alternative but to repeat his previous orders.[35] The last of the constitutions in this category, *Sirm.* 6, sets matters right in Gaul (and, in the related texts in the Theodosian Code, in Rome and Italy) after a time of civil war.

It is not, of course, that in the latter situations the emperors really had received no information and had been subjected to no pressure before proposing legislation—only that there is no mention of it in the text of their laws. There is an important point in this. To readers, and especially to later readers of the texts, it might seem to make a difference whether the emperors' legislation arose from their own inspiration or from situations that happened to have come to their notice through petitions or in some other way. It was with this in mind that the definition of general laws offered in the constitution to the Roman Senate of 426 made it clear that generalitas was inherent in the way in which the legislation was expressed, and not in the circumstances that may have given rise to its expression. It might be spontaneous, or it might arise from some particular circumstance requiring attention: "sive eas spontaneus motus ingesserit sive precatio vel lis mota legis occasionem postulaverit." This last category of texts from the Sirmondian Constitutions might exemplify those in which the emperor's own inspiration—his "spontaneus motus"—gave rise to a law. The other cases, however, in which the emperor responded to circumstances, whether to suggestio of prefect or bishop, to petition read out in the consistory, to commonitorium, or to request for a ruling sent to the emperor by the praetorian prefect, were equally "general laws," because the responses were addressed to public officials with the instructions to ensure that they were published.

Having given some account of his reasons for resorting to legislation, the emperor proceeds, through an explanatory conjunction or phrase (*igitur, itaque, quapropter*), to the substance of the enactment. From the cases just surveyed, one can see that this was often the cue for the editors of the Theodosian Code to pick up the text of the law. The point of substance is usually characterized by the use of a strong verb, frequently *sancimus*—though other, less highly characterized words are used, and the emperor sometimes merely uses verbs in the indicative or imperative mood, describing the behavior that is expected or required. At or near the end of the text will be set out any penalty that is applicable, and it is often at this point that the emperor, with the usual abstractions ("our Clemency to your Magnificence"), addresses the recipient directly with the intimate form of address used for

35. "Tam in praesens quam in futurum inpellit exitium et deo simul ac nobis perdit infelicium vitas, quas et hic legibus dedit et illic ferre iudicium."

men of senatorial rank, "most dear and devoted to us." He then instructs him to ensure that the law be made known to all whom it concerns through letters sent by the prefect to provincial governors under his jurisdiction, which will then be displayed by them under their own gubernatorial edicts. The text of one constitution, *Sirm.* 12, preserves both this instruction and the annotation by the proconsul of Africa that it had been carried out.[36] Sometimes, the prefect may in writing to governors add some special emphasis; in *Sirm.* 6, he is told to make clear to governors, in addition to the specific provisions of the text, the stipulation that the privileges extended to the clergy in legislation of previous emperors should be observed in their entirety. This point would not necessarily find its way into a governor's edict, though he might choose to include it; it was a reminder to him that the laws existed and were to be enforced.

This aspect of the procedures for the promulgation of imperial legislation, whereby laws were addressed to high officials with the instructions to forward them for publication to the governors under their jurisdiction, has emerged repeatedly in the examples discussed here and has relevance to the situation with which the editors of the Theodosian Code were faced.[37] A consequence of the procedures is that laws existed in many versions, as published in different places, and that it might be the copies sent out to officials of lesser standing, rather than the original versions sent to the prefects, that were available for recovery by the editors. *Sirm.* 12, just mentioned, is a case in point: the law was addressed to the praetorian prefect but, as its protocol shows, derives in this version from the copy promulgated by the edict of the proconsul of Africa. The two excerpts in the Theodosian Code preserve only the place of issue, Ravenna, but through errors and variations in their protocols betray the traces of a date of acceptance or publication that had already slipped from the text when the editors came to it. Despite first appearances, therefore, these two texts derive from a provincial version of the law, which may or may not be that posted at Carthage, as represented by *Sirm.* 12. In the case of *Sirm.* 4, a law of Constantine of 336, the place where the law was received is again given as Carthage, a detail preserved by one but not the other of the two excerpts in the Theodosian Code. Both excerpts, however, give the place of issue of the law as Constantinople, a detail absent from the transmitted text of *Sirm.* 4. If this is not simply a question of losses in the later transmission of the text, then the two excerpts in the Theodosian Code must derive from a more complete copy of the law than is represented in the Sirmondian Constitutions—one also made in Africa but preserving the place of issue as well as that of publication in the province.

36. It is worth noting that the constitution, transformed into proconsul's edict, still bears the name of the prefect to whom it was originally addressed, and not that of the proconsul.

37. It occurs in texts edited there—cf. *CTh* 8.5.13, 22, etc.

The most complex case is *Sirm.* 6. This is a copy of a law in the version sent to the praetorian prefect of Gaul and contains elements relevant only to his jurisdiction. None of the three certain extracts in the Theodosian Code derives from this copy. One is taken from the version addressed to the prefect of Rome, refers specifically to his jurisdiction, and is recast in other ways also. The other two extracts are from the version addressed to the comes rei privatae. They share linguistic and other features with the version addressed to the prefect of Rome but omit a point of substance (the employment of pagans and Jews in the imperial service) which is not relevant to the jurisdiction of this official. Whether the emperor addressed the *comes* directly, or whether the praetorian prefect—in this case, of Italy—sent on the relevant parts of a law addressed to him is not clear,[38] but in either case a law addressed to a comes rei privatae will have a different ancestry from one addressed to a prefect of Rome. The presence of a law to this official also implies the existence of versions addressed to others which have not survived—namely, to the magister officiorum (for the point about employment) and the comes sacrarum largitionum. In addition, two laws addressed to the proconsul of Africa are enmeshed in this phase of legislation, although the linguistic connections with it are much looser than in the other cases. In this group of texts, we therefore possess or can assume the existence of versions addressed to the three western prefects, of Gaul, Italy and Africa, and Rome, and at least two further officials, the comes rei privatae and the proconsul of Africa; while the instructions in the version addressed to the praetorian prefect of Gaul to make the law known to governors under their jurisdiction were no doubt repeated in that addressed to the prefect of Italy and Africa. This would generate many more copies. Further, the six texts carry six different dates of issue, and although some of these can be reconciled, it is not clear that all should be. It is just as likely that in such circumstances, when legislation was issued to different officials with different jurisdictions, it was at different times and with variations of expression.

Study of the Sirmondian Constitutions and their related texts in the Theodosian Code touches many aspects of the editorial procedures used in preparing the Code, enabling these to be considered with reference to a surviving body of primary material. The number of texts in the Code for which we possess this advantage is a tiny proportion of the texts that it contains. Nevertheless, it is an important advantage. In the following chapters we are going to survey from different perspectives the methods used by the emperors for the distribution and publication of their legislation, and those used by the editors of the Code in assembling and presenting

38. The survival of a law in versions addressed to the praetorian prefect of Gaul and the prefect of Rome naturally implies the existence of one addressed to the prefect of Italy and Africa.

it. The procedures revealed by the Sirmondian Constitutions and described in this chapter will serve as a constant point of reference.

## *Appendix: Some Points of Linguistic Usage in the Sirmondian Constitutions*

### INSPIRATION AND INFORMATION: REASONS FOR LEGISLATING

*Sirm.* 1. Itaque quia a nobis instrui voluisti, olim promulgatae legis ordinem salubri rursus imperio propagamus. 2. Suggerentibus episcopis didicimus quosdam sacerdotes Christianae legis. 3. Lectis in consistorio precibus, quibus episcopalis pietas aliquid postulans refragatur in eo, etc. 7. Placida beneficia lenitatis dei omnipotentis arbitrio commoti pro felicitate saeculi publicamus. 8. Et nos quidem praeter hanc velut indictam et a maioribus traditam pro religionis observatione clementiam liberandis paene omnibus, quos legum severitas strinxerat, effusa penitus humanitate operam sacrae mentis exserimus. 10. Religiosi sacerdotis fida suggestio exigit probabilem saeculo disciplinam. 11. Ad confirmationem privilegiorum, quae ecclesiis dicavit vetustas, magnificentiae tuae suggestio religiosa commonuit. 12. Conpulsi igitur Donatistarum pertinacia, furore gentilium . . . , necessarium putamus iterare quae iussimus. 13. Scimus enim idque crebris aditionibus supplicatum. 14. Per provinciam Africam tantum quorundam temeritati licuisse conperimus . . . ignorari ab his potuisse non credimus, quod commissum in civitatibus publice memoratur. 15. Quae fori aequitas, responsis veterum et legum nostrarum aeternitate solidata, cunctis est delata personis, debet clericis nunc prodesse. 16. Hinc denique bellorum curis mixta ratio et salubris constitutio admonuit faciendum, etc.

### "THEREFORE, . . . "

*Sirm.* 1. Itaque quid a nobis instrui voluisti, olim promulgatae legis ordinem salubri rursus imperio propagamus. 2. Sancimus itaque hac lege. 3. Idcirco continua lege sancimus. 6. Inl. itaque auctoritas tua omni aevo mansura quae iussimus. 7. Ideo denique pro festivitate paschali . . . noxas remittimus. 8. Quin per omne hoc, quod inter venerandos et celebres dies medium fluit tempus. 9. Ne tamen crimina deprehensa luxurient et sit libera peccantibus pertinacia, placet, etc. 10. Quae cum ita sint, inlustris et praecelsa magnificentia tua, etc. 11. Placet igitur rationabilis consilii tenore perpenso. 12. Conpulsi igitur Donatistarum pertinacia. 13. Convenit, nostris praescita temporibus ut iustitiam inflectat humanitas. Nam cum plerique, etc. 14. Quapropter iubemus. 15. Quapropter placitura omnibus legis aeternitate sancimus. 16. Hinc denique bellorum curis mixta ratio et salubris constitutio admonuit faciendum.

THE AFFIRMATION OF AUTHORITY

*Sirm.* 1. Olim promulgatae legis ordinem salubri rursus imperio propagamus. Sanximus namque. . . . 2. Sancimus itaque hac lege. 3. Continua lege sancimus. 4. Iam dudum quidem constitutionis nostrae saluberrima sanctio promulgata est, quam nostrae repetitae legis veneratione geminamus. . . . Illud etenim hac eadem sanctione praecipimus. 6. Privilegia ecclesiarum vel clericorum . . . prona devotione revocamus; clericos etiam . . . episcopali audientiae reservamus, his manentibus, quae circa eos sanxit antiquitas. 9. Ne tamen crimina deprehensa luxurient et sit libera peccantibus pertinacia, placet, etc. 10. Inlustris et praecelsa magnificentia tua praesentis oraculi sanctionem propositis ubique divulget edictis. 11. Oraculi praesentis adque in omnem aevum perpeti firmitate duraturi . . . roboratis omnibus, quae sacrosanctae venerationis intuitu huiusce sanctionis auctoritate praescribimus. 12. Conpulsi igitur Donatistarum pertinacia, furore gentilium . . . necessarium putamus iterare quae iussimus. Quapropter omnia, quae a nobis generalium lege auctoritate decreti sunt, non solum manere decernimus, verum in exsecutionem plenissimam effectumque deduci . . . Ea, quae generalibus legibus statuta sunt, impleantur, indulsimus. 14. Quapropter iubemus . . . si quidem praesentis legis aeternitate cunctis observanda constituimus, etc. 15. Quapropter placitura omnibus legis aeternitate sancimus. 16. Bellorum curis mixta ratio et salubris constitutio admonuit faciendum . . . cum saluberrimae sanctionis exsecutionem deferri ab omnibus quidem, sed iudicum maxime et officiorum cura obsequioque iubemus.

FORMS OF GREETING

*Sirm.* 1. Ablabi, parens karissime atque amantissime. 2. Hadriane parens carissime atque amantissime. Hanc igitur legem sublimis magnificentia tua, etc. 3. Optate carissime et iucundissime. Quare laudabilis auctoritas tua, etc. 4. Felix parens carissime. 7. Eutropi parens carissime atque amantissime; 8. Antiochine carissime ac iucundissime. Quocirca spectabilis tua, etc. 9. Theodore parens carissime adque amantissime. Quod inlustris magnificentia tua, etc. 14. Theodore parens carissime adque amantissime, quod inl. magnificentiae tuae praelatum litteris, etc. 16. Theodore parens carissime adque amantissime, inlustris magnificentia tua, etc.

PUBLICATION IN THE PROVINCES

*Sirm.* 2. Hanc igitur legem sublimis magnificentia tua cunctas per dioceses sibi creditas publicabit edictis. 4. Volumus, ut excellens sublimitas tua litteris suis per dioecesim sibi creditam commeantibus iudices moneat instantissime huiuscemodi debitam reverentiam custodiri. 6. Inl. itaque auctoritas tua omni aevo mansura quae iussimus in provinciarum notitiam praecipiet etiam sub poena sacrilegii custodiri, specialiter id inlustribus conprehensura praeceptis, ut in omnibus circa ecclesiastica privilegia veterum principum statuta serventur. 9. Quod inlustris magnificentia tua in omnium notitiam datis ad singularum iudices provinciarum litteris faciet pervenire, ut universis id proposita sollemniter edicta declarent. 10. Inlustris et praecelsa magnificentia tua praesentis oraculi sanctionem propositis ubique divulget edictis, ut noverint cuncti, etc. 11. Quapropter sublimis magnificentia tua . . . provinciarum iudices scribtis currentibus admonebit, quo evidenter agnoscant, etc. 12. Quod ad continendos hominum mores religionemque provisum et ad rectores provinciarum sublimis magnificentia tua faciet pervenire et digno per omnes iubebit vigore servari. 14. Quod inl. magnificentiae tuae praelatum litteris, proponendum edictis, in omnium volumus notitiam pervenire, ita ut noverint rectores, etc. 16. Et ne quis contumaciae suae culpam praecepti ignoratione tueatur, Theodore parens carissime adque amantissime, inlustris magnificentia tua legis tenorem litteris suis edictisque propositis ad omnium iudicum et provincialium notitiam faciet pervenire, ita ut noverint rectores universi, etc.

# 7

# *Delivering the Law*

The Sirmondian Constitutions illustrate both the procedures for the issuing and circulation of late Roman legislation and the regular practice of the editors of the Theodosian Code in dealing with them. Concentrating on the substantive matter of the texts before them, the editors excerpted them verbatim, adapting language and syntax insofar as this was required by the removal of the contexts from which the chosen passages were extracted. Their concentration on substance led them to omit certain features of the original legislation. We miss the emperors' explanations of their motives for legislating, descriptions of the situations in need of remedy, and the instructions given to recipients of the legislation to circulate it to governors and officials under their jurisdiction and to ensure that it was known by the public. The personal forms of address used by the emperors in writing to those among their supporters who were more elevated in rank were replaced by more formal conventions. It was not that the editors necessarily or on every occasion excluded these features, which survive in some texts in the Theodosian Code. The editors applied their judgment to what lay before them. If they formed an integral part of the substantive excerpts made by the editors, such features might be retained; if they did not do so they were omitted.

The editors were, however, careful to preserve the indications of origin, date, and recipient of the legislation, in the form of opening and closing protocols of the texts. They kept these details for two reasons, both explicit in the editorial instructions set out in the laws of 429 and 435. In the first place, until such time as

Theodosius' projected "magisterium vitae" containing only currently valid law together with the opinions of jurists was published, the relative validity of the laws assembled in the Theodosian Code was to be determined by their date of issue: "Validiora esse, quae sunt posteriora" (*CTh* 1.1.5). The editors were to show this by retaining the consular year of laws and their day of issue and by arranging the edited texts under their titles in chronological order. Recording the date of the texts was thus no less essential a part of the editorial process than identifying points of substance in the laws. In the second place, the Code was to be a compilation of general legislation. In his law of 435, Theodosius confirmed the definition that Valentinian III gave in his address to the Senate of 7 November 426; not only texts explicitly framed as imperial edicts of general application fell under the category of general law but also texts addressed to individual governors and published under the authority of governors' edicts in specific provinces and places: "in certis provinciis seu locis valere aut proponi iussae" (*CTh* 1.1.6). The editors would need to include in the protocols of the texts information that made clear their status as general laws. The names of the public officials or corporations that received them and, where known, the places and circumstances in which they had been received were part of this information.

With all its elements present, the protocol of a law would trace its history from the giving of a text by the emperor to a named official, corporation, or other addressee through to its acceptance, where appropriate,[1] by the addressee, and its communication by public reading, followed by display, to the public.[2] In practice, the extent to which the full range of possible annotations is preserved in the edited texts of the Code varies widely. Few are as complete as this description would imply. The most frequent form of annotation will by now be familiar. It records at the beginning of the text the names of the emperors, and the name and office of the addressee, whether individual or collective, as with an edict addressed to the people of Rome or Constantinople or to a province, city, or provincial council. At the end are recorded the day, place and consular year of issue. The great majority of texts in the Theodosian Code are documented in this way. A minority, though still a substantial number of texts, records the place and date of the acceptance or public display of a law rather than the place and date of issue. A still smaller minority preserves some elements of the circumstances both of issue and of acceptance or display.

The completeness of the protocols, as preserved, depends on a number of factors

1. I say "where appropriate," because when laws were addressed as edicts to collective recipients, the question of "acceptance" did not arise.

2. Cf. the schematic presentation of the full panoply of annotation by Boudewijn Sirks, in Harries and Wood (eds.), *The Theodosian Code*, p. 46. It is represented as follows: ⟨text⟩-data-(D-P-C)1-acc-(D-P-C)2-pp-(D-P-C)3, where D is date, P is place, C is consulate.

to be discussed later, among them the sources used by the editors. It is natural, however, to expect that laws recovered from archives or other forms of collection made at the point of issue of a law would not possess annotations referring to the place and date of acceptance. Such annotations might have existed in copies of texts kept in central archives if their recipients had to certify to the emperor that they had received a law and if the certification was recorded centrally, but there is no evidence that this was the normal procedure; indeed, if it had been, one would expect a far greater number of such certifications, and a greater uniformity than we find among those that exist. The likeliest account of these annotations is that they were added locally to express the circumstances in which a law was received. If a law is recorded as posted or displayed ("proposita") at Beirut, Carthage, or Rome, then it is likely prima facie that Beirut, Carthage, or Rome was the place where the law was copied and from which it was recovered, directly or indirectly, by the editors of the Code.

The textual transmission of the protocols is in itself extremely hazardous, for Roman numbers and dates, and the names of places and consuls, are readily confused and corrupted.[3] This is particularly true of imperial consulships, especially in the time of Constantine and his sons, where combinations of similarly named Augusti and Caesars hold office repeatedly, only varying in the precise form of their names and the number of their consulships (confusion between the names Constantinus and Constantius is an endless source of trouble in the transmission of late Roman texts, and frequently recurs in modern books). It is equally confusing that the emperors Valentinian and Valens held the consulship together in four years of their joint reign, and Honorius and Theodosius II no fewer than six times between 407 and 422; and these are not the only such cases. Nor does the problem begin with the textual transmission of the Theodosian Code itself; as we shall see in Chapter 8, on many occasions errors in the dating of some texts had already led the editors to place laws in an incorrect sequence. Any student of the Code will be familiar with such difficulties and will be prepared to accept or suggest corrections where necessary. Despite the many individual problems that they generate, the protocols retain unique value as evidence of the procedures involved in later imperial legislation.

In what follows, the protocols will be used as the basis for the reconstruction of a collective "life history" of imperial constitutions. Each stage in the history will be

3. See the discussion of the problems, with examples and reference to Seeck's *Regesten*, by Alan Cameron, in *Consuls of the Later Roman Empire* (1987), pp. 71–84. Cameron is prepared to argue that in some cases the editors invented or guessed the month and day dates of laws in an effort to fulfill their instructions to put them in chronological order. This may be so, but it is a dangerous way to solve problems.

taken in sequence, and illustrated where possible from external evidence. The Sirmondian Constitutions will provide support, as will the well-preserved protocols of the Novels of Theodosius II and Valentinian III from the dozen or so years following the publication of the Theodosian Code. The discussion will however focus on that substantial number of texts in the Code itself, where a greater level of detail than usual is preserved in the protocols. It will be left to the last chapter to set out the possible implications of this information for such questions as the sources of the Code.

In reconstructing this life history, we should naturally begin with conception, or with the gleam in the emperor's eye that preceded even this: the "predrafting" stage that is documented in the Sirmondian Constitutions, and especially in Valentinian's address to the Senate of 426, of which the relevant extract is preserved in the Codex Justinianus (1.14.3). As we saw in Chapter 4, this law sets out the various routes that might lead to the making of a law, including the emperor's own inspiration or "spontaneus motus," petitions, reports, and litigation. What mattered for generalitas was not the origin, but the formal character of legislation. The Sirmondian Constitutions offered cases that could be assigned to the emperor's "spontaneus motus", and also references to the other situations envisaged in the law of 426—a *suggestio* of praetorian prefect or bishop, an inquiry from a prefect, a petition of bishops read out in the consistory, a memorandum informing the emperor of remedies needed in Africa. The Theodosian Code preserves traces of these processes, for instance in the reference to a *suggestio* of the quaestor Eustathius in a law of 415, from which the emperor had learned of a matter needing attention in the imperial bureaucracy.[4] The law begins with a specific reference to its origin with the words, "viro illustri quaestore Eustathio *suggerente* cognovimus"—a phrase recalling some used in the Sirmondian Constitutions (*Sirm.* 2, 10, 11; see Chapter 6).

The procedure by which legislation was drafted, revised, and approved can be reconstructed from a law of Valentinian III of 446, also preserved in the Codex Justinianus (1.14.8).[5] The first stage is that in which a prima facie need for legislation has arisen in one of the ways just described. The proposal is discussed in the consistory, or more informally among the emperor's advisers. If it is decided that legislation is needed, the quaestor is instructed to draft a version. This is brought to

4. *CTh* 1.8.1; Chapter 8, "Variants and Anomalies," no. 1.

5. On what follows, see esp. J. D. Harries, "The Roman Imperial Quaestor from Constantine to Theodosius II," *JRS* 78 (1988), pp. 148–72, at 164–69f.; W. E. Voss, *Recht und Rhetorik in den Kaisergesetzen der Spätantike* (1982), pp. 22–39; Tony Honoré, "Some Quaestors of the Reign of Theodosius II," in Harries and Wood (eds.), *The Theodosian Code,* p. 74; and *Law in the Crisis of Empire*, pp. 133–35.

the consistory for discussion and amendment, and a revised version is read out for approval. Whether this reading out of the approved version takes place at the same meeting of the consistory that has heard the first draft or later is a practical rather than a procedural matter, reflecting the complexity of the issue and the amount of redrafting that is required. In any event, it is essential to put before the emperor the final version of the text, to which he can add his annotation *manu divina,* to show that he has approved it.[6] The law is then promulgated, a term that covers a process or a series of events rather than a single moment. Copies are sent to the relevant officials for implementation and, where appropriate, further circulation; the protocols of the law of 415 inspired by the *suggestio* of Eustathius show that it was addressed to the magister militum Florentius, with copies to the others it affected: the other magister militum, the magister officiorum, and Eustathius himself.[7] No further circulation or public notification was necessary, for a matter concerning the internal workings of the bureaucracy. In most cases, a chain of communication reaching out from emperor to provinces delivered the law to the communities for whose attention it was intended.

On a very few occasions in the Theodosian Code, verbatim excerpts from the *acta* of the consistory are cited as sources of general law. These represent points of legal interest raised in the consistory that were not put into legislation, but were recorded in some other way by an interested party. One each of the five instances is attributed to Constantine, Julian, and Gratian, the other two are attributed to Theodosius.[8] All are rulings on points of private law or legal procedure; indeed, the text of Constantine, in which he replies in Latin to a Greek-speaking petitioner, looks more like a private rescript, though like many such texts it asserts a principle of general application. The text of Julian, by contrast, dated 23 March 362 at Constantinople, is given in Greek with Latin protocols. It is on the force of written instruments in legal proceedings and is of particular interest in recording who was present "standing" (only the emperor sat) at the consistory: "Adstante Iovio viro clarissimo quaestore, Anatolio magistro officiorum, Felice comite sacrarum largi-

6. For the annotation *manu divina* see *Nov. Val.* 1.3, 9, 16, 17, 19. Eusebius, *On the Life of Constantine* 2.33, claimed to possess an authentic copy of an edict of Constantine to the provincials of Palestine with a signature "in the emperor's own handwriting." What he probably means is the subscription "manu divina" (which was itself copied) with the order to publish the edict in the "eastern provinces" (*sic*), 2.42.

7. *CTh* 1.8.1: "Scripta eodem exemplo Sapricio magistro militum, Helioni magistro officiorum et Eustathio quaestori"; cf. 6.28.8, naming nine officials who were the recipients of copies "eodem exemplo"; also 8.7.11 and 11.28.9, and nn. 34–35 to this chapter.

8. *CTh* 8.15.1 (Constantine); 11.39.5 (Julian); 1.22.4 (Gratian); 4.20.3, 11.39.8 (Theodosius).

tionum."[9] All five texts quote the actual words of the emperor and, except for the text of Constantine, for which no protocol survives, have a formula, "pars actorum habitorum in consistorio" or "apud acta," indicating that they were spoken in the consistory. To these may be added a text of Constantine quoted in Chapter 3, consisting of a transcript of a meeting in his principia with an assembly of military officers and others, where a verbatim exchange between the emperor and some veterans concludes with his grant of the privileges for which they petitioned.[10]

It is generally accepted that the central role in the preparation of imperial legislation was that of the quaestor, sometimes called the quaestor sacri palatii; although its continuous history cannot be traced, the office descended from that of the quaestor Caesaris whose function it was in the early empire to read imperial communications to the Senate.[11] Sources from the later fourth to the sixth centuries consistently describe the quaestorship as involving two duties; replying to petitions and drafting legislation. The entry in the Notitia Dignitatum puts the matter succinctly, listing in two lines what fell "under the disposition" of the quaestor: "leges dictandae, preces."[12] The accompanying illustration portrays these duties by a picture of an inscribed stele bearing the words *leges salubres* (or *salutares*), and rolls of paper indicating the petitions to which it was the quaestor's duty to respond (Figures 3 and 4). We saw in Chapter 6 how the Sirmondian Constitutions sometimes allude to the "salubrious" properties of imperial legislation.[13]

The same combination of duties recurs in literary texts of the same period referring to the quaestorship. For Symmachus, writing to Ausonius after Valentinian I's promotion of Ausonius to quaestor, his friend was now "consilii regalis particeps, precum arbiter, legum conditor."[14] The last two phrases echo the expressions used in the Notitia Dignitatum, while the first refers to Ausonius' membership of the

9. Of whom Felix died suddenly within a year, and Anatolius was killed on Julian's Persian campaign. Jovius survived to become prefect of Constantinople in 364.

10. *CTh* 7.20.2: "Idem A. cum introisset principia et salutatus esset a praefectis et tribunis et viris eminentissimis," etc. The law is entered by Mommsen, Prolegomena p. ccxv as "acta in castris," but this phrase does not occur in the original text. By an anomalous editorial intervention, this law and 4.20.3 have "dat(a)" in the closing protocol.

11. See esp. J. D. Harries, "The Roman Imperial Quaestor," pp. 153–54; Honoré, *Law in the Crisis of Empire,* pp. 11–23. The post was revived or re-created by Constantine, see n. 19.

12. Not. Dig., Occ. 10.4–5; Or. 12.4–5. The surviving version of the Notitia belongs to the period between around 394 and 425, but there must have been earlier editions, not extant.

13. See the appendix to Chapter 6.

14. Symmachus, *Ep.* 1.23. For this and other references, see Voss, *Recht und Rhetorik,* pp. 36–39; Honoré, "Some Quaestors," p. 68 (reading "consilii" for "concilii"); Honoré, *Law in the Crisis of Empire,* p. 12.

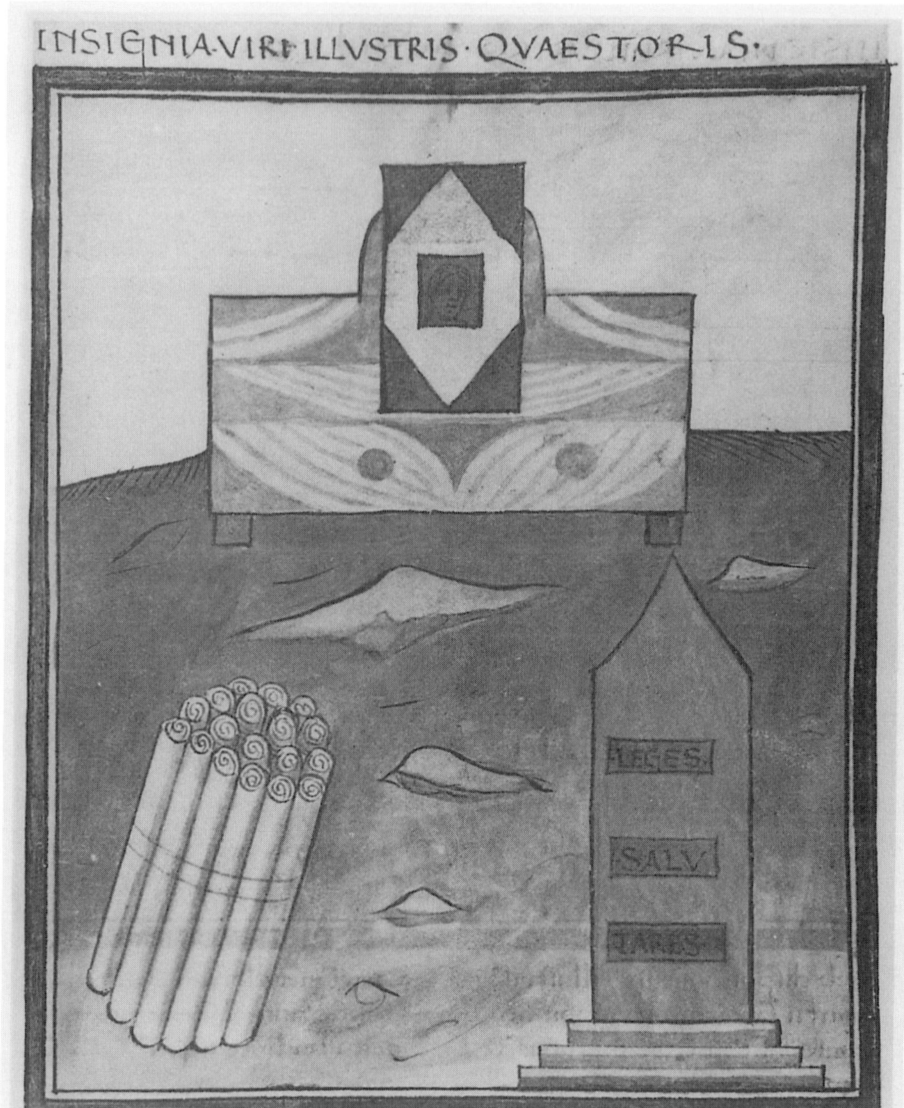


The insignia of the eastern and western *quaestor sacri palatii,* as shown in the Notitia Dignitatum, in a fifteenth-century copy, at two removes from the late Roman original. The insignia are, however, accurately portrayed. They represent the twofold duties of the quaestor in replying to petitions and drafting laws. The former are shown as scrolls, the latter in the form of an inscribed stele. As explained in the present book, the vast majority of laws did not enjoy this degree of permanence, but the image well represents the scope of the emperor's intentions.

The object standing on the table is a diptych of ivory and gold, bearing on the outside the emperor's portrait and on the inside the quaestor's codicils of appointment. H. Omont, *Notitia Dignitatum Imperii Romani: Reproduction réduite des 105 miniatures du manuscrit latin 9661 de la Bibliothèque Nationale* (Paris, 1911), figures 30, 74.

imperial consistory; that is the way in which he now "shared in the royal counsel." Later, after the appointment of his friend Nicomachus Flavianus as quaestor at the court of Theodosius at the end of 388, Symmachus greeted a law emanating from Milan, in a laudatory letter to Flavianus. This is explained, not merely by Symmachus' need to put himself on the right side of Theodosius after his recent support of a usurper but by his assumption that Flavianus was the author of the text.[15] Another quaestor known to Symmachus, Proculus Gregorius, had received letters from him praising an *oratio* of the Emperor Gratian—composed by Gregorius—that had been read to the Senate. Again, Symmachus regarded the promotion as a reward for his friend's literary distinction.[16] In the east at a later time, bishop Theodoret of Cyrrhus wrote to an unnamed prefect, almost certainly the Antiochus Chuzon who was the guiding genius behind the Theodosian Code itself, referring to an earlier correspondence (not extant) "at the time when you were drafting the imperial laws"—as quaestor sacri palatii.[17]

Consistent as it is, this portrayal of the role of quaestor derives from the period—the later fourth and early fifth centuries—in which the office had reached its definitive form. The office of quaestor may indeed, as is stated by Zosimus, be a creation (or revival) of Constantine the Great,[18] though there is no certain attestation of it until the time of his son Constantius II.[19] Nor, until the last decades of the century, is there much positive definition of the duties of the office. The recorded activities of earlier fourth-century quaestors relate more to political and especially diplomatic functions than to those of advising emperors and drafting texts later associated with the office.[20] As for legal expertise, the first occasion on which a

15. On this, see esp. Tony Honoré, "Some Writings of the Pagan Champion Nicomachus Flavianus," in W. Schuller (ed.), *Xenia* 23 (1989), p. 15, with my "Nicomachus Flavianus' Quaestorship: The Historical Evidence," ibid., pp. 18–25, esp. p. 24. The law exists in the Theodosian Code, in a version addressed from Milan on 23 January 389 to the urban prefect of Constantinople (*CTh* 4.4.2).

16. *Ep.* 3.18, cf. 17: "pontificio litterati honoris auctus."

17. Theodoret, *Ep.* 33; *PLRE* 2, p. 103 (Antiochus 6). It was Antiochus Chuzon who drafted *CTh* 1.1.5, initiating the Theodosian Code.

18. Zosimus 5.32.6; cf. Jones, *Later Roman Empire,* p. 1144.

19. The case of *PLRE* 1, Hermogenes 9 (p. 425; under Constantine, 330/37), is likely but not certain. Those of Montius Magnus (*PLRE* 1, Magnus 11; pp. 535–36) and Leontius (*PLRE* 1, Leontius 22; p. 503), under Gallus Caesar in 351–353/54 and in 354, respectively, are certain, and imply the presence of such an official under the Augustus; Taurus is attested as quaestor of Constantius, also in 354 (*PLRE* 1, Taurus 33, p. 879). For some reason the Fasti of *PLRE* 1 (p. 1061) lists Hermogenes under Constantius II. J. D. Harries, "The Roman Imperial Quaestor," p. 171, does not include him.

20. Harries, pp. 153–59.

quaestor is recorded as having given such advice to an emperor is that on which Eupraxius corrected Valentinian I on some not very recondite implications of the law of *maiestas*,[21] and looking at the actual holders of the office even from that time forward, one is hard pressed to show that legal expertise was the overriding criterion in their selection. It was certainly less significant than literary expertise, though this does not exclude the likelihood that the emperors could choose candidates with a knowledge of the law from among those whose formal education had been mainly literary in character. The late Roman educational system would ensure that those who trained as lawyers had also received a literary education.[22] The converse is however not true. The "legal expertise" of those whose literary education was not followed by the study of law would depend on whatever experience of the law and legal procedures they had acquired in the course of a career in the government service. Further, the rank of quaestor was given as a political reward, and as a stepping-stone to higher things, more often than could guarantee that its holders would always possess the relevant experience. The legal expertise of later fourth- and of fifth-century quaestors must be evaluated case by case and not made part of any general assumption about the qualifications required for the office.

Unusually for its early books, the three laws "De officio quaestoris" in Book 1 of the Theodosian Code form a completely preserved title.[23] It is therefore the more interesting that all three texts, in fact two late moments of legislation at Constantinople in 415 and 424,[24] refer to a quite different aspect of his duties from those mentioned so far and one in no way implied by them; the control of the register of minor military appointments known as the *laterculum minus* or Lesser Registry (the document is not extant; the Notitia Dignitatum itself is the *laterculum maius*). In the first law—that inspired by a *suggestio* of the quaestor Eustathius—control over the Lesser Registry is restored to the quaestor after an innovation of "certain persons" that had taken it elsewhere; the predators are no doubt to be found in the department of the magister officiorum, to whom, as well as to the magistri militum, the law was also sent.[25] This rather anomalous duty—appointments do more naturally fall under the magister officiorum—is quite unconnected with the quaestor's role in composing imperial legislation. From the third of the

21. Amm. Marc. 28.1.25, concerning the liability of senators to examination by torture.

22. Like Augustine's friend Alypius, who was among Augustine's pupils at Thagaste but later appears at Rome as a student of law (*Conf.* 6.7.11, 6.8.13; *PLRE* 1, pp. 47–48, under Alypius 8).

23. *CTh* 1.8.1–3, supported by *T.*

24. *CTh* 1.8.3 informs the magister officiorum on 29 April 424 of what had been written to the quaestor four days earlier (1.8.2).

25. *CTh* 1.8.1; for the protocol see Chapter 8, "Variants and Anomalies," no. 1.

laws, of 29 April 424, it appears that it was the magister militum who was then, with still better claims to administrative logic than the magister officiorum, intent on annexing these appointments.

Leaving aside these flurries of bureaucratic infighting, two of the laws have the incidental but important merit of showing that the quaestor exercised a supervision over the functions of the magister memoriae; for it was from the scrinium memoriae, but on the decision of the quaestor, that letters of appointment to the military commands listed in the laterculum minus were issued.[26] If he had this authority over the magister memoriae, it is a safe inference that the quaestor exercised a similar jurisdiction over the magistri epistularum and libellorum; all three departments are listed under a single rubric in both eastern and western sections of the Notitia Dignitatum.[27] In this case, the quaestor will have exercised a general authority over what was earlier, following A. H. M. Jones, called the legal and secretarial side of the imperial service. The close relations between these departments, and especially between the scrinium memoriae and the quaestorship, are also shown by the frequency with which quaestors were promoted from among the magistri memoriae. We saw earlier the circumstances in which Fl. Eupraxius, the first quaestor on record as giving legal advice to an emperor, was promoted to this office from magister memoriae as a reward for his role in the elevation of Gratian as Augustus in 367. We noted too that the career progression from magister memoriae to quaestor recurs among the members of the editorial commissions appointed to work on the Theodosian Code.

The connections between the quaestor and the scrinium memoriae have a bearing on the production of late Roman legislation. According to the Notitia Dignitatum, the quaestor possessed no regular officium but recruited assistants at his discretion from other departments, more precisely from the scrinia memoriae, epistularum, and libellorum.[28] It was here that he was likely to find the experience required by the functions of the quaestor. The duties of the three magistri, as set out in the Notitia, concerned, respectively, "adnotationes," "consultationes," and "cognitiones" (in all three cases "preces"), any of which might involve rulings on points of law; this undoubtedly contributed to a tradition of departmental expertise that could compensate in cases where individual heads of department did not

26. Cf. esp. 1.8.2: "Laterculi curam totius scias ad tuae sublimitatis sollicitudinem pertinere, ita ut *tuo arbitratu ex scrinio memoriae* totius laterculi minoris dignitates . . . iuxta consuetudinem priscam clementiae meae auctoritate deinceps emittantur."

27. Not. Dig., Or. 19, Occ. 17. This authority of the quaestor is more specific than the general subordination of the scrinia to the magister officiorum noted by J. D. Harries, " 'Sacra Generalitas': The Administrative Background to the Theodosian Code," in *Estudios de Historia da Derecho Europeo* (1994), p. 39 (not citing this evidence).

28. Cf. Not. Dig., Or. 12.6: "Officium non habet, sed adiutores de scriniis quos voluerit."

have training as lawyers.[29] A poem of Claudian on the consulship (in 399) of Fl. Mallius Theodorus describes the duties of the magister memoriae in language very like that applied to the quaestor by Symmachus and the Notitia Dignitatum: "terris edicta daturus, / supplicibus responsa, venis; oracula regis / eloquio crevere tuo."[30] That is to say, the magister memoriae, just like the quaestor, issued legislative texts (the precise technical meaning of *edicta* perhaps escapes Claudian's poetic language) and replies to petitions, and put eloquence into imperial utterances. In a cause célèbre of 386 it was not the quaestor but a pious magister memoriae, Benivolus, who resigned his office rather than draft a law permitting the assembly of Arian heretic congregations.[31]

The role of the quaestor in drafting imperial legislation was then not unique, and it may have developed over time. Even when, as in the later fourth and fifth centuries, the duty was unquestionably his, we are in no position to say how often, confronted with the task of drafting a piece of imperial legislation, the quaestor may have delegated the work to a subordinate whom he had chosen from the scrinia to work for him, or to the magister memoriae if that official possessed the necessary skills. For the two main reasons discussed here—the variety of the other duties assigned to the quaestor, and the fact that others too were involved in composing imperial pronouncements—we cannot assume that because a text was included in the Theodosian Code it was drafted by a quaestor.[32]

Consideration of this question leads to a further distinction relevant to the Theodosian Code and the authorship of its constitutions; the distinction between "leges," understood in their primary sense as texts agreed on by the consistory and

29. For these duties see Jones, *Later Roman Empire,* p. 1144; cf., on the magister libellorum and the law, Honoré, *Emperors and Lawyers,* 2nd ed., pp. 139–40.

30. Claudian, *Paneg. dict. Manlio Theodoro cons.,* 34. Identified as a quaestor by Honoré, p. 68 and n. 8; cf., however, *PLRE* 1, p. 901 (Theodorus 27).

31. Rufinus, *Hist. Eccl.* 11.16; Sozomen, *Hist. Eccl.* 7.13.5ff.; *PLRE* 1, p. 161 and my *Western Aristocracies and Imperial Court,* pp. 185f., 189. The law survives as *CTh* 16.1.4, cf. 4.1 (Chapter 8, "Variants and Anomalies," no. 7). Jones, *Later Roman Empire,* p. 1144, comments that it "is not clear why Benivolus, the magister memoriae, instead of the quaestor, was directed to draft [the law]"; my suggestion is that this delegation of duties was more frequent than may appear.

32. These observations impinge on the attempts of Tony Honoré to identify and characterize quaestors by the style of the laws they composed; see "Some Quaestors" and his discussion of the quaestors Eupraxius, Ausonius, and Nicomachus Flavianus in "The Making of the Theodosian Code," *ZSS* 103 (1986), pp. 189–216; *Law in the Crisis of Empire,* pp. 58–70 (on Flavianus). Because of the uncertain character and evolution of the office, one would doubt the method for the earlier period, but Honoré's studies relate to the later phases of the development of the office, when its duties and governmental procedures were more formalised, and yield better to his analyses.

usually drafted by the quaestor, and the administrative letters by which laws, or relevant parts of them, were sent to the officials concerned for enforcement under their jurisdictions.[33] We saw in Chapter 6 the variant texts generated by the lost counterpart, addressed to the praetorian prefect of Italy, of the law addressed to the prefect of Gaul and preserved as the sixth Sirmondian Constitution.[34] The versions of this text addressed, respectively, to the prefect of Rome, the comes rei privatae, and the proconsul of Africa were sent out at different times, with different selections of material and with variations in expression. Although the original text as discussed in the consistory and subscribed by the emperor was no doubt drafted by the quaestor, the secondary versions were not necessarily written by him; the version addressed to the praetorian prefect of Gaul already contains variations appropriate to his particular jurisdiction. In general, it seems unlikely that every text assembled in the Theodosian Code had passed through the full procedure of discussion in the consistory described earlier. Many were regulatory and administrative documents of a routine sort, which hardly needed discussion at that level of formality. Some were such as would in modern usage have been delegated to the chairmen of subcommittees for action contingent on decisions taken elsewhere. It was not always the quaestor, rather than the magister memoriae or a subordinate official from this or one of the other scrinia, who was responsible for drafting them.

The stage at which a text, once agreed upon, was given to its recipient of first destination is marked in the protocols of the Code by normal epistolary conventions. The emperors, speaking always as a college, address the public official or other recipient of the text, and the communication is dated by day and month, together with the place (wherever the emperor happens to be) and the consuls of the year. By far the most frequent word used to describe the issuing of a text is the epistolary *data,* but on occasions another word is used, such as *emissa.*[35]

The significance of these variations is unclear. Mommsen argued that when high officials such as praetorian prefects forwarded laws to governors under their jurisdiction, the correct form for them to use was not *data,* as if they themselves, rather

33. Harries, "'Sacra Generalitas,'" pp. 37–41.

34. Cf. *CTh* 11.28.9 (9 April 414); the law is addressed to the praetorian prefect, and in other copies ("de eadem re scribtum") as an edict to the people, to the comes sacrarum largitionum, to the praepositus sacri palatii as it concerned the imperial household ("domus sacra"), to provincial governors, and, as it concerned the *metallarii,* as an edict to the people of Illyricum.

35. Regarding the use of *emissa: CTh* 6.27.9, 8.1.3, 11.20.20, 11.30.50, 12.1.112. 8.7.11 is addressed "Severo mag. militum" and noted as "emissa ad magistros militum et comites et duces omnes." Possibly some of these texts represent laws forwarded by prefects or other high officials — perhaps Severus himself sent on 8.7.11 to the other recipients noted.

than the emperor, were the source of the legislation, but *missa* or *scripta*.[36] This convention is explicit in a law of Valentinian addressed to the praetorian prefect and "sent" by the prefect to an unidentified subordinate, and it is implied by some other instances, where texts in the Theodosian Code appear to be letters sent by praetorian prefects to other officials, rather than letters sent to them by emperors.[37] This is not to say that the word *data* was not occasionally used in error by praetorian prefects; some apparent anomalies in the protocols of laws are best resolved on this assumption. A law "given" on 15 May 382 "at Tyre the metropolis" and posted at Berytus cannot be an imperial letter but must be part of a praetorian prefect's edict, sent on to a provincial governor and displayed by him. Another text is more carefully annotated, as "given in a letter" by the praetorian prefect at Milan to an unknown official on 22 May 358, when the emperor was at Sirmium; another was "given by the praetorian prefect" at Viminacium on the lower Danube when the emperor—Jovian if the transmitted date is correct—was at Antioch.[38]

The next stages in the life history of a law are its acceptance by its addressee, and his promulgation of the text by announcement and display in a public place. These stages are shown, respectively, by the words *accepta* and *proposita*, usually in the abbreviations *acc.* and *pp*. That acceptance and posting were formally separate stages is implied by the protocols, and clear from other evidence. A letter of a proconsul of Africa to Constantine cited by Augustine begins with an acknowledgment that he had "*received and worshipped* Your Majesty's divine writing," and in a late martyr-act the persecuting "praeses" is described as "embracing" an imperial edict—a theatrical exaggeration, no doubt, but still a reminiscence of late Roman practice.[39] The same image recurs in a Greek legal text, where a law of Constantine is referred to as "divine and adored" (θεῖον καὶ προσκυνητόν); that is, the law, like

36. Mommsen, Prolegomena, p. clv, citing *CTh* 8.11.3, 8.6.1 (see n. 37); and 7.22.9 + 12.1.83, "scribta Petro consulari Phoenices Damasco prid. id. Mai.," etc.

37. *CTh* 8.11.3, "missa a ppo"; cf. 8.6.1, "emissa sub die VIII kal. Feb. Rom(a)," at a time when the emperor was in Gaul (Paris or Reims). For the date (366, not 365), see *PLRE* 1, p. 783.

38. Respectively, *CTh* 7.13.11, "dat. id. Mai. Tyro metropoli, pp. Beryto"; 8.4.6, "dat. epistula ⟨a⟩ praefecto, cui haec sacra fuerat antelata"; 8.1.8, "dat. epistula ⟨a⟩ ppo. v kal. Dec. Viminacio" (27 Nov. 363). Cf. 16.2.15 to the Ppo Italiae, "dat. epistula prid. kal. Iul. Med."—by the prefect in 360, when the emperor was in the east; 5.14.34, addressed to the Ppo. Orientis, "dat. Tyro metropoli" on 6 November 394, when the legislating emperor was at Milan; cf. also n. 47. I discuss *prae-/antelata litteris* and similar expressions later.

39. "Scripta caelestia maiestatis vestrae *accepta atque adorata*," Augustine, *Ep*. 88.2; "amplexatus," *Acta S. Paphnutii*, in *Acta Sanctorum, September*, vol. 6 (24 Sept.), p. 686D. For these and other refs., see S. Lieberman, "Roman Legal Institutions in Early Rabbinics and in the Acta Martyrum," *Jewish Quarterly Review*, n.s. 35 (1944–45), pp. 1–57.

the divine emperor who issued it, exacted adoration (προσκύνησις) as of something sacred.[40] This adoration was presumably expressed by the recipient's lowering his head and raising the document to his lips, much as an official would bend to touch the imperial purple in the court ceremonial of *adoratio purpurae*.[41] Like other aspects of late Roman ceremonial, this convention precedes the fourth century, and its application to imperial legislative texts is a special case of a more general practice. A text of the early third century describes how a famous Sophist actually breathed his last after "worshipping" (προσκυνήσας) the letter that had appointed him imperial secretary.[42] As applied to imperial constitutions, this moment of "adoration" is clearly separate from and earlier than their public display.

Occasionally, as when an emperor addressed a praetorian prefect or other official resident with the *comitatus* in the same place as himself, the date of issue of a text is the same as its date of acceptance; the law was simply handed to its recipient or sent the short distance to his quarters and accepted immediately.[43] In other cases, even when emperor and recipient were residing in the same place, a delay is indicated between the "giving" and the "acceptance" of a law. A law of 381, issued at Constantinople on 6 July, was received there by the comes sacrarum largitionum on 21 July; another, addressed to the comes sacrarum largitionum Proculus on 7 May 386, was received by his successor, evidently some time later.[44] One of the Novels of Valentinian was given at Rome on 26 December 446, received there on the next day, and posted the day after that; another was given, again at Rome, on 13 March, received on 27 March and posted there on 6 April 447.[45] In such cases, we may have to imagine a local reason for the hiatus, such as a backlog of administrative work, holidays, distraction, illness or dilatoriness, or some other cause of delay within the government.[46]

40. Riccobono, vol. 3, no. 101 (at p. 321).

41. On *adoratio purpurae* see my *Roman Empire of Ammianus*, pp. 245–48, with the references cited on p. 515, n. 23.

42. Philostratus, *Vit. Soph.* (ed. Loeb), p. 232.

43. As with *CTh* 2.1.3 (Milan), 2.6.4 (Antioch), 7.22.5 (Constantinople).

44. *CTh* 4.13.8, 6.30.11. The gap of a month (1 August to 1 September 331) between the issue and the posting at Constantinople of the edict represented by *CTh* 11.30.16–17, 11.34.1, and other texts may be explained by Constantine's absence for a visit to Nicomedia—Barnes, *New Empire*, p. 78.

45. *Nov. Val.* 21.2, 23; cf. *Nov. Maj.* 2 (Ravenna).

46. Jones, *Later Roman Empire*, p. 1161, n. 75. In eight cases among the Novels of Valentinian, of laws issued and received or posted in the same place, delays range from one to twenty-four days. In Jones's magnificently sober judgment, the cases "illustrate bureaucratic promptitude or dilatoriness."

Circumstances in which the same date is recorded for the giving of a law and its acceptance or public display may be the exception in our evidence, but they were obviously much commoner than they seem. It was presumably not unusual for praetorian prefects residing in the same place as the emperor to receive laws on the same day that they were sent to them, and it was no doubt regular practice for provincial governors to publish texts as soon as they arrived, but from the point of view of the validity of a law there was no need to record every last detail of its history; to note that any two stages took place on the same day would be gratuitous, when it was normal for them to do so.[47]

In almost all cases where more than one date is recorded in the protocols of a law, these are the dates on which a law was "given," and on which it was either accepted or posted. The difference between the dates expresses a banal but inescapable reality, the physical distance from the emperor to the destination of his laws. The availability to the emperor of the cursus publicus, and his ability to requisition sea transport and to exploit the corn fleets that plied seasonally between Rome and Carthage and between Constantinople and Alexandria, gave him inestimable advantages in speed and reliability over private citizens. But no force on earth could transmit an imperial letter faster than it could be carried by a rapid horseman or exempt the emperor from the delays and hazards of adverse winds, bad weather and the change of seasons. "We are not able," said the emperor Honorius in a law on sea transport, "to abolish accidents or to restrain unkind fortune."[48]

The fifty or more "double-dated" texts in the Theodosian Code are among the best evidence available for the speed of travel between stated origins and destinations in the Roman Empire.[49] Yet, despite the fact that they form a substantial dossier of material, it is difficult to see them as more than examples of journey times, reflecting a number of obvious, and known, variable factors. Eighteen recorded journeys from imperial residences in various places to destinations in Africa reveal striking divergencies—from extremes of a very brisk 31 days for a journey

47. A question attaches to a number of laws annotated as "dat. et pp. Romae" on the same date, at times when the emperor was not resident at Rome; cf. 1.9.1 ("ad agentes in rebus"), 5.15.17 (to the *PPo*), 10.10.2 ("ad populum"), and the edict of 7 April 397 represented by 14.10.2 + 14.11.1 + 14.14.1 + 15.12.3 (Chapter 8, " 'Palingenesia': Laws Reconstituted," no. 10). The explanation may be that the laws were sent to the urban prefect or other official, "given" or announced by him (see n. 38), and posted on the same day as the announcement.

48. Cf. *CTh* 13.9.5: "Excludere casus et inclementem non possumus cohibere fortunam."

49. Jones, *Later Roman Empire,* pp. 402f. and nn. 75–76 at pp. 1161–63; R. Duncan-Jones, "Communication-Speed and Contact by Sea in the Roman Empire," chap. 1 in *Structure and Scale in the Roman Economy* (1990), esp. pp. 17–23. See, for the more general evidence, L. Casson, *Ships and Seamanship in the Ancient World* (1971), chap. 12.

from Sirmium to an unknown destination in Africa in 321 to the extravagant 349 days taken for a law to travel from Ravenna to Carthage in 414/15.[50] The fact that this law was directed to an official (the *tribunus voluptatum*) normally resident at Rome but on this occasion, for some reason, to be found in Africa merely illustrates one of many possible sources of delay; governors and officials were not always where they were thought to be when a letter was sent to them.[51] The other journeys to Africa fall in a range between 60 and 200 days, the only discernible variable being the longer traveling times in the winter months (November through March), when the seas were officially closed for commerce;[52] even this does not prevent times of 180 and 208 days for two journeys made in the calm days of summer.[53] The times taken for imperial letters to reach Italy from origins in Illyricum, and to travel in either direction between Gaul and Italy, are shorter than the journey times to Africa but show comparable variations, from 35 to 82 days in the former case and from 22 to 60 days in the latter; again, this very small sample is consistent with shorter journey times in the summer for communications between Illyricum and Italy (with a crossing of the Adriatic Sea), but that is no cause for surprise.[54] What is at issue is not only the speed of vessels at sea, but the unpredictable lengths of time taken for suitable opportunities for travel to arise, and delays incurred in the course of journeys. A further complicating feature is that, since late Roman emperors spent much of their time away from the immediate environs of the Mediterranean, their dispatches often involved combinations of travel by land

50. *CTh* 11.19.1, 15.7.13; cf. Jones, *Later Roman Empire,* p. 1162; *PLRE* 2, p. 361, s. Diogenianus 2.

51. In the words of Jones, *Later Roman Empire,* p. 1162, the constitution "evidently went astray in the post."

52. *CTh* 9.9.3, §3 (380), defines the open season as 13 April to 15 October, with the earlier part of these months allowed for the acceptance of cargoes. The assumption must be that no one would sail before 13 April and that a voyage begun on 15 October would be completed by the end of the month. Vegetius 4.39 provides similar though not identical data; Casson, *Ships and Seamanship,* pp. 270–71.

53. As Duncan-Jones, "Communication-Speed and Contact by Sea," points out in discussing the African evidence, the sample is too small to allow long-term change for other reasons to be separated from seasonal variants; this acknowledgment follows his remark about "some slowing down" in the later part of the period, which he bases on the observation that "the three edicts despatched after 383 account for three of the four slowest journey times." But of these three instances, one was the exceptional journey of 349 days just discussed, and one was a law issued in November. That leaves one unimpeachably slow journey, 208 days from Aquileia to Hadrumetum for a law issued in June 391. The journey of 180 days from Nasonacum (near Trier: Chapter 8, "'Palingenesia': Laws Reconstituted," no. 3) to Africa was made between 30 May and 26 November 372.

54. Jones, *Later Roman Empire,* pp. 1162–63; Duncan-Jones, pp. 22–23.

and by sea. This can only increase the uncertainties in analyzing them—just as it will have increased the emperor's own uncertainties about when some of his laws would reach their recipients.

Rather than noting the acceptance or display of laws, the protocols of a few texts mention their public reading or recitation in a named location. This is most often the Roman Senate, where laws are said to have been "read" (*lecta* or *recitata*), usually by the urban prefect[55] but sometimes by other officials—in one case by the vicarius of Rome, in another by the primicerius notariorum, whom the emperor, then resident at Rome, evidently sent along for the purpose.[56] Another law affecting the Senate was read in the Pantheon, another in the Palatium. Both locations are unique in our evidence, but the latter coincides with the presence of Constantine at Rome in 326, when the Senate was presumably invited to come to the emperor's Palatine residence to hear the law read out.[57] A law of Valentinian, addressed to bishop Damasus, was "read in the churches of Rome" on 30 July 370—a notable and possibly embarrassing occasion, given the critical remarks in the law about the disreputable conduct of *ecclesiastici* at Rome, as they frequented the homes of vulnerable females in quest of gifts and inheritances.[58] Leaving Rome, two laws, in fact parts of a single text, were "read" at Carthage, one at Capua, another in the senate at Constantinople by the proconsul of the city.[59] Occasionally, by the phrase *lecta apud acta* (or *lecta actis*), a law that has been received by a praetorian prefect or other official and read out by him in public session, or else cited in proceedings held before him, is noted as having been read into his acta, and thereby put on the record.[60]

The final stage in the promulgation of a law was that in which the prefect or governor responsible ordered its public display in the provinces or cities under his

55. Cf. esp. *CTh* 8.18.1: "Dat. XV kal. Aug. Aquil(eiae), recitata aput Vettium Rufinum p.u. in senatu non. Sept." For "lecta in senatu," 9.1.3, 10.19.8 + 15.1.19; "lecta" simply, but addressed to the prefect of Rome, 2.2.1, 9.38.4; to the Senate, 6.4.11, 6.4.22 + 23. *CTh* 11.16.4 was "lecta Rom(ae)" but addressed to the (otherwise unknown) praetorian prefect. There are several cases of laws addressed to praetorian prefects being "pp. Romae," e.g. 7.18.4 and 6, 7.22.3, 8.8.3, 9.19.4 (to a *PPo Galliarum*), 11.16.9, 13.1.1, etc. An especially interesting case, "proposita" at Aquileia on 3 November and "accepta" at Rome on 23 November 386, is 2.8.18 = 8.8.3 = 11.7.13.

56. *CTh* 9.38.6 (381); 6.2.25 (426).

57. Pantheon, *CTh* 14.3.10 (370); Palatium, 10.8.3 (326).

58. "Lecta in ecclesiis Romae," *CTh* 16.2.20 (370).

59. Carthage, *CTh* 4.6.2 + 3 (336); Capua, 11.16.14 (382); Constantinople, 6.4.8 + 9 (356).

60. "Lecta apud acta/actis": 11.16.2 (323), 16.2.14 (357), 2.12.1 (363), 13.9.2 (?372). The Breviarium text of 2.26.2 (?317) has "lecta apud acta," whereas the Gromatici have "lecta apud senatum."

jurisdiction. This was done by his appending to the law an edict whereby he published it under his authority as governor. As we saw in the discussion of the Sirmondian Constitutions, praetorian prefects were regularly told when receiving laws to send them to provincial governors with letters instructing the governors to promulgate the texts by posting edicts. In *Sirm.* 9, perhaps the clearest account of the procedure, the prefect is instructed to bring the regulation to the knowledge of all by means of letters issued to the governors of provinces, so that "edicts posted in the usual fashion" would publish it to the whole world.[61] Similar formulae are found at the end of nearly all the Novels of Theodosius, and the great majority of those of Valentinian. In *Sirm.* 12 we see the entire process, from the delivery of a law to its publication by the proconsul of Africa. The law was given to the praetorian prefect of Italy and Africa at Rome, where the emperor then resided, on 25 November 407. It was then sent by the prefect to Africa, and—still bearing its original address to the praetorian prefect—"posted at Carthage in the forum under the edict of Porphyrius the proconsul" on 5 June of the following year.[62] All that is here omitted is explicit reference to the "letters" by which the prefect would convey the imperial constitution to the proconsul with instructions to publish it with his edict; when this element in the procedure is present, it is described by the formula *antelata* [or *praelata*] *litteris,* meaning that an imperial text is attached to the prefectoral or other letters by which it was conveyed to the receiving official. A well-known example of this procedure from nonjuridical sources is the so-called Edict of Milan of Constantine and Licinius, published at Nicomedia on 15 June 313 by the provincial governor, who, "in order that the contents of the command of our benevolence should come to the notice of all," was instructed "to post this letter everywhere, preceded by your edict [*praelata programmate tuo haec scripta*]"; another, known from a papyrus copy, is the Edict of Aristius Optatus on taxation, from the year 297, which refers to "the imperial edict which has been published and the schedule attached thereto, to which I have prefixed for public

61. *Sirm.* 9: "Quod inlustris magnificentia tua in omnium notitiam *datis ad singularum iudices provinciarum litteris* faciet pervenire, ut universis id *proposita sollemniter edicta* declarent." See also *Sirm.* 14, 16 (texts cited in the appendix to Chapter 6). Some of the material in what follows, and some evidence not mentioned here, are discussed in a different perspective in my "Eternity in Perishable Materials: Law-Making and Literate Communication in the Roman Empire," in T. W. Hillard and others (eds.), *Ancient History in a Modern University* (1998), vol. 2, pp. 253–65.

62. See under "*Sirm.* 12," Chapter 6, for the protocol and dating; cf. *Nov. Val.* 27, "pp. in foro Traiani XIII kal. Aug. sub edicto Firmini viri inl. p(raefecti) p(raetori)o." See also *Nov. Val.* 21.1, 23, and 25 for the phrase *antelata edicto Albini v. inl. ppo.,* or some such, in the sense of a law "prefixed to" or "placed" before the prefectoral edict.

display the copies of this edict of mine."[63] It is repeatedly made clear in passages referring to the publication of legislation, whether by praetorian prefects themselves or by officials under their jurisdiction, that the purpose was to make the emperor's will known to those whom it concerned, "in order that no person may defend the fault of his own contumacy because of ignorance of Our regulation."[64]

The impact of Roman legislation owed its force—and the legislation its validity—to its promulgation and display in the communities to which it was sent. Of all the stages in the life history of a law, this was the culminating moment and the most dramatic. Since the protocols do not record the spirit of enthusiasm, reluctance, or indifference with which laws were received, to capture a sense of the moment we have to look outside the legislative texts themselves. We find for instance in Rabbinical commentaries testimony indicating something of the social experience it generated. Until an edict "which has been written and sealed and brought to a city" was made known by promulgation in the public place, the people were not punishable in respect of it, declared R. Eleazar in the late third century, while the impact on the life of a community of the arrival of such pronouncements is vividly evoked by R. Isaac, also in the time of Diocletian: "A king sent out his order to a city. What did the people in the city do? They rose to their feet, uncovered their heads, and read it in awe, fear, trembling and trepidation."[65]

The intimidating atmosphere, not to mention the theatrical possibilities of such occasions, are conveyed with equal vividness in John Chrysostom's description of the reception of "royal letters (βασιλικὰ γράμματα)" in a city. Chrysostom evokes

63. Edict of Milan: Lactantius, *De Mortibus Persecutorum* 48.12; cf. Eusebius, *Hist. Eccl.* 10.5.13 (Greek version); Edict of Optatus: *P. Cairo Isid.* 1, lines 8–10; on both texts, Simon Corcoran, *Empire of the Tetrarchs*, pp. 158–60, 174–75, and 246. For the examples from *CTh*, Mommsen, Prolegomena, pp. clvi-clvii; e.g., *CTh* 8.4.6, "data epistula ⟨a⟩ praefecto, cui haec sacra [the law itself] fuerat antelata"; cf. 8.5.22, "praelata [MSS prolata] litteris sub die XII k. Mart. Rom.; acc. IIII k. Apr. Venabri [that is, Venafri]," a law addressed to the prefect of Rome and prefixed to his letters to a provincial governor (the consularis of Campania) who received and published it at Venafrum; 9.3.4, "praelata litteris v.c. vicarii," a law prefixed to letters from the vicarius of Spain to a subordinate governor; 11.12.4, "praelata litteris v. inl. com(itis) s(acrarum) l(argitionum)," a law prefixed to and published with letters from the c.s.l.; 7.8.11, "praelata litteris ad Eutychianum praef. urbi," a law addressed to the c.s.l. and sent by him with letters to the prefect of Constantinople.

64. Pharr's trans. of *Sirm.* 16: "Ne quis contumaciae suae culpam praecepti ignoratione tueatur."

65. S. Lieberman, "Roman Legal Institutions," esp. pp. 6–10; and Lieberman, *Hellenism in Jewish Palestine: Studies in the Literary Transmission of Beliefs and Manners of Palestine in the I Century* C.E.*–IV Century* C.E. (1950), pp. 7–10.

in a sermon the effect of their arrival, in order to show how his congregation should stand in still greater fear of the Word of God. For his point to be understood, the (lesser) fear of the emperor would need to be familiar to his listeners: "A profound silence reigns when those letters are read. There is not the slightest noise; everyone listens most attentively to the orders contained in them. Whoever makes the slightest noise, thereby interrupting the reading, runs the greatest danger. All the more should one stand with fear and trepidation . . . in order to understand what is read" to one.[66] The force of the comparison is brought home by descriptions elsewhere of the atmosphere in Chrysostom's churches, clearly no place for the fainthearted, but "fearful and filled with shuddering. For within is the God that has power over life and death—so fearful is the place. And within, ten thousand sermons on eternal punishment, on the rivers of fire, on the poisonous worm, on unbreakable bonds and furthest darkness."[67] In very different circumstances, the same atmosphere of trepidation is conveyed by Ammianus' description of a bogus proclamation made to an unnamed Syrian town by the Maratocupreni, bandits who impersonated imperial officials, in this case the *rationalis,* or financial officer, of the province. Announcing through a herald that they had come with authority to confiscate the property of a leading citizen and having been admitted to the town, the impostors had stripped bare the house of a leading citizen and gotten away before the townspeople realized they had been duped. They had fallen victim to a successful enactment of imperial authority.[68]

Apart from the dramatic impact of heralds and awesome proclamations made to a silent public, imperial letters were distinguished, not only by the sealing mentioned by R. Eleazar, but by a particular form of writing. A law of Valentinian addressed to the proconsul of Africa asserts the imperial monopoly of the script against its improper use by the proconsul's office in making reports to the emperor. In the words of the law, his Serenity the emperor had observed that his Gravity the proconsul had adopted the practice of imitating the "celestial letters" in composing referrals of cases and reports, using the same script (*apices*) as that used by the imperial bureaus. The emperor called a halt to the abuse: "This custom, a teacher of forgery, shall be abolished and everything which must be written either from a province or by a governor shall be entrusted to commonly used letters [*communibus litteris*], so that no person shall have the right to appropriate a copy of this style [*stili huius exemplum*] either privately or publicly."[69]

66. From his *Homilies on Genesis, PG* 53.112.

67. *Hom. I in Iud.,* 4 (*PG* 48.848), as paraphrased by Ramsay MacMullen, *Christianizing the Roman Empire,* A.D. *100–400* (1984), p. 64.

68. Amm. Marc. 28.2.11ff., with my *The Roman Empire of Ammianus,* p. 264f.

69. *CTh* 9.19.3 (trans. Pharr), under the title *Ad legem Corneliam de falso.*

The imperial script referred to is identified as the so-called chancellory hand found on a number of papyri. It is an upright, regular, large, and very clear script derived, it is thought, from an "older Roman cursive" developed by the imperial chanceries and elsewhere obsolete.[70] A law of 470 of the emperor Leo further seems to declare that imperial pronouncements were invalid unless signed in the emperor's own hand in purple—what Leo called the sacred encaustic, referring to a particularly brilliant and durable form of painting with molten wax. No one has the right, on pain of confiscation of property and capital punishment, to usurp the physical form of writing in which the emperor's pronouncements are enshrined.[71] Right down to the writing in which it was expressed, imperial authority was identified and reinforced by a calculated visual—in fact, a strictly "theatrical"—mode of presentation.

If it was perilous to interrupt the public reading of a law by making a disturbance, the defacement or forcible removal of an imperial proclamation once it had been posted was a crime almost unthinkable, producing certain death for treason if the perpetrator was caught. Such an occasion is again described in Rabbinical commentaries, supplementing an episode also known from a Classical source. The commentaries begin with the now familiar description of the "ritual anxiety" with which the laws were received, but then take an unexpected turn: "In every city, when the king's letters arrived the people embraced and kissed them, rose to their feet, uncovered their heads and read them in fear, in awe, in trembling and in trepidation. But when they arrived at the king's own city the people read them, tore them down and burnt them."[72]

We have here a comprehensive and now familiar summary of the circumstances attending the reception of an imperial proclamation. The "embracing and kissing" of imperial edicts is a theme that recurs elsewhere; we have seen it in a letter of a proconsul to the emperor Constantine and a legal text of the same period, and, as part of a fictitious narrative, in a late martyr-act. The burning of the "king's letters" is an additional touch in the Rabbinical source, deriving from an episode described in the Book of Jeremiah (36.23).[73] Otherwise, we recognize the story of the Christian activist who, seeing the first edict of persecution posted at the "king's own city" of Nicomedia, pulled it down and tore it up in protest with sarcastic remarks about (non-existent) Sarmatian victories, thereby securing his desired martyrdom.

70. B. Bischof, *Latin Palaeography: Antiquity to the Middle Ages* (1986; Eng. trans., 1990), pp. 61–63.

71. *CJ* 1.23.6. Only original copies can be meant.

72. See Lieberman, "Roman Legal Institutions," pp. 6–10.

73. On the other hand, "tearing down and burning" occur together in laws of the Theodosian Code, describing what should be done with illegal *libelli,* as we shall see.

Clearly, news of imperial victories was another subject that one might expect to be covered by promulgation of a notice, as is shown also by a passage of Ammianus referring to the "litterae laureatae" by which imperial victories were reported.[74]

Despite all precautions, the promulgation even of imperial pronouncements had an inbuilt transience. Once an edict is old, says a Rabbinical text, "no-one cares about it, whereas everyone rushes to read a new one."[75] We must also bear in mind an obvious fact, the exposure of posted documents to ordinary wear and tear from the elements. This is illustrated by a passage of Ulpian cited in the Digest, concerning the abrogation of liabilities of managers of businesses appointed by minors.[76] It is required that a notice abrogating liability be displayed permanently in a relevant place, and so as to be readable. Ulpian defines "public notice" as one that is "written in clear letters, in a place where it can be easily read from level ground, in front of the shop or the place of business, not hidden away but in open view." As to whether the notice should be in Greek or Latin, in Ulpian's opinion this would depend on the locality, the essential point being that no-one should be able to claim that he did not understand what was written in it. If anyone should claim this, or maintain that he had not seen the notice, when many people *did* read it and it was posted openly, his claim would not be allowed. An action would be admissible if the notice was not on display at the time the contract was made, or if its text had been obscured. In the same way the owner of the shop would be liable if a notice he put up was removed by a third party or if it was unreadable through "age or bad weather or some such contingency." A whole range of legal liabilities is founded on the assumptions that a notice was put up in an accessible and relevant place, that it remained there in legible condition for an appropriate period, and that it was read by and known to interested parties. Ignorance was no excuse, a premise that also applied to that vast majority of imperial proclamations that were displayed in non-permanent materials.

Ulpian may also remind us that the distribution, reception and publication of imperial laws were part of a situation in which a vast amount of writing of all sorts was constantly being delivered to the populations of Roman communities. We seem to have entered a domain of widespread literate communication, where the posting up of notices is a practical and effective way of communicating with the

74. Lactantius, *De mortibus persecutorum* 13; Amm. Marc. 16.12.69.

75. Cited by M. Goodman, *State and Society in Roman Galilee, A.D. 132–212* (1983), p. 141. The word for "edict" is a transliteration of the Greek διατάγμα. Another passage quoted by Goodman allowed the reading of letters posted in a big city even on a Sabbath, when they affected the safety of the State.

76. Digest 14.3.11.

population, and where imperial pronouncements must compete with a mass of ephemeral communications of all sorts—legal notices, announcements, edicts, pamphlets, and all the other written forms of discourse that form the texture of the political life of Roman cities.

Indeed, Roman government itself was a very wordy business. In the mid-second century, Fronto described the uses of imperial edicts and other types of imperial pronouncement. It fell to the Caesars "to address the people on many important matters, to correct the inequities of the law, to dispatch rescripts throughout the world, to take foreign kings to task, to repress by edicts disorders among the allies, to praise their services, to crush the rebellious and to cow the proud. All these must necessarily be done by speech and writing."[77] Fronto undoubtedly wrote with the self-interest of a literary man, but a glance at the evidence will show the extraordinary range of issues on which emperors could deliver themselves.[78] Edicts were not only used to enact and order; they were used to announce, advise, excuse, exhort, explain, lecture, to create opinion, to respond to abuse. Suetonius claims that as censor Claudius issued twenty edicts in one day, including two disarmingly rustic texts, of which one advised the public to pitch their wine-jars well in view of the abundant vintage, and another pronounced the sap of the yew tree to be an excellent remedy for snake-bite (*Claud.* 16.4)! He also, learning that an eclipse would fall on his birthday, published an edict saying exactly when it would occur and for how long, with an account of its causes, showing that it was bound to happen and should not provoke disquiet (Dio 60.26.1). The intention was prudent, the execution possibly a little pedantic.

The eccentric oddities of Claudius are as nothing compared with the torrent of words emitted by the emperors of the fourth century. We begin with the edicts and rescripts of the emperors of the Tetrarchic period, giving with full argument the reasons for the imposition, and then again for the suspension, of their persecutions of Christianity, and continue with edicts of Constantine to the provincials of Palestine, setting his military successes in the context of the failure of the persecutions and his personal conversion to Christianity, and to the provincials in general on the merits of Christianity and the wickedness of paganism.[79] The reluctance of scholars to believe that these texts could be authentic expressions of the imperial will,

77. "Verbis ac litteris"; Fronto, *Ad M. Antoninum Imp. de eloquentia* 1.7 (ed. Loeb, Vol. 2, pp. 58–59).

78. Margareta Benner, *The Emperor Says: Studies in the Rhetorical Style in Edicts of the Early Empire* (1975).

79. To the provincials of Palestine, Eusebius, *On the Life of Constantine* 2.24–42 (but "published in the eastern provinces," 42); to the eastern provinces, ibid. 48–60. The former was the text of which Eusebius claimed to possess a copy with the emperor's signature (n. 6).

was overcome by the discovery of one of the most unlikely passages of Constantine's edict to the provincials of Palestine on a contemporary papyrus.[80]

After the Tetrarchs and Constantine, the most disconcerting case of this imperial flow of words is provided by Julian the Apostate. Among Julian's collected writings are familiar sorts of text such as edicts to the Alexandrians reproving them for the violent murder of their bishop, and to the people of Bostra and Edessa on the subject of religious discord.[81] The first of these texts ended with the instruction that it should "be displayed to my citizens of Alexandria," in the second the emperor "publicly commanded" the citizens of Edessa "to abstain from all feuds and rivalries." Other writings of Julian resist any clear distinction between what we might naturally call "legislation" and much broader categories of imperial pronouncement. There are his letters to the Athenians and to other Greek cities, defending his civil war against Constantius and posted in public places, just like imperial legislation, for all to read. Above all there is the *Misopogon* or "Beard-Hater," interpreted in a brilliant article by Maud Gleason.[82] In the *Misopogon,* Julian affected to join the people of Antioch in criticism of his own beard (and general character), a logical inversion enacting the traditions of masquerade and role-reversal attached to the New Year's festival for which it was composed.[83]

It is hard to imagine anything less resembling general legislation than a satirical tract whose basic logic derived from the circumstances of a public holiday; one wonders how many citizens of Antioch appreciated their emperor's literary brilliance when they saw the *Misopogon* posted in public "outside the palace, at the place called the Tetrapylon of the Elephants by the Regia."[84] The "Regia" was a short colonnaded street leading from a cross-roads near the palace, serving, in the words of the Antiochene Libanius, as a sort of Propylaea to it.[85] How is one to imagine the scene? Presumably as a row of notice-boards with the leaves of the *Misopogon* pasted up, to be read by curious citizens or by practiced readers who

80. A. H. Jones, "Notes on the Genuineness of the Constantinian Documents in Eusebius' Life of Constantine," *JEH* 5 (1954), pp. 196–200; repr. in his *The Roman Economy* (ed. P. A. Brunt), pp. 257–62.

81. *Epp.* 60 Bidez/21 Wright (Alexandria); 114–15 Bidez/40–41 Wright (Bostra and Edessa).

82. "Festive Satire: Julian's *Misopogon* and the New Year at Antioch," *JRS* 76 (1986), pp. 106–19.

83. Gleason, pp. 110f. and n. 43.

84. See now on the literary complexity of the text Jacqueline Long, "Structures of Irony in Julian's Misopogon," *The Ancient World* 24.1 (1993), 15–23—another fine article, exploring a further dimension of the topic opened up by Maud Gleason.

85. Malalas, in Bonn ed., p. 328B; Libanius, *Or.* 11.205; cf. G. Downey, *A History of Antioch in Syria* (1961), pp. 393f. and nn. 88–89.

gathered in the streets of cities when such documents arrived, and proceeded to regale unlettered passers-by with their contents; a scene not unlike that when legislation arrived in a city, when, according to the Rabbinical text mentioned earlier, everyone "rushed up" to read a new edict when it was displayed there.

The *Misopogon* is a particularly complex example of those "edicts of chastisement" for which Roman emperors are well known, and it belongs, still more broadly, to the context of the history of lampoons, libelli, pamphlets, and posters that is familiar from the fourth and earlier centuries.[86] Such lampoons and pamphlets could be a significant element in political crises and, in the hands of emperors and others, influential in the formation of public opinion. According to Optatus of Milevis, a church deacon fell afoul of the law of maiestas on account of a "famosa epistula," or lampoon, in which he accused the emperor Maxentius of being a usurper.[87] In the same period, the Christian persecutions instigated by Maximinus Daia were supported by the ideologue Theotecnus of Antioch, who produced forged "memoirs" of Pontius Pilate and Jesus and sent them around Maximinus' territories with edicts (προγραμμάτα) ordering that they be publicly posted everywhere, in country as well as town, and given to schoolteachers with instructions to make children learn them by heart. Another gleefully malicious contribution was made by the military commander of Phoenice, who got confessions from prostitutes of Damascus that they had been Christians, sent them to the emperor, and at his instructions had them posted up "in every place and city"—that is to say, again, both in towns and in country settlements.[88] The points of contact with the diffusion of imperial legislation are obvious. In a text preserved in the Theodosian Code, the emperor Honorius met claims by Donatists that they had received a rescript in their favor from Julian by ordering that the rescript, or what was claimed to be such, should be prefixed to a prefectoral edict and posted publicly in the most frequented places of cities, and that the Gesta, or records of the proceedings allegedly containing it, should be subjoined, in order that "the steadfast constancy of the Catholic belief and the desperation of the Donatists, that is falsified by perfidy, may become known to all."[89] This text does more than show

86. Gleason, "Festive Satire," pp. 117–18.

87. Or of tyrannical behavior—Opt. Mil. 1.17 (ed. C. Ziwsa, *CSEL* 26, p. 19): "Per famosam nescio quam de tyranno imperatore tunc factam epistulam reus appellatus est."

88. Eusebius, *Hist. Eccl.* 9.5.1–2.

89. *CTh* 16.5.37: "*Rescribtum,* quod Donatistae a Iuliano tunc principe impetrasse dicuntur, *proposito programmate celeberrimis in locis volumus anteferri et gesta, quibus est huiuscemodi allegatio inserta, subnecti,* quo omnibus innotescat et catholicae confidentiae stabilita constantia et Donatistarum desperatio fucata perfidia. Dat. V kal. Mar. Rav. Stilichone et Aureliano conss." (25 February 405, corrected date). See my earlier comment on the expression *anteferri* (*antelata*).

analogies between the procedures for the dissemination of religious propaganda and for the promulgation of imperial legislation; it completely assimilates them. It also suggests the high level of public comprehension of relevant issues that is implied by this mode of communication.

Although the emperors were the most persistent protagonists in this endless campaign of public information and misinformation, they by no means held the monopoly on it. It was part of the general tone of public life. Among innumerable examples, the Council of Elvira in the early fourth century anathematized "those who are found posting libelli famosi in church" (Canon 52)—from which one might guess it to be a not uncommon occurrence in suspicious Christian communities, still exchanging reproaches in the aftermath of the persecution. Basil of Caesarea later described how a dedicated virgin was harassed by a man of poor reputation, whose advances she rejected. He then, according to the woman, "filled the whole city with slanders against me, and pilloried me with a public placard that was affixed to the doors of the church."[90] We may recall that one of the earliest confrontations of Christianity with the Roman authorities involved the posting in a town of Pontus of an anonymous libellus "containing the names of many people."[91] Declaring against the admissibility of such documents in any accusation, Trajan rightly commented that it would set a very bad precedent; but the episode again takes us into the poisoned atmosphere of a provincial town affected by discord, gossip, and rumor.[92]

The Theodosian Code contains a title of ten laws *De famosis libellis,* in which the same principle as that enunciated by Trajan is repeated.[93] The fundamental point of law is that no accusation may be anonymous; an accuser must openly stand behind what he alleges and show that there is a public interest in the matter and that his involvement is not captious or based on personal enmity. So, on pain of assumed complicity in its distribution, no one may tell to another person anything that he has read in a libellus but, rather, must report, if he happens to know, the identity of its instigator;[94] otherwise, the offending document must be torn down and burnt.[95] In describing the methods by which libelli were disseminated,

90. *Ep.* 289; Loeb trans., neatly adapted by Gleason, p. 116 ("pilloried" for στηλιτεῦσαι).

91. Pliny, *Ep.* 10.96.5–6: "Propositus est libellus sine auctore multorum nomina continens," distinguishing these from "alii ab indice [that is, by an identified informer] nominati."

92. Pliny, *Ep.* 10.97.2: "Sine auctore vero propositi libelli ⟨in⟩ nullo crimine locum habere debent. Nam et pessimi exempli nec nostri saeculi est."

93. *CTh* 9.34. Two of the laws, 9.34.1 and 9, were transcribed with interpretationes in the Breviarium of Alaric.

94. *CTh* 9.34.9–10.

95. On tearing down and burning, see *CTh* 9.34.3, 4, 7, 9 (with interpretatio, cf. n. 96), and 10. Compare the Edictum de accusationibus, discussed in Chapter 9.

the sixth-century interpretatio of the first of the ten laws goes beyond the text under commentary, in saying explicitly that they might either be posted or thrown down where they would be found.[96] The methods are exactly as described in a passage of Eunapius found in the Suda, telling how the return of the emperor Jovian from the disastrous Persian campaign of 363 was greeted by lampoons: "Some of them thrown on the ground so that whoever wished could pick them up and read them; others they posted up on walls.[97] Of the ten laws in this title of the Theodosian Code, the first four happen to be recorded as "posted" in cities of the empire—two at Carthage, one each at Rome and Tyre. In a neat irony, both offense and remedy exploit the same means of communication with the public.

As contrasted with this transient deluge of words written on perishable materials, laws were, on relatively rare occasions, to secure their perpetual observance, engraved on bronze or stone. To pursue the idea of the "life history" of a law, this is what one might call its apotheosis, eternal life reserved for a select few. How they were chosen is not always very clear. The Theodosian Code itself occasionally refers to the preservation of legislation for all time by engraving on bronze tablets. A law of 336/37, for example, issued by Constantine from his eastern capital on an unknown date, was addressed to the provincial council of Africa; by coincidence it was posted at Carthage on the very day before the emperor's death in the east. It exempted certain categories of former municipal office-holders from "compulsory public services of an inferior kind," and closes with the provision that, "in order that this regulation may be confirmed by perpetual observance, We order this law to be published by being engraved on bronze tablets. Posted on the twelfth day before the kalends of June at Carthage in the year of the consulship of Felicianus

96. See *CTh* 9.34.1: "Scribtionis auctor requiratur et repertus cum omni vigore cogatur de his rebus, quas *proponendas* credidit, conprobare," with the interpretatio, "Qui famosam cartham ad cuiuscumque iniuriam et maculam conscripserit in secreto *aut in publico adfixerit inveniendamque proiecerit,* illum, *contra quem proposita est carthula,* non nocebit nec famae eius aliquid derogabit"; cf. the interpretatio to 9.34.9: "Si quis carthulam famosam in cuiuscumque iniuriam vel infamiam *in publico propositam viderit et non statim discerpserit,* et cuicumque, quae in ea legit, fortasse rettulerit, ipse velut auctor huius criminis teneatur."

97. Eunapius, frag. 29.1, Blockley (from Suda Ἰ(οβιανός) 401; ed. Adler 1.2, p. 638. The Greek word προσεκόλλιζον means strictly "pasted"), and the passage continues, "These said such things as 'You came back from the war. You should have come to grief there!,' and 'Ill-omened Paris, most handsome to look at!,' and so on, including, 'If I do not take you and strip your clothes from you, your cloak and tunic, which hide your shame, and send you off in haste wailing to the land of the Persians!' " As will be clear, the content of these "famosi" could be extremely circumstantial, assuming a high level of public (and even literary) appreciation of what was said in them.

and Titianus."[98] As its protocol shows, the text of the law preserved in the Code derives not from the bronze tablets mentioned there, but from the copy displayed at Carthage. Even when laws were engraved on bronze or stone, it is usually not from this source that they have come down to us, but through the copying of posted versions.

Another text from the Code contains regulations about pigs, including the delightfully salutary caution that their weight "is to be sought by the tongue of the balance" and not estimated "by the liberty of the eyes." Addressed to the prefect of Rome, the admonition concludes with the provision that all the regulations must be engraved on a bronze tablet and placed in the swine market as an eternal memorial.[99] In another law of Constantine, the exemption of *palatini* from menial public services is engraved on bronze tablets, to which the palatini could appeal if their exemptions were challenged.[100] A law of Valentinian ordered that the names and entitlements of the citizens of Rome receiving free bread distributions should be listed in bronze at the place where the distributions were made;[101] and a late law of Theodosius II had set in bronze the provisions whereby a sum of 611 pounds of gold was made available for the purchase of grain for distribution at Constantinople.[102]

These texts embody a very ancient epigraphic convention. From early times we find written into pieces of Roman legislation the provision that they be displayed in public places, in such a way as to be easily legible by those concerned: in clear letters, at eye level, in the most frequented places of cities. Already in the senatusconsultum *De Baccanalibus* of 186 B.C., it is decreed that "you shall announce these things on no fewer than three occasions in a public meeting, and so that you shall know the Senate's opinion, this was their opinion, . . . and you shall engrave this on a bronze tablet, . . . and you shall order it to be fastened up where it can be easily known: *utiquei eam figier ioubeatis, ubei facilumed gnoscier potisit.*"[103] The

98. *CTh* 12.5.2, trans. Pharr: "Quod ut perpetua observatione firmetur, legem hanc incisam aeneis tabulis iussimus publicari. P(ro)p(osita) XII kal. Iun. Karthagine Feliciano et Titiano conss." The law may have been issued in the later part of 336 to be received at Carthage in May 337. For Constantinople, see Barnes, *New Empire,* p. 80.

99. *CTh* 14.4.4: "Suariis aestimandi licentia denegetur pondusque porcorum trutinae examine, non oculorum libertate quaeratur. . . . Haec autem omnia aeneae tabulae in foro suario collocandae ad aeternam memoriam oportebit insculpi. Dat. III id. Octob. Remis, Lupicino et Iovino conss."

100. *CTh* 6.35.4.

101. *CTh* 14.7.5.

102. *CTh* 14.16.3, issued on 26 Nov. 434, during the period in which the Theodosian Code was being compiled.

103. Riccobono, vol. 1, no. 30 (also *ILS* 18), vv. 22ff., cf. the *Lex de repetundis,* Fragmentum Tarentinum, lines 12ff.: "[In tabulam aheneam scriptum litteris inc]isi fictamque apud

Roman Empire provides many instances of the dissemination of such written materials, together with the instructions that they should be accessible for consultation by the public.[104] To choose only from recently published examples, in the Tabula Siarensis from Baetica the Senate decrees that posthumous honors are to be awarded to Germanicus Caesar. In order to make the decree known, the consuls are to issue an edict, instructing magistrates and legati of municipalities and colonies of Italy, and colonies in the provinces, to publish it, while governors of provinces are advised that they would do well to display the text in the most frequented place in communities under their jurisdiction.[105] In the Lex Irnitana from the same Spanish province, now by far our fullest version of a Roman municipal charter, several provisions relate to the posting of information in a more or less permanent form; rental agreements and conditions, the governor's *album*, the names of *iudices* and of candidates for office, public notices, and so on. The final rubric of the inscription reads:[106] "Concerning the inscription of the statute on bronze. Any duumvir who is in charge of the administration of justice in that municipium is to see that this statute is inscribed on bronze in the most prominent place in that municipium so that it may be properly read from ground level."[107]

The formula, defining the conditions in which an inscription or public notice could be read, was not just a convention of no practical concern. Not only was it by hearing the law announced in public places and reading it when displayed that the populations of the empire were expected to have knowledge of it; still more important, when we consider how legislative texts might enter the juristic tradition, it

forum unde de plano recte legi possit." See esp. Callie Williamson, "Monuments of Bronze: Roman Legal Documents on Bronze Tablets," *Classical Antiquity* 6.1 (1987), pp. 160–83, at 171 n. 43, with M. W. Frederiksen, "The Republican Municipal Laws: Errors and Drafts," *JRS* 55 (1965), pp. 183–98, at 184.

104. W. Williams, "Formal and Historical Aspects of Two New Documents of Marcus Aurelius," *ZPE* 17 (1975), esp. pp. 41f., 44f. with 50 n. 3.

105. "Ut quam celeberrumo loco figeretur," as in *CTh* 16.5.37, cited earlier; cf. Tabula Siarensis, frag. 2(b), lines 23–27; see J. González, "Tabula Siarensis, fortunales Siarenses et municipia civium Romanorum," *ZPE* 55 (1984), pp. 55–100.

106. J. González, "The Lex Irnitana: A New Copy of the Flavian Municipal Law," *JRS* 76 (1986), pp. 147–243 (trans. Michael Crawford pp. 182–99). The clause quoted, chap. 95, is followed by chap. 96, "Sanction," with an addendum on the rights of patrons over freedmen and freedwomen (§97), and a letter of Domitian on marriage, issued at Circei on 10 April and recited at Irni on 11 October A.D. 91 (§98).

107. Often abbreviated, as here, "*u*[*t*] *d*[*e*] *p*[*lano*] *r*[*ecte*] *l*[*egi*] *p*[*ossint*]." For the Greek equivalent, compare Josephus' transcript of an edict of Claudius: "I desire magistrates of cities, colonies and municipalities, both in Italy and outside it, and kings and rulers . . . to have my edict inscribed and displayed for not less than thirty days, in a place where it can be clearly read by a man at ground level (εξ ἐπιπέδου)" (*Ant. Iud.* 19.291).

was in this way that legal authorities and other interested parties took note of it by making copies for themselves. This common habit of copying down legislation can be easily illustrated: Caligula aroused criticism because he imposed new tax laws and had them engraved in tiny letters and in an awkward corner, so that they could not be copied;[108] while Eusebius, in Greek versions of Latin originals, quoted Galerius' edict of toleration, and, later, Maximinus' rescript against the Christians. Eusebius explicitly says of the rescript that it was copied (and, presumably, translated) from the copy engraved on a bronze stele at Tyre.[109] Two Latin versions are also known from inscriptions in Asia Minor; one, with a fragment of the city's petition in Greek, from Arykanda in Lycia, the other a recently published text from Kolbasa in Pisidia.[110] "And so these orders against us," says Eusebius at the end of his translation of the rescript, "were published in inscriptions in every province, depriving us of all hope of human aid."[111] One may reflect on the oddity of such texts being inscribed in Latin in places such as Arykanda and Kolbasa, where that language was barely known, but for Eusebius they were a real threat to the security of Christians. Presumably they were widely known in translation, possibly displayed in the more ephemeral form of painted placards or paper notices. Of the two versions we possess of the so-called Edict of Milan of Constantine and Licinius offering toleration and rights of property ownership to Christians, one was cited by Eusebius in a Greek translation of the original, one in Latin by Lactantius from the copy displayed under the governor's edict at Nicomedia, where the writer was living at the time (it was the city where the Christian martyr mentioned earlier tore down the edict of persecution). It is worth adding that the only surviving text of one of the most important of all Roman legal enactments, the so-called Constitutio Antoniniana of A.D. 212 giving the Roman citizenship to all free inhabitants of the empire, comes down to us as part of a dossier of legal documents assembled by an individual who apparently wished to use it to support his title to residence at Alexandria, or some other privilege to which the *Constitutio* was relevant. It too was perhaps transcribed by the petitioner or on his behalf from a publicly displayed version of the law; in any case, it is a good illustration of the importance to individuals of possessing copies of legislation that affected them, and of one of the means by which laws were transcribed and entered the juristic tradition.[112] We saw

108. Suetonius, *Caligula* 41.1: "minutissimis litteris et angustissimo loco, uti ne cui describere liceret." *Describere* is the term for "copy out."

109. *Hist. Eccl.* 9.7.2ff. On Tyre as the metropolis of Phoenicia (or Phoenice), see n. 38.

110. Stephen Mitchell, "Maximinus and the Christians in A.D. 312: A New Latin Inscription," *JRS* 78 (1988), pp. 105–24.

111. *Hist. Eccl.* 9.7.15.

112. *P. Giss.* 40; F. M. Heichelheim, "The Text of the *Constitutio Antoniniana* and the

in Chapter 2 how private rescripts were displayed at the place where they were given to petitioners, where they could be transcribed by other interested parties for the precedents and points of law they might contain.

The vast majority of imperial pronouncements were recorded not on bronze or stone, but in various perishable forms; in addition to the small number of texts ordered to be inscribed on bronze for reference in perpetuity, the Theodosian Code also refers to the publication of texts on painted tablets or linen sheets—in one text to all three media.[113] Even these are cases of conspicuous public display, and stand apart from the vast majority of texts that were written on paper under governors' edicts, displayed on public notice boards, and after an initial flurry of interest left to suffer the deterioration of time and weather, or to enjoy the modest claim to perpetuity entailed by their transcription by a lawyer or other interested party. It is, however, this habit of individuals of transcribing for their own use the texts of imperial legislation that stands behind the question of the sources of the Theodosian Code, a topic to be discussed in the final chapter of this book.

---

Three Other Decrees of the Emperor Caracalla Contained in Papyrus Gissensis 40," *Journal of Egyptian Archaeology* 26 (1940), pp. 10–22, esp. 21–22. See Williamson (n. 103), pp. 165f., for the copying of military *diplomata* in the interests of the individuals whose privileges they recorded.

113. *CTh* 11.27.1, "Aereis tabulis vel cerussatis aut linteis mappis scribta per omnes civitates Italiae proponatur lex."

# 8

# *The Editors at Work*

## Three Approaches

The preceding chapters have described in two ways the character of the texts included in the Theodosian Code. This was done in Chapter 6 by comparing, in the Sirmondian Constitutions, a group of texts transmitted in their unedited form with the versions of these texts as they appear in the Code; and in Chapter 7, by reconstructing the life history of a law, from the moment at which the need for legislation was accepted and a law drafted, through the hazards of its journey to often distant parts, to its promulgation in a province by the governor to whom it was sent. The description touched upon the manner in which the law was received by the population of a province and offered a perspective of imperial legislation beside the other forms of written materials, mostly ephemeral, with which it had to compete for the attention of the public.

The present chapter looks at the Theodosian Code itself, taking certain situations and categories of material confronting the editors, in the belief that their responses to this material may throw light on its general characteristics. It falls into three parts. In the first are studied the activities of the editors in one selected title of the Code. The second offers the converse of this approach (though the question is also raised in the first part), reconstructing a number of more extensive laws from excerpts disposed by the editors in different places of the text. In the third part are set out some anomalies and special situations that may throw light on the origin of the material in which they occur. In all three parts, more general conclusions will be indicated from time to time, to be drawn together in the final chapter of this book.

## *A Selected Title*

*CTh* 11.30 *De appellationibus et poenis earum et consultationibus*,[1] is a title containing sixty-eight laws on the rules of procedure, time limits, and other restrictions governing appeals to higher courts. The topics covered concern mainly litigation and civil jurisdiction, with a certain emphasis on fiscal matters, but criminal jurisdiction is also included. The edited laws range from a few words of legal definition (nos. 7, 38, 42, 43, 51, and 52) to substantial texts running up to half a page in length (11, 64). They cover the period from 313 to 429 and are relatively evenly distributed. The longest space of time between two adjacent laws is eight years, with two gaps each of seven and six years. There is some bunching of laws—for example, in certain parts of the reign of Constantine—but in general the texts are sufficiently well spaced to form a coherent body of material. The title is used here to illustrate some of the procedural and other matters discussed in the previous chapter and to indicate patterns in the distribution of some editorial procedures that, if found more widely, may have a bearing on the composition of the Code and on its sources.

A. To begin with questions internal to the title, two pairs of texts were issued on the same date and possess identical or near-identical protocols, showing that each pair originally formed parts of a single law. The pairs are 5 and 6, addressed on 13 August 316 to Petronius Probianus, whose office is not stated but who is known to have been proconsul of Africa, and posted at Theveste on 15 October; and 16 and 17, two of many extracts in the Code addressed "ad universos provinciales" on 1 August 331. The law was posted on 1 September, at Constantinople according to the first of the extracts—a detail absent from the manuscript tradition of its successor but safely restored to it. It will receive further discussion in the second part of this chapter.

B. In a far greater number of cases we find complementary extracts elsewhere in the Theodosian Code, from which missing details in the protocols can be restored or mistaken details amended:

1. The first law in the title bears the name of the same addressee, Claudius Plotianus, *corrector Lucaniae et Brittiorum* and, except for a minor inconsistency as to the day of the month, the same date and consuls, 30 [27] December 313,[2] as

1. "Appeals and the Penalties Thereof: Reference of Cases to the Emperor" (trans. Pharr).

2. Viz., *III* (or *VI*) *kal. Ian. Trev(eris) Constantino A III et Licinio III conss.*

the first law in the preceding title, 11.29 *De relationibus*. That version, however, adds to the date of issue of the law at Trier a date and place, 6 February at Rhegium, for its acceptance by the *corrector.* It is safe to assume that the two texts were edited from the same original version; that 11.29.1 begins with the annotation *post alia* and 11.30.1 ends with *et cetera* suggests that in this original text the excerpts came in the opposite order from the one in which they appear in the Theodosian Code. If so, then we should also restore to 11.30.1 the annotation *acc. VIII id. Feb. Regio* that occurs in its companion text. It would be logical to prefer the more complete protocol of 11.29.1 and to accept VI rather than III kal. Ian. as the day of issue of the law, giving 27 rather than 30 December.

As to the consular year, when a law was issued late in one year and accepted or posted early in the next, it is more usual for the consular date, sometimes given as a postconsulate, to record the date of acceptance than that of issue.[3] In this case, because Constantine was at Trier at the end of 313 but not at the end of 312, either the consular date of the law is by exception the date of issue, in this case 27 December 313, or it should should be amended by one of two methods: the replacement of a consular by a postconsular date or an increase from "III" to "IIII" in the number of the imperial consulships. According to these respective corrections, the law was given at Trier on 27 December 313 and received at Rhegium on 6 February 314, or on the corresponding dates two years later.[4]

2. The second law in the title has the same addressee, date, and protocols as both *CTh* 9.40.1 (*De poenis*) and 11.36.1 (*Quorum appellationes non recipiantur*), which treat closely related subjects; the protocols of all three laws, clearly edited from a single text, show that this was issued at Trier on 3 November 313 and received at Hadrumetum on 17 April 314; according to the principle just stated, the consular year is that in which the law was received in Africa, not that in which it was issued at Trier.[5] *CTh* 11.30.2 has at the beginning *post alia* and at the

3. R. Delmaire, "Etude sur les souscriptions de quelques lois du Code Théodosien: Les lois reçues à Regium," in M. Christol and others (eds.), *Institutions, société et vie politique* (1992), pp. 315–28; cf. Seeck, *Regesten,* pp. 14–15, and Alan Cameron, in *Consuls of the Later Roman Empire,* pp. 79–84, arguing that "post-consular" datings reflect provincial practice and are signs of provincial origin for the texts. This is true, and important in considering the sources of the Code.

4. Delmaire, pp. 317–18, 325. Seeck, *Regesten,* pp. 78, 162 (misreported by Delmaire), replaced the consular with a postconsular annotation to give a date of issue as 313 and a date of acceptance as 314.

5. Delmaire, "Etude sur les souscriptions," pp. 318–19, 325. The law was placed after 11.30.1 by the editors of the Code because of its apparently later consular date. This was however the date of *acceptance;* the law was actually issued earlier than its predecessor.

end *et cetera,* the annotations suggesting that it might have made up the middle portion of the original text. The office of the addressee, Catullinus, is not given in any of the three texts; he is however identified as Aco Catullinus, later proconsul of Africa[6] but at that point praeses of the province of Byzacena, of which Hadrumetum was the chief city.

3. *CTh* 11.30.4 is addressed to Amabilianus, praefectus annonae Africae, with a transmitted "proposita" date (but no place) of 30 December 315:

> pp. III kal. Ian. Constantino A. IIII et Licinio IIII conss.

Two other laws, 13.5.2–3 in the title *De naviculariis,* addressed to the same person as praefectus annonae ("Africae" is missing), have discrepancies in their annotations of date and place but are evidently connected with each other, and with 11.30.4:

dat. kal. Iun. Trev(iris) Constantino A. IIII et Licinio IIII conss.;
pp. V. kal. Iun. Constanp. Constantino A. V et Licin(io) Caes. conss. [319].

The second of these excerpts adds the name of a place at which the text was posted, supposedly Constantinople. This is impossible at such an early date, and anyhow inappropriate for a law directed to an official in Africa. It is a persuasive suggestion that it is a misreading of the recently renamed "Constant(inae)," Constantina, or Cirta, in Numidia, and that these three texts represent a law issued at Trier and posted at Constantina some time later.[7] The corrections required to achieve this result are extremely uncertain. One suggestion, accepting the protocol (but not the consuls) of 13.5.3 and in the other two texts amending "Ian." to "Iun." and vice versa, would see in it a law issued at Trier on 1 January and published at Constantina on 28 or 30 May 315. An alternative, accepting the date and place of issue of 13.5.2 and emending "Iun." to "Ian." in 13.5.3, would have it issued at Trier on 1 June 315 and posted at Constantina on 28 or 30 December of the same year. Other possibilities can be devised, however, and it is not clear that the protocols are reliable enough to give any particular reconstruction an advantage over others.[8]

6. Seeck, *Regesten,* pp. 57–58; *PLRE* 1, p. 187 (Catullinus 2).

7. Seeck, *Regesten,* pp. 98, 110, against Mommsen's judgment that the inconsistencies are merely copyists' errors.

8. *PLRE* 1, p. 49, under Amabilianus, writes of it as a single law, "possibly issued at Trier on 315 Dec. 30 and published at Constantina on 316 May 28," but the only explicit "data" notification, in 13.5.2, gives a date on the first of a month. Barnes, *New Empire,* p. 71, and J. Gaudemet, "Constitutions Constantiniennes destinées à l'Afrique," in *Institutions, société et vie politique,* p. 351, enter it (after Seeck) as a law of 1 June 314, but this dating takes no

4. *CTh* 11.30.11 is a law addressed to Maximus, without designation of office, on the transmitted date "prid. id. Ian."—that is, 12 January in the consular year 321; this is right for the praefectus urbi Valerius Maximus *signo* Basilius, whose attested tenure runs from 1 September 319 to 13 September 323.[9] The companion of this law is found (from the Breviarium) with identical protocols as the first text of *CTh* 2.18 *De iudiciis*. If the annotation *post alia* at 11.30.11 is correct, and if no further extract is missing in the earlier books of the Code, then this extract should have stood in the original text as the earlier of the two.

5. *CTh* 11.30.12, addressed by Constantine to the holder of an unspecified magistracy, carries the same protocols as 12.1.8, except that the name of the recipient varies, appearing as either Florentinus or Florentius. As with 13.5.3, just discussed (no. 3), the date of issue, in this case 13 April 323, is inconsistent with the place, Constantinople, which did not yet exist. In any case, it is known that in spring 323 Constantine was resident at Thessalonica.[10] Whatever correction is accepted, the error goes back to the common source of the two texts separated by the editors.

6. The companion text of *CTh* 11.30.19 is found at 12.1.28 (*De decurionibus*), a law about nominations for curial status. Both texts are addressed to Anatolius, vicarius Asiae, and the protocols are in agreement in giving a date, without place of origin, of 26 November 339. The annotations *et cetera* in 12.1.28 and *post alia* in 11.30.19 suggest that the fragments stood in this order in the original text, as would be logical, nominations of curial status coming before appeals about them.

---

account of the consular dates. As for 1 June 315, Constantine is recorded at Trier from October 314 until 28 April 315; then comes "Sirmio" on 2 June 315 (*CTh* 2.30.1). It is unclear whether of two unlikely options this is Constantine at Sirmio (mod. Sirmione on Lake Garda in northern Italy) or Licinius at Sirmium in Pannonia (that is to say, "Sirmio," with the manuscripts); see Simon Corcoran, "Hidden from History: The Legislation of Licinius," in Harries and Wood (eds.), *The Theodosian Code,* pp. 113–14, or *Empire of the Tetrarchs,* p. 287 (no. 5),—citing a third, and in my view better, option, that of retaining Sirmium but redating *CTh* 2.30.1 to 319. This removes it from the scene and permits Constantine to legislate from Trier on 1 June 315.

9. Chastagnol, *Fastes,* no. 29 (pp. 72–74). The exact dates are recorded by the *Chronographer of 354* (Mommsen, *Chron. Min.* 1, pp. 66–68).

10. Barnes, *New Empire,* p. 75. See Corcoran, "The Legislation of Licinius," p. 113, or *Empire of the Tetrarchs,* p. 286, for Seeck's fanciful idea (*Regesten,* pp. 110–11) that Constantine might have temporarily occupied Byzantium (in Licinius' territory) in 323 and issued a law in the city, later renamed by the editors as Constantinople. The notation is more likely a textual error deriving from the transposition of the name of emperor into that of city—though as Corcoran points out, it is not easy to turn this into a specific emendation, since the emperor's name does not occur among the consuls.

The corresponding text at *CJ* 7.63.1 combines *CTh* 11.30.19 with an earlier text in the same title (11.30.10). This is however an innovation in *CJ*, and does not affect the interpretation of the Theodosian Code texts.[11]

7. A similar observation about the order of the extracts applies to *CTh* 11.30.26 and 11.36.12, parts of a law addressed to the praetorian prefect Volusianus on 29 or 30 July ("IIII," or "III kal. Aug.") in the year 355. In addition to their recipient, the subject matter of the law, appeals in matters concerning *bona vacantia* and payments due to the fiscus, associates the two texts. The first text is annotated *post alia,* the second *et cetera,* which, if no other part is missing from the incomplete books, may indicate that the two extracts originally stood in the reverse order from that in which we find them in the Code.

8. *CTh* 11.30.32 is a law of Valentinian and Valens addressed to the council of Carthage. The form of address, "Impp. Valentinianus et Valens AA. salutem dicunt ordini Karthaginis," is identical with that of its companion text at 11.36.15 (*Quorum appellationes non recipiantur*), with the trivial change of one word, *Karthaginis* to *Karthaginiensium.* Both texts bear the transmitted date of 4 February 364, with the place of issue given as Milan. Valentinian, the actual author of the law, did not, however, take up residence at Milan until late October 364. It is not clear whether the solution is to correct the year from 364 to 365 allowing the month and day to stand, or to amend the transmitted month to one late in 364 (by reading "prid. non. Dec." for "prid. non. Feb."). Whichever correction is preferred,[12] it must be made to both extracts, and in either case the effect will be to transpose the texts to a later place in their respective titles. This is another case where the error in the transmitted date goes back to the sources before the editors of the Code.

9. In the case of *CTh* 11.30.36 we find two companion texts elsewhere in the Theodosian Code. They are 11.29.5 (*De relationibus*) and 11.36.21 (*Quorum appellationes non recipiantur*). The three texts, which concern the prompt hearing or correct form of reference to the emperor of appeals in matters pertaining to civil and criminal jurisdiction (including taxation), are addressed to the praefectus urbi Eupraxius and agree on the date XVI kal. Mart., or 14 February, as that of the posting of the law, presumably at Rome, though none of the texts preserves this detail; the consular year is 374. They bear the respective annotations *et cetera* (11.29.5), *post alia* and *et cetera* (11.36.21) and *post alia* (11.30.36), which would

11. Seeck, *Regesten,* p. 199, followed by *PLRE* 1, p. 59 (Anatolius 3), place them in 352, but there seems no real reason for this.

12. Seeck, *Regesten,* p. 220, opts for 4 February 365. Mommsen, ad loc. and in Prolegomena, p. ccxxxviii, implicitly preferred to change the month.

suggest—again, if the annotations are accurate and there is no missing portion—that they stood in this order in the original text from which the editors worked.[13]

10. *CTh* 11.30.37 was addressed by Valens, Gratian, and Valentinian II—in practice by Gratian—to the proconsul of Africa Thalassius in the consular year 378.[14] The transmitted date of issue is "III kal. Sept.," or 30 August, and the place "Trev[eri." By the end of August, however, Gratian was no longer at Trier, nor was Valens still alive. Gratian was somewhere in the Balkans, having failed to bring timely help to his colleague, who was killed on the battlefield of Hadrianople on 9 August. The problem of dating can be solved by adducing the three companions of the law elsewhere in the Theodosian Code: they are found in succession at 11.36.23–25. From these texts the correction of "III kal. Sept." to "III kal. Feb.," that is 30 January, is transparent, and suits Gratian's known whereabouts at that time. Of the three companion texts, one—the first in the sequence—also gives a date of acceptance of the law as "VI kal. Mai.," or 26 April. The place of acceptance is not recorded, but the office of the recipient would suggest it to be Carthage. (Parallel examples for the time lag between 30 January and 26 April for a law issued at Trier and received in Africa were presented in Chapter 7.) The laws contain annotations relating them to each other in terms of the original text; 11.36.23 has *et cetera,* 11.30.37 and 11.36.24 have both *post alia* and *et cetera* and 11.36.25 has *post alia.* This seems to be the sequence of the extracts in the original text; it would be unclear whether 11.30.37 or 11.36.24 stood earlier, but the annotations in 11.36.23–25 suggest the reasonable inference that these three extracts stood in this order in the text that lay before the editors. On the likely assumption that all four extracts derive from the same original text, the notification of the date of acceptance of the law, preserved in only one extract, ought to be read in all four; it should certainly be read in the three fragments edited together in 11.36.23–25.

11. A less clear case is presented by *CTh* 11.30.38, a law of Gratian, Valentinian II, and Theodosius (again, in practice a law of Gratian) addressed from an unspecified location (probably Aquileia)[15] to the praefectus praetorio Syagrius on 18 June 380. Seeck connected with this law a text without date or place of origin, addressed to the same official and posted at Rome on 15 July of the same year

13. A point of interest is that Eupraxius was a former quaestor of Valentinian who has won some recognition for his knowledge of the law and is praised by Ammianus Marcellinus for his firmness and integrity in legal matters, even when confronted with the aggressive demands of his master; see Chapter 7.

14. For Thalassius, the son-in-law of Ausonius and the father of Paulinus of Pella, see Matthews, *Western Aristocracies and Imperial Court,* p. 70.

15. Seeck, *Regesten,* p. 254.

(7.18.4).[16] The subject of this second law, military deserters, bears no obvious connection with that of the first, but the time lag of a month between the issue and publication of the law makes it possible to take them as parts of a longer communication addressed to the praetorian prefect on 18 June and sent on by him to be posted at Rome on 15 July.

12. A companion text to *CTh* 11.30.44 is provided by 4.17.4. The laws, addressed to the praefectus urbi Symmachus, bear the same protocols and date of 29 November 384, and the connection of subject matter is clear (4.17.4 concerns the giving of judicial sentences in writing). The first text has the annotation *post alia,* and the only difference between them is that the second has the place of origin, Mediolanum, written out in full rather than abbreviated. The special interest in this case lies in the fact that the text of 4.17.4, in a very incomplete part of the Code, is supported only by the Appendix to the Breviarium edited by Krüger (1.23); it appears neither in any manuscript of the Code nor in the Breviarium itself.[17] That it can be associated with an extant text elsewhere in the Theodosian Code attests the reliability of the citations preserved in the Appendix.

13. Some comment is required regarding *CTh* 11.30.45, addressed from Milan on 15 February 385 by "idem Augusti"—that is to say, referring back to 11.30.38, by Gratian, Valentinian II, and Theodosius—to the comes rei privatae Pelagius; its companion text is found, as in other cases, in 11.36 *Quorum appellationes non recipiantur* (as 11.36.29). The first of the texts has the annotation *post alia* the second *et cetera,* which should mean, with the usual reservations, that this extract stood earlier in the original version before the editors. The difficulty with these texts is that by February 385 the college of emperors should not include Gratian, who was overthrown and killed by the usurper Maximus in 383; the date of his death was 25 August of that year. "Idem Augusti" should in 385 refer to Valentinian and Theodosius, omitting Gratian but with the addition of Theodosius' son Arcadius, raised to the rank of Augustus on 16 January 383; as far as this title of the Code is concerned, the imperial college should have been revised from 11.30.40 (31 August 383) but in fact appears in its correct form only at 11.40.47 (26 January 386). The first of the edited texts before us, 11.30.45, has taken some account of the new situation by showing "idem Augusti et Arcad(ius) A.," but without shedding the name of Gratian, which is still inherent in the phrase "idem Augusti." The reason for the anomalies can only be conjectured. It may be that the name of Maximus had been added to the imperial college in 386 (when he was

16. *Regesten,* p. 254; *PLRE* 1, p. 862 (Syagrius 3), makes no connection between the two laws.

17. See Chapter 5.

recognized by Theodosius and the name of his consul Euodius accepted into the formulae of imperial laws)[18] but eliminated after his overthrow of Valentinian in 387 and defeat by Theodosius in the following year. The editors, or their sources, avoided these complications by retaining the titulature "idem Augusti"; having so "unwritten" Maximus, they had little choice but to revert to the previous legitimate imperial college, despite the death of Gratian two years earlier. In *CTh* 11.30.45, but not in its partner or in any of the relevant laws 11.30.40–46, the name of Arcadius was added, as if by an afterthought.

14. The next law in the title is *CTh* 11.30.46, a text of 25 November addressed to the comes sacrarum largitionum Florentius. A companion text is found at 11.36.30 with the same protocols but with the name of the recipient given as Florentinus; the first of the texts carries the annotation *post alia,* the second *et cetera.* Secure inferences about the order of the extracts in the original text are undermined by a further companion, which is found, preserved by manuscript *A,* at 1.10.3. The manuscript gives a slightly variant date of "V [for VII] kal. Dec.," and presents the name of the recipient as Florianus. It also omits the second of the consuls' names: "Arcadio A. I [et Bautone conss.]." These are idiosyncrasies of the manuscript itself and do not affect the conclusion that these three laws derive from a single original text.

15. *CTh* 11.30.49 is a law of Theodosius, issued at Rome to the praefectus urbi Albinus during the emperor's residence in the city in the summer of 389; its date is 29 July. The companion of this law is preserved at *CJ* 6.1.8, as part of a title derived from a seriously incomplete part of the Theodosian Code, namely, Book 5; Krüger inserted the law as 1e in his title XVI, *De inquilinis et colonis.*[19] It might possibly have occurred in the preceding title XVI, *De fugitivis colonis inquilinis et servis,* but this is of no very great moment. In either case, the law extant in the Theodosian Code has allowed us to confirm the identification of a companion text in the incomplete books of the Code.

16. *CTh* 11.30.52, of 28 September 393, is associated with three texts found at other places in the Theodosian Code—more accurately, in the Breviarium, the only source for these passages, where again the full text of the Code is not extant (*CTh* 2.12.5, 4.3.1, 4.8.9). A minor discrepancy in dating is resolved by the smallest of corrections ("IIII" for "VII kal. Octobr." in 4.8.9). Only the Breviarium versions name the recipient, Rufinus, as praetorian prefect, where *CTh* 11.30.52 preserves the original address of an emperor to his friend, with no mention of his office:

18. "*Codex Theodosianus* 9.40.13 and Nicomachus Flavianus," *Historia* 46 (1997), p. 207 and n. 42.

19. See Chapter 5 for Krüger's reconstruction of Book 5 of the Code.

"Have, Rufine k(arissime) n(obis)." Given these discrepancies, it seems possible that *CTh* 11.30.52 derived from a different version of the law than the source of those provided by the Theodosian Code to the compilers of the Breviarium.[20]

17. *CTh* 11.30.53, a law of 16 May 395 addressed by Arcadius and Honorius—that is to say, by Honorius—to the proconsul of Africa Ennoius, possesses no fewer than five companions, edited in succession as 12.1.141–45 (*De decurionibus*). The annotation *post alia* appears in 11.30.53 but of the other texts only one bears the complementary annotation, *et cetera,* 12.1.142. The texts present no problem of dating, all the protocols agreeing in every detail. There is however a difficulty, in that the successive texts 12.1.143 and 144 are practically identical in substance and expression, the former differing only by an additional opening clause, in which the emperors remark on their observation of the intolerably fraudulent practice that has arisen. The laws are among those annotated by Mommsen as *geminae,* or doublets, identical or near-identical texts that occur twice in the Theodosian Code.[21] One can understand why such texts, which might have more than one point of relevance, should be found edited twice in different parts of the Code. It is not so clear why they should occur as adjacent laws in the same title, unless it is simply that the editors were following very literally their instructions to include all the leges generales recovered by them. That is to say, they included two successive versions of the same text because they had recovered more than one copy and did not venture to omit either.[22] If so, it is another indication of the multiplicity of their sources.

18. The likely companion of *CTh* 11.30.56, a law addressed to Nebridius as proconsul of Asia on 22 July 396, is found not in the Theodosian Code but at *CJ* 11.50.2, under the title *In quibus causis coloni censiti dominos accusare possunt.* Its source is again to be found in the incomplete Book 5 of the Theodosian Code, where Krüger inserted it into his title XVII (Mommsen's title 18), *Ne colonus inscio domino suum alienet peculium vel litem inferat civilem.* The wording of the title and its location in Book 5 are confirmed by the Breviarium, and also by the Lex Romana Burgundionum, in which the law is cited with this reference.[23] This is certainly the right place for it, but it is not clear that the two parts of the text derive

20. Seeck, *Regesten,* p. 282, separates 11.30.52 entirely from the other three texts, but this seems unnecessary.

21. Cf. his list at Prolegomena, p. cxix—not including this example, though it is noted in his text.

22. For a similar case of adjacent "twins," 9.42.12–13, see the last section of this chapter.

23. *Lex Romana Burgundionum* 14.6 (Riccobono, vol. 2, p. 728): "vel Theudosiani legem libro V, sub titulo: Nec colonus inscio domino suo alienet peculium vel litem inferat ei civilem, ad Nebridium vicarium Asie."

from a single original version. The *CJ* text is addressed to Nebridius as comes Asiae (corrected by Krüger to read "proconsulem"), and it bears no date. To complete the confusion, the Lex Romana Burgundionum names the addressee as "vicarium Asiae."

19. *CTh* 11.30.57 is a law addressed to the praefectus praetorio Orientis Eutychianus on 27 July 398. It is repeated verbatim as the first part of a longer version at 9.40.16, *De poenis,* and other parts of a clearly substantial archetype appear in three other places: at *CTh* 9.45.3, *De his, qui ad ecclesias confugiunt;* at 16.2.33, *De episcopis, ecclesiis et clericis;* and at *CJ* 1.4.7, *De episcopali audientia* . . . .[24] All versions preserve the same date, "VI kal. Aug.," and the unusual place of issue "Mnizo"; this is Mnizos, a station on the main road from Nicaea to Ancyra, where the emperor Arcadius traveled in the summer of 398.[25] Elements of the last sentence of 9.40.16 also seem to be expanded at 16.2.32, a law with almost the same transmitted date as the others but addressed to the wrong individual as praetorian prefect and with no place of issue.[26]

20. There is no need to comment at length on *CTh* 11.30.67, a law of Theodosius II addressed from Constantinople to Asclepiodotus, praefectus praetorio Orientis, on 30 March 423. Two companions appear with identical protocols in the following title—one at 11.31.9, the other at 4.18.2 from the Breviarium. The first of the three texts carries the annotations *post alia . . . et cetera,* and the second *post alia.* In the case of an eastern law of such recent date, there is no reason to suspect a source other than imperial archives found at Constantinople.

21. The situation is rather different with the last case to be discussed here (and the last law in the title), *CTh* 11.30.68, addressed from Ravenna to Celer, proconsul of Africa, on 25 February 429. The law and its three companions, 11.1.34 (*De annona et tributis*) and 12.1.185–86 (*De decurionibus*), defend African landowners from improper and unreasonable tax demands. There are two reasons to suspect that these laws came to the editors of the Code in two groups. First, the two texts edited as *CTh* 11.30.68 and 11.1.34 open with the epistolary form of address used by emperors to their supporters: "Impp. Theodosius et Valentinianus AA. Celeri suo sal(utem)." The texts edited as 12.1.185–86 have the regular address, "Impp. Theodosius et Valentinianus AA./Idem AA. Celeri proc(onsuli) Afric(ae)." Second, in two of the texts is found a reference to the vir spectabilis and comes

24. For the restoration of this text to *CTh,* see Chapter 5.

25. Seeck, *Regesten,* p. 295, with ref. to Claudian's *In Eutropium,* 2.97–102, 416. For the place, see Pauly-Wissowa, *Realencyclopädie* 30, col. 2290. The *CJ* excerpt misreads as "Mediolani."

26. The only difference in the dating is "VII kal. Aug.," for "VI kal. Aug." in the other texts mentioned. The recipient is given as Clearchus, PPo, but this is incorrect for 398.

Bubulcus, whose services as envoy had secured the benefits in question for the African provincials, but he is referred to in a different style in each case. In 11.1.34 the edited text ends with a fine acknowledgment of the forcible effect of his eloquence on the imperial mind: "Quae pietatem nostram viri spectabilis Bubulci comitis et legati decernere coegit eloquium." In 12.1.186 the same services are described in a more formal and objective style: "Legatio proconsularis provinciae per Bubulcum spectabilem virum comitem curiales pro aliis, qui nec in eodem territorio possident, deflevit adstringi," etc.[27] It is unlikely that the original text contained both these statements as we read them, and there was no need to say the same thing twice in these different ways. The explanation is that the two pairs of laws derived from different copies; one, to venture a speculation, in the form addressed at once to the proconsul and delivered to him by Bubulcus himself, the other drafted and sent in the usual way by the imperial scrinia.

These twenty-one texts from 11.30 thus lead to a further thirty-six companion texts edited elsewhere in the Theodosian Code,[28] and three (nos. 15, 18, and 19) from the Codex Justinianus, one of which (no. 18) is also referred to in the Lex Romana Burgundionum. In the three cases from *CJ*, and one from the Appendix (no. 12), we are able to confirm texts lost from the manuscript tradition of the Code by associating them with texts in the fully preserved books. In several places comparison of the protocols of the complementary texts requires correction of the annotations in the texts before us, and justifies the restoration of missing details relating to the acceptance of laws (nos. 1, 3, 10, and ?11). Although in most cases the companion texts derive from a single original in the hands of the editors, this cannot always be assumed to be the case. Some divergences are best explained on the supposition that the editors already possessed more than one copy of the original version.

C. In a few cases from the same title, in addition to those mentioned above (B, nos. 1, 8), the editors of the Code inserted laws in an incorrect sequence, from which it follows that they already had before them inaccurate protocols:

1. The recipient of 11.30.13, with the transmitted date of 3 August 326, was the prefect of Rome Iulianus; this is Amnius Anicius Julianus, who is known to held the prefecture from 12 November 326 until 7 September 329; 3 August 326

27. Trans. Pharr, "The eloquent statement of the delegate, the Respectable Count Bubulcus, has impelled our piety to decree these measures" (11.1.34): "The delegation of the Proconsular Province, as represented by the Respectable Count Bubulcus, has lamented the fact that decurions are being constrained," etc. (12.1.186). Unfortunately, this is all that is known of the splendid Bubulcus—*PLRE* 2, p. 242. His name (Ploughman) is an antiquarian invention, being found historically in the republican *gens Iunia:* Pliny, *Hist. Nat.* 18.3.10 (with the explanation of its origin); Livy 9.20.7, etc.

28. Including no. 11 and *CTh* 16.2.32 from no. 19.

falls clearly outside his tenure.[29] The most likely correction adopts the consular dating "Constantino A. VIII et Constantio C. IIII" for the transmitted "Constantino A. VII et Constantio C. III conss.," thereby moving the law to 329. That the editors of the Code already had the transmitted date is shown by their placing of the text in sequence after a law of 13 April 323 and before laws of 29 July 327 and 31 July 329.

2. The same prefect, here addressed as Anicius Iulianus, was the addressee of 11.30.18, given at Serdica on 19 June and posted at Rome on 27 July in the transmitted but erroneous consular year 339, "Constantio A. II et Constante conss." The editors of the Code duly inserted the text between laws of 1 August 331 and 26 November 339, but it is clear that it should stand before its three predecessors in the title. This is again achieved by an amendment of the consular date, to read "Constantino A. VIII et Constantio Caes. IIII"—that is to say, 329.[30]

3. A similar observation applies to 11.30.20, addressed to the eastern praetorian prefect Philippus, who held office at the earliest from 344, and posted at an unspecified location on the transmitted postconsular date of 9 June 340.[31] The editors clearly had before them the transmitted date, for they put the text in its place for the year 340, after a text of 26 November 339 and before texts of 28 November 340, February 343, and July 345. The best redating of this law, again involving an amendment of the number of the imperial consulships, in this case from "Constantius A. II and Constans" to "Constantius A. IIII and Constans III," while retaining the "post consulatum" convention, would locate it in 347.[32] We have seen that "post consulatum" datings, combined with *proposita* annotations, often mean that a law has been received in a province early in the year following its

29. Chastagnol, *Fastes,* pp. 78–80 (no. 32); Barnes, *New Empire,* p. 111. The prefecture is precisely delimited by the *Chronographer of 354* (see n. 9).

30. Only 328 and 329 are possible (in June 327 the emperor was at Constantinople). Although one or the other must be accepted, the supporting evidence for either is less than conclusive. The emperor's presence at Serdica in May and June 329 is otherwise documented only by an amendment of the date of *CTh* 9.9.1. The preceding year, 328, is similarly "documented" for 18 May by an amendment of *CTh* 11.7.4—Barnes, *New Empire,* pp. 77–78. The easier corruption of the consular dating of 11.30.18 makes 329 the better option, but it is a marginal judgment.

31. "Post cons. Constantii iterum et Constantis AA."; cf., for the date of Philippus' prefecture, *PLRE* 1, p. 696 (Philippus 7), with the Fasti at p. 1049. I do not know why Cameron, in *Consuls of the Later Roman Empire,* p. 81 (no. 20), gives him as prefect of Italy, Illyricum, and Africa.

32. Seeck, *Regesten,* pp. 41, 199, puts the law in 353; this would even reinforce the argument made earlier.

issue, before the names of the new consuls are known there, but this is an unlikely explanation for a law posted as late as 9 June. Here is a persuasive argument for emending the transmitted "V id. Iun." to "V id. Ian.," to give a date early in the new year, before the official who had received the law from the praetorian prefect and now published it had been notified of the names of the new consuls.

4. *CTh* 11.30.55, addressed to Messala, the praetorian prefect of Italy, carries the transmitted date 19 May 396. Messala held the prefecture in 399 and 400, to either of which years the law in question could be assigned.[33] The transmitted date is impossible, but was clearly that before the editors of the Code, who inserted the law in sequence for that date.

5. To these four instances should be added 11.30.12 + 12.1.8, mentioned earlier, for which any correction retaining Constantinople as the place where the original law was issued would entail displacement of its excerpts in both titles in which they occur. In both places the editors inserted the texts in sequence for a law with the transmitted date of April 323.

In the great majority of the cases discussed above, the changes required to the transmitted protocols of laws are not designed, in the usual manner of textual critics, to restore the text of the Theodosian Code to that produced by the editors, but in a second level of intervention to correct their work by identifying errors already present in the material in their possession. It will be clear that in some cases boldness is required of the modern commentator in handling the texts. This is rather a mixed blessing. Confronted with the more recalcitrant difficulties, the commentator may welcome the proven necessity to be bold; at the same time, it is all the more difficult to judge which of several bolder solutions may be best. What will however also be clear is the extent of the restoration that is needed in this single title to restore its contents to their original condition.

As to some more general features illustrated by this title of the Theodosian Code, we may note that the laws were issued in the usual range of places, where the emperors had their residence at different times in the fourth and early fifth centuries. By far the greater number originate in the west, where two laws were, unusually, issued at Rome, at times when the emperors are known to have been there—Constantine in 315 and Theodosius I in 389, respectively (3, 49). Of the laws issued in other places, three each were issued at Trier (1, 2, and 37) and Sirmium (7, 11, and 27), three also, and a probable fourth, at Aquileia (9, 33, 46, and cf. 38), nine at Milan (32, 34, 44, 45, 48, 53, 54, 58, and 60) and four at Ravenna (62, 64, 65, and 68); one each at Arles (5 + 6), Serdica/Sofia (18),

33. For 399, Seeck, *Regesten,* p. 77; cf. *PLRE* 2, p. 760 (Messala 3).

Singidunum/Belgrade (28), Verona (59), Brixia/Brescia (61), and at an otherwise unknown place transmitted as "Messadensi" (25). This last place marks the emperor Constantius' presence in Raetia, on a campaign against the Alamanni which he is known to have conducted in the year in question (355); otherwise, the places are a good selection of regular court capitals and more occasional imperial residences in the period. Arles early in his reign, and Serdica in its later years, were favored by Constantine (he renamed Arles Constantina, and it was said that he had once contemplated founding at Serdica the new capital that was ultimately built at Constantinople), and Ravenna replaced Milan as the western emperor's main Italian residence in the very early fifth century.[34] Sirmium was one of the main, and Singidunum one of the more occasional Balkan imperial residences; Verona was quite often host to emperors in their journeys across north Italy between Aquileia and Milan, while Brixia only rarely acted as such. As the case of Messadensi suggests, however, there was hardly any location so insignificant (and Brixia was very far from this) that it might not, in certain circumstances, receive an emperor.

The east produces a smaller number of laws than the west, and a proportionately narrower range of places of issue, reflecting in this the more stable political circumstances of the eastern empire. Ten laws, excluding the doubtful case of 11.30.12, were issued at Constantinople (42, 43, 47, 50, 51, 52, 56, 63, 66, and 67), and one each at Heraclea (13), Antioch (29), Marcianopolis in Thrace (35), and Mnizos in Asia Minor (57)—the last-named insignificant in history except for its presence in itineraries, its occasionally mentioned bishop, and the visit of the court of Arcadius in 398.

The recipients of the legislation follow the same pattern of a predominance of western over eastern addressees. In the west, there is a strong emphasis on Italy and Africa. This is not surprising in a title on civil law, with some prominence given to fiscal matters. These provinces were densely urbanized and heavily exposed to taxation but enjoyed access to the imperial court to alleviate the impact and to facilitate a certain taste for litigation. Prefects of Rome were the recipients of ten of the laws (7, 8, 11, 13, 18, 34, 36, 44, 49, and 61), praetorian prefects of Italy also of ten (25, 26, 27, 28, 31, 38, 48, 51, 55, and 58), proconsuls of Africa of eleven (3, 5 + 6, 21, 23, 37, 53, 60, 62, 64, 65, 68). One each went to the praetorian prefect of the Gauls (30), to the vicarii of Rome (29) and of Africa (33), to a western vicarius of an unspecified region, probably Italy (9),[35] to the corrector Lucaniae et Brittiorum (1), to the praeses Tripolitanae (59), to the rationalis urbis Romae (14), and to the praefectus annonae Africae (4). The "ordo civitatis Karthaginis" received a

34. The first law issued there was *CTh* 7.13.15, of 6 December 402.

35. *PLRE* 1, p. 836 (Iulius Severus 25), accepting Seeck's correction of 11.30.8 from 319 to 318, where it joins other laws, every one placed in 318 by correction of transmitted dates.

law (32), and so did the "concilium provinciae Africae" (15). Of a cluster of western laws narrowly dated between 381 and 385, three were sent to the comes sacrarum largitionum (39, 40, and 46) and two to the comes rei privatae (41, 45), all on fiscal matters. A possible explanation is that these already formed a little dossier of texts acquired by the editors of the Code.[36]

In the east, eight laws were addressed to the praetorian prefect of the Orient (20, 35, 47, 52, 57, 63, 66, and 67), but below this level the numbers both of governors and of the laws addressed to them are also much lower than in the west. A single law was addressed to the prefect of Constantinople (54), two to the proconsul of Asia (50, 56), and one each to the vicarius of Asia (19), the proconsul of Palestine (42), the praeses Ciliciae (24) and the dux Aegypti (43). One text was addressed "ad universos provinciales" (16 + 17), and one to an unknown official in the east (22).

The places at which laws are noted as having been "posted" show a similar preponderance of locations in the west, especially at Rome and in north Africa. Four laws were explicitly, and a fifth by sure inference, posted at Rome (8, 18, 23, 28, cf. 36),[37] two at Carthage (15, 39), one each at Capua (25), Theveste (5 + 6), Hadrumetum (2), and Tacapae (33). By reference to companion texts in different titles, a law can be seen to have been posted at Rhegium in south Italy (1 + 11.29.1), one at Cirta/Constantina in Numidia (4), and a third example at Carthage (37).[38] In the east, only two "proposita" locations are recorded in this title: Constantinople for the edict "ad universos provinciales" (16 + 17) and Cyzicus (22).

The laws, supplemented by evidence from related texts in the same title and elsewhere, provide several examples of the double-dated laws described in the previous chapter. I list them in geographical order, from western to eastern points of origin:

11.30.1 + 11.29.1, Trier to Rhegium, 27 Dec.–6 Feb.
11.30.37 + 11.36.23, Trier to ?Carthage, 30 Jan.–26 April.
11.30.2, Trier to Hadrumetum, 3 Nov.–17 April.
11.30.4 + 13.5.2–3, Trier to ?Cirta, either 1 Jan.–28/30 May, or 1 June–28/30 Dec.
11.30.5 + 6, Arles to Theveste, 13 Aug.–15 Oct.
11.30.25, "Messadensi" to Capua, 25 July–(no date).
?11.30.38 + 7.18.4, ?Aquileia to Rome, 18 June–15 July
11.30.33, Aquileia to Tacapae, 12 Sept.–15 Dec.
11.30.28, Singidunum to Rome, 18 June–23 Aug.

36. Compare the laws and rescripts of 365 preserved "ex corpore Hermogeniani" in the *Consultatio veteris cuiusdam iurisconsulti;* Chapter 2, n. 14.

37. Excluding the doubtful case of 11.30.38 + 7.18.4, discussed earlier (no. B.11).

38. See nos. B.1, 3, and 10.

11.30.18, Serdica to Rome, 19 June–27 July.
11.30.16 + 17, ?Nicomedia to Constantinople, 1 Aug.–1 Sept.[39]

Allowing for the times of year at which they were made, none of these journeys falls outside the normal range of journey times surveyed in Chapter 7, and some are noticeably brisk. The five or seven months taken by 11.30.4 and its associated texts to reach ?Cirta/Constantina from Trier are subject to very uncertain reconstructions of their dates of issue and publication.

Two aspects of the distribution of certain characteristics among the sixty-eight laws of this title are worth indicating for their possible significance if they are found to occur more widely.

First, the laws recorded as other than "data" simply—that is to say, as "accepta" or "proposita"—form a minority of texts within the title as a whole. However, they achieve near-parity in its earlier part; of the first forty-one laws in the title (down to the year 383), twenty are so recorded, in the final twenty-seven there are none.[40] If the inference is correct that annotations relating to the acceptance and publication of laws owe their presence to the circumstances in which they were accepted and published, it will be of some interest if they are found to be more frequent in the earlier than in the later laws assembled by the editors of the Code. It suggests that, as they went back in time, the editors relied more heavily on provincial sources than they did for the more recent period.[41]

Second, there is a change between the earlier and the later parts of the title regarding the linguistic conventions by which the recipients of the texts are addressed: whether by the use of *ad* with the accusative case, as in "ad Bassum p.u." (7), or by the simple dative case, as in "Apodemio ppo Illyrici et Ital(iae) II" (51). The latter convention is more elaborately expressed in the form "Petronio Probiano suo sal(utem)" (5 + 6); or, in the case of the Augusti to a public body, "salutem dicunt ordini civitatis Karthaginis" (32).

The distinction between the two modes of address may seem to be merely a matter of convention and to be otherwise insignificant. Nevertheless, it is the case

39. Cf., on this last case, Chapter 7, n. 44.

40. The figures include 11.30.1, on the assumption that *accepta* be supplied from 11.29.1 (no. B.1), and 11.30.37 (no. B.10), and on the other side exclude two cases of the annotation *emissa* (11.30.30, 50).

41. A similar pattern of distribution of annotations within titles is found with four or more instances in each in *CTh* 6.4, 7.22, 9.34, 10.10 (with one very late instance), 12.1, 13.1, 13.5, and 15.1; and with three instances in 1.15, 2.16, 4.12, 6.29, 6.35, 8.1, 9.38, 13.3, and 14.17. The number of such annotations is generally proportionate to the length of titles, and the same pattern is found in titles with only one or two instances.

both that their relative frequencies change quite markedly as one goes through the title, and that this reflects a change of practice visible throughout the Code.[42] In this title alone, of those among the first 23 original texts that were addressed to individual recipients,[43] there are just six that use the form of address with the dative (4, 5 + 6, 14, 18, 20, and 24); the rest use *ad* with the accusative case. No more examples of the dative usage occur from 25 to 42, inclusive, by which time it is a very small minority of texts; but in the final part of the title, from 43 to 68, the dative usage is strongly preferred, with nineteen instances in the last twenty-six laws, and fifteen in the last twenty. Furthermore, of the six texts in the sequence 43–68 that use *ad* with the accusative, five, falling early in the sequence (44, 45, 46, 48, and 52), are of western origin, and one (57) is a doublet of a law elsewhere in the Code (9.40.16), where the dative form is used. One text (52) has the more intimate form of address, "Have Rufine, k(arissime) n(obis)"; and again, the three related laws preserved in the Breviarium all preserve the address with the dative, "Rufino ppo," presumably deriving this form of address from their now lost exemplars in the Theodosian Code.[44] The last law in the title, and a companion text elsewhere in the Code, retain the address "Celeri suo sal(utem") (69 + 11.1.34) where two other versions of the same original text have the regular form of address, again in the dative (12.1.185–86). I earlier offered an explanation for this.[45]

The meaning of this change of preference merits reflection. Broadly speaking, the difference between them is that the dative usage expresses the form of an epistolary address from writer to recipient, while *ad* with the accusative is a more descriptive form that might be used by a third party; that is to say, it is a more "editorial" idiom. It is particularly striking how closely the evidence of this single title conforms to an analysis of the Theodosian Code as a whole. Boudewijn Sirks has compiled figures on the basis of Mommsen's Prolegomena, covering year by year the period 366–400.[46] They can be summarized as follows:

42. Seeck, *Regesten,* pp. 16–18; cf. Sirks, "The Sources of the Code," in Harries and Wood (eds.), *The Theodosian Code,* pp. 52–53.

43. Three were addressed "ad concilium provinciae Afric(ae)" (15) and "ad universos provinciales" (16 + 17), respectively. These texts are not included in the survey of the title, but they share its characteristics; cf. the address to 11.30.32, cited earlier.

44. See no. B.16.

45. See no. B.21.

46. Boudewijn Sirks, "The Sources of the Code," pp. 52–53, and Appendix 2, pp. 66–67. Sirks does not say whether his year-by-year figures allow for necessary corrections to Mommsen's Prolegomena; however, the patterns are clear, and Sirks follows the figures derived from Mommsen with a summary of those derived from Seeck's *Regesten,* with very similar results. Honoré, *Law in the Crisis of Empire,* p. 139, argues that "no firm conclusion" can be drawn from the changing convention, but this is unsatisfactory; the figures need *some* explanation.

| | East | | | West | | |
|---|---|---|---|---|---|---|
| address | dative | *ad* | dat: *ad* | dative | *ad* | dat: *ad* |
| 366–79 | 19 | 39 | 0.49 | 16 | 196 | 0.08 |
| *p.a.* | 1.36 | 2.79 | | 1.14 | 14.0 | |
| 380–94 | 277 | 33 | 8.39 | 41 | 108 | 0.38 |
| *p.a.* | 18.47 | 2.20 | | 2.73 | 7.20 | |
| 395–400 | 111 | 11 | 10.09 | 132 | 7 | 18.86 |
| *p.a.* | 18.50 | 1.83 | | 22.0 | 1.17 | |

In the east, we must allow for an increase, beginning in 380, in the amount of surviving legislation; even so, the figures show a decisive change in that year, sustained thereafter, towards a preference for the dative form. Whether the increase in the number of laws represents more legislation or a higher level of recovery, or both, will be parts of the explanation of the phenomenon, which is in itself unquestionable.

In the west, although there are years between 387 and 394 in which, because of the prevailing political turbulence, little legislation was issued, the same change, combined with a similar increase in the volume of surviving legislation, occurs with almost equal distinctness in 395. The figures both for east and west seem to reflect a change of practice rather than a progressive shift of style, which would not be so abrupt. That the change originated in an eastern milieu is also suggested by the two higher figures for the west in the period 387–394; namely, those for 389 and 390, producing, respectively, ten usages with the dative out of fourteen laws, and nine cases out ten. These were the two years of Theodosius' presence in the west after his defeat of the usurper Maximus, when the political situation was more stable, and either western legislation was influenced by eastern practice, or the manner in which it entered the records and was recovered by the editors of the Code was subject to a similar change; or, of course, both.

The change of idiom was surely not an innovation of the editors of the Code themselves; one can imagine neither why they should have introduced it, nor how, across the hundreds of diverse topics and titles emerging from their labors, they could have imposed it so consistently. It must have been a feature of the material before them.[47] As with the decreasing proportion of *proposita* and *accepta* annota-

47. Sirks, "The Sources of the Code," p. 53, thinks of the change of idiom as expressing a preference of "Theodosius or his aides," as contrasted with Seeck, *Regesten,* who saw a change in the compilers' source material from copybooks or *commentarii* (*Abschriftenbücher*) to the

tions, the change might suggest that as they approached their own day, the editors of the Code were more able to use material from central archives that had not already been worked over by others.[48] The clear dating of the change would then suggest that the archives existed in their improved form, in the east from 380 (following the accession of Theodosius) and in the west from 395 (the accession of his sons), and that the legislation for those earlier years of Theodosius in the west for which the later convention applies was also found in the eastern archives.[49]

A final aspect of the conventions found in *CTh* 11.30 is worth noting, since it too occurs elsewhere. In thc Theodosian Code the recipients of constitutions are generally addressed by the single name by which they were known. In four cases in this title, representing three original texts, recipients are, however, addressed more fully, in a fashion resembling an earlier Roman style of nomenclature, *gentilicium* or family name followed by *cognomen* or personal name: "ad Claudium Plotianum correctorem Lucaniae et Brittiorum" (1, cf. 11.29.1); "Anicio Iuliano p(raefecto) u(rbi)" (18); "Petronio Probiano suo sal(utem)" (5 + 6).[50] The recipient of 11.30.9, addressed "ad Severum vic(arium)," may be the same as the "Iulius Severus" (or "Verus") addressed by a fuller name in two other texts in the Code; 6.35.4 "ad Iulium (Se)verum vic(ari)um Italiae," and 8.18.2, "Iulio Severo."

This practice of using fuller forms of the names of the recipients recurs in the Theodosian Code, as a characteristic of laws of Constantine that is found only rarely after his time; so, in laws that are all from the Constantinian period and all of western provenance, we encounter the following individuals (only those offices are listed in which the recipients of laws were actually addressed in this way). The predominance of Roman, Italian, and African, that is to say broadly "senatorial" magistracies[51] is obvious:

---

original texts themselves (*Aktenbücher*); I would interpret the former category more broadly, to cover all derivative sources, as described earlier. Sirks rightly observes that both forms of address are found at all times throughout the empire, but the point at issue is the change of idiom within the Theodosian Code.

48. This seems compatible with the arguments of Honoré, *Law in the Crisis of Empire*, pp. 136–41, suggesting on other grounds that for laws issued in 398 and later the editors relied heavily on records available at Constantinople.

49. Sirks, p. 53 n. 55, suggests that "if Seeck had been right, the change would have occurred simultaneously in East and West," but this is not necessarily so. The progressive establishment of the regime of Theodosius would permit either interpretation at issue here—a change in the conventions of composition or in the character of the sources. For the reasons given earlier, the latter seems to me more likely.

50. But cf. 11.30.3, "ad Probianum proc(onsulem) Afric(ae)."

51. Matthews, *Western Aristocracies and Imperial Court*, esp. pp. 23–31.

Vettius Rufinus (4.11.1—cf. 8.18.1) prefect of Rome, 315–16;
Septimius Bassus (1.2.3), prefect of Rome, 317–19;
Locrius (Lucrius) Verinus (2.19.1, 12.11.1, 14.4.2, etc.), governor/vicarius, 314; vicarius Africae, 318–21; prefect of Rome, 323–25;
Iulius (Se)verus (mentioned earlier), vicarius Italiae, 318;
Silvius Paulus (1.15.1), "magister Italiae" (meaning vicarius?), 325;
Aconius (or Aco) Catullinus (8.12.2) proconsul of Africa, 317–18;
Domitius Celsus (1.22.1, 9.18.1), vicarius Africae, 315–16;
Annius Tiberianus (12.1.15), comes Africae, 325–27;
Mecilius Hilarianus (9.19.1 + 12.1.3), corrector Lucaniae et Brittiorum, 316;
Iunius Ruf(in)us (4.13.1), consularis Aemiliae, 321;
Ulpius Flavianus (11.16.2), consularis Aemiliae et Liguriae, 323;
Barbarus Pompeianus (1.2.6), consularis Campaniae, 333;
Antonius Marcellinus (11.3.1), praeses Lugdunensis Primae, 319 (correct to 313?);
Versennius Fortunatus (8.7.1), consularis aquarum, 324;
Iulius Antiochus (1.2.1), praefectus vigilum, 313/4–19;
Paternus Valerianus (6.38.1), governor/vicarius, 312/337 (?330);
Crepereius Donatianus (1.2.4), western (?) governor, 319;
Furius Felix (2.11.1), western governor (praeses Corsicae??), 320;
Aurelius Helladius (11.39.1, dat. Naisso/?Nasseti), provincial governor/vicarius, 325;
Maximilianus Macrobius (9.12.2, dat. Sirmio), (?) provincial governor, 326 (correct to 329?);
Lucretius Paternus (12.1.17), (?) provincial governor, 329.

Mecilius Hilarianus, listed here as corrector Lucaniae et Brittiorum in 316, is found similarly addressed, as the holder of the praetorian prefecture, among the few post-Constantinian examples (6.4.3–4; 339, corrected to 354), while the "Aco(nius) Catullinus" who was so addressed as vicarius Africae in 12.1.24, of 338, was the son of his Constantinian homonym the proconsul. The number of cases belonging exclusively to the post-Constantinian period is very small; only four or five cases can be found.[52]

This phenomenon, distributed among many books of the Theodosian Code, is less likely to reflect an idiosyncrasy of its editors than to be an original feature of their material of the Constantinian period; that is to say, their material derived

52. For the few exclusively post-Constantinian examples, cf. Egnatius Faustinus (11.9.2, 12 December 337), Aurelius Mimenius (11.39.4, 346), Bibulenius Restitutus (11.7.7, 353/346), and Vindaonius Magnus (1.28.3, 376). The fuller name of Marius Artemius is preserved at *CJ* 10.26.2 (364), no doubt from a lost law in *CTh,* but not in the other laws addressed to him that are extant there.

from sources that already contained this convention of nomenclature. It would not be surprising if a period that produced such important and such diverse legislation as that of the Tetrarchs and Constantine had attracted the interest of jurists and legal historians; indeed, we shall see in the next chapter that some legal texts of the period were already subject to selective compilation and publication. In all this we have pointers to the possible sources and methods employed by the editors of the Theodosian Code.

## *"Palingenesia": Laws Reconstituted*

As we saw in the first part of this chapter and in the discussion of the Sirmondian Constitutions in Chapter 6, we commonly find excerpts of the same original text entered at different points in the Theodosian Code. This is what one would expect, given the editors' instructions of 429, repeated in 435, to classify the points of substance in their texts under appropriate titles, dividing them where necessary. For the modern user of the Code, there is an obvious corollary. If late imperial legislation is to be understood in anything like its original form, a routine but essential task may involve the reversal of the editors' efforts, in order to reconstitute these excerpts from their various locations in the Theodosian Code (and, where appropriate, from the Codex Justinianus). Many elements in the presentation of laws, discarded by the editors, will never be recovered, but the benefits of this reconstitution of texts have been shown at many points in the foregoing discussion. In particular, Valentinian's so-called Law of Citations of 426 takes on quite a different aspect when its full range of contents is made clear in this way—no longer the nadir or low-water mark of Roman jurisprudence but a comprehensive statement of the authority of different types of legal pronouncement, together with some difficult rulings in testamentary law.[53]

The second part of this chapter develops this approach from a selection of cases where laws have been divided into several titles. The examples have been chosen for their inherent interest and in one or two cases for their complexity; they have also been chosen because they are cases where the reconstituted texts add up to more than the sum of their parts.[54] Where there seems to be some basis for it, an attempt is made to determine the original order of the excerpts. This part of the reconstruction is of course extremely speculative.

1. Valentinian's law of precedence was issued on 5 July (III non. Iul.) 372 at Nasonacum, modern Nassogne, an imperial residence situated in the Ardennes just

53. Compare the two texts reinstituting higher education at Constantinople, taken together in Chapter 2.

54. See also the examples from *CTh* 11.30 discussed in the first part of this chapter.

over hundred kilometers west of Trier, where the emperor resided in the summer of 372.[55] The textual variation between the forms *Nasonacum* and *Nasonnacum* is hardly of any great significance. All the excerpts were addressed to the urban prefect Ampelius, three of them providing also the date of acceptance by him as "III non. Sept." The space of two months (5 July–3 September) from the issue of the law near Trier to its acceptance at Rome is well within the sample time scales set out in Chapter 7. A comprehensive law, it must also have been issued to other officials, certainly to the western praetorian prefects, to whom many of its provisions were more relevant than they were to the urban prefect, but there is no trace of any of these further copies. The editors must be presumed to have made their extracts from the single copy addressed to Ampelius. There is no indication whether such a law was also promulgated by Valens in the east, though one might expect consistency of practice between the two *partes imperii* on such a matter.

As to the content of the individual texts, 6.7.1 gives equal standing to prefects of the city, praetorian prefects and magistri equitum and peditum, their precedence over each other to depend on the order of their appointment. Further provisions concern the order of ranks to be observed in visiting judges in their chambers or at extraordinary sessions, and in the Roman Senate, where the "ancient ordinances" are to be observed; the law does not say what these were. *CTh* 6.9.1 ranks members of the *sacrarium,* or imperial consistory, that is to say the quaestor, the magister officiorum, and the comites largitionum and rei privatae, in precedence over proconsuls. *CTh* 6.14.1 ranks comites rei militaris over proconsuls, while 6.22.4 gives similar precedence to those holding the honorary title of magister equitum. *CTh* 6.11.1 ranks magistri scriniorum (that is, the magistri memoriae, epistularum, and libellorum) over vicarii.

Two of the laws, 6.14.1 and 6.22.4, use identical language in ranking the officials in question above proconsuls, diverging only in their identification of the honorands:

| | |
|---|---|
| 6.14.1. Post alia: Qui<br>contemplatione meritorum ducto<br>intra provincias transmarinas<br>strenuissime milite primi<br>ordinis comitivam fuerint<br>consecuti, ea reverentia<br>altissimarum dignitatum viris | 6.22.4. Post alia: Qui<br>contemplatione meritorum<br>honorarios magisterii equitum<br>adepti sunt codicillos, ea<br>reverentia altissimarum<br>dignitatum viris subiugantur, ut<br>his locum praestent, qui |

55. For Nasonacum/Nassogne, possibly an imperial estate, see E. M. Wightman, *Roman Trier and the Treveri* (1970), pp. 126, 184 with map, at p. 136. Also issued there in 372 was *CTh* 8.7.12, of 30 May, received in Africa on 26 November.

subiugantur, ut his locum praestent, qui proconsulatus insignibus adornantur. Et cetera.

proconsulatus insignibus adornantur. Et cetera.

Presumably, the original text joined military comites primi ordinis and honorary magistri militum in some such way as this: "Qui contemplatione meritorum ducto intra provincias transmarinas strenuissime milite primi ordinis comitivam fuerint consecuti, ⟨sive⟩ qui honorarios magisterii equitum adepti sunt codicillos, ea reverentia altissimarum dignitatum viris subiugantur, ut his locum praestent, qui proconsulatus insignibus adornantur."[56] The editors of the Code separated the points of substance and inserted them under their relevant titles *De comitibus rei militaris* and *De honorariis codicillis,* repeating the text from one to the other and adding the phrase "contemplatione meritorum" where it was lacking in the now divided text. Whether the discrepancy of dating between "III non. Iul." (6.14.1) and "IIII non. Iun." (6.22.4) occurred at this or some other stage of transmission is impossible to say. It can hardly reflect the circulation of different copies, since all the surviving excerpts are from the version addressed to the prefect of Rome.

Four of the five texts incorporate the annotations *post alia . . . et cetera;* the first text has neither, from which, and from its subject matter, one might possibly infer that it came first in the series. Since all the other extracts have both *post alia* and *et cetera,* it is not possible on these grounds to determine which stood last. No doubt they were arranged according to the seniority of the officials whose precedence was discussed in them.

2. An edict of Honorius addressed in 397 to the Senate and people exists in eight fragments, seven from the Theodosian Code, one surviving only in the Codex Justinianus. With one exception the extracts are addressed "ad senatum et populum" and are dated, with minor discrepancies, "XVII kal. Mai." (15 April). The texts concern the grain supply, with passing reference to the oil supply, of Rome, and aspects of the senatorial land tax (*collatio glebalis*) and *munera,* or public duties. It is possible to reassemble the fragments in at least a plausible order of topics, with some support from expressions in the laws and from certain elements in their editorial presentation.

The first, *CTh* 14.15.3, as transmitted, is addressed to the Senate alone rather

56. The following is a composite translation derived from Pharr: "Those persons who have very gallantly led their soldiers in transmarine provinces and in consideration of their merits have obtained the countship of the first order, ⟨and those also⟩ who have obtained honorary letters patent conferring upon them the title of master of the horse, shall be subjoined to men of the loftiest ranks, and such respect shall be paid to them that those who are decorated with the insignia of the proconsulate shall yield precedence to them."

than to the Senate and people, but it begins with a direct appeal to "patres conscribti" and affirms the emperor's concern for them and the people. To judge by the conventions seen in the Sirmondian Constitutions and other texts, one might suppose this to be the opening move in an *oratio* of the emperor addressed to the Senate and intended to be implemented by that body for the benefit of the populus Romanus.[57] The text covers two topics: it disallows remissions granted, by special favor, of the obligation to provide corn and oil for the city, and it forbids anyone to touch grain held in Africa for public consumption at Rome and the diversion of such cargoes elsewhere. These points were not necessarily continuous in the original text. The derivative version at *CJ* 11.23.2 has the first point only, the second being of no interest in sixth-century Constantinople, at a time when Rome itself was in any case no longer supplied with grain from Africa. The second point, concerning grain held in Africa, does, however, connect in a different way with *CJ* 4.40.3, prohibiting the sale of corn supplies held "in diversis litoribus."[58] As edited in *CJ*, this topic falls under the law of sale and is so classified under the title *Quae res venire non possunt et qui vendere vel emere vetuntur*. This title is not extant in the Theodosian Code, where it will have stood, with *CJ* 4.40.3, among the opening titles of Book 3, somewhere after 3.1 *De contrahenda emptione*.

The third law, *CTh* 13.5.27, instructs *navicularii* to pay one-third of the payments due from them at the beginning of the sailing season and specifies that deterioration in their vessels will be restored at the expense of the praetorian prefecture. Further, anyone who qualifies for service among the navicularii must serve in this capacity. In the fourth, *CTh* 13.9.5, deliveries of corn frustrated by shipwreck shall be reported to the praefectus annonae and vicarius (of Rome); any delay or negligence in doing so shall be punished. In the fifth, the praefectus annonae and vicarius are also involved in *CTh* 12.6.24, concerning *susceptores* and *praepositi* of the imperial granaries. They are to make annual reports to these two officials; in addition, they are to be liable for office for five years, their successors being chosen from municipal councils. If coherence of subject is any guide, these three extracts might have stood together in the original text.

Two further excerpts touch broader questions of senatorial taxation. In the sixth, *CTh* 6.2.17, the regular tax assessors (*censuales*) are relieved of the burden of collecting the collatio glebalis. In view of their great knowledge of the situation, however, they are still to investigate and make declarations to the emperor. This law is worthy of note for its indication that the censuales were themselves the

57. Seeck, *Regesten*, p. 7.10–13, argued that the compilers of the Code recovered the law in two forms, as a letter to the Senate and as an edict to the people.

58. Cf. the assertion of this principle by Valentinian, in the episode reported by Ammianus, 28.1.17f.

source of the emperor's knowledge of the difficulties in dealing with senators.[59] Further indicating the scope of senatorial ingenuity in the evasion of taxes, *CTh* 6.2.18, the seventh, permits the transfer of senatorial properties to others only if the transfers are properly recorded, with reasons, in the provincial records. It is natural to suppose that these two laws, edited in sequence and on the same subject, belonged together in the original text of Honorius' law.

Finally the brief fragment of the eighth law, *CTh* 6.4.31 declares as invalid exemptions given by rescript from the provision of public games; the due order of obligations is to be maintained.[60] The phrases *post alia* and *et cetera* at the beginning and end of this text show that it stood neither first nor last in the sequence of extracts. It is of course possible that more excerpts of the law once existed in the early books of the Code, to which these phrases referred; otherwise, this fragment might have stood after the first clause of *CTh* 14.15.3 (the clause disallowing remissions), covering other remissions by special favor. That 14.15.3 should be placed first in the sequence is confirmed by the absence at the beginning of this text of any *post alia* annotation, while the phrase *et cetera* is present at the end. As we saw, the second point of *CTh* 14.15.3 leads directly to *CJ* 4.40.3, while there is little doubt that *CTh* 6.2.17 and 18 belong together. Although both of these extracts possess the annotation *post alia* at the beginning, neither, as transmitted, has *et cetera*. This combination would be consistent with the conclusion that they stood at or near the end of the original text.

3. Constantine's extensive edict of 331 on civil law is preserved in eight extracts, six from the Theodosian Code or Breviarium, two from the Codex Justinianus. Issued on 1 August 331, it was addressed "ad universos provinciales" or, in one case, from the Breviarium, "ad provinciales" merely (*CTh* 5.4.1). That this variant was present in the original text of the Theodosian Code is suggested by its appearance also in the version of this text preserved in the Codex Justinianus (8.36.2). Two texts, edited in sequence in the Theodosian Code (11.30.16–17; see the first part of this chapter) add to the date of issue a date of publication of the law, 1 September, one of these versions but not the other (and it alone among all eight extracts) giving also the place of publication as Constantinople (11.30.16).[61] The anomalous delay of one month between the issuing of the law and its publication at Constantinople may be explained by the emperor's absence on a short visit to Nicomedia, as

59. Cf. *CTh* 6.2.16 & 20, of Sept. 395 and Dec. 397, on the related question of the exaction of the *aurum oblaticium* from senators living in provinces. The duty of exaction is transferred in 6.2.20 from the censuales to the provincial governor.

60. Praetorian games were promised ("quos votivi sumptus designarit electio") ten years ahead of time; cf. *CTh* 6.4.13, 22, etc.

61. I would assume that, even though it is only recorded in this one case, all the surviving extracts of the law derive from a text published at Constantinople.

already conjectured, on quite different grounds, by T. D. Barnes.[62] The two texts surviving only in the Codex Justinianus give the date of issue as X kal. Aug. (3.19.2) and that of publication as k. Oct. (3.13.4), respectively, but the Theodosian Code annotations are clearly preferable. They are earlier; though incomplete they are without contradiction in what they do preserve; and they are better transmitted, in three cases through the full text of the Theodosian Code, in two cases through the Breviarium, in one through the Gromatici.

The edict concerns litigation over property but raises also general questions of procedure relating especially to appeals. The questions relating to procedure concern 1) the conduct of litigation by representatives of minors (3.30.4); 2) appeals from proconsuls, comites, and vicarii (but not from praetorian prefects), and complaints that lesser judges were not allowing appeals (11.30.16); 3) the neglect by litigants of regular channels of appeal, in which case no remedy is available from the emperor (11.30.17); 4), a subcategory of 3), concerning people who neglect regular channels of appeal claiming '"fear" of judges, in which case the emperor or praetorian prefect will give judgment; 5), an extract preserved only by the Codex Justinianus, declaring that no one should decline the scrutiny of a regular judge and seek remedy from the praetorian prefect or any judge of spectabilis rank (proconsuls and vicarii) but rather should make an appeal directly to the emperor (*CJ* 3.13.4).

The issues relating directly to property concern, in the remaining three extracts, the nontransferral to a third party of any object currently under litigation (4.5.1); arbitration of boundary disputes where less than five feet of land is concerned (2.26.3); and litigation over immovable property where the owner is absent and refuses to appear or to appoint a legal agent or procurator (*CJ* 3.19.2).

As indicated, our sources for this extensive text are various. Only three survive in the full text of the Theodosian Code; these are *CTh* 11.30.16–17 and 11.43.1 (of which the first two recur, under different titles, in the Codex Justinianus). *CTh* 3.30.4 and 4.5.1 are from the Breviarium, of which 4.5.1 recurs in the corresponding title *De litigiosis* at *CJ* 8.36.2. *CTh* 2.26.3 occurs neither in the Breviarium nor in the Codex Justinianus but is securely restored to the Theodosian Code as one of several laws assigned to this title by the Gromatici. The two laws preserved only in the Codex Justinianus are from the titles *De iurisdictione omnium iudicum et de foro competenti* (3.13) and *Ubi in rem actio exerceri debet* (3.19), neither title being extant in the Theodosian Code; Krüger restored both texts to Mommsen's existing titles in Book 2.[63] Together with the cases mentioned in the first part of this

62. *New Empire*, p. 78; see Chapter 7, n. 44.

63. Respectively, as 2.1.1b (*De iurisdictione et ubi quis conveniri debet*) and 2.5.1a (*De dominio rei quae poscitur vel consortibus ab eo cui denuntiatum fuerit nominandis*).

Chapter on *CTh* 11.30, these observations further justify the conclusions set out in Chapter 5 about the text of the early books of the Theodosian Code.[64]

4. Constantius' letter of 356 to the Senate on nominations to senatorial office and other questions of procedure is a relatively straightforward example. It consists of three laws, all addressed "ad senatum" and edited in sequence in the Theodosian Code under title 6.4 *De praetoribus et quaestoribus*. Despite some discrepancies, the subscripts of the laws show them to be parts of the same original text. It was issued at Milan during Constantius' well-documented visit to the west, on III id. Apr. (11 April) and, according to the first two extracts, "read by the proconsul Araxius" on VI (6.4.8) or VII (6.4.9) id. Mai., that is, on 9 or 10 May 356. That the senate in question is that of Constantinople is clear, both from the name of the official who read out the law and from his office. It was not until 359 (to be precise, on 11 December) that Constantinople joined Rome in being governed by a praefectus; before then, the governor held the rank of proconsul, as in this law.[65] The third extract records that the law was given on VII id. Mai., but no place of issue is named, and it is certain that the subscript is incomplete in other ways also. The date as well as the place of issue have fallen from the text, and the transmitted VII id. Mai. is the date not of issue but of the reading of the law by Araxius; so the text of the subscript should be restored to conform to its predecessors, as "dat. ⟨III id. April. Med., lecta ab Araxio procons. die⟩ VII id Mai.," etc.[66] With the support of this correction, the date of the reading of the law as VII (rather than VI) id. Mai. might be marginally preferable. Not that the difference of a day matters much. In either case, there will be the lapse of a month between the issue of the law at Milan and its reading at Constantinople.

The first of the three texts (6.4.8) is a brief statement that nominations (of quaestors and praetors) be made according to the regular procedures rather than by the interventions of high officials; the second (6.4.9), an almost equally brief excerpt laying down a quorum of fifty senators for meetings of the Senate—it being certain, as the emperor put it, that such a number would contain "ample virtue" for the task. The third excerpt (6.4.10) is a much longer text prescribing that nominations in future be made on the Emperor Constantius' birthday (which the transmitted text gives as "id. Aug." but was in fact VII id. Aug.), and continue for as many days as necessary to complete the task. It proceeds by invalidating

64. In the first part of this Chapter, nos. B15 and 18.

65. Jones, *Later Roman Empire*, p. 692 and n. 11; *PLRE* 1, p. 94 (s. Araxius) and Fasti, p. 1056.

66. I do not see why Mommsen should think that some letters may have fallen from the text after the word *procons.* in the subscript of *CTh* 6.4.8. The abbreviation is straightforward and intelligible.

enrollments among the class of *functi* (senators who had already held the office in question and could claim exemption from its duties) that had been secured by bribery,[67] and it prohibits the transfer of the obligations resulting from nomination to sons, grandsons, or any other persons. This third and longest extract also, like *CTh* 14.15.3 discussed above, contains a direct address to the senators as "patres conscribti."

Although the three excerpts, from the same original text, were edited in sequence under the same title, *CTh* 6.4.9, on the senatorial quorum, does not seem to belong to it, unless the meetings under discussion are specifically only those concerned with the nominations of praetors and quaestors.[68] In this case the extract, taken by itself, is misleading, since it reads as if it were a general provision covering all senatorial meetings on any subject. The loss of context has produced a false impression of the substance of the law.

It seems impossible to say which of the extracts stood first, particularly if the editors of the Theodosian Code were already working with a truncated version of the subscript of 6.4.10. In this case the text would have appeared to the editors to be later than the other two, to which it in fact belonged. If this were so, and bearing in mind the address to "patres conscripti" (not to mention the emperor's reference to his own birthday), which would stand well near the beginning of a text, we might infer that this excerpt was originally the first of the three. None of the three texts recurs in the Codex Justinianus, nor is any related text there found that should be restored to the Theodosian Code. One would not expect this, since the relevant title in Book 6 is attested by *R*.

5. Constantius to the Senate in 361. Reconstruction of this substantial text can suitably follow that of the same emperor's letter to the senate of Constantinople of 356. The law is found in no fewer than eleven extracts in the Theodosian Code, most of them short, but two, edited in succession in *CTh* 6.4 *De praetoribus et quaestoribus,* texts of considerable length. The extracts are addressed "ad senatum" and are dated, without discrepancy, V non. Mai. (3 May) of the year 361. The two long texts edited as 6.4.12–13 also preserve a place of issue, "Gyfyrae" (13 "[Gyf]yrae"). This is Gephyra, "the Bridge" in Greek, a location outside Antioch on the road to the Euphrates frontier, where Constantius was marching when he issued the law.[69]

To begin with these two long texts, the first follows up the letter of 356 in specifying in greater detail the senatorial quorum required for the election of prae-

67. These are distinguished from the bona fide recipients of imperial favor.

68. As tacitly assumed by Jones, *Later Roman Empire,* p. 540.

69. The emperor never returned to Constantinople from his eastern campaign but died in Bithynia while returning west to confront the rebellion of Julian.

tors and then proceeds to the replacement of praetors who died before their term of office came around.[70] Especially noteworthy is the naming of "Themistius the philosopher" as one whose presence was required in the Senate on these occasions. The second excerpt is a detailed paragraph setting out the financial obligations of various categories of praetor, with measures to ensure willing compliance. Although these two texts can be separated by content into the two subjects of nomination and financial duties, they can easily be read continuously. There is no reason to doubt that they stood in this order in the original document.

The other extracts cover a variety of legal and financial issues affecting senators, in general favoring their interests. *CTh* 1.28.1 requires the selection of suitable men as *defensores senatus* and defines the scope of their powers in relation to the emperors and praetorian prefects. *CTh* 7.8.1 declares that the duty of *hospitalitas* (billeting) is not to be imposed on unwilling senators, and 11.15.1 assures senators that their agents and managers will not be troubled to undertake the purchase of certain kinds of supplies. Similarly (13.1.13), senatorial farmworkers and tenants are not to be enrolled among the class of *negotiatores* if they simply trade in the regular produce of the land, while senators are not held liable for the tax dues of coloni who have fled from their property (11.1.7). Nor are senatorial estates in provinces to be made liable for the costs of building undertaken by governors (15.1.7). Senators are made responsible for the exaction of recruits only on their own estates, if necessary jointly with other senators, and may not incorporate with their own the liabilities of any nonsenators (11.23.1). Decurions who had entered the senate of Constantinople to the detriment of their civic duties are to be restored to their cities, and any moneys owing to the cities or to the imperial fiscus are to be repaid (12.1.48). Finally, in *CTh* 1.6.1, judicial appeals from the eastern provinces (which are named) are referred to the praefectus urbi—the urban prefect of Constantinople, appearing under his recently acquired title. It is not clear at what point of the original text this excerpt would have appeared.

It is difficult to go further in reconstructing this law, though its coherence of subject matter is obvious. None of the texts possesses the annotations *post alia* or *et cetera* that might suggest the original order of at least certain extracts, and only the two texts edited as *CTh* 6.4.12–13, which one would think did occur in this order, preserve the place of issue; in all other respects the protocols are identical. The additional information in their protocols might suggest that these two longer extracts, related to each other in subject matter, came from a different version of the original text than the others. An alternative explanation from editorial practice might be that the longer extracts invited the more complete annotation, or that in the shorter extracts the editors omitted allusion to Gyfyrae because they had not

70. Elections were made ten years in advance (see n. 60).

heard of any such place-name and did not understand it; or else it is simply a matter of differing levels of attentiveness among the working committees who handled the material. Nevertheless, the differences in the style of annotation between these two texts and the others, and the complete absence of any *post alia* and *et cetera* indications, would be unusual if the editors knew that they were dealing with a single text divided into many parts. It is at least possible that the discrepancies already existed in the material that came into their hands.

6. The Roman Senate is the recipient of three laws sent to it by the emperor Gratian (in the name of his colleagues) in 376, all of them addressed "ad senatum" and all "read in the Senate," but with different transmitted dates. *CTh* 9.1.13 carries the date III id. Feb., 10.19.8 that of id. Aug., while 15.1.19 lacks a day-and-month date but has the same consular year as the other two laws. Mommsen took the three texts to be parts of a single communication of Gratian to the Senate, adopting the date of III id. Feb. for all three.[71] A glance at their respective contents makes it clear that this cannot be so. *CTh* 9.1.13 is a very important law, relating to members of the senatorial order found guilty of criminal offenses; their cases may be heard by provincial governors but must be referred for sentencing to the emperor and the "inclytae potestates," namely, the urban and praetorian prefects. Cases so referred to the praefectus urbi are to be heard by that official and a panel of five senators known as the *iudicium quinquevirale,* its members to be chosen by lot. The significance of this law is that it follows the period of judicial conflict between the Senate and the agents of Valentinian described by Ammianus Marcellinus and expresses the reconciliation between emperor and Senate that followed the accession of Gratian in November 375.[72] The date of the law, read in the Senate on 11 February and sent from the imperial court some time earlier, falls early in this period of rapprochement.[73]

The other two texts can be associated with each other, but not with the law of 11 February. They concern the quarrying of stone in Macedonia and Illyricum, as to which senators are given immunity from indirect taxation and customs duty on the imported stone (10.19.8), and building at Rome; no urban prefect or other official may start any new building but must restrict himself to restoration of the old, and any (presumably private) person who wishes to undertake new building must do so at his own expense, and without digging up the foundations of existing

71. Prolegomena, p. ccliii; cf. Seeck, *Regesten* (see my n. 73). Nevertheless, in his note on 15.1.19 (p. 805), Mommsen associates its date with that of 10.19.8, that is, id. Aug.

72. *Western Aristocracies and Imperial Court,* pp. 56–69; A. Chastagnol, *La préfecture urbaine à Rome sous le Bas-Empire* (1960), pp. 123–27.

73. Seeck's dating of all three laws (with *CJ* 3.24.2, see my n. 74) to 1 January 376 to conform to the reference to an imperial *oratio* in Symmachus, *Ep.* 1.13, involves some serious manhandling of the evidence—*Regesten,* pp. 105, 246.

structures or despoiling them for materials (15.1.19). This undated law, beginning *post alia,* can readily be joined to 10.19.8, ending *et cetera,* and share its transmitted date of 13 August. The law of 11 February on criminal jurisdiction involving senators is a quite separate issue; although it carries both annotations *post alia* and *et cetera,* the references are not to these texts.[74] It so happens that we possess parts of two laws of 376, each of them addressed to the Senate and read there at different times of the year.

7. Among the many laws issued by Theodosius I at Thessalonica during his residence there in 379 and 380 are several addressed to his praetorian prefect Eutropius.[75] Of these laws, at least seven, and possibly nine, derive from a single extensive text given to Eutropius on XV kal. Iul. (17 June) 380. It covered a number of topics in family and property law. Three of the laws concern the payment and return in various circumstances of betrothal gifts. The first of these texts, *CTh* 3.5.11, survives in the Breviarium; before it in Mommsen's text stands a second law, 3.5.10, where only the number of the law and a fragment of its title are attested in *T*. Nothing survives of the actual text of the law, or of the name of the addressee. Both can however be restored from *CJ* 5.1.3, concerning the return of betrothal gifts in the event of the death of either party.[76] *CTh* 3.6.1, again from the Breviarium, denies the right of governors, officials, and members of their families to secure betrothal gifts by intimidation, such gifts being permitted only where all parties freely consent. This is the only text of this series with a reference to excerpts edited elsewhere, in this case *post alia,* but this adds nothing except to confirm what one would guess from the subject of the law, that it is a subsidiary point in the matter of betrothals; whether this entire topic stood first in the original text there is no way of saying.

Passing on to other topics, *CTh* 4.19.1 is a ruling on the question of interest payments on sums of money exacted by adjudication; while the successive laws *CTh* 9.42.8–9 address the related questions of the disposition of the property of exiled persons and the succession to the property of those who have suffered execution. The second of these texts is remarkable for its citation of the law of the

74. Nor can one find any complementary text elsewhere in the Theodosian Code; no doubt the references are to laws in the now incomplete books. Seeck, *Regesten,* loc. cit., added to the cluster of laws *CJ* 3.24.2, addressed "ad senatum" on 1 March with no year but the imperial college of 375/383. On grounds of subject matter, however (matters arising from the residence of senators), this law should be taken with *CJ* 10.40.8, given on 1 March 390.

75. There is a good case for seeing him as the author of the historical Breviarium dedicated to Valens, later consul of 387, and friend of the orator Symmachus: *PLRE* 1, p. 317 (Eutropius 2); *Western Aristocracies and Imperial Court,* pp. 8–9, 96–97.

76. The title is *De sponsalibus et arris sponsalibus et proxeneticis,* corresponding to *CTh* 3.5 *De sponsalibus et ante nubtias donationibus;* see Chapter 5.

Twelve Tables and the Praetor's Edict. Somewhat apart from the topics raised so far, 9.27.2 prevents governors found guilty of maladministration from holding further public office.

A further text addressed to Eutropius, *CTh* 6.10.1, was connected by Mommsen with the law of 17 June.[77] That its transmitted date is XVII rather than XV kal. Iul. is no objection to the identification, but the difference in subject matter suggests that this is an entirely separate text. *CJ* 9.29.3, however, a law with the transmitted consular year 385 and the date XVI k. Aug., has to be removed from 385 and may well form part of the text here under discussion; it forbids the holding of office by anyone in the province of his origin without the willing consent of the emperor and could be associated with *CTh* 9.27.2 on governors guilty of maladministration.[78] So too, *CJ* 6.23.16, a law on testamentary dispositions and fideicommissa and the obligations that arise out of these, was connected by both Mommsen and Krüger with the law of 17 June[79] and may well, with correction of its transmitted date of k. Iul. to XV k. Iul., be part of it. It goes without saying that both these texts from the Codex Justinianus, like *CJ* 5.1.3 just mentioned, derive from the now incomplete books of the Theodosian Code.

8. The next example is from an editorial point of view by far the most difficult of those presented here, and no general explanation appears to give a satisfactory account of its characteristics. It is a group of nine laws divided among six titles of the Code and deriving from a letter of Constantius (or Constantine) addressed collectively to the praetorian prefects, who are not named. Three of the texts (8.4.5, 8.7.4, and 12.1.18) are addressed "ad vv. cc. ppo" ("ad viros clarissimos praefectos praetorio"), the rest "ad ppo," similarly to be understood in the plural, as the "college" of prefects. The form of address is unparalleled in the Theodosian Code. There is no need to describe the content of the texts in detail; they concern terms of service in the imperial army and administration, recruitment, and the relationship of these matters to the membership of city councils. This matter is raised in seven of the nine texts. Escape from city councils to the Senate in order to avoid municipal service is also forbidden. The texts form a coherent group of regulations, and this finding is consistent with the *post alia* and *et cetera* annotations, one or both of which occur in all but one of the texts.[80] Not a single text among the nine mentions a place of origin, an omission which, though generally unhelpful, is another sign that they belong together.

77. Prolegomena, p. cclvii.

78. The connection was made by Seeck, *Regesten,* pp. 95.32–39, 255, cf. *PLRE* 1, p. 317, but not by Mommsen, Prolegomena, pp. cclvii (s.a. 380), cclxiv (s.a. 385).

79. Mommsen, Prolegomena, p. cclvii; Krüger, note on *CJ* 6.23.16. In this case, the connection was not made by Seeck or by *PLRE.*

80. *CTh* 12.1.14 has neither annotation; 7.13.1, 8.7.6, and 12.1.18 have only *post alia.*

The difficulty with this text is that the nine excerpts are assigned to four different consular years and, remarkably enough, to nine different month-and-day dates. The question of the consular years should in principle be the easier to resolve, but one only has to set out the evidence to see the difficulties that can result when the consulships of similarly named Augusti and Caesars occur in such profusion. The following are the consular datings as set out by Mommsen;[81]

6.27.1: VIII id. Mart. Constantio A. VII et Constante C.
7.13.1: prid. non Iul. Constano[82] A. VI et C
7.21.2: k. Mai. Constantio A. VI et Constante II C
8.4.5: prid. non. Mai. Constantino A. VII et Constante C. II
8.7.4: prid. id Mai. Constantio A. VII et Constante II C
8.7.5: XV k. Iun. Constantio A. VII et Constante C. II
8.7.6: prid. non. Oct. Constantio A. VII et Constante C. II
12.1.14: VIII k. Dec. Constantino A. VII et Constantio C
12.1.18: VII k. Dec. Constantino A. VIII et Constantio IIII

If the only excerpts of the law to survive had been the last two, critics would have little difficulty in associating them, reconciling the day as VII or VIII k. Dec., and choosing the consular year of one or the other; the consuls of 12.1.14 are correct as they stand for 326, those of 12.1.18 are correct for 329 with the emendation of *Constantinus II* for *Constantius IIII* Caesar to give "Constantino A. VIII et Constantino C. II." A Constantinian date for the laws would be confirmed by the editors of the Code having in a very dense title, put them in sequence for 326 and 329.[83] The address "ad praefectos," fully attested in 12.1.18, would suit either year in the reign of Constantine, given one Augustus and several Caesars with whom praetorian prefects were associated. Then 8.4.5 might be claimed for Constantine with the acceptance of his seventh consulship as 326 and the correction of the text by his colleague to read "Constantius Caesar I," or else amending his seventh to his eighth consulship to give 329 and correcting the name of his colleague to read "Constantinus Caesar IIII."

If this view has attractions (it at least provides some structure to the problem), it also presents difficulties. Only three of the nine texts name Constantine as first consul. Five of the other six give the name of Constantius, whose sixth and seventh consulships fell in 353 and 354; in each case he held the office with his nephew Gallus, normally known as Constantius Caesar. On this basis 7.13.1 also, reading

81. In his ed., p. 282 (on 6.27.1); cf. Cameron, in *Consuls of the Later Roman Empire*, p. 75.

82. "Constano" [*sic*] is the reading of *R*, the only witness. At 8.7.7 "constanus" (*T*) is read for "constantius" (*R*).

83. *CTh* 12.1 contains 192 texts (the most of any title). 12.1.13 is 17 May 326; 1.15 is 21 April 327, and 1.16–17 are 29 Sept. and 25 Oct. 329, respectively. For another example of confusion between 326 and 329, see the first part of this chapter, no. C.1.

"Constantio" for the abbreviated "Constano" of *R*, yields a consular dating of 353, as would 7.21.2, reading "Constantio" for "Constante" Caesar, and preferring the numeration of the Augustus' consulship to that of his Caesar's consulship. The alternative, to prefer the numeration of the Caesar's consulship as the less likely to suffer alteration or error than that of the Augustus, would yield 354, and this date is that offered by 8.7.4–6.[84]

The name of Constans Caesar presents a difficulty on any reading of the evidence. Constantius held the consulship three times with his brother Constans, in 339, 342, and 346, but it is more likely that the name of Constans in the laws under review is either a misreading of the official name of Gallus Caesar or a piece of editorial "tidying up" inspired by the disgrace and death of Gallus in 354. His name could conveniently be replaced by that of the most recent and better-known imperial figure who had preceded him. The retention in all but one case of *C(aesar)* in the imperial titulature is perhaps a hint that this is what has happened.

On the assumption that a single text is involved, the most likely solution is put the date at 354, as better attested than 353, and to remove 12.1.14 and 18 from 326 and 329 and relocate them in 354, while bearing in mind that the editors of the Code understood both texts to be of Constantinian date. Indeed, Seeck took the law to be one of Constantine, accepting the consular indications of 12.1.14 and 18 and amending all the other headings to conform.[85]

The question of the consular year fades into insignificance when we observe that each of the nine laws bears a different day-and-month date. Taking the laws in the order in which they occur in the Code, we find VIII id. Mart. (6.27.1), prid. non. Iul. (7.13.1), k. Mai. (7.21.2), prid. non. Mai. (8.4.5), prid. id. Mai. (8.7.4), XV k. Iun (8.7.5), prid. non. Oct. (8.7.6), VIII k. Dec. (12.1.14), and VII k. Dec. (12.1.18). Whatever may be said of the consular years, it is obvious that these discrepancies of months and days cannot be resolved by any rational or noncoercive method of textual correction.[86]

It is hard to find a general explanation of the discrepancies. The most obvious beginning is to ask whether all the excerpts do in fact derive from a single text. Possibly the texts assigned to 326 and 329 are after all parts of a law of Constantine, while the other seven fragments are parts of a different and later text. This

84. This group of texts is "closed in" by laws of 349 and (?) 356 (MSS 358); this defines the originator as Constantius but does not decide between 353 and 354.

85. *Regesten,* 42–43, 177; see Cameron, in *Consuls of the Later Roman Empire,* p. 75.

86. As explained, one might resolve the discrepancy between VIII and VII k. Dec. (12.1.14 and 18), then assign to these two laws a common consular year. For the rest, if coercive methods were employed, one might correct "prid. id. Mai." (8.7.4) to "prid. non. Mai." (8.4.5), then make the other two "pridie" dates conform to these by changing "Iul." (7.13.1) and "Oct." (8.7.6) to "Mai." But apart from the violence of the solution, it would still not produce the single date that is needed.

explanation is unconvincing, because the address "ad praefectos praetorio" is unparalleled in the Theodosian Code; it is true that it is attested in full in only three of the texts, but the abbreviation *ppo* without the name of a recipient would be equally unusual and is best explained as an abbreviation of the plural.[87] The connections in the subject matter of the laws, and the presence of *post alia* and *et cetera* annotations, also suggest a single origin for the nine excerpts.

If the correct consular date is 354, then it is worth noting that this is the period of Constantius' residence in the west after his defeat of the usurper Magnentius, at a time when Gallus Caesar represented imperial government in the east. No fewer than four praetorian prefects are recorded or suggested in the course of the year 354; in Gaul, Italy and Africa, Illyricum, and the East.[88] There is thus ample opportunity for multiple datings of a text sent "ad praefectos" and distributed by them in the usual manner to subordinate officials. Indeed, an explanation of the discrepancies could be that some of the variant month-and-day dates of the laws are not connected with the date of issue but are those on which copies or excerpts were accepted or published in different locations; we have seen many examples of this shift of *acc./pp.* to *dat.* in the transmitted texts of laws.

There are, however, difficulties with this view. If the editors of the Code recovered the text as distributed in this way, we should need to explain why no trace of an *acc.* or *pp.* occurs in any of the nine excerpts, and also how the editors came to realize that the fragments did in fact form part of a single text. That they did realize this is implicit in the usual understanding of *post alia* and *et cetera* annotations as interventions of the editors of the Code, in cases where they began with a single text and divided it up according to their normal working procedure. The suggestion of Alan Cameron, that the month-and-day dates are sheer guesses and that the original text or texts in the editors' hands had no such dates at all, is attractive, but it at once runs into an objection; the editors would have had no reason to guess three different dates for the three texts they themselves edited in sequence as 8.7–4.6. If they were aware that these were parts of a single text, they should at least have invented the same date for them all.

That at least some of the editors' errors were already present in the material before them is shown by their having placed the excerpts that appear as 12.1.14 and 18 in the sequence of their transmitted dates, in 326 and 329, respectively. If it occurred to them that even these two extracts belonged together, the editors made no attempt, apart from adding a *post alia* annotation to 12.1.18 (which can only refer back to 12.1.14), to show this in their editing.

One possible explanation of this difficult situation might be that the editors

87. And 8.7.5 and 6 can be seen as continuing the fuller annotation of 8.7.4.

88. *PLRE* 1, Fasti, p. 1049. The details of the reconstruction do not matter; what is important is the relationship between a single Augustus and a college of prefects.

came into possession of the various fragments of the text already divided with their different dates, but then somehow realized, or had it brought to their attention, that the fragments were part of the same text. They then registered this in their usual way by *post alia* and *et cetera* annotations but made no attempt to regularize the transmitted dating of the separate fragments, even to the extent of putting together 12.1.14 and 18 or assigning the same date to 8.7.4–6. The problem with this view is that we would not know how the editors came to realize that they had the parts of a single text before them without acquiring a copy of it, which would presumably have resolved the contradictions of dating.

A second explanation would be that they recovered the fragments singly or as little groups of texts from existing collections that came into their hands, and that the *post alia* and *et cetera* annotations were already written into these earlier collections. This explanation would offer an advantage for understanding the present case, with a corresponding disadvantage when its implications are considered. The advantage would be that the editors do not need in the present case to have realized that all nine fragments were part of a single text. The disadvantage would be that the same observation might apply to other, so far unsuspected occasions in the Theodosian Code on which the annotations occur; perhaps they were not in all cases original to the editors of the Code but were already to be found in the earlier sources from which they drew their material. As far as the present case is concerned, it seems most likely that the variant dates were already present in the material before the editors of the Code saw it. The variations were neither invented by the editors nor introduced by them into the subsequent transmission of the text.

9. The Codex Justinianus contains three brief excerpts from an imperial edict on the law of succession, none of which survives in the Theodosian Code, although it is clear that they once stood there. The texts are attributed to Constantine, but with a transmitted date of 339 that would locate the edict in the early years of the reign of Constantius. They come from the sequence of titles in Book 6 on property and testamentary law, where they correspond to the first few, very incomplete, titles of the fourth book of the Theodosian Code, and to sections XXV–XXVII of the Praetor's Edict. The first excerpt (*CJ* 6.9.9, *Qui admitti ad bonorum possessionem possunt et intra quod tempus*) concerns the attestation of claims to inheritance, stating that such claims should be made before any iudex or duumvir (so covering both imperial and municipal jurisdiction) within the time limits laid down by ancient practice. The point of law made in this text is that claims in the second and lower degrees of inheritance are not invalidated if they are in strict terms made prematurely, before the lapse of the period for claims in the first degree. The text begins with an expression of the wish to eliminate arguments based merely on forms of words ("ut verborum inaniam excludimus captiones"), and this is the essential point in the other two fragments of the constitution. In the first (*CJ*

6.23.15, *De testamentis: Quemadmodum testamenta ordinantur*), it is said that wills are valid in any form of words that expresses the testator's intention, and on whatever physical materials they are written; in the second (*CJ* 6.37.21, *De legatis*) that legacies and fideicommissa do not require the use of any particular formula, nor are they rendered invalid by any oddity or irregularity of language. Given a clear intention, the exact form of expression was not essential, for words that might have issued from the faltering tongue of a dying man: "quae forte seminecis et balbutiens lingua profudit." It was of no matter whether in naming an heir a testator said, "Heredem facio" or "instituo" or "volo" or "mando" or "cupio" or "esto" or "erit" (6.23.15).

The three texts are often taken as part of a larger group forming a single act of legislation, not of Constantius but of Constantine.[89] The other components of the group are four texts from the Theodosian Code, all addressed as edicts "to the people" and concerning inheritance and property law. Of these texts, the first two, *CTh* 3.2.1 and 4.12.3, derive from the Breviarium, 3.2.1 being preserved also in the Codex Justinianus (8.34.3). The third and fourth texts, *CTh* 8.16.1 and 11.7.3, preserved in *R* and *V*, respectively, are also to be found in the Codex Justinianus (8.57.1, 10.19.2); neither of them is in the Breviarium. The first of these corresponding pairs of texts is Constantine's law removing the penalties for celibacy laid down in the time of Augustus.

The reassembly of the act of legislation of which these texts are believed to be part requires some hard work with the transmitted protocols of the laws. In the first place, the consular datings of the four Theodosian Code texts give two different years—326 (*CTh* 3.2.1, 4.12.3), and 320 (8.16.1 and, with a minor correction, 11.7.3):

3.2.1: Dat. prid. kal. Febr. Serdic(ae) Constantino A. VII et Constantio C. conss.
4.12.3: Dat. VI kal. Sept. Serdicae Constantino A. VII et Constantio conss.
8.16.1: Dat. prid. kal. Feb. Serdicae, pp. kal. April. Rom(ae) Constantino A VI et Constantino C. conss.
11.7.3: Dat. kal. Feb. Constantino A. VI et Constanti⟨n⟩o Caes. conss.

The place of issue, given as Serdica by three of the texts, favors 320 as the date of the legislation and the relocation of *CTh* 3.2.1 and 4.12.3 to this year by emendation of the consular dates.[90] This is generally accepted. There is now the difficulty that the transmitted dates present three different, and two significantly different, days and months of issue: "prid. kal. Febr." (3.2.1 and 8.16.1), "kal. Feb." (11.7.3),

89. Judith Evans Grubbs, *Law and Family in Late Antiquity: The Emperor Constantine's Marriage Legislation* (1995), pp. 118–23 and 128–29.

90. See Barnes, *New Empire*, pp. 74–75, for Constantine's movements in this period.

and "VI kal. Sept." (4.12.3). The advantage would seem to lie with 8.16.1, where we find a full protocol, with the dates of issue as 31 January at Serdica, and of publication as 1 April at Rome. It is not unreasonable to amend the dates of issue of the other three texts to conform to this, though a glance at Seeck's *Regesten* will show just how much change is necessary to secure the desired reconciliations.[91]

The connection of the Codex Justinianus texts with this "general legislative 'package'"[92] also involves changes to their transmitted date and place of issue. Two of the three texts (6.23.15, 6.37.1) bear the consular date of 339, while two give the place of issue not as Serdica but as Laodicea (written in full, 6.9.9, 6.23.15). All agree on the kalends of February, rather than the last day of January, the reconciled date of the Constantinian edict, as the date of issue. If this last correction is accepted in the case of *CTh* 11.7.1, there can be no fundamental objection to making it also in the texts from the Codex Justinianus; it is a small change, well within the range of those one has routinely to make in the dates transmitted by the Codes. As to the year, the consular date under the reign of Constantius is contradicted by the name of the issuing emperor, Constantine. In the case of *CJ* 6.9.9, this is with the abbreviation *idem A.*, referring to the preceding law. This is indeed assigned in the Codex Justinianus to Constantine, but it is a mistaken assignment. A corresponding text in the Theodosian Code establishes that the correct date—at least, of publication—of this law is 339 and that the emperor is Constantius (*CTh* 8.18.4; cf. *CJ* 6.9.8). Krüger thought that the compilers of the Codex Justinianus took *CJ* 6.9.8 to be a law of Constantine, but mistakenly, for it is certainly a law of Constantius. Possibly, then, its successor is also. Given this possibility as well as the general one of confusion between the names of Constantine and Constantius in textual transmission, the argument from imperial nomenclature is inconclusive.

A connection with the legislation of Constantine further requires that *Laodicea*, the transmitted place of issue of *CJ* 6.9.9 and 6.23.25, be regarded as a corruption of *Serdica*.[93] There is no evidence for an imperial visit to at Laodicea (taking this to be the Syrian city of the name) in 339, but it is not an impossibility. Constantius was at Antioch on 27 December 338 and led a campaign to the eastern frontier the following year.[94] We know of no particular reason the emperor should have been at Laodicea in January/February 339, but there is nothing to preclude it either. The two cities were close together. The early fourth-century papyrus itinerary of The-

91. *Regesten*, pp. 59, 169. Barnes, *New Empire*, p. 74, accepts Seeck's corrections without comment.

92. Evans Grubbs, *Law and Family in Late Antiquity*, p. 120.

93. It is going too far to regard this, as Evans Grubbs does (ibid., p. 120 n. 72), as "certain."

94. *CTh* 2.6.4, dat. et pp. Antioch(iae); Seeck, *Regesten*, p. 186.

ophanes has him traveling from Laodicea to Antioch, in an admittedly huge journey stage of sixty-four miles covered in one day.[95] Alternatively, to admit another uncertainty, the laws from the Codex Justinianus might have been "posted" rather than "given" at Laodicea on 1 February 339. Like that from imperial nomenclature, the argument from place of issue is inconclusive.

As to the content of the laws, there is no overriding need for the Codex Justinianus texts to be connected with those attributed to Constantine. Any emperor or emperors might legislate at various times on such issues, repeating or modifying earlier legislation. There is, however, a specific item of evidence in favor of the connection.[96] In his *Life of Constantine* (4.26.6), after describing Constantine's abolition of the old law on celibacy (as in *CTh* 8.16.1), Eusebius attributes to the emperor a law permitting a man at the end of his life "to set out his intentions in plain language and everyday expressions, and to declare his will in any convenient form of writing, even by word of mouth if he wishes, requiring only that it be done in the presence of witnesses able honestly to maintain his trust." This seems close enough to the provisions of *CJ* 6.23.15, quoted above, to justify attributing that law, with its companions in the Codex Justinianus, to Constantine, correcting the consular date to produce this end, and reconciling the month-and-day dating with that of the Constantinian texts discussed here. The first of the three excerpts, *CJ* 6.9.9, may then be the "Constantiniana lex" referred to in a law of Justinian himself, where it is said to have replaced the ancient action of "petitio bonorum possessionis," by which, after his inheritance had been confirmed, an heir had also to petition a magistrate for a decree to enable him to enter into possession of it (*CJ* 7.70.7.3a, of 530). That in two of the three Codex Justinianus excerpts Laodicea is read instead of Serdica would suggest that these texts derived from an original—the now lost version in the Theodosian Code—already containing the error.

That Eusebius, writing in the east in the 330s, could cite an edict of Constantine promulgated at Rome in 320 suggests that the legislation had become widely known throughout the empire, by some other process than its promulgation by an imperial colleague (there being no reason to suppose that Constantine and Licinius would have acted in concert at this time). Eusebius' source is not necessarily the "imperial or ecclesiastical" archives suggested by some commentators.[97] One would expect such an interesting and substantive law, on such a generally important matter as the law of succession, to have been copied and discussed by practicing lawyers and to have entered into the juristic literature, as it surely entered into

95. *P.Ryl.* 627, lines 331–33: Laodicea–Hydata–Daphne–Antioch.

96. Evans Grubbs, *Law and Family in Late Antiquity,* pp. 128–29. I am not persuaded that the orator Nazarius (pp. 124–27) has anything to offer in this context.

97. Ibid., p. 129.

the work of the courts. The process may well have multiplied the types of error that we see in the various fragments of the law as transmitted to us. As we see in other cases, for instance that of the Edictum de accusationibus discussed in Chapter 9, the editors of the Theodosian Code may have found their texts, with variant dates and other details, already excerpted in earlier collections and exposed to the vagaries of actual use. As for the law on celibacy, it is doubly important that this should be considered in the context of the range of topics with which it was associated in Constantine's edict of 320. Whatever was (and has been) made of it by posterity and by interested contemporaries, the law has nothing to do with Christian celibacy.[98]

10. Honorius' interesting law banning the wearing of Oriental shoes and trousers ("tzangae" and "bracae") in the city of Rome has been referred to earlier. The law does not stand by itself but is one of four extracts from an edict of 397 addressed to the people of Rome. A second extract prevents the erection of huts and cottages in the Campus Martius. In both cases the penalty, expressed in identical terms, is confiscation of goods by the prefect of Rome, and exile without term. The original edict was no doubt divided in the manner described for Valentinian's law of precedence of 372, the description of penalty being repeated for the two edited texts:

> 14.10.2[99]: *Impp. Arcadius et Honorius AA. ad populum.* Usum tzangarum adque bracarum intra urbem venerabilem nemini liceat usurpare. Si quis autem contra hanc sanctionem venire temptaverit, sententia viri inl. p(rae)f(ecti) spoliatum eum omnibus facultatibus tradi in perpetuum exilium praecipimus. Et cetera. *Dat. pp. Romae in foro divi Traiani Caesario et Attico conss.*

> 14.14.1: *Impp. Arcadius et Honorius AA. ad populum.* Post alia: Eos, qui in campo Martio casa seu tuguria conlocare temptaverint, sententia viri inl. p(rae)f(ecti) spoliatos eum omnibus facultatibus tradi in perpetuum exilium praecipimus. Et cetera. *Dat. et pp. Romae in foro divi Traiani Caesario et Attico conss.*

A third extract (14.11.1), with both *post alia* and *et cetera* annotations, prohibits agentes in rebus and palatini of lower rank, on pain of deportation, from entering the city without the reason of some official duty or function. This is the only text of the four to give the date of 7 April for the posting of the law in the forum of Trajan. As transmitted, this is the same as the date of issue. The emperor

98. Ibid., p. 120; Antti Arjava, *Women and Law in Late Antiquity* (1996), pp. 78–79.
99. See Chapter 7, n. 47.

being at Milan at the time, either this is a case of a *data* annotation referring not to the emperor but to an announcement by the prefect preparatory to his posting of the law, or the editors used a copy of the edict from which the date and place of issue had fallen, and attempted to repair the damage by using a formula found elsewhere to indicate the posting of a law on the same day and at the same place as those of issue. The fourth text, annotated *post alia,* forbids men from the gladiatorial school to join the service of Roman senators (15.12.3).

The four texts derive from a single edict, concerned with various abuses affecting the public life and appearance of the capital. In the extracts on the wearing of bracae and tzangae and building on the Campus Martius, the enforcement of the law is entrusted to the prefect of Rome, and it is this officer who is addressed in a sequel, a law of 6 June 399 reiterating the ban on these outlandish garments. There is a development between the two texts, in the way in which neglect of the imperial will is described—it is no longer those who "venture" ("temptaverint") to ignore it who are threatened with punishment, but those who long persist in their obstinacy: "si quisquam post praeceptum nostrae clementiae in hac contumacia perduraverit" (14.10.3). It was not just a repetition of the law, but a way of reminding the prefect that he had been given this duty, and that the emperor expected it to be performed. Seeck proposed that the successive laws 14.10.2–3 be taken together, one as part of the edict to the people, the other addressed at the same time to the prefect of Rome. In this case, the date of tenure of the prefect addressed, Nicomachus Flavianus, would locate the entire group of texts in 399. This reconstruction would eliminate the apparent doublet between the two texts on Oriental shoes and trousers and make plausible administrative sense, the edict to the people being reinforced by the letter to the prefect. However, the hypothesis would require extensive changes to the protocols of the texts, and on the suggestion presented here there is no need for it.[100]

## *Variants and Anomalies*

The interpretation of the procedures employed by the editors of the Theodosian Code shows a connection with—indeed, offers one way of approaching—the question of the sources from which they recovered the texts of their laws; whether, as has recently been restated by Boudewijn Sirks, they were to be found in central archives or copybooks in which the emperors entered copies of the legislation they issued, or in the provincial archives favored by Seeck, or in the variety of sources,

100. *Regesten,* pp. 77, 296. The prefect in April 397 was the Gaul Florentinus; the law of 399 is addressed to Nicomachus Flavianus. Intervening were the tenures of Lampadius, Felix, and (?) Quintilius Laetus—Chastagnol, *Fastes,* pp. 248–352.

especially the family papers of former officeholders, as suggested by A. H. M. Jones.[101] These questions will be brought together in the final chapter of this book. For the moment all that needs to be said is that it is important not to work with too restrictive an idea of the variety of sources that were available. It would be perverse to deny to the editors the use of imperial archives, in whatever form they may have been kept. At the same time, Seeck's observation that the fourth century, with its frequent civil and foreign wars and the endless itinerancy of its emperors, was not conducive to the ordered preservation of central archives, retains its force.[102] The purpose of the third part of this chapter is, however, to show from discrepancies within the Code itself that central archives cannot have been the only, or a uniquely important, source for the compilers of the Code. Discrepancies between laws, and between different versions which can be found of the same laws, are best explained on the grounds that their texts were derived from different sources.

1. We begin, however, with two contrary examples, cases of recent eastern legislation, where it seems more than likely that central archives were involved.[103] The edited protocols of these laws suggest either that the editors had found various copies of laws, which they gave in a single text while indicating the alternative sources that had come to their notice, or that they found a copy already annotated in the fashion shown. Both laws are discussed in much the same sense by Seeck:[104]

> 1.8.1: *Impp. Honorius et Theodosius AA. Florentio magistro militum. Viro illustri quaestore Eustathio suggerente, . . . . dat. id. Oct. Constantinopoli Honorio X et Theodosio VI AA. consul. Scripta eodem exemplo Sapricio magistro militum, Helioni magistro officiorum et Eustathio quaestori* (15 October 415).

As we saw in Chapter 7, the law concerns the restoration to the quaestor of certain military appointments listed in the laterculum minus, or Lesser Register. To secure the enforcement of the law, copies were sent "eodem exemplo" to all the relevant officials, including the magister officiorum, who had general supervision of administrative arrangements and had claimed these for his jurisdiction. The law

101. Sirks, "The Sources of the Code," in Harries and Wood, *The Theodosian Code,* pp. 49–52 (with full discussion of the arguments of Seeck); Jones, *JRS* 54 (1964), p. 79, also in *The Roman Economy,* ed. P. A. Brunt, pp. 376–77. Some but not all of what follows derives from my treatment of this subject in Harries and Wood, pp. 31–41.

102. Seeck, *Regesten,* p. 2.

103. What follows should be taken in association with the arguments of Honoré, *Law in the Crisis of Empire,* pp. 136–41.

104. *Regesten,* pp. 4f. In most of the examples that follow, the argument is developed from the protocols of the laws rather than the content, which is indicated by ellipses ( . . . . ), without any indication of the length of the substantive text. The presentation of the names of emperors, either in full (as *Impp. Honorius et Theodosius AA.*) or as abbreviated (*idem AA.*), simply transcribes editorial practice in the text in question.

is a success for the influential quaestor Eustathius who "suggested" it. It does not follow that it was among his departmental records that it was found, but a central archive, whether the quaestor's or that of any other of the officials mentioned, who had retained the law for their reference, is probably the best interpretation of the style of annotation of this recent law.

> 11.28.9: *Idem AA. Anthemio ppo. . . . . Dat V id. April. Consta(nti)nop(oli), Constantio et Constante conss. De eadem re scribtum edictum ad populum: ad Marcianum com(item) s(acrarum) l(argitionum): Musellio praeposito sacri cubiculi de titulis ad domum sacram pertinentibus: ad rectores provinciarum: et de metallariis edictum ad populum per provincias Illyrici et ad rectores provinciarum* (9 April 414).[105]

In this case, it is a likely deduction from the reference to the publication of the part of the text "de metallariis" as an "edictum ad populum per provincias Illyrici et ad rectores provinciarum," that the document was recovered as annotated at an early stage from the archive of a central official, possibly that of the praetorian prefect who had responsibility for its further diffusion, before it was divided into sections for enforcement by the separate agencies mentioned. Had this "edict concerning mineworkers" been recovered only in the version published in Illyricum for these particular recipients, it would not have contained the cross-references to others; there would be no need for the "people of Illyricum" to know to whom else it had been sent, or what else was contained in it.

2. Certain very late inclusions in the Code might be viewed in the same way. The last dated laws in the Theodosian Code, from summer 436 and spring 437, were addressed to successive praetorian prefects of the Orient, Isidore and Darius. We might take for granted that these laws—one of those to Isidore, of 4 June 436, being edited in six extracts, three of them in succession (12.1.189–191)[106]—were given to the editors of the Code by sources close to the centre of power. Another very recent eastern law with multiple addressees is *CTh* 6.28.8 (29 Jan. 435), addressed to the magister officiorum and sent "eodem exemplo" to the praetorian and urban prefects, to eastern deputy prefects and the *praefectus Augustalis,* and to the proconsul of Achaia. This text also is best seen as having been recovered so annotated from a central archive.

3. Matters are however not always so straightforward even for this very recent

105. Trans. Pharr: "On the same matter an edict was issued to the people; to Marcianus, Count of the Sacred Imperial Largesses; to Musellius, Grand Chamberlain, with reference to accounts pertaining to the sacred imperial household; to the governors of the provinces; and, with reference to the miners, an edict to the people throughout the provinces of Illyricum and to the governors of the provinces."

106. The others are 11.5.3; 14.26.2; 14.27.2.

period. In a further example, three edited laws deriving from a single pronouncement of 3 April 436 were addressed to the praetorian prefect Isidore, two of the extracts (but not the third) preserving in slightly different ways the annotation that the same law was also being issued to the praetorian prefect of Illyricum:

> 8.4.30: *Idem AA. Isidoro ppo. Post alia: eodem exemplo Eubulo ppo Illyrici . . . . Dat. III non. April. Const(antino)p(oli) Isidoro et Senatore conss.*

> 12.1.187: *Idem AA. Isidoro ppo . . . . Et cetera. Dat. III non. April. Constant(ino)p(oli) Isidoro et Senatore conss. Eodem exemplo Eubulo ppo Illyrici.*

The interest here lies partly in the fact that the prefect of Illyricum mentioned, Eubulus, was a member of the editorial panels of 429 and of 435 but had been promoted from his work on the Code to take up the prefecture;[107] he, if anyone, was in touch with the proceedings of the panel and in a good position to ensure that the commission received new legislation in its most authentic state. Despite this, the third version of this law (12.1.188), largely duplicates but also differs in detail from 8.4.30, and its protocol makes no mention of the prefect of Illyricum. It seems that even in this very recent case the compilers of the Code worked with not one "master copy," but with at least two versions of the law.

4. If this may happen even for recent eastern legislation, the situation for the more distant past, and especially for the western empire, is infinitely more complicated. Here we find anomalies impossible to understand in reference to an archive maintained at the center of power. By what process of recovery, for example, do we possess the text of a single law of Constantine "accepted" at Hispalis (Seville) on 18 April 336, apparently four years after it was issued at Constantinople?[108]

> 3.5.6: *Idem A. ad Tiberianum vicarium Hispaniarum . . . . Dat. Id. Iul. Constant(ino)p(oli). Accepta xiiii k. Mai. Hispali Nepotiano et Facundo conss.*

Such a gap between issue and acceptance, even between two such distant locations, is excessive in light of any assumptions of delays in communication between

107. See Chapter 4.

108. Barnes, *New Empire,* p. 145 and n. 17. The question of the date of issue of the law turns on the date, or dates, on which Tiberianus can have held office as vicarius (or comes) of Spain. *PLRE* 1, p. 911 (Tiberianus 4) has him as comes Hispaniarum in 332 (17 October; *CJ* 6.1.6), replaced by Severus in 333–35, and returning as vicarius Hispaniarum in 335 (if we take this to be the date of *issue* of *CTh* 3.5.6, which would then have been addressed to Tiberianus one year, and not four years, before it was posted). But first of all, *CTh* 13.5.8 to Severus has him still in office on 19 May 336 (*PLRE* solves this by moving the law to 335), and second, a return of Tiberianus to be vicarius of Spain does not seem likely. Seeck, *Regesten,* p. 183, lists 3.5.6 without comment under 335.

east and west. It may be that this is a special case, to be solved by a more radical approach than any so far thought of to problems of textual transmission or Constantinian prosopography.

5. A convincing historical context can however be found for discrepancies in a law of Valens addressed to the comes sacrarum largitionum, which survives in two fragments of what—given their diversity of subject matter—was clearly a much longer law issued at Noviodunum on 3 or 5 July 369. One extract, but not the other, is recorded as "accepted" at Marcianopolis on 18 July:

> 10.16.2: *Idem AA. et Gratianus ad Archelaum com(item) Or(ientis) . . . . dat. III non. Iul. Novioduno Val(entini)ano n(o)b(ilissimo) p(uero) et Victore conss.*
>
> 10.21.1: *Impp. Val(entini)anus et Valens AA. Archelao com.s.l. . . . . dat. V non. Iul. Nevioduni; acc. XV kal. Aug.27 Marcianopoli Val(entini)ano nob. p. et Victore conss.*

It is not hard to see what has happened here. In 369 Valens made Marcianopolis his winter quarters in preparation for his third campaigning season against the Goths. It appears from 10.21.1 that the emperor left behind his court administration at Marcianopolis and sent this law back to his comes sacrarum largitionum from his campaign headquarters at Noviodunum.[109] The edited text clearly derives not from an original version issued by the emperor and copied into some central file, but from that received by the comes sacrarum largitionum. The different protocol of 10.16.2 (with the correct inclusion of Gratian in the imperial college), the discrepancy in the date, and the error in the office of the recipient ("com. Or." for "com.s.l."), all show that this part of the law was recovered from a different source. This cannot have been a central archive. Had it been so, the compilers would have found both laws together as part of the same text, without the discrepancies between them that we find in the published versions. Instead, they recovered two partial, already separated versions of the same law but because of the differences in dating and protocols did not realize that they were dealing with a single pronouncement.

6. In another example, subtly different versions are found of a law addressed to the vicarius of Africa on the evasion of municipal duties under the assumed guise of high office. One version is recorded as "accepted" at Carthage on 12 December 338, the other as "posted" on 27 November at some unspecified location—not at

109. Amm. Marc. 27.7.5–6, mentioning both places. In 378, by contrast, Valens took with him to Hadrianople "thesauri . . . et principalis fortunae insignia cetera cum praefecto et consistorianis" (31.12.10, cf. 31.15.2, "potestatum culmina maximarum et fortunae principalis insignia thesaurosque").

Carthage, since the date is earlier than the "acceptance" of the first version there—and "accepted" at Timgad on 15 December.[110] As with the Sirmondian Constitutions and their corresponding texts discussed in Chapter 6, bold characters in the longer version indicate material shared with the shorter, and italics indicate variations in language. In both cases the full text of the law is given:[111]

> 6.22.2: *Imp. Constantius A. Aconio vic. Afric.* Ab honoribus mercandis per suffragia vel qualibet ambitione quaerendis certa multa prohibuit. Cui addimus, ut **quicumque fugientes obsequia curiarum umbram et nomina adfectaverint dignitatum, tricenas libras argenti inferre cogantur,** manente illa praeterea inlatione auri, qua perpetua lege constricti sunt. *pp. V kal. Dec., acc. XVII kal. Ian. Thamugadi Urso et Polemio conss.*

> 12.1.24: *Idem A. Aconio Catullino vic. Afric.*
>
> Quicumque fugientes obsequia curiarum affectaverint *adumbratae* nomina dignitat*is, etsi eos spes falsi honoris inluserit,* XXX argenti libras inferre cogantur. *acc. Karthag. prid. id. Dec. Urso et Polemio conss.*

The anomalies in the protocols of the laws, in which one version appears to have been displayed (in one place) at a date before it was received (in another), and before its counterpart was received at Carthage, may be explained on the basis of the assumption that the texts represent a stage of distribution beyond the vicarius to whom they were addressed. The first version, in which the vicarius' name is also transmitted in a less complete form, would represent a copy posted by him at an unknown location and sent on to Timgad to be received there by someone else—for example, the consularis Numidiae; the second would represent the copy received from the vicarius by the proconsul of Africa.[112] It arrived later than the copy

110. Reading with Mommsen "XVII kal. Ian." for "XVII kal. Iun.," to accommodate the dating to that of 12.1.24. The attribution of both texts to Constantius derives from the exclusion from the titulature of the names of Constantine II (337–40) and Constans (337–50), after the civil wars that eliminated them.

111. Pharr's translation of 6.22.2: "Trafficking in honours through patronage or acquiring them through any corrupt solicitation whatever is forbidden under an established penalty. We add that if any person should attempt to evade the duties of his municipal council and should seek to obtain the shadow and the name of high rank [even though he should be deceived of his hope of this false honour], he shall be compelled to pay thirty pounds of silver, and the fine of gold shall also remain, to the payment of which he is constrained by the eternal law." The phrase in square brackets is found only in 12.1.24; it adds to the proof that the shorter text cannot derive from the longer.

112. Known from other sources as Aurelius Celsinus: *PLRE* 1, p. 192 (Celsinus 4).

sent on to Timgad because the vicarius was nearer to Timgad than to Carthage when he received the original version of the law from the emperor.[113] At some stage, the law was "improved" by someone who fancied his hand at retouching the style by writing "adumbratae nominae dignitatis" for "umbram et nomina dignitatum." In any event, it is clear that the compilers of the Code recovered two versions of the law and not a single copy from some central archive. One might in any case wonder how many laws would have survived in their original form from the western reign of Constans, to whom this law must be assigned. That emperor had been killed early in 350 and replaced by a usurper who was himself shortly afterwards suppressed by Constantius after notoriously bloody battles. Where were the imperial archives in all of this?

It is also of interest that the successors of *CTh* 12.1.24 in the text of the Code nevertheless possess earlier dates, being issued, respectively, on 28 October and 1 November. The editors must have realized that, although the recorded date of *acceptance* at Carthage of 12.1.24 was later, it was *issued* earlier than its successors. That this was an editorial inference is clear from the fact that the date and place of issue of the law are not recorded in either version.

7. At 16.1.4 the Theodosian Code preserves one of the most widely reported of late Roman laws, that issued by Valentinian II at Milan on 23 January 386 permitting the free assembly of Arian congregations.[114] The circumstances that led up to and the consequences which followed the publication of the law are described by various writers, including Ambrose, bishop of Milan, and Augustine, who was in the city at the time as professor of rhetoric, and the church historians Rufinus and Sozomen. From Rufinus and Sozomen, and from Gaudentius, bishop of Brescia, we hear about the latter's parishioner the magister memoriae Benivolus, who resigned his office rather than draft the legislation.[115] That the law involves Milan and concerns the relations of the imperial court, influenced by the Arianism of the empress and her supporters, with the Catholic community of the city and its bishop

113. It may or may not be significant that there is no attested praetorian prefect of Italy and Africa at this moment; see the Fasti of *PLRE* 1, pp. 1048–49. Perhaps the vicarius was performing the prefectoral role of distributing legislation in his diocese—a role that must frequently have fallen to him in any case—with laws that retained their original address to the praetorian prefect.

114. Trans. Pharr: "If those persons who suppose that the right of assembly has been granted to them alone should attempt to provoke any agitation against the regulation of Our Tranquillity, they shall know that, as authors of sedition and as disturbers of the peace of the Church, they shall also pay the penalty of high treason with their life and blood. Punishment shall also await those persons who may attempt to supplicate Us surreptitiously and secretly, contrary to this Our regulation."

115. Matthews, *Western Aristocracies and Imperial Court*, pp. 184–86, 189.

is beyond any doubt. It is puzzling, therefore, to find at *CTh* 16.4.1 a single sentence of the law cited almost verbatim and with the same date as 16.1.4, but presented as if issued at Constantinople:

| 16.1.4 | 16.4.1 |
|---|---|
| 16.1.4: *Imppp. Val(entini)anus, Theod(osius) et Arcad(ius) AAA. Ad Eusignium ppo. . . .* Conveniendi etiam quibus iussimus patescat arbitrium, scituris **his, qui sibi tantum existimant colligendi copiam contributam,** quod, **si turbulentum quippiam contra nostrae tranquillitatis praeceptum faciendum esse temptaverint, ut seditionis auctores pacisque turbatae ecclesiae,** etiam **maiestatis capite ac sanguine sint supplicia luituri,** manente nihilo minus eos supplicio qui contra hanc dispositionem nostram obreptive aut clanculo supplicare temptaverint. *Dat. X kal. Feb. Med(iolano) Honorio nob. p. et Euodio conss.* | 16.4.1: *Imppp. Val(entini)anus, Theod(osius) et Arcad(ius) AAA. Eusignio ppo.* His, qui sibi tantum*modo* existimant colligendi copiam contributam, si turbulentum quippiam contra nostrae tranquillitatis praeceptum faciendum esse temptaverint, ut seditionis auctores pacisque turbatae ecclesiae, maiestatis capite ac sanguine sint supplicia luituri. *Dat. X kal. Feb. Constantp. Honorio nob. p. et Euodio v.c. conss.* |

The textual variations are slight but from an editorial point of view significant. Apart from the different and mistaken place of issue, the epistolary form *Eusignio* is read for *ad Eusignium,*[116] and the consul Euodius is given his rank as—"v(ir) c(larissimus)"; Euodius was the consul of the western usurper Magnus Maximus, and his name is here recorded, as in several other laws, in the one year in which Maximus was recognized by Theodosius.[117] The minor discrepancies of phraseology do not suggest that the shorter text was edited from the longer, or that either was edited from a common original; compared with 16.1.4, 16.4.1 omits the

116. See the first part of this chapter. The "dissertatio" of Maximinus (n. 118), though apparently deriving from *CTh* 16.4.1, nevertheless transmits the address as "ad Eusignium pf. pretorio." The discrepancy between the two forms also occurs in 10.16.2 and 10.21.1, discussed above (No. 5).

117. Matthews, *Western Aristocracies and Imperial Court,* p. 179; *Historia* 46 (1997), at pp. 207–8.

words *quod* and *etiam* but on the other hand has the longer "tantummodo" where 16.1.4 has merely "tantum." Although it is true that it concerns the most general aspect of 16.1.4, it is hard to see how 16.4.1 ever became connected with the eastern empire. For present purposes, it is relevant only to observe that the editors of the Theodosian Code must have acquired these two laws from different sources. Had they extrapolated 16.4.1 from 16.1.4 they would not have incorporated these discrepancies in the protocol.[118]

8. The following two laws, given on the same day, 12 June 393, and edited in succession under 9.42 *De bonis proscribtorum seu damnatorum*, relate to another well-known event of the period, the most serious upheaval in the court politics of the later years of Theodosius; the fall of the Lycian Fl. Eutolmius Tatianus and his son Proculus. They had been, respectively, praetorian prefect of the east and prefect of Constantinople during Theodosius' absence in the west on the campaign against the usurper Maximus, and were brought down after the emperor's return to the east.[119] Tatianus, who had been consul in 391, was sent back to his native Lycia, while Proculus was condemned to death and beheaded at Sycae (Galata); the date of the execution was 6 December 393.[120] The agent of their downfall was Theodosius' western supporter, the magister officiorum and praetorian prefect Fl. Rufinus, who succeeded Tatianus as praetorian prefect,[121] and to whom the first of the two laws was addressed. With variant turns of rhetoric, they order the restoration of property confiscated by Tatianus, either to his impoverished victims if they survived, or to their closest relatives if the owners themselves had been executed.[122]

118. The law is also summarized, from the fuller version at *CTh* 16.1.4, by Sozomen, *Hist. Eccl.* 7.13.7, and cited in full (including protocol) from the shorter version at 16.4.1, hence with the place of issue given as Constantinople, by the fifth-century Arian bishop Maximinus, in his "dissertatio" on the council of Aquileia, §95 (ed. R. Gryson, *Corpus Christianorum* 87 [1982], pp. 195f.); cf. Peter Heather and John Matthews, *The Goths in the Fourth Century* (1991), at pp. 145f. It is remarkable that a law in favour of Arian congregations was included in the Theodosian Code, and shows how strictly the editors observed their instructions to record "cunctas/omnes constitutiones" (laws of 429 and 435). Maximinus actually failed to realize that 16.4.1 was a law issued *in favour of* the Arians, as he would have done had he made the connection with 16.1.4.

119. *PLRE* 1, pp. 876–78 (Tatianus 5) and 746–47 (Proculus 6); they held their offices from 388 till the late summer of 392, Theodosius having returned to Constantinople by July 391.

120. Zosimus 4.52, cf. Eunapius, fr. 59 Müller/57 Blockley; for the date of the execution, *Chron. Pasch.*, s.a. 393. As prefect of Constantinople, Proculus had in 390 erected the obelisk that still stands in the Hippodrome; his name was erased from the dedicatory inscription after his fall, and later re-inscribed after the rehabilitation of his memory (*ILS* 821).

121. *PLRE* 1, pp. 778–81 (Rufinus 18); Matthews, *Western Aristocracies and Imperial Court*, pp. 113, 134–36.

122. Seeck, *Regesten*, p. 281–82, accepting the obvious correction of the MSS (*VT*) reading

The similarities in the texts are picked out by the numbered sections (i)-(iv), section (v) being present only in the second text:

| 9.42.12: *Idem AAA. Rufino ppo.* | 9.42.13: *Idem AAA. Drepanio com.r.p.* |
|---|---|
| (i) Omnia proscribtorum bona, quae fisco iusserat Tatianus adnecti, | (i) Omnia proscribtorum bona, quae fisci nomine singulis quibusque Tatianus eripuit, |
| (ii) vel ipsis, qui propriam nuditatem, | (ii) vel ipsis, qui gladio acerbiorem stilum passi aerumnas suas nuditatemque fleverunt |
| (iii) vel illis, qui suorum mortem in extrema positi egestate lugent, | (iii) vel eorum filiis ac propinquiis, qui cruentas excepere sententias, |
| (iv) sine dubitationis obstaculo reddi praecipimus. | (iv) restitui mox iubemus, |
| | (v) ita ut omnes, qui aliquid ex huiusmodi bonis nostra liberalitate meruerunt, restituere indepta cogantur. |
| *Dat. prid. id. Iun. Constantinop. Theod. A. III et Abundantio v.c. conss.* | *Dat. prid. id. Iun. Constantinop. Theod. A. III et Abundantio v.c. conss.* |

What is interesting about these texts is, first, that both appear in the Code, it being obvious that they related to the same event and expressed the same ordinance about it, an identity of reference that is only emphasized by their being edited in succession in the same title; and second, that their language varies as widely it does. The first of them is addressed to Rufinus, the actual architect of Tatianus' destruction;[123] the second is addressed to Rufinus' subordinate the comes rei privatae, whose department would be concerned with the restoration of the

"ian." in 9.42.13. The following are Pharr's translations of the two laws: "All the property of proscribed persons which Tatianus has ordered to be annexed to the fisc, We order to be returned, without the hindrance of doubt, either to those persons who lament their own want or to those persons who are placed in extreme poverty and mourn the death of their own kinsmen" (9.42.12). "All the goods of the proscribed persons which Tatianus has seized from any individual in the name of the fisc We order to be restored at once, either to those persons who have suffered a written sentence harsher than the sword and have wept over their hardship and want, or to the children and near kinsmen of those who have received death sentences, and We order that all those persons who have acquired any property of this kind by Our liberality shall be compelled to restore what they have received" (9.42.13).

123. It was after Rufinus' fall late in 395 that the reputation of Tatianus and the Lycians was restored: *CTh* 9.38.9 (31 August 396), with direct allusion to the enmity of an unnamed individual who is certainly Rufinus. The fallen prefect is named at 9.42.14 (13 February 396).

confiscated property to its owners.[124] Yet the second, and one would have thought derivative law is longer and contains a more elaborate rhetoric than its companion. It does not look as if either text were simply an expansion or a contraction of the other. If 9.42.12 were a contraction of 13, the letter to the praetorian prefect would have had to be abbreviated from the longer version addressed to his subordinate, an unlikely conclusion. It is possible, no doubt, that the second text represents an expanded communication from the prefect's office to that of his comes rei privatae, but this would require the prefect's staff to have elaborated the rhetoric contained in the emperor's letter to him. This assumption seems gratuitous; the expanded references to sentences of poverty and misery as fates worse than death are more than is needed in a memorandum addressed by a praetorian prefect to his subordinate. It is also possible that the texts are not related in this way, but that each, with the same substantive logic, is a separate expression of a common rhetorical idea.[125] Perhaps the emperor wrote independently to his prefect and to the comes rei privatae, in which case we may be looking at two literary hands in the office of the quaestor, working to the same brief with the same rhetorical idea suggested to both.[126]

As to the presence of both texts in succession in the Theodosian Code, where either one would have covered the situation, the explanation is presumably that its editors followed literally their instructions to include every text recovered by them that possessed the quality of generalitas. They obtained these two texts from different sources and entered them in the Code without attempting to resolve their differences of expression.

A third text, addressed on the same day to Rufinus and edited under title 11.1, *De annona et tributis,* may help to explain the situation. It orders the abolition of additional tax burdens imposed without precedent by Tatianus on the shoulders of provincials:

> 11.1.23: *Imppp. Theod(osius), Arcad(ius) et Honor(ius) AAA. Rufino ppo.* Aerariae praestationis adiectio, quam citra priscam consuetudinem provincialium

124. Drepanius is the panegyrist Latin(i)us Drepanius Pacatus, a political associate of Rufinus: *PLRE* 1, p. 272 (Drepanius); Matthews, *Western Aristocracies and Imperial Court,* pp. 228; and *Latomus* 30 (1971), pp. 1078–82.

125. Apart from certain formal expressions and the name of Tatianus, the texts share only the word *nuditatem. Fleverunt* in 13 corresponds to *lugent* in a different clause of 12, while the idea of the need (*egestate*) of those whose relatives have been executed occurs only in 12. 13 has the more elaborate references to punishment by execution.

126. The case is not unlike that involving the envoy Bubulcus discussed in the first part of this chapter under the heading "A Selected Title" (no. B.21), and the letter and law of Constantine discussed in Chapter 9.

> umeris Tatianus inposuit, a cunctis penitus salubri moderatione removenda est. *Dat. prid. id. Iun. Constantinop. Theod. A. III et Abundantio v.c. conss.*[127]

It looks from all this as if the editors recovered a single text addressed to Rufinus, of which they edited one part in 9.42 and the other in 11.1. They recovered separately the version sent on the same day to the comes rei privatae and, applying their instructions faithfully and literally, included it together with that addressed on the same subject to his superior. Being from the eastern empire at a relatively recent date, both original texts, one to the praetorian prefect and one to the comes rei privatae, may well have been recovered from central archives. In any case, they already possessed the variations of language found in them.

9. The best explanation of a law addressed to the consularis of Campania *or* (*sic*) the consularis of Picenum is that the compilers recovered two copies of a law originally issued more widely—to all provincial governors, to all governors of Italian provinces, or to a praetorian prefect with the instructions to forward it to them:

> 12.1.71: *Idem AA. et Gr(ati)anus A. ad Amphilochium cons. Campaniae sive ad Sofronium cons. Piceni . . . . dat. III non. Mai. Trev(iris) Val(entini)ano et Valente III AA. conss.* (5 May 370).

To say that a law was issued to one *or* another of two officials is, in the words of Seeck, just nonsense ("Unsinn"). The compilers clearly had before them two copies of the law, which they combined in this strange fashion—"in jener wunderlichen Weise"![128] As Seeck also observed, the successor of this law in the same title, on a closely related subject—the performance of municipal obligations by people claiming exemptions—carries the same date and is addressed to another Italian provincial governor, the consularis of Tuscia.[129] The editors of the Code seem to have recovered three separate texts containing two parts of a single original pronouncement, one part in copies addressed to the governors of Campania and Picenum, the second part in a copy addressed to the governor of Tuscia.

10. A similar explanation may hold for a law addressed to the proconsul *and* the vicarius of Africa but beginning with a phrase in the singular, and so clearly addressed to each separately:

127. Trans. Pharr: "The additional tax payment of bronze, which without the authority of ancient custom was imposed by Tatianus on the shoulders of the provincials, shall be completely removed from all by Our salutary regulation." Another text, *CTh* 14.17.12, of 20 November 393, invalidates entitlements to food distributions made by Proculus, presumably as part of his bid for popular support.

128. For this and the following case, cf. Seeck, *Regesten,* p. 6.

129. Ibid., p. 35.

> 1.12.6: *Idem AA. Victorio proconsuli Africae et Dominatori vicario Africae.* Apparitioni *tuae* et legatorum quadringentos de his dumtaxat, quos rei publicae membra non querentur sibi esse detractos, etc. [including also the phrases *arbitrii tui* and *officii tui*] . . . . *dat. XII k. Iun. Med*[*iolano*] *Honorio A. IIII et Eutychiano consul.* (21 May 398).[130]

These examples of their procedures, to which many others could be added, support the arguments offered earlier, that the editors of the Theodosian Code did not work with central archives across the whole span of the period with which they were concerned. Had they done so, they would have recovered more laws in total and there would have been fewer discrepancies between different versions of the same laws and fewer indications of the circumstances in which laws were received, read out, and posted in public places. A total of around twenty-seven hundred "basic texts" originally recovered by the editors is not an especially impressive haul of legislation over a 125-year span, if the original texts survived in central archival sources that approached anything like completeness.[131] It is much more impressive if the laws had to be recovered from diverse provenances. Furthermore, the argument that laws were recovered from such archives leaves out of account one of the most obvious ways in which legal texts are known to have been preserved in the Roman empire, as mentioned in Chapter 7: through the transcribing by interested parties of publicly displayed copies. As in earlier centuries, this custom of transcription continued during the period of the legislation contained in the Theodosian Code.

No single or narrow range of possibilities relating only to officially preserved versions of imperial legislation will explain the discrepancies and anomalies that occur in the published texts of the Code. The answer to the question of its sources similarly lies not at one or two but at many points in the wide area between the central records consulted in the case of recent laws issued in the east and the diverse and the scattered locations in which some of the laws recovered were originally received. The probability, supported by some observations in the first part of this chapter, also exists that the sources of material available to the editors changed over the period that concerned them. These questions will be taken up in the final chapter of this book.

130. Trans. Pharr: "For your office staff and that of the legates, [We decree] that four hundred apparitors shall be assigned from those persons only whom the members of any municipality do not complain of as having been withdrawn from them."

131. For this estimate of the number of "basic constitutions" see Sirks, "The Sources of the Code," Appendix 1, pp. 64–66.

# 9

# *Edicts and Letters*

## Four Last Examples

This final substantive chapter presents four cases (to add to the Sirmondian Constitutions), where the edited texts of laws in the Theodosian Code can be compared with more extensive or differing versions surviving elsewhere. The first two examples involve laws of Constantine. The first is a legislative text of which an excerpt appearing in the Code also exists more or less complete, but with significant differences, on contemporary inscriptions; the second is an intriguing case in which the edited text in the Theodosian Code can be compared with the emperor's own version of the same law in a letter describing its contents. Both these cases have a bearing on the processes of conception and early transmission of imperial legislation. The third example is Julian's law about public education, and the fourth is a law of Theodosius I on male prostitution in the city of Rome, preserved in the Theodosian Code and also, derived from a different original copy, in an independent juristic, or quasi-juristic, source of the late fourth century.

### *Edictum de Accusationibus*

*CTh* 9.5.1 is—surprisingly, given the historic importance of the subject—the sole law to be included in the Code under the title *Ad legem Iuliam maiestatis.* Assigned in the transmitted text to Constantine as sole emperor and addressed to a p.u. (*praefectus urbi*), Maximus, the law lays down stringent conditions for accusations in cases of maiestas, including torture both for those of any social rank accused under the law, and for those unable to sustain their accusations, and crucifixion for slaves and freedmen who accuse their masters and patrons.

As it stands in the Theodosian Code, the law contains a difficulty, and a point of special interest. The difficulty is that it carries a "proposita" dating by the consuls of 314, whereas the addressee of the law, if Maximus is the urban prefect Valerius Maximus *qui et* Basilius, held office from 1 September 319 to 13 September 323; since the day of posting is 1 January, the year would be one of the years 320 to 323.[1] The point of special interest is the crucifixion of slaves and freedmen. For centuries this had been the regular mode of punishment for those of servile status in cases where a so-called aggravated capital penalty was thought appropriate. It is reported by Aurelius Victor that Constantine abolished the "ancient and most dreadful penalty" of crucifixion with the breaking of legs.[2] The historian gives no indication of when Constantine effected this change in policy, and there can be no inherent objection to the attribution of *CTh* 9.5.1 to a time in the reign before he had implemented it.

The interpretation of the law is complicated, and made more interesting, by the occurrence of the same Theodosian Code extract as two paragraphs of a longer text in the form of an edict now known from six Latin inscriptions, five of them certainly, the sixth possibly, from the eastern provinces. The most complete of the inscriptions, from Lyttos in Crete, supplemented by an inscription from Tlos in Lycia and by one no longer extant but copied at Padua in the sixteenth century, provided the basis for the standard versions of the edict in handbooks of legal sources, and for the text with translation and commentary by Heichelheim and Schwarzenberger (1947).[3] The three inscriptions discovered more recently, from Sinope on the Black Sea, from Pergamum, and now from Ephesus, in Asia Minor, have permitted distinct improvements, especially to the preamble and the final

1. "Pp. kal. Ianuar. Volusiano et Anniano conss."—Chastagnol, *Fastes,* pp. 72–74 (no. 29); Barnes, *New Empire,* p. 111. The exact dates of Maximus' tenure are given by the *Chronographer of the Year 354*. There is no possibility of confusion with the prefect of Rome in 314, who was named Aradius Rufinus: *Fastes,* pp. 59–62 and 63 (nos. 22 and 24). See further n. 28.

2. Aurelius Victor, *Caesares* 41.4: "Eo pius, ut vetus teterrimumque supplicium patibulorum suffringendisque cruribus primus removerit."

3. Lyttos: *Ephemeris Epigraphica* 7, p. 416, re-edited with photograph by M. Guarducci, *Inscriptiones Creticae,* vol. 1, no. 188 (pp. 226–28); Tlos: *CIL* 3.12133; "Padua": *CIL* 5.2781, with Mommsen's notes. From these versions derive Riccobono, vol. 1, no. 94 (pp. 458–61), and, better presented, Bruns, no. 94 (pp. 266–67); F. M. Heichelheim and S. Schwarzenberger, "An Edict of Constantine the Great: A Contribution to the Study of Interpolations," *Symbolae Osloenses* 26 (1947), pp. 1–19.

paragraphs of the text.[4] The version copied at Padua (ancient Patavium) has also long been supposed, because of the provenance of the other texts, to have originated in Asia Minor, but because the actual stone is lost, there is no way of confirming this.[5] The variations of expression between the inscriptions, and between the relevant sections of these and the version of the text in the Theodosian Code, are in most cases trivial, but in two instances import a different substantive reading clearly not intended by its original author. Further, if either of the dates suggested by the Theodosian Code is accepted, the provenance of the five extant inscriptions in the regions then controlled not by Constantine but by Licinius poses an obvious question in relation to the version addressed in the Code to the prefect of Rome.

The text of the edict presented here incorporates the more recent discoveries, without attempting to resolve the few textual problems that remain; it is not an epigraphic study. Supplements are indicated selectively and obvious restorations not at all, comment being provided in footnotes where it seems necessary.[6] The numbering of paragraphs is for convenience in discussion, although the separation of the paragraphs themselves is indicated by the arrangement of the epigraphic texts.[7] The translation is mine, but I have consulted those by Heichelheim and, for the extract preserved in the Theodosian Code, by Pharr. Variations in the Theodosian Code version of the text, to be discussed below, are shown in italics.

Exemplum sacri edicti

[Reb]us ips[is] nobis probatum est plurimos non contentos fortunis s[uis . . . *about eighteen letters missing*][8] accusationem in[ . . . ] [(?) nonnumquam a]dque ex

4. Sinope: J. Moreau, "Fragment, découvert à Sinope"; Pergamum: C. Habicht and P. Kussmaul, "Ein neues Fragment"; Ephesus: D. Feissel, "Les Constitutions des Tétrarques," and "Deux Constitutions Tétrarchiques." The most pertinent discussions, in addition to those by Habicht and Kussmaul, and in particular by Feissel, are Barnes, "Three Imperial Edicts," (cf. *New Empire*, pp. 127–28); and Simon Corcoran, "Hidden from History: The Legislation of Licinius," in Harries and Wood (eds.), *The Theodosian Code*, at pp. 115–16 (cf. *Empire of the Tetrarchs*, pp. 190–91, 288–91).

5. An eastern origin is supposed by Habicht and Kussmaul, "Ein neues Fragment," p. 137; Barnes, *New Empire*, p. 128; Corcoran, *Empire of the Tetrarchs*, pp. 190, 288; and Feissel, "Les Constitutions des Tétrarques," p. 49 with n. 88.

6. The epigraphic situation is not entirely satisfactory, a new inspection of the longest text, from Lyttos, being needed. Despite her note that she had inspected the inscription ("revisi"), Guarducci's text derives heavily from earlier printed versions and shows in square brackets parts of words that can be read on her photograph (from an impression of the stone).

7. On the divisions of the text, see Feissel, "Les Constitutions des Tétrarques," p. 49.

8. The words *non contentos* were given by the Sinope fragment, "fortunis s[uis]" being then an obvious supplement; people "not content with their own fortunes," are trying to enrich themselves by accusing others for the financial rewards. Feissel's restoration ("Les

eiusmodi causis tam eos qui accus[an]tur quam qui [ad tes]timonium voc[an]tur gravissimis vexationibus adfici.

(Ia) Unde consulentes securitati provincialium nostrorum[9] eiusmodi remedia prospeximus, ut accusator quidem non omnimodo de iudicio repellatur, verum quicumque intentionibus suis probationes addere confidit, habeat adeundi iudicis liberam potestatem ac manifestis indiciis commissi reum in eum qui convictus fuerit vindicetur. Quod detegat, ut pro qualitate factorum conpetentur si minime potuerit ea quae intentaverit conprobare, scire debet severiori se sententia subiugandum.

I(b) Sane si quis alicui maiestatis crimen intenderit, cum eiusmodi obiectus minime quemquam privilegio dignitatis alicuius a strictiori inquisitione tueatur, sciat se quoque tormentis esse subdendum, si aliis manifestis indiciis *atque argumentis* accusationem suam non potuerit conprobare, cum in eo, qui huius temeritatis deprehendetur, illut quoque tormentis erui oporteat, cuius consilio atque instinctu ad accusationem accessisse videatur, ut ab omnibus tanti commissi consciis vindicta possit reportari.

*CTh* 9.5.1: *Imp. Constantinus A. ad Maximum p.u.* Si quis alicui maiestatis crimen intenderit, cum *in huiuscemodi re convictus* minime *quisquam* privilegio dignitatis alicuius a strictiore inquisitione *defendatur,* sciat se quoque tormentis esse subdendum, si aliis manifestis indiciis accusationem suam non poterit conprobare. *Cum eo,* qui huius esse temeritatis deprehend*itur, illum* quoque tormentis *subdi* oport*et,* cuius consilio atque instinctu ad accusationem accessisse videbitur, ut ab omnibus conmissi consciis statuta vindicta possit reportari.

II Delatoribus autem quod adeundi quoque iudicis tam statutis parentum nostrorum quam etiam nostris sanctionibus interclusa sit facultas, omnibus cognitum est, cum eiusmodi hominibus audientia non debeat commodari, quando quidem eos pro

---

Constitutions des Tétrarques," p. 50) of the opening words, "[reb]us ips[is nob]is probatum est," at the beginning of the inscription is a decisive improvement over previous versions and is fully compatible with what can be seen on Guarducci's photograph.

9. *Provincialium nostrorum* (for Guarducci's *provinciarum nostrarum*) is given by the Sinope fragment.

tanti sceleris audacia poenae conveniat subiugari.

III In servis quoque sive libertis, qui dominos vel patronos accusare aut deferre temptant, eiusmodi legem iuxta antiqui quoque iuris statutum observandum esse censuimus, ut scilicet professio tam atrocis audaciae statim in admissi ipsius exordio per sententiam iudicis conprimatur ac denegata audientia patibulo adfixus qui ad eiusmodi desperationem processerit, exemplum ceteris praestet, ne quis in posterum audaciae similis existat.

In servis quoque vel libertis, qui dominos aut patronos accusare aut deferre temptaverint,

professio tam atrocis audaciae statim in admissi ipsius exordio per sententiam iudicis conprimatur ac denegata audientia patibulo adfig*atur*. *Pp. kal. Ianuar. Volusiano et Anniano conss.*

IV. Sane ut undique versum securitati innocentium consulatur, placet etiam famosos libellos non admitti. Quos sine nomine propositos si qui invenerit, statim detrahere atque scindere vel igni debebit exurere. In quibus etiam iudicum eiusmodi observantiam esse oportebit, ut, si forte ad se talis libellus perlatus fuerit, igni eum praecipiat concremari, cum eiusmodi scripturam ab audientia iudicis penitus oporteat submoveri; manente contra eos inquisitione qui libellos eiusmodi proponere ausi fuerint, ut reperti debitis temeritatis suae poenis subiciantur.

V. Super itaque omnibus tam ad praefectos nostros quam etiam ad praesides[10] et rationalem et magistrum privatae scripta direximus, quorum exempla [alio?] edicto nostro subdita cuiusmodi legem statutumque contineant, plenissime declaratur.[11]

Copy of the Sacred Edict.

The facts themselves have proven to us that a great many men, not satisfied with their own fortunes, [enrich themselves by engaging in the accusation of others],

10. *Tam* is omitted by error from the Pergamum text. Barnes' claim, "Three Imperial Edicts" *ZPE* 21 (1976), p. 276 n. 5; *New Empire,* p. 128 n. 20) to the reading "etiam ad praesides," confirmed by the Pergamum fragment, amounts to the replacement of the regularly printed "et" by the clearly preferable "ad"—an old correction already reported by Mommsen in his notes on the Padua version.

11. See Habicht and Kussmaul, "Ein neues Fragment," p. 136, for the text of these last lines as preserved in the Pergamum inscription: "quorum e[xempla alio edicto]/nostro subdita cuiusmodi legem [statutumque con]/tineant p(l)enissime declaratur."

and that from cases of this sort both those who are accused and those who are called to give witness are subjected to very serious harassments.[12]

I(a) Therefore, pursuing our concern for the peace of mind of our provincials we have provided remedies as follows [*eiusmodi*]: that an accuser should indeed not be altogether rejected from the court, but that any person who is confident that he can provide proof of his allegations may have liberty and power to approach a judge and by clear evidence expose the guilt of the accused, in order that retribution may be fittingly imposed on him in proportion to the nature of his crimes. But, if a person is quite unable to prove what he has alleged, he should know that he is to be disciplined by a more severe penalty.

I(b). Further, if a person directs against anyone a charge of maiestas, since an accusation of this sort offers no protection by privilege of any rank against the more stringent sort of examination, let the accuser know that he, too, is to be put to the torture if he is unable to prove his accusation through additional proofs and arguments. In addition, in the case of a man who is caught out in such reckless audacity, the following information also must be drawn from him by torture: namely, with whose advice and at whose instigation he seems to have undertaken the accusation. So retribution may be exacted from all the participants in so great a crime.

II Now, of course, with regard to *delatores,* it is known to everyone that their rights of access to a judge have been restricted both by the statutes of our predecessors[13] and by our own laws, since no hearing ought to be granted to men of that sort. Rather, it is right that they should be subdued by punishment for their audacity in committing so great a crime.

III. In the case also of slaves or freedmen who attempt to accuse or to inform against their masters or patrons, alongside the provision of the old-established rule [*antiqui iuris*] we order that a law [*legem*] be observed as follows: namely, that the confession of such outrageous audacity should be quashed by sentence of the judge at the very outset of the admission, and that anyone who has ventured to an act of desperation of this sort should be denied a hearing and fastened to the cross. He may so provide an example to others, that in future no perpetrator of a similar act of audacity may ever appear.

IV. Furthermore, not to omit any consideration of the peace of mind of the innocent, it is our pleasure that defamatory flysheets [*famosi libelli*] also be not admitted. If anyone finds such documents posted up [*propositos*] anonymously, it will be

12. Namely, torture; see n. 17 below.

13. See n. 44 for the interpretation of this phrase.

his duty at once to pull them down and tear them up or burn them. In such matters the same course of action must be followed also by judges—namely, that if on any occasion such a libellus is produced before a judge, he should order it to be burned; for a written text of this kind ought to be completely withdrawn from the hearing of a judge. An inquiry should be directed against those who bring themselves to post libelli of this sort, so that they may be found and subjected to due penalties for their temerity.

V. On all these matters, therefore, we have sent letters both to our prefects and to provincial governors, to the rationalis and to the magister privatae, copies of which are appended to [another?] edict of ours; in these letters it is very fully stated how they incorporate the law and statute.

The Theodosian Code version[14] consists of two extracts of the text as it is preserved epigraphically, separated by one omitted section, and also omitting four others. The character of two of the missing sections will be familiar from the Sirmondian Constitutions, as discussed in Chapter 6. The first is a preamble describing the problem to be addressed and declaring the emperor's concern for his provincials in doing so. The expression in the edict "unde consulentes securitati provincialium nostrorum," marking the transition between preamble and substantive legislation, is equivalent to the "therefore" expressions noted in the Sirmondian Constitutions. There is also a concluding section (§V) ordering letters explaining the law to be sent out "to our prefects and to the provincial governors, to the rationalis and the magister privatae"; this will be discussed further. Two other minor omissions, embodied in the same section of the original text (§III), are also of the sort found elsewhere—namely, a statement about the deterrent purpose of the punishment ordained for slaves and freedmen, and a reference to legal prece-

14. Trans. Pharr: "*Emperor Constantine Augustus to Maximus, Prefect of the City.* If any person should bring the charge of high treason against another, since a person convicted in a case of this kind is not protected by the privilege of any high rank from a very severe inquisition, the accuser shall know that he also must be subjected to torture if he should not be able to prove his accusation by other clear evidence. Along with the person who is discovered to be guilty of such rash criminality, that person must also be subjected to torture by whose advice and instigation he appears to have undertaken the accusation, in order that the established penalty may be exacted of all persons who are accomplices of this deed. In the case of slaves also, or of freedmen who attempt to accuse their masters or patrons, respectively, or to report them to the authorities, the assertion of such atrocious audacity shall be repressed immediately at the inception of the guilty act itself, through the sentence of the judge, a hearing shall be denied such slave or freedman, and he shall be affixed to the cross. *Posted on the kalends of January in the year of the consulship of Volusianus and Annianus.*"

dent, "antiqui iuris statuta." These changes are well within the terms of reference laid down for the editors of the Theodosian Code, as we saw them in Chapter 4.

As to omissions relevant to the substance of the law, the first is a statement of the conditions under which "accusatores" might be heard in the courts—that is to say, when they claimed to have clear proof of their allegations—and of the penalties that attach to a failure to prove them (§Ia). This section contains material relevant to the Theodosian Code, particularly to title 9.1, *De accusationibus et inscribtionibus,* but it is not found there.

Next omitted is a shorter section (§II) referring to legislation of previous and the present emperors affecting "delatores."[15] Although it separates the two extracts run together as *CTh* 9.5.1, the section is of no real substance, and one can imagine that editors with the full text before them might not trouble to excerpt it; even so, the text is as substantial as some others assembled under *CTh* 10.10, *De petitionibus et ultro datis et delatoribus,* and one might expect it to have been included.

This is emphatically true of the third omitted section, a definitive statement on the subject of "famosi libelli" (§IV). We saw in Chapter 7 that the Theodosian Code contained an entire title *De famosis libellis* (9.34), and many of the themes covered in that title are found in this section of the epigraphic text; notably, that anyone finding anonymous libelli should pull them down and tear them up or burn them, and that a judge should likewise consign them to flames if they are brought before him, while any persons suspected of posting such documents should be questioned and if guilty subjected to the due penalties. This part of the text is germane to the Theodosian Code title and is as clear a statement of the principles involved as any of the texts that survive there. It is inconceivable that, had the editors known of the edict in its complete form, they would have omitted this part of it.[16]

No less significant than its omissions is the fact that in two places the Theodosian Code version, with small changes to the text of the original edict, has substantially changed its meaning. Both occur in §Ib of the edict, yielding the first part of the Theodosian Code text:

1. The edict refers to the provision that in accusations of maiestas torture may be applied to the accused person, whatever his social rank: "cum *eiusmodi obiectus* minime quemquam privilegio dignitatis alicuius a strictori inquisitione tueatur."[17]

15. "Tam statutis parentum nostrorum quam etiam nostris sanctionibus." For the language, see the Appendix to Chapter 6.

16. Constantius referred in 338 to a law of his "inclytus pater" on the subject: *CTh* 9.34.5. If the present edict is indeed a law of Constantine, it is more likely to be that referred to by Constantius than would any other preceding text in 9.34, but it may not be so (as we shall see).

17. *Eiusmodi obiectus* is a strange expression for "accusation of . . .," although *obiector* is

The principle is familiar from legal and other texts from all centuries of the Roman Empire.[18] In the Theodosian Code, however, through changes in language and syntax, it is not the accused, but the man already convicted of maiestas who is liable to this treatment: "cum *in eiusmodi re convictus* minime quisquam . . . defendatur." This language changes the point of law covered by the edict.[19]

2. In the second case, yet smaller changes in the text have an equally substantial effect on the point of law involved. In the edict, torture is to be applied to an accuser who fails to make good his case, not only in virtue of his own failure but for a second reason — in order to extract the names of those who may have put him up to the accusation: "*illut* quoque tormentis *erui* oporteat, cuius consilio atque instinctu ad accusationem accessisse videatur."[20] This is an application in penal law of a rule known from the Digest, referring to the legal liabilities of a "mandator," the person who authorizes or commits another to initiate proceedings on his behalf. Callistratus had cited a rescript of Antoninus Pius referring to a ruling of Hadrian, to the effect that a delator was compelled to publish the name of his mandator and, if he did not publish it, was to be put in prison. The aim of the rule was not that an accuser should escape punishment if he had a mandator, but that the latter also should be punished, just as if he himself had laid the information before the court.[21] In penal law, a mandator is "the person who orders another to commit a crime," as the jurist Paul understood in stating that in a case of murder, even when the actual murderer was known, a judicial inquiry should be held to find

found in the sense of "accuser" (Lewis and Short, ad loc.). The text badly overuses *eiusmodi* (eight occurrences, and one of *cuiusmodi*). As to torture, Heichelheim's translation "a somewhat stiff cross-examination" misses the precise point of law involved. A "more severe" examination is one with torture.

18. Ammianus Marcellinus refers at 19.12.17 to the "Corneliae leges," and at 28.1.11 to ancient practice and imperial regulation ("iuris prisci iustitia, divorumque arbitria") as permitting torture in cases of maiestas; cf. *CTh* 9.35.1 (of 369), "excepta maiestatis causa, in qua sola omnibus aequa condicio est"; 9.16.6 (of 358), etc.; cf. Peter Garnsey, *Social Status and Legal Privilege in the Roman Empire* (1970), pp. 141–47 (cf. p. 216 on the torture of witnesses); L. Angliviel de Beaumelle, "La torture dans les *Res Gestae* d'Ammien Marcellin," in M. Christol and others (eds.) *Institutions, société et vie politique* (1992), pp. 91–113, esp. 92–96, 101–2, 111 (citing also Digest 48.18.10.1 and Paul's *Sentences* 5.29.2).

19. As to syntax, the accusation (*obiectus*) becomes the convicted person (*convictus*), with a shift from the active deponent (*tueatur*) to the passive voice (*defendatur*). The essential point in the original version is that the accused may be tortured *before* being found guilty, as part of the process of examination.

20. The change of mood from *oporteat* to *oportet* in the Code follows from the radically changed usage of *cum,* from causal conjunction (*cum oporteat*) to preposition (*cum eo*).

21. Digest 49.14.2.5.

out who had ordered it.[22] This foreshadows the situation envisaged in the edict. The Theodosian Code version of the text, however, merely states that torture is to be applied to the instigator of the accusation: "*Illum* quoque tormentis *subdi* oportet, cuius consilio et instinctu." This is not a true statement of the law of the edict, where the issue is not the torture of the mandator of the crime, but the discovery of his name from the accuser whom he has instigated.

As for the omission of passages as between the edict and the Theodosian Code, the best explanation is that the editors of the Code were working, not with the full text of the edict, but with an excerpted copy already lacking the provisions about accusatores and delatores and those relating to famosi libelli. It does not seem possible that, if they had had the full text of the edict before them, they would have omitted these passages.[23] As to whether the substantive changes just described were part of the earlier fragmentation of the text of the edict, or whether they were introduced by the editors of the Code themselves, the former alternative seems by far the more likely, given the instructions to the editors of the Code that they were not to change the substance of the law, and that they were to include all laws meeting the formal criterion of generalitas, even if they were superseded by later legislation.[24] That is to say, both the omissions from the edict and the changes to the text as it appears in the Theodosian Code precede the work of the editors themselves. That the text from the Code does, like others, have a "prehistory" of distribution and editing is clear from the last clause of the edict, according to which explanatory letters are to be sent to prefects and governors, and to the rationalis and the magister privatae, with apparent reference to a further edict, not extant. (The latter two officials were included in the circulation list because of the interest of the treasury in cases of maiestas, when property would fall into the emperor's hands by confiscation). The *proposita* annotation in the Theodosian Code indicates that this text derives ultimately from the copying down of a version of the law in the form of a letter to one of these officials and published under his authority in the manner described in Chapter 7.

22. A. Berger, *Encyclopedic Dictionary of Roman Law,* s.v. *mandator;* Paul, in Digest 49.5.6: "Etsi percussor certus sit, tamen habenda quaestio est, ut caedis mandator inveniatur."

23. The view of Heichelheim and Schwarzenberger, "An Edict of Constantine," pp. 11–12, that these sections were omitted as "superfluous" by the editors of the Code, contradicts these instructions, which the evidence of the Code shows that they observed throughout.

24. Similarly, Heichelheim and Schwarzenberger, "An Edict of Constantine" (cf. Corcoran, *Empire of the Tetrarchs,* p. 190 n. 86), cannot be right in their general argument that the editors of the Code adapted the edict to conform to later legislation (as in *CTh* 9.1.19, of 423, on judicial torture). This would have far exceeded the mandate given to them.

Support for the idea that the edict had a prehistory of transmission, is provided by an unusual aspect of the epigraphic evidence. In five of the six examples so far known, the edict accompanies other legislative texts of the same period, sometimes engraved on the same stone, and in all cases closely associated with it. The writer of the manuscript version from Padua moved directly from the edict to a fragment of an enactment about the abuses of the imperial tax officials known as Caesariani, apparently taking the two texts as parts of a continuous document.[25] The same two texts have been shown to belong together in the epigraphic fragments from Ephesus, where fragments of the law about Caesariani give a date for that text of 305/6. This is confirmed by a Greek version of the same enactment from Athens, referring to abuses that had occurred in the period before 19 September 305.[26] At Tlos, the edict is associated both with the legislation about Caesariani and, following the edict on the same stone, another legislative text of 310/11, while the Lyttos version of the edict is associated with a closely related pronouncement of the same period, on the restoration to private individuals of property confiscated by Caesariani.[27] At Sinope, the edict is connected with two pieces of Tetrarchic legislation: namely, the Edictum de pretiis of 301 and an edict of Galerius dated to 310. Only the text of the edict from Pergamum is at present without an epigraphic context of this sort.

We are witnessing the engraving for permanent display, in prominent eastern cities, not only of single laws but of groups of laws of the Tetrarchic period—a sort of epigraphic dossier of legislation on certain related subjects from the first decade of the fourth century. The question of the dating and other problems of interpretation associated with the edict and its relationship with the Theodosian Code must clearly take this epigraphic context into account.

The problem began with the contradiction between the consular dating of 314 of *CTh* 9.5.1 and the tenure in office of the urban prefect Maximus to whom the law was addressed, if we assume this to be the Valerius Maximus who held the office in 319–23. The solution involved choosing between consuls and recipient to

25. The two texts are presented in sequence (though correctly, following Mommsen, as parts of separate pieces of legislation) in Bruns, nos. 94–95 (pp. 265–68). For what follows, see Feissel, "Deux Constitutions Tétrarchiques," esp. pp. 288–99.

26. In the Ephesus fragment, Galerius is mentioned in the imperial titulature, but not in first place—hence, before the death of Constantius on 25 July 306; Feissel, "Deux Constitutions Tétrarchiques," pp. 274–75, developing and refining his earlier discussion (1995), pp. 51–53. For the Athenian text, Feissel, pp. 278–81.

27. *Inscr. Cret.* vol. 1, no. 189 (pp. 229–30); Corcoran, *Empire of the Tetrarchs,* p. 191. To judge by Guarducci's report, and by differing conventions of orthography in the printed texts, nos. 188 and 189 were not inscribed at exactly the same time, but their relationship seems clear.

support one or the other date; general preference has lain with the recipient, and the law dated to his tenure of the prefecture.[28] It will be obvious that this approach barely scratches the surface of the problem.

We saw in the last paragraph of the edict that letters also were to be sent to the prefects, as well as to provincial governors and other officials. The text in the Theodosian Code represents one of these letters. It seems likely that the provision for circulation was initially intended to cover praetorian prefects rather than prefects of the city of Rome. At the same time, prefects of Rome exercised jurisdiction, and whoever its primary recipients were, there is no inherent reason that such a text should not have been received by a *praefectus urbi,* who would then have posted the law at Rome on 1 January of whichever consular year is accepted.

There arises at once the problem of the eastern provenance of the epigraphic evidence for the edict from which this letter was derived. If we accept Constantinian authorship of the letter transmitted by the Theodosian Code, and a date in the first part of his reign, the law has to be seen in one of three ways: as an edict of Constantine promulgated also by Licinius in the parts of the empire controlled by him; as an edict of Licinius promulgated also by Constantine in a letter to the prefect of Rome; or as an edict agreed upon and promulgated jointly by the two of them.[29] Any of these possibilities seems much less likely in 319–323 than in 314, when the so-called Edict of Milan of the previous year, promulgated jointly by Constantine and Licinius but known to us from two epistolary copies from the eastern provinces, was at least a recent memory. The Edict of Milan itself is not a good formal parallel, having been approved and issued jointly in consequence of an actual meeting between Constantine and Licinius. This has not been suggested for the text now under discussion, but the close relations between Constantine and Licinius in the aftermath of their meeting at Milan in February 313 and the marriage of Constantine's sister to Licinius might provide the context for the joint promulgation of the Edictum de accusationibus, posted by an agent of Constantine in the west on New Year's Day of 314.[30]

A refinement of this position is that the law is not one of Constantine at all but of

28. Chastagnol, *Fastes,* p. 73 and *PLRE* 1, p. 590 (Maximus 48), both opting, with Seeck (*Regesten,* pp. 75, 169), for 1 January 320 (as the *proposita* date). Seeck argued that the names of the consuls of 314, 316, and 320 had replaced successive "postconsular" datings by Constantine and Licinius, and that confusions between these are the source of confusion in the dating of laws.

29. I.e., actively promulgated by the two emperors, not simply issued by one emperor while bearing collegiate titulature; cf. Corcoran, *Empire of the Tetrarchs,* pp. 103–7.

30. The dating 1 January 314 seems too late for the publication at Rome of a law agreed on at a meeting of the two emperors held at Milan in early February 313. See Barnes, *New Empire,* p. 71, for the chronology of 313.

Licinius, and that its recipient was not a prefect of Rome, but a hitherto unknown praetorian prefect in the east named Maximus.[31] Now, Licinius undoubtedly possessed a praetorian prefect, and, for all we know, his name may have been Maximus. Many individuals and their offices are known only from laws addressed to them in the Theodosian Code, and the case before us may be just one more example of this. The argument also has the merit of giving weight to the provenance of the epigraphic evidence. It is, however, not the most secure approach to a difficulty to invoke an otherwise unattested individual for the one purpose of solving it, and there is certainly no justification for entering this new Maximus as a proven office holder in a register of praetorian prefects of the period.[32] The arguments offered in support of this reconstruction are of very doubtful value. That Constantine abolished crucifixion does not preclude his authorship of the law before he had effected this change of policy;[33] moreover, the observation that accusations for maiestas fit the circumstances after the defeat of Maximinus in 313 might apply to other contexts or require no explanation so specific for an enactment of such general benefit.[34]

An alternative view suggests that the address to Maximus as *p.u.* does not refer to a prefecture at all, urban or praetorian, but is an abbreviation of *perfectissimus vir,* the designation of imperial officials of equestrian rank. In this case, Maximus could be the rationalis or one of the praesides to whom copies of the edict were sent with explanatory letters (§V), posted by him on 1 January 314 at the place where he received it.[35] This solution has the virtue of economy, and it is true that laws in the Theodosian Code of relevant date can be found in which both a rationalis and a praeses are addressed as *v.p.* (*vir perfectissimus*).[36] The reverse order *p.v.* is not, however, found in the Code (nor is any parallel with the ranks of *clarissimus, spectabilis,* or *inlustris*), while the confusion between *p.u.* (for *praefectus urbi*) and

31. Barnes, *New Empire,* pp. 127–28, with Habicht and Kussmaul, "Ein neues Fragment," p. 136 n. 5, referring to a publication of 1957 by A. Ehrhardt (Barnes's contribution is the addition of Maximus as *praefectus praetorio* of Licinius). The solution appeals to Corcoran, *Empire of the Tetrarchs,* pp. 288–91; cf. Feissel, "Deux Constitutions Tétrarchiques," p. 289.

32. *New Empire,* pp. 127–28, cf. 138 (under the rubric "Attested Prefects and Their Dates").

33. "It is *unwelcome* [my italics] to have Constantine ordaining crucifixion as a punishment after his conversion to Christianity," writes Barnes in favor of Licinian authorship, "Three Imperial Edicts," *ZPE* 21 (1976), p. 276. This begs some rather obvious questions.

34. And as Corcoran observes (*Empire of the Tetrarchs,* p. 289), Crete had not fallen under Maximinus' rule.

35. The suggestion of Benet Salway, reported by Corcoran, *Empire of the Tetrarchs,* p. 190 n. 84.

36. *CTh* 10.18.1 (to a rationalis, 313), 13.10.2 (to a praeses, 311/313). See also 9.40.4 (praeses, ?346), 2.26.1 (diocesan comes, 330), 11.7.5 (comes largitionum, 345).

*p.po.* (for *praefectus praetorio)* is common. It seems more likely that, whatever other confusions and errors may be involved, the latter is the best approach to this particular question.

A more radical solution would be that the law is indeed one of Constantine but that it was promulgated after his defeat of Licinius and acquisition of the eastern provinces in 324. The text preserved in the Theodosian Code would then have to be regarded as both seriously misdated and misattributed, possibly by confusion of the Valerius Maximus *qui et* Basilius who was prefect of Rome in 319–23 with the Valerius Maximus who is attested as praetorian prefect of Constantine at various times in the period 326–33—in what sequence or combination of tenures is not clear, but an eastern tenure from late 326 to early 329 seems sufficiently well supported.[37] The difficulty with this reconstruction lies in its distance in time from the epigraphic context to which the original edict belongs. This, as we have seen, draws us to the first decade of the century. A date approaching 330 for its derivative text in the Theodosian Code seems incompatible with this context and should for this reason be rejected.

Whatever plausibility these various solutions may possess, the one thing that is clear is that they cannot all be right. The aim of this discussion is not to solve the problem of the Edictum de accusationibus but to consider its bearing on the character and editing of the Theodosian Code. Yet this may itself lead, if not to a solution, at least to a more complete statement of the problem, for an argument not so far drawn into the debate arises from the relationship between the epigraphic text of the law and the epistolary version of it found in the Theodosian Code.

We have seen that this consists of two extracts of the text, separated by one omitted section and omitting four others. As to these omitted sections, and one in particular (the paragraph on libelli famosi), it seems impossible that if the editors of the Theodosian Code had known of them, they would have excluded them from a Code in which their instructions were to include *all* texts of general or edictal significance, whether or not they were still valid law at the time of the editing of the Code. The *proposita* annotation in the Theodosian Code indicates that the text derives ultimately from a letter written to a praetorian or urban prefect and published under his authority in the manner described in Chapter 7, but the omission of these sections shows that the derivation was from a secondary and incomplete version of that text. At some stage also, the already mentioned changes in the text

37. *PLRE* 1, pp. 590–91 (Maximus 49), has him successively as *PPo Orientis* from late 326 to early 329 (he was *cos.* 317), under Constantius Caesar in Gaul in 332–33, and of Dalmatius on the Danube in 337; Barnes, *New Empire*, pp. 132, 138.

were introduced — and not by the editors of the Code — which, despite their apparently trivial nature, have the effect of changing the substantive meaning of the law.

It is generally assumed that the edict must be a text of 312 or later, in order for a version of it to qualify for inclusion in the Theodosian Code.[38] This argument is not as conclusive as it looks. To accept a law for inclusion in the Code, the editors must indeed have believed that it had been promulgated in or after 312, and they clearly did so in this case, placing the text, though with contradictory indications, in the time of Constantine. But we saw in Chapter 8 that the editors were sometimes mistaken in their dating of laws, putting texts in sequence within titles on the basis of incorrect transmitted dates. There is no warrant for assuming that such errors took place only within the period after 312, and not between that and the preceding period. It is at least a possible approach to the Edictum de accusationibus to suggest that, like the rest of the epigraphic dossier to which it belongs, it is a text of the later Tetrarchic period, mistakenly associated in the Theodosian Code with Constantine. Because the editors of the Code worked with an already excerpted version of the text, there is an additional stage at which a mistaken attribution can have been brought into it.

Further to this argument, it might also be worth reopening the question of the provenance of the Padua text of the edict. Because of the distribution of the surviving inscriptions, this is generally taken to be of eastern origin; the stone could have been imported to northern Italy at some unspecified later date, possibly carried as ballast in a Venetian merchant ship returning from the east. There is nothing impossible in this understanding of the situation, and a parallel can be found in a fragment of the Edictum de pretiis found in Italy but clearly of eastern origin, being written in Greek and engraved on Greek island marble.[39] In the case of the inscription from Padua, the possibility of import from the east cannot be tested, for the stone has long been lost and its text survives only in a Renaissance transcript. There is, however, a different way of approaching the question. The extant copies of the edict are found in important eastern cities, provincial capitals such as Ephesus, or cities that were on a governor's assize circuit, where it made sense for a text — indeed, for a dossier of texts — of a significant judicial character to be placed on permanent display (Athens, Pergamum, Sinope, Lyttos). Now, Patavium was just such a city in northern Italy: not the provincial capital of Venetia and Istria (which was Aquileia), but an important city, and surely an assize center, within the province.[40] It is the location of two important inscriptions of the late third century

38. Cf. Feissel, "Les Constitutions des Tétrarques," p. 50. For a possible exception, see n. 44.

39. Corcoran, *Empire of the Tetrarchs,* p. 230, with Michael Crawford, "The Pettorano Fragment of the Prices Edict," *Athenaeum* n.s. 62 (1984), pp. 315–16.

40. By way of parallel: Jerome's first letter concerns a capital offense judged at Vercellae by

documenting the early divisions of Italy as a province in the Tetrarchic period—respectively, of Paetus Honoratus, corrector Italiae, and of Insteius Tertullus, corrector Venetiae et Histriae, the first securely attested governor of the province under that designation.[41] Padua is an inherently convincing location for such a text as the edict, and in general it is a bold assumption that of more than three hundred extant inscriptions of unquestioned provenance at Padua, this one text, which happens not to be extant, should have come from the east.[42]

There is a warning in this difficult case. If no version of the edict had survived in the Theodosian Code, the epigraphic evidence would clearly have been taken to indicate a Tetrarchic date—possibly of 305/6, the date of the edict about Caesariani associated with it that bears the names of Constantius and Galerius.[43] The reference in §II of the edict to "statuta parentum nostrorum" would then be read, not as a general reference to the predecessors of the present Augusti, but to these predecessors as also their relatives—the now retired Tetrarchs, Diocletian and Maximian.[44] If, on the other hand, the inscriptions bearing the text of the law had not survived, the debate concerning the version in the Theodosian Code would have been confined to a discussion between the consular date of 314 and the years of office of the supposed addressee. In either case, the debate would have been conducted on incomplete premises.

The presence of an earlier stage of transmission in the Theodosian Code text affects the situation in two ways. By increasing the possible sources of error that might have been incorporated into the text of the Code, it expands the possible range of solutions to the problem, while at the same time making it more difficult to give decisive preference to any particular one. There is a corollary that affects our understanding of the Theodosian Code itself. It cannot be taken for granted of a text found there that even if its origin, date, and addressee can be reconciled internally or with other information in the Code, this is its correct date, or that the

---

the governor of Aemilia and Liguria; he is *PLRE* Anonymus 90 (p. 1019). The chief city of the province was Milan; Vercellae was an assize center.

41. *CIL* 5.2817–18; see *PLRE* 1, pp. 441 (Honoratus 11) and 883 (Tertullus 6), and G. A. Cecconi, *Governo imperiale e elites dirigenti nell'Italia Tardoantica* (1994), pp. 52–53 (Aquileia), 178 n. 21 (Patavium), and 210–11 (Fasti).

42. I should make it clear that I accept the correction *orbis Romani* for *CIL*'s *urbis Romanae* in line 4 of the text on Caesariani that follows the edict in the Padua transcript—Feissel, "Les Constitutions des Tétrarques," pp. 51–52. This removes a specifically western reference, while enlarging the reference to cover the entire Roman empire.

43. See note 26.

44. In an intriguing parallel, *CTh* 13.10.2 refers to an order made "sub domino et parente nostro Diocletiano seniore A[ugusto]"—written after the death of Maximian in 310 (or his name would have been mentioned). The *CTh* text (MS 313) may be of 311 or 312.

transmitted date of a law, however uncontested and uncontroversial it may seem, is correct. Many errors surely remain which we have no way of detecting.[45]

## *A Letter and Law of Constantine*

On 5 February 330 Constantine wrote from Serdica to the consularis of Numidia giving exemption from municipal duties to members of the Catholic clergy who had been forced into them by Donatist rivals.[46] The edited text, providing both for the present situation and for future cases, appears in the Theodosian Code title *De episcopis, ecclesiis et clericis*.[47]

In a letter written from the same place on the same day (the year is not given in the text, but is obviously also the same), Constantine wrote to a group of Catholic bishops in Africa. He told them that he had ordered letters to be sent to the rationalis requiring him to arrange the necessary financial support through the transfer of an imperial property to the ownership of the Catholic church, and to the consularis of Numidia to give all possible help to the bishops in constructing, at the emperor's expense, a new basilica in the city of Constantina (formerly Cirta). The emperor goes on to summarize an order he had given on the question of the curial duties of members of the clergy. The ground covered in this part of his letter is the same as that of *CTh* 16.2.7, and the language has many points of similarity. Identical or near-identical words and phrases are shown in bold type in the text of Constantine's letter, related expressions in italics, and enough of the preceding text is given to show the context of the emperor's action as his response to a petition of the bishops.[48]

45. See Chapter 7, with the remarks of Alan Cameron in *Consuls of the Later Roman Empire*, p. 73.

46. Seeck, *Regesten*, pp. 14, 180; Barnes, *New Empire*, p. 78. On the consularis, *PLRE* 1, p. 936 (M. Aur. Val. Valentinus 11). He is known from *CIL* 11.5381 (Assisi), which mentions his governorship of Numidia as well as the (earlier) correctorship of Flaminia and Picenum.

47. *CTh* 16.2.7, trans. Pharr: *The same Augustus [Constantine] to Valentinus, consularis of Numidia*. Lectors of the divine scriptures, subdeacons, and the other clerics who through the injustice of heretics have been summoned to the municipal councils shall be absolved, and in the future, according to the practice of the Orient, they shall by no means be summoned to the municipal councils, but they shall possess fullest exemption. *Given on the nones of February at Serdica in the consulships of Gallicanus and Symmachus*.

48. This petition, according to my customary policy, I have gladly embraced and have immediately given an official letter to the rationalis, saying that he should see to the transfer of a house belonging to us with full legal rights into the ownership of the catholic church, which I have made a gift with prompt generosity and have ordered to be handed over to you forthwith. Now, as to the place in which I commanded a basilica to be built at the expense of the fisc, I

Optatus, *Appendix* 10 (ed. Ziwsa, p. 215); Quam petitionem more instituti mei libenter amplexus sum et statim ad rationalem competentes litteras dedi, ut domum bonorum nostrorum transgredi faciat cum omni iure ad dominium ecclesiae catholicae, quam promta liberalitate donavi ac vobis tradi protinus iussi. In quo tamen loco sumptu fiscali basilicam erigi praecepi,

ad consularem quoque scribi mandavi Numidiae, ut ipse in eiusdem ecclesiae fabricatione in omnibus sanctimoniam vestram iuvaret. **Lectores** etiam ecclesiae catholicae **et hypodiacones, reliquos quoque** ⟨*qui*⟩ *instinctu memoratorum* pro moribus ad munera vel *ad decurionatum* **vocati sunt,** iuxta statutum legis meae ad nullum munus statui evocandos. Sed et eos, qui ducti sunt haereticorum instinctu, iussimus protinus molestis perfunctionibus **absolvi. De cetero** etiam *legem meam super ecclesiasticos catholicos datam* custodiri mandavi,

quae omnia, ⟨ut⟩ vestrae patientiae palam fierent, harum litterarum testificatione perscripta sunt, etc. *Data non. Februar. Serdica.*

*CTh* 16.2.7; *Idem A. Valentino cons*(*ulari*) *Numidiae.* Lectores divinorum apicum et hypodiaconi ceterique clerici, qui per iniuriam haereticorum ad curiam devocati sunt,

absolvantur, et de cetero ad similitudinem Orientis minime ad curias devocentur, sed immunitate plenissima potiantur. *Dat. non. Feb. Serdica Gallicano et Symmacho conss.*

---

have also ordered a letter to be written to the consularis of Numidia, instructing that he himself should in every way aid your holy persons in the construction of the church. Further, where readers of the catholic church and subdeacons, and others too, who at the instance of the aforesaid persons have on account of certain customs been called to public duties or the decurionate, I have stated that according to the statute of my law, they are not to be called up for any duty; and those too, who were brought in at the instance of the heretics, we have commanded to be absolved of their onerous obligations. For the rest, I have ordered that my law concerning the catholic clergy is to be observed. All these things are prescribed by the witness of this letter, that they may be done in open view of your longsuffering patience. (Trans. Mark Edwards, *Optatus: Against the Donatists* (Translated Texts for Historians, 1997), pp. 200–201; with revisions).

In describing his law, Constantine diverges from the exact wording, but keeps to the substance and order of the text preserved as *CTh* 16.2.7, and he repeats the distinction made in the Theodosian Code between the present situation and future practice. In both texts this distinction is marked by the words *de cetero,* and since in each case this phrase follows the word *absolvantur/absolvi,* it is likely that it represents a common point of division. This may help us identify the emperor's references to preceding legislation, in the phrases *iuxta statutum legis meae* in the earlier part of his ruling about the clergy, and *legem meam* in the last quoted sentence.

The first reference is sometimes taken to be to the law preserved as *CTh* 16.2.2 of 21 October 319, addressed to the corrector Lucaniae et Brittiorum, a brief extract of what may have been a piece of legislation of more general bearing.[49] This earlier law contains both the elements present in the first part of *CTh* 16.2.7—namely, the exemption of clergy from curial service and their harassment by others inspired by "sacrilegious malice"—but says nothing about the identity of these enemies of the clergy, whether heretic or pagan, or simply curial orders protesting the loss of leading members to the class of exempt persons, now expanded by the inclusion of Christian clergy. Another possible candidate is Constantine's letter of 313 to the proconsul Anullinus, preserved by Eusebius.[50] This text exempts from curial service clergy "of the Catholic church over which Caecilianus presides," but speaks only in general terms of the "error or sacrilegious fault" that might impede the performance of their religious duties. It attributes none of these obstacles to the agency of any named enemies of the Catholic clergy, and in this respect falls short of Constantine's law and letter of 330, both of which are explicit on the role of "heretics."[51]

Since neither law fully meets the terms of Constantine's back-reference, an alternative possibility might be considered: that the expressions *iuxta statutum legis meae . . . statui* and *iussimus* in these two sentences of Constantine's letter refer not to any existing law at all, but to the current legislation now initiated in the instruction given to the consularis of Numidia. The words should be read as part of a series of narrative perfect tenses in which Constantine explains to the bishops what he has ordered to be done in immediate and willing response to their petition: first,

49. Cf. Mommsen, ad loc. (p. 837). The entire extract reads as follows: "Qui divino cultui ministeriis religionis inpendunt, id est hi, qui clerici appellantur, ab omnibus omnino muneribus excusentur, ne sacrilego livore quorundam a divinis obsequiis avocentur."

50. Eusebius, *Hist. Eccl.* 10.7. Constantine may have remembered his earlier legislation as more explicit than it actually was.

51. In the phrases *per iniuriam haereticorum* in *CTh* 16.2.7, and *haereticorum instinctu* and *instinctu memoratum* in Constantine's letter.

the building of a basilica at imperial expense, and second, the issuing of legislation in the interest of the Catholic clergy.[52]

On any interpretation, the reference in the second part of *CTh* 16.2.7 and in the following sentence of Constantine's letter (after the phrase *de cetero* in both cases) is to a different and later act of legislation than those considered here, since it refers to an eastern precedent now applied to the west; this would necessarily date from the years after Constantine's acquisition of the eastern provinces in 324. It is to this legislation that Constantine's letter refers in his words *legem meam super ecclesiasticos catholicos.*[53] We saw that in some of the Sirmondian Constitutions a general order that existing laws should be observed was added to the terms of new legislation, and here too it is possible that something to this effect was omitted by the editors of the Theodosian Code.

Since Constantine, writing on the same date as that of *CTh* 16.2.7, must mean that he has just this very moment ordered a letter to be sent to the consularis, it may be that we have in his words something like the version of his law that was sent to the imperial bureaus for composing; the expression *divini apices* in the Theodosian Code, meaning "Holy Scriptures," looks rather like a contribution from the pen of an imperial draftsman,[54] who may also have added the reference to eastern precedent left unspecified by the emperor in his letter to the bishops. The differences between Constantine's version of the law in his letter and that in the Theodosian Code would then derive from the fact that in the letter he was summarizing something that he had just — on the very same day — sent for drafting. In this respect, the emperor's language makes an important and relevant distinction; he wrote directly and in his own person to the African bishops, but had "ordered a letter to be written" ("scribi mandavi") conveying his instructions to the consularis of Numidia. The situation takes us "behind" the Theodosian Code, to a moment very close

52. The sequence runs as follows, omitting inessentials but emphasizing the perfect tenses and indications of promptitude: "Petitionem *amplexus sum* . . . *statim* litteras *dedi* . . . (domum) quam *promta* liberalitate donavi ac vobis tradi *protinus iussi* . . . basilicam erigi *praecepi,* ad consularem scribi *mandavi* . . . iuxta statutum legis meae *statui* . . . *iussimus protinus* molestis perfunctionibus absolvi." Throughout, Constantine is explaining, not what he had done previously, but what he has ordered to be done on this present occasion; there is in this part of the letter no reference to earlier legislation.

53. The nearest possibility in the Theodosian Code is 16.5.1 (1 September 326), posted somewhere in the east ("Gerasto": Gerasa or Berytus?) by Dracilianus, the vicarius mentioned also in Eusebius' *Life of Constantine* (*PLRE* 1, p. 271; Seeck, *Regesten,* p. 177, with 11.20, 106.11). However, this text is rather the converse of 16.2.7, in that it excludes heretics from the privileges extended to Catholic clergy, without saying anything substantive about the latter.

54. For *apices,* see Chapter 7.

to the original conception and drafting of a piece of imperial legislation. It suggests something of the procedures that were involved, and enables us to restore the extract surviving in the Code to its context in the financial and other assistance also offered by the emperor in response to the petition of the African bishops.

## *Julian on Public Education*

One of the best-known texts in the Theodosian Code is a law of Julian issued on 17 June 362, on the procedures for the appointment by city councils, and approval by the emperor, of candidates for public teaching positions:[55]

> *CTh* 13.3.5: *Idem A.* Magistros studiorum doctoresque excellere oportet moribus primum, deinde facundia. Sed quia singulis civitatibus adesse ipse non possum, quisque docere vult, non repente nec temere prosiliat ad hoc munus, sed iudicio ordinis probatus decretum curialium mereatur optimorum conspirante consensu. Hoc enim decretum ad me tractandum referetur, ut altiore quodam honore nostro iudicio studiis civitatum accedant. *Dat XV kal. Iul., acc. IIII kal. Augustas Spoletio Mamertino et Nevitta conss.*

The law, expressed as an edict and intended to apply to all individual *civitates*, on both counts meets the criteria of generalitas put to the editors of the Theodosian Code in the laws of 429 and 435. It was no doubt sent to praetorian prefects with the usual instructions to arrange for its publication in the provinces under their jurisdiction; of the scores, if not hundreds of copies that must have existed, that preserved in the Theodosian Code is the version published at Spoletium (Spoleto) in the province of Tuscia and Umbria on 29 July 362, exactly six weeks after its issue in the east. The precise place of issue of the edict is not recorded, but it must have been somewhere on Julian's route across Asia Minor from Constantinople to Antioch, from where he was to mobilize the great Persian campaign of the following year. The latest extant law issued at Constantinople in 362 is dated 12 May

55. Trans. Pharr: "Masters of studies and teachers must excel first in character, then in eloquence. But since I cannot be present in person in all the municipalities, I command that if any man should wish to teach, he shall not leap forth suddenly and rashly to this task, but he shall be approved by the judgment of the municipal senate and shall obtain the decree of the decurions with the consent and agreement of the best citizens. For this decree shall be referred to Me for consideration, in order that such teachers may enter upon their pursuits in the municipalities with a certain higher honor because of Our judgment. *Given on the fifteenth day before the kalends of July. Received on the fourth day before the kalends of August at Spoleto in the year of the consulship of Mamertinus and Nevitta.*" See esp. Thomas M. Banchich, "Julian's School Laws: *Cod. Theod.* 13.5.5 and *Ep.* 42," *The Ancient World* 24 (1993), pp. 5–14. "*Ep.* 42" refers to Julian's letter about education, which will be discussed; it is no. 42 in Hertlein's 1876 edition of Julian's letters.

(*CTh* 13.3.4), and Julian is stated by Ammianus Marcellinus to have entered Antioch at the time of the celebration there of the rituals of Adonis; the city was full of weeping, a bad omen for the emperor's arrival.[56] The date of the festival was in July, which means that the law about professors was sent out before Julian arrived there; the first law certainly issued at Antioch after Julian's arrival is of 28 July (*CTh* 1.16.8). A possible place of origin for the edict might be Ancyra, where, again from Ammianus, we know that Julian enforced other measures to do with the recruitment of the curial orders of the cities. Perhaps the edict, as extant, was part of a more extensive document on the broader subject of civic life.[57]

In any case it has no explicit connection with Julian's equally famous enactment, reported by Ammianus in the general context of Julian's early residence at Antioch, prohibiting Christian teachers of rhetoric from practicing their profession—a measure that seemed to Ammianus out of keeping with the virtues of an emperor whom he admired above all for the even-handed justice of his legislation.[58] Together, no doubt, with the recipients of the edict of 17 June, one might reflect on the criteria likely to be employed in his reviews of appointments, by an emperor of openly pagan sympathies and notoriously officious temperament, who regretted that he could not himself be present in every single city of the Roman Empire to give personal approval to their decisions. But if there is an implied threat here, none of it appears in the text of the edict, which possesses a different context and says nothing about Christianity. The edict represents a different act of legislation from that reported by Ammianus. Indeed, in its distinction between public and private education it even has something in common with the law of Theodosius II of 425 establishing a public professorate in literature, philosophy, and law in the city of Constantinople and restricting private teachers to the homes of those who employed them (see Chapter 2).

By the same token, the edict of Spoletium is to be distinguished from the well-known pronouncement of Julian on the subject of education that has been transmitted (in imperfect condition) among the emperor's letters.[59] There is indeed common ground between the texts, in that both start with the assertion that the foundation of teaching is the moral character of the teacher. To quote the opening

56. Amm. Marc. 22.9.15; for the date ("mense Iulio," Jerome, *Comm. in Ezech.* 3.8.13f.; CC 75, p. 99), see esp. J. den Boeft, J. W. Drijvers, D. den Hengst, H. C. Teitler, *Philological and Historical Commentary on Ammianus Marcellinus XXII* (1995), pp. 178–80. Like others (cf. Banchich, p. 13), I was misled, in *The Roman Empire of Ammianus,* p. 108, in supposing the date to be 18 July precisely.

57. Julian at Ancyra: Amm. Marc. 22.9.8–12.

58. Amm. Marc. 22.10.7; cf. 25.4.20 (in the obituary of Julian).

59. *Ep.* 61b Bidez/36 Wright. I do not know why Bidez inserts the letter in the section of his edition relating to Julian's sojourn at Constantinople.

words of Julian's letter, "It is our belief that a correct education consists, not in the rich harmony of words and speech, but in the healthy disposition of a rational judgment, and in true opinions as to what is good and evil, beautiful and base." The assertion is however worked out in different ways in the two texts. In the edict of Spoletium, it is an enunciation of the general principle, given canonical expression by Quintilian, that the teacher should be a man of virtue as well as a master of eloquence: "vir bonus, dicendi peritus."[60] In Julian's letter, the principle is applied to the particular situation of a teacher whose religious persuasion prevents his believing the truth of what he teaches—namely, the texts of the Classical writers; such men may take themselves to "the churches of the Galileans" to educate their public in the writings of Matthew and Luke. Although the letter in the standard English translation bears the heading "Rescript on Christian Teachers," it carries neither a heading nor any other form of address in the manuscripts. In some ways it reads more like a section of one of Julian's polemical letters or tracts than a piece of legislation. We saw in Chapter 7, however, that Julian's public pronouncements are often hard to classify in formal terms, and the emperor goes on to offer Christian teachers a choice: either to decline to teach what they do not believe, or to declare to their pupils that the authors Homer, Hesiod, and the others whom they teach, are not guilty of "impiety, foolishness and error with regard to the gods." The choice was offered to such teachers either to renounce their religion in order to teach or to renounce their profession in order to retain their belief. Julian adds at the end of the text that no young pupil who wishes to learn is to be excluded from school. This is the only passage in which the word *law* is mentioned, but it does seem clear that the entire text is intended as an authoritative pronouncement, and likely that, in substance if not in form, it is the law mentioned by Ammianus Marcellinus.

Julian's letter has no connection in substance or form, however, with the edict of 17 June 362 posted at Spoletium. Even if the same emperor and the same policy are involved, the texts cover different subjects and are differently directed. One concerns the public procedures for the appointment of candidates, the other the private motivations of practicing teachers, and in point of expression they possess no significant common ground. It is misleading to regard Julian's letter as an "explanation" of the edict of Spoletium, and very unlikely that the Theodosian Code text was edited in such a way as to deprive it of an openly religious content that it had

60. Quintilian, *Inst. Or.* 12.1.1. M. Winterbottom, "Quintilian and the *Vir Bonus*," *JRS* 54 (1964), pp. 90–97, may be right in seeing a new urgency attaching to the principle in Quintilian's day, but the principle is an old one. It also stated in *CTh* 13.3.6, the law of Jovian cited in n. 62.

once possessed.[61] Jovian's legislation of early 364 picks up both aspects of Julian's policy, for it implicitly sets aside his procedures for the appointment of candidates suitably qualified by moral character and eloquence and permits established professors to resume careers that had been interrupted.[62]

## *Theodosius on a Moral Scandal*

The fourth and last example concerns two versions of a law of Theodosius I of 390, posted in different places and at different dates in the city of Rome, on the issue of male prostitution. One version is preserved in edited form in the Theodosian Code, the other in the *Collatio Legum Mosaicarum et Romanarum,* a work of unknown provenance that reached its final form in the last decade of the fourth century or soon after.[63] The text is the latest that is contained in the collection:[64]

*Coll.* 5.3 (Riccobono, vol. 2, p. 557): *Imp⟨p⟩. Valentinianus Theodosius et Arcadius Auggg. ad*

61. For proponents of these views, see the long footnote of Banchich, p. 6 n. 3.

62. *CTh* 13.3.6 (11 Jan. 364): "Si qui erudiendis adulescentibus vita pariter et facundia idoneus erit, vel novum instituat auditorium vel repetat intermissum." The law is attributed in the manuscript (*V*) to Valentinian and Valens, but if its transmitted date is correct, it is a law of Jovian. All commentators refer to the cases of Prohairesios of Athens and Victorinus of Rome as teachers who responded to Julian's law by resigning their chairs; see Banchich, pp. 10–11.

63. See the discussion by J. D. Harries, "How to Make a Law-Code," in M. Austin, J. Harries, and C. Smith (eds.), *Modus Operandi: Essays in Honour of Geoffrey Rickman* (1998), pp. 66–71; Detlef Liebs, *Die Jurisprudenz im spätantiken Italien, 260–640 n. Chr.* (1987), pp. 162–74, and the references collected by Corcoran, *Empire of the Tetrarchs,* p. 11 nn. 27–29.

64. *The Emperors Valentinian, Theodosius, and Arcadius Augusti to Orientius, vicarius of the city of Rome.* We cannot tolerate that the city of Rome, mother of all the virtues, should any longer be polluted by the corruption of male decency made effeminate, nor do we permit that sturdy rustic strength, inherited from our first founders, to be weakened and the people broken by a softening of their character, in reproach to the centuries of our founders and of the emperors, Orientius, our most dear and delightful friend. Therefore all those, whose criminal practice it is to dispose a man's as a woman's body, to condemn it by the passive submission of an alien sex and to hold no distinction between themselves and females, your admired Experience will, as the enormity of their crime demands, seize and drag out, shame to say, from the brothels of males, and in the sight of the people expiate the crime with the vengeance of fire, so that all may understand that the lodging place of a male soul [that is, his body] should be sacrosanct to all, and that no one will escape the supreme punishment who indecently abandons his own sex to seek out another's. *Posted on the day before the ides of May, in the atrium of Minerva.*

*Orientium vicarium urbis Romae.* Non patimur urbem Romam virtutum omnium matrem diutius effeminati in viro pudoris contaminatione foedari et agreste illud a priscis conditoribus robur fracta molliter plebe tenuatum convicium saeculis vel conditorum inrogare vel principum, Orienti k(arissime) et iuc(undissime) nobis. Laudanda igitur experientia tua **omnes, quibus flagitii usus est virile corpus muliebriter constitutum alieni sexus damnare patientia nihil**que **discretum habere cum feminis,** occupatos, ut flagitii poscit inmanitas, atque omnibus eductos, pudet dicere, virorum lupanaribus **spectante populo flammae vindicibus expiabit,** ut universi intellegant sacrosanctum cunctis esse debere hospitium virilis animae nec sine summo supplicio alienum expetisse sexum qui suum turpiter perdidisset. *Prop. pr. id. Maias Romae in atrio Minervae.*

*CTh* 9.7.6: *Idem AAA. Orientio vicario urbis Romae.* Omnes, quibus flagitii usus est virile corpus muliebriter constitutum alieni sexus damnare patientia, nihil esse discretum *videntur* habere cum feminis, *huiusmodi scelus* spectante populo flammae vindicibus expiab*unt. Pp. in foro Traiani VIII id. Aug. Valentiniano A. IIII et Neoterio conss.*

As in the case of the Sirmondian Constitutions, the *Collatio* preserves the original rhetoric omitted by the editors of the Theodosian Code, following their editorial instructions concerning matters not relevant to the force of sanction. It is enough for legal purposes that the criminal offense be defined and that burning alive be prescribed as the penalty. It is not necessary to vent the emperor's outrage at the situation brought to his notice, to describe the arrest and hauling out of the criminals from their dens of unnatural vice (a scene reminiscent of a police raid in a 1930s gangster movie), or to evoke the improving effect of the awful penalty upon onlookers. All these aspects are expressed in the original version of this law but are omitted in the shorter version found in the Theodosian Code. The emperor's in the circumstances incongruous address to Orientius as his "most dear and delightful friend," as found so often in the Sirmondian Constitutions, is also omitted. Apart from these changes, and the introduction of the word *videntur* so that *habere* is no longer governed, as in the original version, by *quibus flagitii usus est,* the amendments in the Theodosian Code are minor syntactical adjustments made to accommodate the way in which the text has been excerpted.[65]

The compilers of the Code might in principle have recovered any of several copies of the law, which the vicarius would have had posted at various places in the city in order that they might be read by the public, and where they might be copied by interested parties in the manner described in Chapter 7. The Theodosian Code represents one of these copies, the *Collatio* another, the divergencies between their dates and places of publication showing how the publication, and therefore the enforcement, of imperial legislation could be a prolonged process of diffusion rather than a single moment of authority expressed at one time and in one place. If this was true of a single, though very large city like Rome, it was still more so of the provincial urban, village, and rural communities of which the empire was composed.

65. The phrase *huiusmodi scelus* is inserted to cover an omitted section; while *omnes* has in the abbreviation become the subject of *expiabunt* in the sense of "all (the criminals) will pay for" rather than the object of *expiabit,* "(the vicarius) will punish all (the criminals)." In both texts *flammae vindicibus* is difficult ("vengeance of fire"?). A correcting hand in *V* reads *vindices* in *CTh,* which is easier but does not look right; and *Coll.* agrees with the transmitted text.

# 10

## *Conclusion*

## The Code and Its Sources

It is a fundamental principle in interpreting any historical source to inquire into its context and function: to ask what sort of text it is, who wrote it for whom, with what purpose or agenda, and how it was received. The principle is as relevant for a collection of legal texts as for any other source—and certainly no less difficult to apply, for the context of such a work is not the relationship of a known author and his text with other writings which he may be supposed to have known, but the relationship of many, largely unknown authors to nothing less than the society of their times, both as it was and as their masters wished it to be. The Theodosian Code presents acute problems of context: those inherent in the book itself, and in the individual texts that form it. I have tried to address both aspects. I have described by which processes the Code was conceived and implemented, how it was published and distributed, what methods were impressed upon its editors, how they fulfilled them, and who the editors were. I have given an outline of the character of late Roman legislation, indicating how this legislation was framed, drafted, and circulated and how it was received in the provinces of the empire. In this final chapter I return to some questions raised in earlier parts of this book but so far not drawn together, in particular that of the sources of the Code.

The question has two dimensions, concerning the intrinsic nature of the text, and the working procedures of the editors who accomplished it. Both are important issues, with interesting implications concerning the methods best employed to address them. They involve a combination of that essential but subjective faculty, common sense, with textual evidence that is by its nature incomplete. It is a matter of common sense that the solution to the question of sources lies at some point, or points, on the scale of possibilities suggested by two alternatives: official archives maintained by the emperor and his functionaries who composed and issued the legislation, and local sources of various types, having in common that they originate with those who received or acquired legislation rather than with those who issued it. As to the evidence of the laws themselves, however, only a minority can be shown from the contents or protocols of the texts to belong definitely to one category or the other. It is a matter of judgment how typical of the majority that give no such indication is this minority of texts that do.

Both types of source are realistic possibilities. The emperors did maintain archives, though in what shape or form is not easy to say. Nor is it clear how it affects one's view of the situation whether one imagines archives from which many items are missing, or archives so complete that nothing can ever be found in them. Anyone with experience of university administration will know that both varieties are quite common, and the same was undoubtedly true of the later Roman Empire.[1] In the early second century, Pliny, as governor of Pontus and Bithynia, asked Trajan to confirm from his archives the validity of certain letters and edicts of earlier emperors, of whose accuracy and authenticity he felt doubtful, and received the reply that among the original documents that could be found, none applied unambiguously to all provinces (*Epp.* 10.65–66). The incompleteness of Trajan's records may relate to the transfer of the province from senatorial to imperial control, which left it uncertain what precedents applied to it, but such changes of authority are precisely the sort of hazard that lies in wait for an administrative archive. If there were a change of duties affecting, for example, the magister officiorum in relation to the quaestor sacri palatii (as described in Chapter 7), it is entirely a matter of guesswork whether the appropriate files were transferred to

1. See A. N. Sherwin-White, *The Letters of Pliny* (1966), p. 653: "The [imperial] *commentarii* . . . contained all the *constitutiones* of whatever type of each Princeps, arranged according to the appropriate *scrinium* . . . , and must have resembled the minute book of an Oxford college in the diversity of their material." This is an apt, if somewhat parochial, comparison. Governing body meetings of Oxford colleges cover every aspect, academic, financial, political, and personal, of college business, and are written up in great ledgers, under the headings according to which the business has been discussed. No two colleges record their business in uniform fashion, and indexing is a rather recent habit. It may depend on the memory of senior fellows whether a matter has been discussed before, and with what outcome, and those who know its history have an advantage in discussion. In an oration referred to earlier (Chapter 7, n. 56), Libanius mentioned a claim that an alleged law was to be found in a departmental archive — but he did so in the process of denying the existence of the law.

reflect the new division of responsibility, and things like this were happening all the time. Fourth-century emperors, like their predecessors in less bureaucratic centuries, kept records of taxes paid and due, dispositions of armies, lists of officials and records of their duties, grants of privilege made to individuals and corporate bodies, and so on — including, of course, legal files. By far the most likely source of the Codex Hermogenianus, with its concentration of texts from just two years of the reign of Diocletian, was copies of imperial rescripts preserved in the archives of the magister libellorum in the form in which they were issued to individual petitioners.[2] The Codex Gregorianus, by contrast, with its much broader time span reaching back to the early third century, was proportionately more dependent on sources recovered from elsewhere than administration — an observation directly relevant, as we shall see, to the question of the sources of the Theodosian Code.[3]

The preceding chapters have given examples of texts in the Theodosian Code, mainly recent texts of eastern origin, where imperial archives are the most likely source.[4] Even here, we find cases where the compilers seem to have recovered a single act of legislation in several versions deriving from different stages of its circulation to the officials affected by it. The sixth Sirmondian Constitution, of 425, is addressed to the praetorian prefect of Gaul. The excerpts of the law contained in the Theodosian Code derive from related but not identical texts, one of them directed to the praetorian prefect of Italy but extant only in secondary versions sent by the prefect to the comes rei privatae and the proconsul of Africa, another directed to the prefect of Rome; and all six versions of the text bear different dates, beyond reconciliation by plausible conjecture. The most likely explanation is that even if imperial archives were the source of this recent law, they did not yield a single "authorized" text, but derivative versions addressed to different officials at different times.[5]

That "local" sources as well as central archives come into consideration is also clear. Not only is there extensive evidence, from all centuries of the empire, that interested parties did in fact copy down legislation that affected them — the Great Persecution and its aftermath are the best known of many examples of this common procedure, which is discussed in Chapter 7 — but the source of many texts in the Theodosian Code is shown by their annotations to have been the point of

2. From the year 293, 376 rescripts; from 294, 492 rescripts: see Honoré, *Emperors and Lawyers*, table 1, p. 189.

3. Honoré, p. 53: "The rescripts of the *Codex Gregorianus* usually give the date of posting up, those of the *Codex Hermogenianus* the date of execution."

4. To wit, cases where a sample text is included in the Code, of which other versions were written "eodem exemplo" to other recipients: see nos. 1–3 under the heading "Variants and Anomalies," Chapter 8.

5. See under "*Sirm.* 6," Chapter 6.

acceptance and publication, rather than the place of issue. This argument, the principal one that Seeck offered for the local provenance of much material in the Code, retains its force.[6] In the absence of evidence that governors and officials to whom laws were addressed were required to certify to the emperor that they had received them, it may be taken that the texts annotated as *proposita, accepta, lecta,* and so on are indeed evidence of a local source, in the sense described above. They were recovered not at the place of issue, but at the place of acceptance and publication. The derivation is of course indirect, for the compilers of the Theodosian Code did not copy down their material from notice boards exactly as it was posted in the cities of the empire—editors working from Constantinople in the 430s did not so recover a law posted at Hispalis (Seville) a hundred years before.[7] As we saw in Chapter 7, the life of an imperial edict posted in a city was a short one, before indifference or familiarity, competition from other forms of communication, and the wear and tear of the elements rendered it a thing of the past. The texts survived thanks to interested parties, jurists and others, who had reason or inclination to copy down the texts of laws. There is also the possibility, advanced by A. H. M. Jones, that copies of laws were retained among their family papers by the officials (especially urban and praetorian prefects from the aristocracy) to whom they were addressed, and that they were recovered from this source by the compilers of the Theodosian Code.[8] The suggestion would help explain the predominance of certain individuals and families, for example Petronius Probus and the Anicii, among the recipients of imperial legislation attested in the Code. However, since the laws themselves would bear no trace of an origin in family papers, it cannot be more than hypothetical.

The answer to the question of the sources of the Theodosian Code lies, neither at one extreme nor at the other, but in some proportion across the whole range of possibilities between them.[9] The possibly unanswerable question is, in what proportion? The reason this question may be unanswerable is that it must be argued from a minority of texts. The great majority appear in the simple form in which the emperors address their governor, public official, or community, with the date and place of origin of the text in question, and that is all. This is what the protocols of a text would look like at their point of composition and issue. The absence of any note of acceptance or publication is, however, no proof of recovery from a central archive, for although such details *may* be transcribed with a text at its point of

6. *Regesten,* pp. 2–16.

7. See Chapter 8, "Variants and Anomalies," no. 4.

8. *JRS* 54 (1964), p. 78 = *The Roman Economy* (ed. P. A. Brunt), pp. 376–77.

9. Cf. Seeck, *Regesten,* p. 16 on the varied ("höchst mannigfach") character of sources before the editors.

acceptance and publication, from the point of view of the validity or interest of a law they *need* not be. Conversely, the argument from the minority of cases in which a local point of recovery is explicitly stated may contribute nothing to the interpretation of the majority. Nevertheless, a number of arguments, some well known, some new, may help to define the possibilities of an answer. In general, they support the notion of a diversity of sources to complement the imperial archives that certainly were used.

The first and most obvious point, emphasized by Seeck, is the preponderance of western laws in the Code as a whole, at least for the earlier period.[10] Despite the ideology of imperial unity, which required that all laws carry the protocols of the entire college of emperors, it is unlikely that many texts were published in both parts of the empire; there was no need, for example, for the many laws affecting Africa, issued by a western emperor with competence to legislate and addressed to the proconsul or vicarius,[11] to be reported to his eastern colleague, nor was there any reason the latter should wish to see them. Uncertainty in one part of the empire regarding the validity of laws issued in the other is shown by a comment of Honorius on an alleged law of his eastern colleague Arcadius relieving Jews of burdens of service as town councillors.[12] The law had been adduced in their cause by Jews of Calabria, but the emperor's response was that since the law, *if it existed,* was clearly injurious to his domains, its validity could not be admitted. This was from a time when relations between eastern and western courts were a live issue between them, both regimes claiming a priority bestowed by the late emperor Theodosius I. The inhabitants of southern Italy were perhaps more exposed than most to the influence of eastern claims, and sufficiently emboldened to put to the western emperor an argument based on his colleague's legislation. In more usual circumstances, ignorance of and indifference to the legislation of the other *pars imperii* was surely the prevailing sentiment. It seems unlikely that much fourth-century western legislation could be found in fifth-century eastern archives. Even the most determined advocates of central sources postulate that the compilers exploited western archives in Rome and the provinces as well as those available at Constantinople.[13]

10. *Regesten,* p. 2. The imbalance is especially clear when one looks beyond the level of praetorian prefects to lower officials, proconsuls, vicarii, provincial governors, and so on (but including prefects of Rome). The proportions shift in favor of the east after 379 (in the east) and 383 (in the west); Honoré, *Law in the Crisis of Empire,* pp. 141–42.

11. Seeck, *Regesten,* p. 2, notes that more than a hundred constitutions were addressed to proconsuls of Africa (and only thirteen to proconsuls of Asia).

12. *CTh* 12.1.158 (13 September 398). The eastern law referred to may be 16.8.13 (1 July 397); if so, it had not been reported to Honorius.

13. E.g., Sirks, "Observations sur le Code Théodosien," *Subseciva Groningana* 2 (1985), p. 22—"archives impériales à Constantinople, mais aussi des archives à Rome et dans les

This general point is reinforced by the observation that political conditions in the fourth-century west, and what A. H. M. Jones called the "migratory character" of the imperial *comitatus* and praetorian prefectures,[14] do not seem likely to have encouraged the systematic maintenance of imperial archives. There are so many breaks in continuity, so many moments at which such archives could have been damaged, lost, or abandoned. To take an example: the Code contains many fourth-century laws issued at the imperial capital city of Trier. In the early fifth century, in view of the insecurity of the north, the emperors abandoned Trier for Arles, in the south. Possibly (we have no way of knowing) the emperor's functionaries gathered together and took with them what they could of the working files and archives of their departments; but how complete were they, and in what state of organization did they emerge from their journey south and installation in new imperial quarters? Most certainly, the compilers of the Theodosian Code did not travel north to Trier in the fourth decade of the fifth century. The strongest statement of the case for recovery from imperial archives would have to concede that the compilers of the Code recovered laws issued at Trier from archives in their new location at Arles, but this reconstruction incorporates some quite hazardous assumptions. Again, we saw earlier the case of a law of 338 preserved in two slightly variant versions, addressed to the vicarius Africae and received at Carthage and at Timgad on 12 and 15 December, respectively.[15] The proof, inherent in the protocols of the law, that it was recovered, in its two extant versions, at its points of reception rather than at its point of issue, is supported by the identification of the emperor who issued it. Although it bears the titulature of the emperor Constantius, the law is one of Constans from the period of his joint rule (337–40) with Constantius and Constantine II. The regime of Constans, who defeated Constantine II in 340 and took over his domains, was ended by the usurper Magnentius in 350. Magnentius was in turn defeated by Constantius after two of the bloodiest of fourth-century battles. It is possible, no doubt, that the imperial archives survived this mayhem and could be found by fifth-century eastern editors of the Code, but far more likely that the implications of the protocols, that this law was recovered by the editors

---

provinces," with (after Mommsen) private archives of "un jurisconsulte africain," a list expanded in his "Sources of the Code," in Harries and Wood (eds.), *The Theodosian Code,* p. 52, to include Constantinople, Rome, and Ravenna, with private collections in Italy and Africa and from the law schools at Berytus and Constantinople. Presumably, by "Rome" is meant the archives of the urban prefects and vicarii; it is not clear how much other legislation would be kept in the city.

14. *JRS* 54 (1964), p. 79.

15. *CTh* 6.22.2 and 12.1.24; see Chapter 8, "Variants and Anomalies," no. 6. For a similar case—a law of Constans received in Italy in 341 and later attributed to Constantius—cf. *CTh* 16.10.2.

from a source deriving from its African points of acceptance, are a true indication of origin. Other anomalies, already discussed, between variant texts of laws show that these particular examples cannot have been derived from central archives.[16] There were clearly intermediate stages in transmission, at which the variants were introduced.

It has been argued that the number of cases bearing explicit indications of local origin is a small proportion of the total number of texts extant in the Code; about 200 texts directly attested in this way with another 50 identified by inference, altogether about 10 percent of the total.[17] Even 250 texts is however quite a significant number, given the uninformative nature, in this respect, of the great majority of the texts in the Code; further, it substantially understates the number of texts for which a local provenance can be inferred. As mentioned earlier, annotations that laws were accepted or posted at certain places were not essential to their validity as texts and might be omitted in transcription; at the same time, although such details may easily drop out of a text, whether by deliberate omission or by mechanical errors of transmission, there is no reason they should ever be added, and no obvious way in which this could be done. The five excerpts of Valentinian's law of 372 on precedence, addressed to the urban prefect Symmachus, almost certainly derive from the same original text; but of these five excerpts, only three carry the *proposita* annotation that clearly belongs to all of them.[18] Only two of the eight excerpts of Constantine's edict of 331 on private law carry a date, and only one a place of publication, but there is no reason to doubt that all eight excerpts derive from the same source, which would have shown both details.[19] On other occasions an annotation of receipt or publication survives in only one or two of a series of texts, to all of which it is appropriate, and there must be many examples of laws where notifications of acceptance or publication have been omitted or lost, and no parallel texts or internal anomalies exist to show that they should be restored.[20]

The same observation applies to those laws with "postconsular datings" to the year after that of the named consuls. It has been shown that the publication of these laws generally belongs to the early months of the year after their year of issue,

16. See Chapter 8, "Variants and Anomalies," nos. 5 and 7.

17. Sirks, "Observations," pp. 22–24; cf. "Sources," p. 50.

18. See Chapter 8, "A Selected Title," no. 1.

19. Six excerpts from *CTh*, two from *CJ;* see Chapter 8, "'Palingenesia': Laws Reconstituted," no. 3; also no. 4, where only two of three closely related fragments give the place of receipt. My own count adds at least 100 more texts where local origin can be proven or inferred, to the 250 adduced by Seeck.

20. See, for instance, Chapter 8, "A Selected Title," nos. B.1, 10, and ?11, and "'Palingenesia': Laws Reconstituted," no. 4.

and that the postconsular annotations were added to the texts when they were received in a province before the names of the new consuls were known there. It was very rarely that the names of the current consuls were not known at the imperial court from which a law was dispatched;[21] these examples seem certain to reflect a local origin for the texts in question. In some cases, problems in the dating of texts can be solved by the textual insertion *of proposita* annotations that have been lost in transmission.[22] Even when this is not so, it is clear that many texts in this and the preceding category were recovered from local sources, although their protocols may bear no trace of it.

Other arguments support the likelihood of intermediate stages between the original versions of laws and their acquisition by the editors of the Theodosian Code. In study of the title 11.30, *De appellationibus et poenis earum et consultationibus,* and on several occasions elsewhere, we saw that laws were entered by the editors not only with incorrect dates, but in the incorrect sequence within titles entailed by these dates; that is to say, the errors are not part of the later transmission of the text of the Code, but were already present in the material before the editors.[23] It is no doubt possible that the laws were entered with inaccurate dates or in inaccurate sequence in imperial commentarii, but far more likely that the errors derive from a period of transmission in which the texts had passed through other hands before they came into those of the editors of the Code. An example of such a prehistory of transmission was found in the Edictum de accusationibus, discussed in Chapter 9, where the excerpts appearing in the Theodosian Code omit important topics that were covered in the edict, and for which appropriate titles exist. These omissions, and the apparently small changes that have the effect of altering the substance of the law, show that the versions in the hands of the editors of the Code must already have been subjected to editorial intervention. These changes were not the work of the editors of the Theodosian Code. Reasons were also given for linking the text with a dossier of other legislation of the later Tetrarchic period preserved in epigraphic sources—in which case, even the Constantinian attribution of the two excerpts included in the Theodosian Code is in question. Traces of little dossiers of texts were found in *CTh* 11.30, in the form of a group of five laws from the years 381–85, addressed to a western comes sacrarum largitionum and comes rei privatae. These may be compared to the group of rescripts of 365 found in the

21. Cameron, *Consuls of the Later Roman Empire,* pp. 77–84; cf. Delmaire, "Etude sur les souscriptions," in M. Christol and others, *Institutions, société et vie politique,* pp. 315–28. Such a situation might occur when, for example, the eastern court was to notify the western of the names of both consuls but had not yet done so; these, however, are very exceptional circumstances.

22. For a clear case see Delmaire, p. 323 (his no. 7).

23. See Chapter 8, "A Selected Title," nos. C.1–5.

Fragmenta Vaticana, where they are in turn ascribed to the Codex Hermogenianus, in what must be a fourth-century redaction of that text.[24]

Legislation addressed to Africa has often been seen as an example of such earlier collecting and editing, and recent study of the material has confirmed the likely existence of private archives composed of laws received in Africa, even when there is no indication in the protocols of the laws themselves that their origin was provincial.[25] We also noted the special character of many laws from the time of Constantine, in which officials were addressed by the fuller, more formal fashion of *nomen* plus cognomen rather than by the simple cognomen (or *signum*) that is the standard form of address in the Code. This surely derives from conventions employed by earlier compilers of this particular body of material, and not from any innovation introduced by the editors of the Theodosian Code. Constantine's juridical activity, especially in private and family legislation, was extensive and important. The legislation must frequently have been at issue in fourth-century courts of law, and it would be in the interests of practicing advocates to have studied and made collections of it.[26]

In considering the alternatives of central archives and local sources, discussion does not seem fully to have addressed the possibility of change over time from one to the other. Yet this is an obvious likelihood, if the quality and completeness of imperial archives improved as the editors advanced toward their own day, and there was also less opportunity (because less time) for the processes of "unofficial" collection suggested here. Two observations made in Chapter 8 are relevant. The first is that, in the title (11.30) subjected to close study, the proportion of *proposita* and *accepta* annotations is greater in the earlier than in the later part of the title. This observation, which is confirmed by a review of other titles in which several such annotations occur and by their distribution throughout the Theodosian Code, suggests that the editors used material deriving from the place of receipt and publication of laws more frequently for the earlier than for the later part of the period covered by them. This would be an endorsement of common sense, for the

24. Chapter 2, n. 14. Rescripts were not included in the Theodosian Code; what is important for the present discussion is the implied existence of such earlier collections of legal texts.

25. Cameron, in *Consuls of the Late Roman Empire,* pp. 79–81. J. Gaudemet, "Constitutions Constantiniennes destinées à l'Afrique," in M. Christol and others, *Institutions, société et vie politique,* pp. 329–52, rather passes over the question of sources. Mommsen (Prolegomena, p. xxix) thought that the archives of an African jurisconsult came into question, a suggestion apparently accepted by Sirks, "Observations."

26. See nn. 13, 24. Gaudemet, p. 349, points to the predominance of Constantine's extant legislation in the earlier years of his reign; 146 texts from the period 313–23, 101 from 326–36 (the corresponding figures from Africa are 50 and 14). Gaudemet does not state whether he has allowed for the rejoining of texts separated in editing.

converse of the situation, that central archives were in a better state for the later part of the period than for the earlier, is inherently likely. The contrast, noted earlier, between the forms of annotation in the laws collected in the Codex Gregorianus and the Codex Hermogenianus, respectively, would reinforce the conclusion that, the broader the time span covered by a compilation of laws, the greater the variety of the sources from which the laws were recovered.

The second observation, again confirmed by a survey of the Code as a whole, relates to the form of address used in the laws of the title studied. In the earlier laws, the form of address using *ad* with the accusative case predominates; in the later, the form of address with the name of the recipient in the dative case is the more common. The interesting phenomenon here is that, in the Code as a whole, the convention shifts heavily in favor of the usage with the dative and does so at distinct points; in the east in the year 380 and in the west in 395. The shift in style is clear, and it occurs too abruptly to be explained by a slow change of taste. It is not likely to be an innovation of the editors of the Code, for one can see neither why they should have implemented it nor how they can have done so with such consistency across the full range of contents of the Code; nor is it likely to express a change in the conventions used by the emperors themselves. What then is the explanation? As Seeck observed, the difference between the two modes of address reflects their distance from the original form used by the emperor; the dative case expresses the epistolary mode used by the emperors, while *ad* with the accusative is a more objective style appropriate for the transcription of a text. In other words, it is a more "editorial" convention. If it was not introduced by the editors themselves, then the difference of style must have been inherent in the material that came into their hands. Exceptions will be found, but it would be consistent with the facts, and again accord with common sense, if for the earlier part of their period the editors of the Code used material in which the shift to a more "editorial" manner had already been made by predecessors who had collected the material before them, while for their later material they had access to archival sources preserving the original form of address of the emperor to his subordinates.[27] The shift to the form of address with the dative coincides with the dynasty of Theodosius in the two phases of its establishment in east and west, and the inference is that during this period the archival material available to the editors of the Theodosian Code increased significantly.

As to the methods used by the editors in working on their texts, we have seen from many examples that they followed the principles set out for them in the two

27. See Chapter 8, nn. 52–53, for arguments on this issue. In any event, the conclusion sits well with Honoré's arguments for a shift in favor of eastern archives after 398: *Law in the Crisis of Empire,* pp. 137–41. In this as in all other respects, the situation in the west is more complex than that in the east.

constitutions of 429 and 435. They classified laws under titles, dividing them where necessary; they set out the texts in chronological order within titles, they eliminated nonessential verbiage but otherwise retained the original wording of texts; and they adapted the language of texts in syntax and vocabulary where their omissions and abbreviations made this necessary. It is worth insisting on one point. The editors were instructed, as we have seen, to include in their work *all* laws possessing the character of generalitas, whether or not they were currently valid; it was not for the editors, but for users and, no doubt, teachers, to observe when earlier laws had been superseded by later. There is no room for the idea that the editors of the Code were empowered to make substantive judgments on the the laws before them, or that they did make such judgments.[28] They could omit legal inessentials, such as the emperors' reflections on how they came to know about situations in need of remedy, their expressions of outrage that such wickedness existed, the fearful character of the punishments they laid down and instructions to their officials to distribute the law in their provinces, but that is all. Comparison of Theodosian Code texts with the fuller corresponding versions found, for example, in the Sirmondian Constitutions, supports this conclusion. There are no grounds for the belief that the editors were authorized to change the substance of laws, to omit obsolete rules, or to reject laws that were no longer relevant. If some law meeting the formal criterion of generalitas cannot be found in the Theodosian Code, it is because the editors did not find it, not because they found but rejected it.

In constructing the Code, the editors began with the sources of law, the legal status of texts of varying sorts, and the powers of imperial officials. They then proceeded to the private law, in which they followed the order of topics laid down by the Praetor's Edict and then (in Book 5) those topics in private law covered not by the edict but by imperial legislation and juristic authority. In the remaining books as far as Book 15, they addressed questions in public, administrative, and criminal law in a more or less systematic order, ending with cities and public works. The final book is on religion, but its position at the end of the Code reflects no more than that the sources of law and the Praetor's Edict came at the beginning. If Book 16 reads as the thematic climax of the entire Theodosian Code, this is the accidental result of an arrangement made for quite different reasons. It was not until the time of Justinian that religion was to appear at the beginning of a book of Roman law, preceding even the sources of law and the powers of the emperor and his officials. This placement would express a change of ideology that had not yet occurred at the time of the publication of the Theodosian Code.

To historians who wish to make use of the Theodosian Code, little can be said that will simplify matters, at the end of a study whose main contribution is to

28. Honoré, *Law in the Crisis of Empire,* pp. 142–49.

demonstrate the complexity of the text and its sources. Certain points may, however, be borne in mind. First, the definition of generalitas was a formal one; a law must either have been an edict or have been a text addressed to a public official and published by him under his own edict, or have contained within itself the statement that it was to be regarded as an edict or observed as a general rule. This obviously does not mean that all laws were relevant at all times and in all places, and we have seen cases (the wearing of trousers at Rome, for example) where the application of the rule in question was in principle and in practice limited.[29] Generalitas entails that a rule should be enforced in all relevant future circumstances, but the scope of these circumstances might be inherently restricted—and subject to argument in the courts on whether they did or did not apply.

A second point arises from the editors' instructions to include all the texts that they recovered incorporating generalitas. It follows from the arguments presented earlier that their success was incomplete. It cannot be assumed that a reference in an external source to a law on any subject is to an extant law on that subject or that, when an emperor refers back to a law of a predecessor, that law can be found in the Code. The law of Julian forbidding Christians to serve as teachers of rhetoric is not a version of the law of 362 extant in the Theodosian Code, though in terms of imperial policy it is related to it.[30] The measures of Gratian against temple properties, well known from the debate of 384 between Ambrose and Symmachus, are referred to in a law of Honorius of 415 but are not extant in the Theodosian Code and, according to the argument presented earlier, never were so.[31] The same argument might apply to the Constantinian legislation in favor of the Christian Church mentioned by Eusebius in his work *On the Life of Constantine*. While the legislation may or may not be authentic or accurately reported, lack of authenticity does not follow from its absence from the Theodosian Code.[32]

29. This law (14.10.2) is part of a longer text about the city of Rome addressed "ad populum" on 7 April 397; see Chapter 8, " 'Palingenesia': Laws Reconstituted," no. 10.

30. "Julian on Public Education," Chapter 9.

31. *CTh* 16.10.20; Matthews, *Western Aristocracies and Imperial Court*, pp. 203–11.

32. See esp. Eusebius, *V. Const.* 3.54–66 and 4.18–27. The account of Constantine's legislation given by T. D. Barnes, *Constantine and Eusebius* (1981), pp. 246–48, is almost entirely derived from Eusebius, and makes no reference to the Theodosian Code. Eusebius' references to legislation on Sunday observance (4.18) and to Jewish ownership of Christian slaves (4.27) are, however, represented in *CTh* (2.8.1; 16.9.1 and 16.8.5). The supposed abolition of gladiatorial combat is perhaps generalized by Eusebius (and *CJ* 11.44.1) from *CTh* 15.12.1 and concerns only the abolition of the penalty of condemnation to the arena (it is followed by other emperors' legislation showing that the institution continued to exist). Nothing survives in *CTh* of general legislation against idolatry except for a law of Constantius [Constans] referring back to it (16.10.2). For the emperor's marriage legislation, see esp. Judith Evans Grubbs, *Law*

Users of the Code, especially those interested in private law, should remember that its first five books are seriously incomplete and require supplementation from many sources apart from the Breviarium of Alaric, the essential source for most of what survives; in particular, the Codex Justinianus comes into play, providing more than 230 texts not included in Mommsen's edition. What we read in the first five books of the Code is thus a sixth-century reconstruction, from these two main sources, of a fifth-century compilation of mainly fourth-century material. Users should also recall that, for the period to which they may wish to apply the texts as historical evidence, the Theodosian Code itself did not yet exist. Contemporary—that is to say fourth- and early fifth-century—knowledge of the law was less comprehensive and well organized than the Code itself makes it appear. The impact of imperial legislation on late Roman society at large will not be doubted, but this does not mean that we can assume the effect of any particular act of legislation of which we happen to know.

It is also necessary to bear in mind that the Theodosian Code was intended as the first installment of a more extensive codification. According to the distinction with which this book began, the Code is a collection of the laws (leges) issued by emperors, not a declaration of how the law (ius) stood on any subject. The principle "The later, the more valid" was a temporary definition pending the preparation of a critical digest, to which the Theodosian Code and its predecessors the Gregorian and Hermogenian Codes, together with the jurists, would contribute. The Theodosian Code should be read in the light of the intention to produce this further volume; we can by no means be sure what proportion of its contents would have passed the scrutiny of its editors and taken its place as *ius*.

As for the interpretation of individual texts, the reader should always bear in mind what may have been omitted. This will relate to expressions of the emperor's intentions, to the improving effect of punishment, and so on; one may regret the loss of this often lively (or deadly) material, but the omissions should not affect the point of substance in a law. It is also advisable, in using a law, to see whether it may be part of a longer text of which other excerpts were placed by the editors elsewhere in the Code. We saw that in *CTh* 11.30 almost one-third, twenty-one out of sixty-six original texts, had companions, sometimes more than one, in other parts of the Code, and in some cases this constellation might affect the interpretation of a text and its protocols, allowing a better understanding of the date of the law or of the circumstances of its reception and publication. Occasionally such companion texts are relevant to the text of the Theodosian Code itself, for instance in confirm-

---

*and Family in Late Antiquity: The Emperor Constantine's Marriage Legislation* (1995), pp. 128–31. For the testamentary legislation mentioned at *V. Const.* 3.26, see Chapter 8, "'Palingenesia': Laws Reconstituted," no. 9.

ing the inclusion of a law in the books of the Code for which the manuscripts are incomplete.[33] In Chapter 8 were presented some examples of laws assembled from many excerpts in various parts of the Theodosian Code (and Codex Justinianus), and others were discussed elsewhere as they arose. The so-called Law of Citations of 426 appears in a new light when it is assembled and studied with the other texts with which it belongs. Indeed, the part of it defining generalitas, preserved only in the Codex Justinianus but clearly present in Book 1 of the original Theodosian Code, has a direct bearing on the principles enjoined on the first editorial commission less than three years later.

The historical interpretation of the texts that make up the Theodosian Code is a difficult matter, not least because the effect of its editors' brief was to deprive the texts of much that might have helped us to understand them. Even so, the laws are not isolated fragments. They bear dates by year, month and day, and places of issue and (less frequently) acceptance, they are gathered under thematic titles, they embody generalitas in the sense described, and they are addressed to public officials of whom something may be known and to public bodies and institutions whose character is familiar to us. They can often be connected with other texts elsewhere in the Code, regaining something of their original character in the process; and the organization of the Code is intelligible. There is no golden rule, but historians, well aware that the most rewarding of their texts are often the most difficult, do not expect such a thing. The Theodosian Code is no exception. It is as difficult a text as it is fundamental to our understanding of late Roman history, and as formidable as those Roman emperors whose endless and so often frustrated efforts it enshrines. Like the emperors, it has enjoyed the respect, without exactly winning the affection, of historians. I would like to think that this book, if not stimulating affection, may have served the understanding of both emperors and the Code in which they are portrayed to us.

33. For examples, see Chapter 8, "A Selected Title," nos. B.12, 15, 18, and 19.

# *Bibliography*

The following is a list of the secondary titles referred to in the course of the book, omitting some standard reference works, editions of texts, and commentaries. Books and monographs are listed before articles.


Angliviel de Beaumelle, L. "La torture dans les *Res Gestae* d'Ammien Marcellin." In M. Christol, S. Demougin, Y. Duval, C. Lepelley, and L. Pietri (eds.), *Institutions, société et vie politique dans l'empire romain*, pp. 91–113 (Collection de l'Ecole française de Rome, 159). Rome, 1992.

Archi, G. G. *Teodosio II e la sua codificazione*. Naples, 1976.

Arjava, Antti. *Women and Law in Late Antiquity*. Oxford, 1996.

Baldwin, Barry. "Acclamations in the *Historia Augusta*." *Athenaeum*, n.s. 59 (1981), pp. 138–49.

Banchich, Thomas M. "Julian's School Laws: *Cod. Theod.* 13.5.5 and *Ep.* 42." *Ancient World* 24 (1993), pp. 5–14.

Barnes, T. D. *Constantine and Eusebius*. Cambridge, Mass., 1981.

———. *The New Empire of Diocletian and Constantine*. Cambridge, Mass., 1982.

———. "Merobaudes on the Imperial Family." *Phoenix* 28 (1974), pp. 314–19.

———. "Three Imperial Edicts." *ZPE* 21 (1976), pp. 275–77.

Benner, Margareta. *The Emperor Says: Studies in the Rhetorical Style in Edicts of the Early Empire* (Studia Graeca et Latina Gothoburgensia, 33). Göteborg, 1975.

Berger, A. *Encyclopaedic Dictionary of Roman Law* (Transactions of the American Philosophical Society, new series, 43.2). Philadelphia, 1953.

Bischof, B. *Latin Palaeography: Antiquity to the Middle Ages* Cambridge, 1990.

Brown, Peter. *Augustine of Hippo: A Biography.* London, 1967.

Brunt, P. A. "Lex de Imperio Vespasiani." *JRS* 67 (1977), pp. 95–116.

Cameron, Alan, with R. S. Bagnall, Seth R. Schwartz, and K. A. Worp. *Consuls of the Later Roman Empire* (Philological Monographs of the American Philological Association, 36). Atlanta, 1987.

——. "The End of the Ancient Universities." *Journal of World History* 10.4 (1967), pp. 653–73.

——. "The Empress and the Poet: Paganism and Politics at the Court of Theodosius II." *Yale Classical Studies* 27 (1981), pp. 217–89.

Casson, L. *Ships and Seamanship in the Ancient World.* Princeton, 1971.

Cecconi, G. A. *Governo imperiale e elites dirigenti nell'Italia tardoantica: Problemi di storia politico-amministrativa.* Como, 1994.

Chastagnol, A. *La préfecture urbaine à Rome sous le Bas-Empire* (Publications de la Faculté des Lettres et Sciences Humaines d'Alger, 34). Paris, 1960.

——. *Les fastes de la préfecture de Rome au Bas-Empire* (Etudes Prosopographiques, 2). Paris, 1962.

Clover, F. M. *Flavius Merobaudes: A Translation and Historical Commentary* (Transactions of the American Philosophical Society, new series 61.1). Philadelphia, 1971.

——. "Olympiodorus of Thebes and the Historia Augusta." *Bonner Historia-Augusta-Colloquium 1979/81* (Bonn, 1983), pp. 127–56.

Collinet, P. *Histoire de l'école de droit de Beyrouth* (Etudes historiques sur le droit de Justinien, II), Paris, 1925.

Corcoran, Simon. *The Empire of the Tetrarchs: Imperial Pronouncements and Government, A.D., 284–324.* Oxford, 1996.

——. "Hidden from History: The Legislation of Licinius." In Jill Harries and Ian Wood (eds.), *The Theodosian Code,* pp. 97–119.

Crawford, Michael. "The Pettorano Fragment of the Prices Edict." *Athenaeum* n.s. 62 (1984), pp. 315–16.

Croke, Brian. "Mommsen's Encounter with the Code." In Jill Harries and Ian Wood (eds.), *The Theodosian Code,* pp. 217–39.

Dagron, G. "Aux origines de la civilisation byzantine: Langue de culture et langue d'état." *Revue Historique* 241 (1969), pp. 23–56.

Davidson, Theresa S. "A Problem of Senate Procedure in the Later Roman Empire." *American Journal of Philology* 67 (1946), pp. 168–83.

Delmaire, R. "Etude sur les souscriptions de quelques lois du Code Théodosien." In M. Christol, S. Demougin, Y. Duval, C. Lepelley, and L. Pietri (eds.), *Institutions, société et vie politique dans l'empire romain* (Collection de l'Ecole française de Rome, 159), pp. 316–328. Rome, 1992.

Downey, Glanville. *A History of Antioch in Syria, from Seleucus to the Arab Conquest.* Princeton, 1961.

Duncan-Jones, Richard. "Communication-Speed and Contact by Sea in the Roman Empire." In *Structure and Scale in the Roman Economy,* pp. 7–29. Cambridge, 1990).

Evans Grubbs, Judith. *Law and Family in Late Antiquity: The Emperor Constantine's Marriage Legislation.* Oxford, 1995.

Feissel, D. "Les Constitutions des Tétrarques connues par l'épigraphie: Inventaire et notes critiques." *L'Antiquité Tardive* 3 (1995), pp. 33–53.

——. "Deux Constitutions Tétrarchiques inscrites à Ephèse." *L'Antiquité Tardive* 4 (1996), pp. 273–89.

Frederiksen, M. W. "The Republican Municipal Laws: Errors and Drafts." *JRS* 55 (1965), pp. 183–98.

Garnsey, Peter. *Social Status and Legal Privilege in the Roman Empire.* Oxford, 1970.

Gaudemet, J. *Institutions de l'Antiquité.* Paris, 1967; 2nd ed., 1982.

——. *Le Bréviaire d'Alaric et les Epitome* (Ius Romanum Medii Aevi, Pts. 1, 2 b). Milan, 1965.

——. "Constitutions Constantiniennes destinées à l'Afrique." In M. Christol, S. Demougin, Y. Duval, C. Lepelley, and L. Pietri (eds.), *Institutions, société et vie politique dans l'empire romain* (Collection de l'Ecole française de Rome, 159), pp. 329–52. Rome, 1992.

Gilson, E. *Scolies ariennes sur le Concile d'Aquilée* (Sources Chrétiennes, 267). Paris, 1980.

Gleason, Maud. "Festive Satire: Julian's *Misopogon* and the New Year at Antioch." *JRS* 76 (1986), pp. 106–19.

González, J. "Tabula Siarensis, Fortunales Siarenses et Municipia Civium Romanorum." *ZPE* 55 (1984), pp. 55–100.

——. "The Lex Irnitana: A New Copy of the Flavian Municipal Law." *JRS* 76 (1986), pp. 147–243.

Goodman, M. *State and Society in Roman Galilee, A.D. 132–212.* Totowa, N.J., 1983.

Gordon, C. D. *The Age of Attila.* Ann Arbor, 1960; repr. New York, 1993.

Habicht, C., and Kussmaul, P., "Ein neues Fragment des Edictum de Accusationibus," *Museum Helveticum* 43 (1986), pp. 135–44.

Harries, Jill (J. D.). *Law and Empire in Late Antiquity.* Cambridge, 1999.

——. "Church and State in the *Notitia Galliarum.*" *JRS* 68 (1978), pp. 26–43.

——. "Sozomen and Eusebius: The Lawyer as Church Historian in the Fifth Century." In C. Holdsworth and T. P. Wiseman (eds.), *The Inheritance of Historiography, 350–900*, pp. 45–52. Exeter, 1986.

——. "The Roman Imperial Quaestor from Constantine to Theodosius II." *JRS* 78 (1988), pp. 148–72.

——. "'Sacra generalitas': The Administrative Background to the Theodosian Code." In *Estudios de Historia da Derecho Europeo,* pp. 31–24. Madrid, 1994.

——. "How to Make a Law-Code." In M. Austin, J. D. Harries, and C. Smith (eds.), *Modus Operandi: Essays in Honour of Geoffrey Rickman* (Bulletin of the Institute of Classical Studies), suppl. 71, pp. 63–78. London, 1998.

Harries, Jill, and Wood, Ian (eds.), *The Theodosian Code: Studies in the Imperial Law of Late Antiquity.* London, 1993.

Heichelheim, F. M. "The Text of the *Constitutio Antoniniana* and the Three Other Decrees of the Emperor Caracalla Contained in Papyrus Gissensis 40." *Journal of Egyptian Archaeology* 26 (1940), pp. 10–22.

Heichelheim, F. M., and Schwarzenberger, S. "An Edict of Constantine the Great: A Contribution to the Study of Interpolations." *Symbolae Osloenses* 26 (1947), pp. 1–19.

Hirschfeld, O. "Die römische Staatszeitung und die Akklamationen im Senat." *Kleine Schriften*, pp. 682–702. Berlin, 1913.

Holum, Kenneth G. *Theodosian Empresses: Women and Imperial Dominion in Late Antiquity.* Berkeley, Calif., 1982.

Honoré, Tony (A. M.). *Gaius.* Oxford, 1962.

——. *Tribonian.* London, 1978.

——. *Ulpian.* Oxford, 1982.

——. *Emperors and Lawyers,* 2nd ed. Oxford, 1994.

——. *Law in the Crisis of Empire, 370–455 A.D.: The Theodosian Dynasty and Its Quaestors.* Oxford, 1998.

——. "The Making of the Theodosian Code." *ZSS* 103 (1986), pp. 133–222.

——. "Scriptor Historiae Augustae." *JRS* 77 (1987), pp. 156–76.

——. "Some Writings of the Pagan Champion Nicomachus Flavianus." In W. Schuller (ed.), *Xenia: Konstanzer Althistorische Vorträge und Forschungen* 23 (1989), pp. 8–17, 26–43.

——. "Some Quaestors of the Reign of Theodosius II." In Jill Harries and Ian Wood (eds.), *The Theodosian Code,* pp. 68–94.

Hunt, E. D. *Holy Land Pilgrimage in the Later Roman Empire, A.D. 312–460.* Oxford, 1982.

Janin, R. *Constantinople byzantine.* Paris, 1964.

Jolowicz, H. F. *Historical Introduction to the Study of Roman Law.* Cambridge, 1932; 3rd ed., Barry Nicholas (ed.), 1972.

Jones, A. H. M. *The Later Roman Empire, 284–602: A Social, Economic, and Administrative Survey,* 3 vols. Oxford, 1964; repr. in 2 vols., 1973.

——. "Notes on the Genuineness of the Constantinian Documents in Eusebius' Life of Constantine." *Journal of Ecclesiastical History* 5 (1954), pp. 196–200; also published in *The Roman Economy,* P. A. Brunt (ed.), pp. 257–62.

——. "Collegiate Prefectures." *JRS* 54 (1964), pp. 78–89; also published in *The Roman Economy,* pp. 375–95.

Klauser, T. "Akklamation." *Reallexikon für Antike und Christentum,* vol. 1 (1950), cols. 213–33.

Krüger, P. "Beiträge zum Codex Theodosianus: Zur Wiederherstellung der Titelfolge im fünften Buch des Codex Theodosianus." *ZSS* 34 (1913), pp. 1–12.

"Über Ergänzung des Theodosianus aus dem Justinianus." *ZSS* 38 (1917), pp. 20–28.

——. "Versuch einer Wiederherstellung der Titelfolge des 4. und 5. Buchs." *ZSS* 38 (1917), pp. 28–34.

Kunkel, W. *An Introduction to Roman Legal and Constitutional History.* Trans. J. M. Kelly. 2nd ed. Oxford, 1973.

Lemerle, P. *Le premier humanisme byzantin.* Paris, 1971.

Lenel, O. *Das Edictum Perpetuum.* 3rd ed., Leipzig, 1927; repr. Aalen, 1956.

Lieberman, S. *Hellenism in Jewish Palestine: Studies in the Literary Transmission of Beliefs and Manners of Palestine in the I Century C.E.–IV Century C.E.* (Texts and Studies of the Jewish Theological Seminary of America, 18). New York, 1950.

——. "Roman Legal Institutions in Early Rabbinics and in the Acta Martyrum." *Jewish Quarterly Review,* n.s. 35 (1944–45), pp. 1–57.

Liebeschuetz, J. H. W. G., *Antioch: City and Imperial Administration in the Later Roman Empire.* Oxford, 1972.

Liebs, Detlef. *Hermogenians Iuris Epitomae: Zum Stand der römischen Jurisprudenz im*

*Zeitalter Diocletians* (Abhandlungen der Akademie der Wissenschaften in Göttingen: Philologisch-Historische Klasse, dritte folge, 57). Göttingen, 1964.

———. "Nichtliterarische römische Juristen der Kaiserzeit." in K. Luig and D. Liebs (eds.), *Das Profil der Juristen in der europäischen Tradition: Symposion aus Anlaß des 70. Geburtstages von Franz Wieacker,* pp. 123–98. Ebelsbach, 1980.

———. *Die Jurisprudenz im spätantiken Italien, 260–640 n. Chr.* (Freiburger Rechtsgeschichtliche Abhandlungen, n.f. 8). Freiburg, 1987.

Long, Jacqueline. "Structures of Irony in Julian's Misopogon." *The Ancient World* 24.1 (1993), pp. 15–23.

Lowe, E. A. *Codices Lugdunenses Antiquissimi: Le scriptorium de Lyon, la plus ancienne école calligraphique de France* (Bibliothèque de la ville de Lyon: Documents paléographiques, typographiqes, iconographiques, fasc. 3–4). Lyons, 1924.

———. *Codices Latini Antiquiores,* 1–11 and suppl. Oxford, 1934–71.

Maas, Michael. *John Lydus and the Roman Past.* London, 1992.

MacMullen, Ramsay. *Christianizing the Roman Empire,* A.D. *100–400.* New Haven, Conn., 1984.

MacCormack, Sabine. *Art and Ceremony in Late Antiquity.* Berkeley, Calif., 1981.

———. "Change and Continuity in Late Antiquity: The Ceremony of *Adventus.*" *Historia* 21 (1972), pp. 721–52.

Mango, Cyril. *Le développement urbain de Constantinople (IVe-VIIe siècles)* (Travaux et Mémoires du Centre de Recherche d'Histoire et Civilisation de Byzance, Monographies 2). Paris, 1985.

Matthews, John (J. F.). *Western Aristocracies and Imperial Court,* A.D. *364–425.* Oxford, 1975; repr. with postscript, 1990, 1998.

———. *The Roman Empire of Ammianus* London, 1989.

Matthews, John (J. F.), and Heather, Peter, *The Goths in the Fourth Century.* Liverpool, 1991.

———. "Olympiodorus of Thebes and the History of the West (A.D. 405–425)." *JRS* 60 (1970), pp. 79–97.

———. "Gallic Supporters of Theodosius." *Latomus* 30 (1971), pp. 1073–99.

———. "Gesandtschaft." in *Reallexikon für Antike und Christentum* 10 (1977), cols. 653–85.

———. "Symmachus and His Enemies." In F. Paschoud (ed.), *Colloque Genevois sur Symmaque, à l'occasion du mille six centième anniversaire du conflit de l'autel de la Victoire,* pp. 163–75. Paris, 1986.

———. "Nicomachus Flavianus' Quaestorship: The Historical Evidence." In W. Schuller (ed.), *Xenia: Konstanzer Althistorische Vorträge und Forschungen* 23 (1989), pp. 18–25.

———. "Ammianus on Roman Law and Lawyers." In J. den Boeft, D. den Hengst, and H. C. Teitler (eds.), *Cognitio Gestorum: The Historiographic Art of Ammianus Marcellinus* (Koninklijke Nederlandse Akademie van Wetenschappen Verhandelingen, Afd. Letterkunde, new series, 148), pp. 47–57. Amsterdam, 1992.

———. "The Making of the Text." In Jill Harries and Ian Wood (eds.), *The Theodosian Code,* pp. 19–44.

———. "*Codex Theodosianus* 9.40.13 and Nicomachus Flavianus." *Historia* 46 (1997), pp. 196–213.

———. "Eternity in Perishable Materials: Law-Making and Literate Communication in the

Roman Empire." In T. W. Hillard, R. A. Kearsley, C. E. V. Nixon, and A. M. Nobbs (eds.), *Ancient History in a Modern University,* vol. 2, pp. 253–65. Grand Rapids, Michigan, 1998.

Millar, Fergus. *The Emperor in the Roman World.* London, 1977.

Mitchell, Stephen. "Maximinus and the Christians in A.D. 312: A New Latin Inscription." *JRS* 78 (1988), pp. 105–24.

Moreau, J. "Fragment, découvert à Sinope, de l'édit de Constantin *De accusationibus.*" *Historia* 5 (1956), pp. 254–56.

Nash, Ernest. *A Pictorial Dictionary of Ancient Rome.* London, 1961; 2nd ed. New York, 1967.

Platner, S. B., and Ashby, T. *Topographical Dictionary of Ancient Rome.* London, 1929.

Roueché, Charlotte. "Acclamations in the Later Roman Empire: New Evidence from Aphrodisias." *JRS* 74 (1984), pp. 181–99.

———. "'Floreat Perge.'" In M. M. Mackenzie and C. Roueché (eds.), *Images of Authority: Papers Presented to Joyce Reynolds on the Occasion of her 70th Birthday* (Cambridge Philological Society, supplementary vol. 16, 1989), pp. 204–27.

Schulz, F. *History of Roman Legal Science.* Oxford, 1946; repr. with addenda, 1953.

———. *Classical Roman Law.* Oxford, 1951.

———. "Paul Krüger." *ZSS* 47 (1927), pp. ix–xxxi.

Sherwin-White, A. N. *Roman Society and Roman Law in the New Testament.* Oxford, 1963, repr. 1965.

———. *The Letters of Pliny.* Oxford, 1966.

Sirks, Boudewijn (A. J. B.). "Observations sur le Code Théodosien." *Subseciva Groningana* 2 (1985), pp. 21–34.

———. "From the Theodosian to the Justinian Code." *Atti dell'Accademia Romanistica Costantiniana: VI Convegno Internazionale* (1986), pp. 265–302.

———. "The Sources of the Code." In Jill Harries and Ian Wood (eds.), *The Theodosian Code,* pp. 45–67.

Syme, R. "Fiction About Jurists." *ZSS* 97 (1980), pp. 78–104; also published in *Roman Papers,* vol. 3. Oxford, 1984, pp. 1393–1414.

Talbert, Richard. *The Senate of Imperial Rome.* Princeton, 1984.

Thompson, E. A. *A Roman Reformer and Inventor: Being a New Text of the Treatise De rebus bellicis.* Oxford, 1952.

Turner, C. H. "Chapters in the History of Latin MSS." *Journal of Theological Studies* 1 (1900), pp. 435–41.

———. "Chapters in the History of Latin MSS, III: The Lyons–St. Petersburg MS of Councils." *Journal of Theological Studies* 4 (1903), pp. 426–34.

Turpin, W. "The Purpose of the Roman Law Codes." *ZSS* 104 (1987), pp. 620–30.

Vessey, Mark. "The Origins of the *Collectio Sirmondiana:* A New Look at the Evidence." In Jill Harries and Ian Wood (eds.), *The Theodosian Code* (1993), pp. 187–99.

Voss, W. E. *Recht und Rhetorik in den Kaisergesetzen der Spätantike: Eine Untersuchung zum nachklassischen Kauf- und Übereignungsrecht* (Forschungen zur Byzantinischen Rechtsgeschichte 9). Frankfurt am Main, 1982.

Wal, N. van der. "*Edictum* und *lex generalis:* Form und Inhalt der Kaisergesetze im spätrömischen Reich," *Revue Internationale des Droits de l'Antiquité* 28 (1981), pp. 277–313.

Watson, Alan. "The Development of the Praetor's Edict." *JRS* 60 (1970), pp. 105–19; also published in *Law Making in the Later Roman Republic.* Oxford, 1974, chap. 3.

Wenger, L. *Die Quellen des römischen Rechts.* Vienna, 1953.

Wightman, E. M. *Roman Trier and the Treveri.* London, 1970.

Williams, W. "Formal and Historical Aspects of Two New Documents of Marcus Aurelius." *ZPE* 17 (1975), pp. 37–78.

Williamson, Callie. "Monuments of Bronze: Roman Legal Documents on Bronze Tablets." *Classical Antiquity* 6.1 (1987), pp. 160–83.

Winterbottom, M. "Quintilian and the *Vir Bonus.*" *JRS* 54 (1964), pp. 90–97.

Wood, Ian. "The Code in Merovingian Gaul." In Jill Harries and Ian Wood (eds.), *The Theodosian Code.* pp. 159–77.

Yavetz, Z. *Plebs and Princeps.* Oxford, 1969.

# *Index of passages discussed*

The index does not collect all passages cited for any purpose whatever, but only those of which something positive is said, or which contribute directly to the argument under review. In references to the *Codex Justinianus* or to the Theodosian Code, the indication "(title)" means that an entire title of the Code in question is at issue, not any particular text or texts that fall within it.

# *General Index*